Functional Gastrointestinal Disorders

This book brings together world experts in the field of functional gastrointestinal disorders (FGIDs) who practise an integrated and holistic approach in their care for patients to provide an up-to-date and comprehensive evaluation of a range of issues associated with the biopsychosocial treatment of FGIDs. Examining topics such as neurological and biological aspects of FGIDs, common concerns faced in relation to diagnosis, and ongoing medical decisions and interventions, each chapter provides crucial practical recommendations, as well as future directions of psychosocial work in multi-team environments.

Functional Gastrointestinal Disorders considers individual conditions in detail, including the current Rome IV diagnostic criteria for FGIDs required to make a positive diagnosis, the role of psychological and other biopsychosocial and biofeedback aspects of treatment, and general recommendations with regard to diet and medications. Each chapter also provides an up-to-date consolidation and evaluation of the current literature as well as practical recommendations, which can then be applied by readers in their own interaction with FGID patients. Topics covered include:

- the common concerns and issues faced by individuals with FGIDs in relation to pre-and post-diagnosis, ongoing medical decisions and interventions
- review of current evidence-based biopsychosocial treatment practices for each FGID condition
- the differences and challenges associated with FGIDs across individual life stages
- special topics, such as the relationship with eating disorders and the role of psychotropic medications
- modern patient-centred initiatives, such as patient empowerment, distance and e-therapies
- the future challenges facing FGID treatment.

Throughout the entire book, common themes and practical recommendations are described. *Functional Gastrointestinal Disorders* has broad applicability across multiple spheres, including treatment, research and teaching, and is accessible to those working in gastroenterology and primary care alike.

Simon R. Knowles is Senior Academic and Clinical Psychologist, Swinburne University of Technology, Melbourne, Australia.

Julian Stern is Consultant Psychiatrist in Psychotherapy and Director of Adult and Forensic Services, Tavistock Centre, London, UK.

Geoff Hebbard is Director of Gastroenterology, University of Melbourne, The Royal Melbourne Hospital, Melbourne, Australia.

Functional Gastrointestinal Disorders

A Biopsychosocial Approach

Edited by
Simon R. Knowles, Julian Stern
and Geoff Hebbard

Routledge
Taylor & Francis Group
LONDON AND NEW YORK

First published 2018 by Routledge

2 Park Square, Milton Park, Abingdon, Oxfordshire OX14 4RN
52 Vanderbilt Avenue, New York, NY 10017

Routledge is an imprint of the Taylor & Francis Group, an informa business

First issued in paperback 2018

British Library Cataloguing-in-Publication Data
A catalogue record for this book is available from the British Library

Library of Congress Cataloging-in-Publication Data
A catalog record for this book has been requested

ISBN: 978-1-138-94703-0 (hbk)
ISBN: 978-0-367-19873-2 (pbk)

Typeset in Bembo
by Apex CoVantage, LLC

Contents

Acknowledgements

The editors would like to thank all of the contributors who provided chapters despite having significant responsibilities outside of this project. The authors would also like to thank Professor Douglas Drossman and the Rome Foundation for their permission to cite the Rome IV FGIDs criteria. We also thank Professor Drossman for providing the foreword to this book and his very kind words. Thank you to Emily Taylor at The Rome Foundation for tracking down several figures used in this book. Finally, the editors thank Ms Sarina Cook for her expert help in providing administrative support and collating the book chapters.

SK: I wish to thank all of the contributors to this book. Each of you has significant research and clinical responsibilities and yet has made time to contribute to this edited book. My own contributions to this book have been influenced by many individuals, including Professors Antonina A. Mikocka-Walus, Laurie Keefer, Finlay Macrae, Michael Kamm, Michael Salzberg, David Castle, Peter Gibson and Brjánn Ljótsson, and Drs Edwin Harari and Kaveh Monshet. To my fellow co-editors, Julian and Geoff, thank you so much for your expert knowledge of FGIDs and passion for making the lives of those with gastroenterological and psychological conditions better. Finally, I wish to thank my patients and the many individuals who have kindly offered their precious time and experiences to give me insight into the complexity of living with FGIDs.

JS: I have been most fortunate to work with some inspiring, thoughtful and caring colleagues, in both my psychiatric and psychotherapy workplaces (Maudsley Hospital and now the Tavistock Centre), and for 17 years at the unique St Mark's Hospital in Harrow, Greater London. Without their guidance, interest and support, my professional life would have been much the poorer. More recently, working with Simon and Geoff on this book has been a pleasure. But the main acknowledgements are to the many patients who have brought their symptoms and suffering to me, and allowed me into their lives, fears and dreams.

GH: My initial experience with patients with functional gastrointestinal disorders was guided by Professors Michael Horowitz and John Dent in Adelaide, both of whom provide significant ongoing support. Professor Werner Schwizer in Zurich has given me an international perspective on FGIDs, and over the more recent years the role of psychological and psychiatric care, with behavioural aspects, has been strongly influenced by others in Melbourne, including Professor Peter Gibson and the group at St Vincent's Hospital (Melbourne) led by Professor Michael Kamm.

Rationale for the book

Functional gastrointestinal conditions (FGIDs) are common, costly and disturbing to clinician and patient alike. Often crossing the divide between medicine and psychology, they are best managed by clinicians able to maintain a number of different thoughts and paradigms in the mind at the same time. Rather than the 'body' or the 'mind', this group of conditions requires clinicians to focus on 'both-and'. Thus, the objective of this book is to bring together world experts who practice an integrated and holistic approach in their care for FGID patients, and to provide reviews of the literature across a range of topics associated with the biopsychosocial treatment of FGIDs. Each chapter, written by leading experts in the field of FGIDs, will endeavour to provide an up-to-date comprehensive consolidation and evaluation of the current literature and then provide practical recommendations which can then be applied by readers in their own interaction with FGID patients.

The structure of the book

Each chapter in this book is guided by the biopsychosocial approach, reviewing the current literature, and also provides practical recommendations which readers can use within their own profession/FGID treating team. To help delineate and cover the multiple theoretical and practical aspects of the biopsychosocial approach to FGIDs and patient care, the book has been organized into five parts.

In Part I, the chapters describe key background information and then describe some clinically oriented epidemiology. An introductory chapter, defining the epidemiology of the FGIDs, is followed by reviews of stress and distress in FGIDs, FGIDs and the brain-gut axis (BGA), and the role of microbiota. Psychosocial and then cross-cultural aspects of the FGIDs are explored.

Part II is entitled "Diagnostic Procedures, Assessment and Biopsychosocial Methods in FGIDs". Here the chapters explore the role of diagnostic procedures, the psychological assessment of the FGID patient, the impact of diet and nutrition, and the role of a particular modality of treatment – that is, biofeedback.

Part III is the largest part of the book. Entitled "FGIDs and Biopsychosocial Approaches across the Age Range", it provides chapters on each FGID, identifying current Rome IV criteria and recommendations for management from biopsychosocial approaches.

Part IV is entitled "Working with Complex Psychological Issues in FGIDs". It contains three chapters on the role of psychotropic medication, the co-existence of eating disorders and FGIDs, and then the role of the patient him/herself, focusing on patient empowerment and working with complex patients with FGIDs.

The last part of the book, Part V, explores future directions in FGIDs.

Here the chapters are wide-ranging, from the ever-increasing importance of eHealth and advances such as microbiota, faecal transplants and new pharmaceutical approaches to modern psychological approaches, the input made by complimentary medicine and a final chapter on integrated and biopsychosocial care approaches. This is a fitting final chapter, as so much of the book is dedicated to the importance of an integrated and holistic approach to patients suffering from these conditions.

We hope and trust that the aforementioned integrated (and international) approach which runs throughout each chapter in this book, colouring and influencing the key themes and practical recommendations, will make the book a helpful resource for practitioners in secondary and primary care.

SK, JS and GH
Melbourne and London
February 2017

Levels of evidence

Throughout this book, chapters will provide an up-to-date summary of research based upon recommended levels of evidence across multiple domains (e.g., medical, pharmaceutical, psychological, dietary, complementary therapies). The following is a description of the levels and their interpretation.

Level	*Evidence*
I	Systematic review of all randomized controlled trials (RCT)
II	At least one randomized controlled trial (RCT)
III-1	Pseudo-randomized controlled trial
III-2	Comparative studies with concurrent controls, non-randomized, interrupted time series with a control group
III-3	Single arm studies, comparative study with historical control, interrupted time series without a parallel control group
IV	Case study, post-test only or pre- and post-test

Source: National Health and Medical Research Council (1999). A guide to the development, implementation and evaluation of clinical practice guidelines. Canberra: Author.

Foreword

To see an educational piece with the title *Functional Gastrointestinal Disorders: A Biopsychosocial Approach* peaks my interest. Why? I was fortunate when in training to have as my mentor Dr George Engel, the internist and psychoanalyst who coined the term 'biopsychosocial model' [1]. Then for over 40 years after becoming a gastroenterologist, the biopsychosocial aspects of FGIDs have guided my life's interest from an investigative, clinical and educational perspective [2].

The FGIDs truly are biopsychosocial disorders: the causes are multi-determined and vary depending on the individual's genetic make-up, microenvironment, psychological state and even the foods eaten. Thus, one must appreciate the immense variability in symptoms and their severity across persons so afflicted and in the same person over time. So while having an FGID means fulfilling certain symptom (Rome IV3) criteria, the clinical expression of this disorder and the personal experience of having it can vary considerably and truly are unique to the individual. This understanding has led the Rome Foundation to take a major position with Rome IV by redefining the functional GI disorders from this well-entrenched but somewhat stigmatized term of limited value to patients and clinicians to something truly biopsychosocial: disorders of gut-brain interaction. They are classified by GI symptoms that relate to any combination of (a) motility disturbance, (b) visceral hypersensitivity, (c) altered mucosal and immune function, (d) altered gut microbiota and (e) altered central nervous system (CNS) processing [4].

To this end, after reviewing the book very nicely edited by Drs Knowles, Stern and Hebbard my interest assuredly grew. Why? Because they brought together a group of skilled academicians and clinicians with vast experience in the field who write well, and who bring to bear a comprehensive sense of what the FGIDs are all about, from a biopsychosocial perspective and in a clear and relatively concise manner.

At a glance, the book could be considered a 'mini Rome IV', and fortunately the key elements of the larger information set are accurately retained. The elements of Rome IV classification and the diagnostic criteria, the attention to cross-cultural factors and the discussion of adult and paediatric disorders are accurately integrated into this book. Overall, while the book is more concise than the Rome IV book (developed for scientists, academicians and regulatory agencies as much as for clinicians), there is an effective presentation style to meet primarily the needs of the clinician, and a breadth of presentation relevant to both the medical and behavioural clinician. The term 'biopsychosocial' is well depicted by additional chapters: "Stress, Distress and FGIDs", "Psychosocial and Individual Aspects of FGIDs" and "Psychological Assessment and Questionnaires in FGIDs". There is also a series of psychological treatment chapters, including "Functional Bowel Disorders: 'Psychodynamic Therapy', 'Hypnosis', 'Cognitive Behavioural Therapy', 'Stress Management and Mindfulness-Based Approaches'". Finally, there are special chapters on eating disorders, the use of psychotropic medication and patient empowerment.

As the field of medicine moves towards a more integrated, biopsychosocial understanding of illness and disease and towards a patient-centred plan of care, persons with FGIDs are likely to benefit. This book I believe will help us to move in that direction by training the practitioners. While it can't replace Rome IV in its comprehensiveness, it complements it by focusing on the biopsychosocial elements in understanding these disorders and the management of the patients so afflicted.

Douglas A. Drossman MD
President, Rome Foundation (www.romefoundation.org) and
Professor Emeritus of Medicine and Psychiatry
UNC Center for Functional GI and Motility Disorders and
Center for Education and Practice of Biopsychosocial Care (www.drossmancenter.com)
at Chapel Hill

References

1 Engel, G.L.: The need for a new medical model: A challenge for biomedicine. *Science* 1977, **196**: 129–136.
2 Drossman, D.A.: Presidential address: Gastrointestinal illness and biopsychosocial model. *Psychosom Med* 1998, **60**: 258–267.
3 Drossman, D.A., Chang, L., Chey, W.D., Kellow, J., Tack, J., Whitehead, W.E., & the Rome IV Committees: Rome IV functional gastrointestinal disorders – disorders of gut-brain interaction. Raleigh, NC: Rome Foundation, 2016.
4 Drossman, D.A.: Functional gastrointestinal disorders: History, pathophysiology, clinical features and Rome IV. *Gastroenterology* 2016, **148**: 1262–1279.

Contributors

Dr Anurag Agrawal
PhD, MRCP
Consultant Gastroenterologist
Doncaster Royal Infirmary
Armthorpe Road
Doncaster DN2 5LT UK

Professor Jane M. Andrews
MBBS, PhD, FRACP
Consultant Gastroenterologist
Head IBD Service & Education,
Royal Adelaide Hospital
The University of Adelaide
SA 5005 Australia

Dr Alissa Beath
BA in Psychology (Hons), PhD
Associate Lecturer
Psychology Department
Faculty of Human Sciences
Macquarie University
NSW 2109 Australia

Professor Marc Alexander Benninga
MD, PhD
Head of the Department Paediatric Gastroenterology & Nutrition
Dept of Paediatric Gastroenterology
Emma Children's Hospital / Academic Medical Centre
Meibergdreef 9, H7-248
1105 AZ Amsterdam, the Netherlands

Dr Catherine Boyd
BSc (Med), MBBS (Hons), PhD, DipCH, FRACP
Paediatrician
Royal Darwin Hospital
Rocklands Drive, Casuarina, NT 0811 Australia

Dr Rebecca E. Burgell
MBBS (Hons), FRACP, PhD
Lecturer and Consultant Gastroenterologist
Consultant Gastroenterologist
The Alfred Hospital
55 Commercial Rd,
Melbourne, VIC 3004 Australia

Dr Brenda Bursch
BA (Hons), MA (Psychology), PhD
Clinical Director, Paediatric Psychiatry Consultation Liaison
Professor of Psychiatry & Biobehavioural Sciences and Paediatrics
David Geffen School of Medicine at UCLA
University of California Los Angeles
760 Westwood Plaza, Semel 48-253C
Los Angeles, CA 90024 USA

Professor Michael Camilleri
MD, FACP, AGAF, FACG, D.Sc. (Hons)
Professor of Medicine, Pharmacology, and Physiology

Atherton and Winifred W. Bean Professor
Consultant, Division of Gastroenterology and Hepatology,
Mayo Clinic
200 First St. S.W.
Rochester, Minnesota 55905 USA

Elspeth Carruthers
BA, MA
Medical student
St. Georges University of London
Cranmer Terrace,
London, SW17 0RE UK

Professor Lin Chang
Vice-Chief and Professor of Medicine
MD, AGAF, FACG
G Oppenheimer Center for Neurobiology of Stress and Resilience
10833 Le Conte Avenue, CHS 42-210
Los Angeles, California 90095-7378 USA

Dr Gareth Drake
BSc, MSc, DClinPsy
Clinical Psychologist
TAP (Team Around the Practice), Tavistock and Portman NHS Foundation Trust
The Monroe Centre, 33a Daleham Gardens, London, NW3 5BU, UK

Dr Rebecca Ellis
BA, DClinPsy
Clinical Psychologist
Clinical Health Psychology Department, Mid Yorkshire Hospitals NHS Trust
Pinderfields Hospital, Aberford Road, Wakefield, WF1 4DG, UK

Dr Anton Emmanuel
BSc, MD, FRCP
Consultant Gastroenterologist
GI Physiology Unit
University College Hospital
London WC1E 6DB, UK

Professor Mark Fox
MD, MA, FRCP
Lead Consultant
Abdominal Center: St. Claraspital
Kleinriehenstrasse 30 4058
Switzerland

Professor Peter R. Gibson
MBBS (Hons), FRACP, MD
Professor of Medicine and Consultant Gastroenterologist
Department of Gastroenterology, Monash University & Alfred Health
55 Commercial Rd,
Melbourne, VIC 3004 Australia

Dr Madhusudan Grover
MD
Assistant Professor of Medicine
Consultant, Division of Gastroenterology and Hepatology
Enteric NeuroScience Program
Mayo Clinic
200 First St. S.W.
Rochester, Minnesota 55905 USA

Livia Guadagnoli
BS
Clinical Psychology Doctoral Student
Department of Psychiatry and Behavioural Sciences
Northwestern University Feinberg School of Medicine
676 North Saint Clair Street, 14th floor
Chicago, IL 60614 USA

Dr Sebastian Haag
MD, PhD, MSc (Epid)
Gastro-Praxis Wiesbaden
Langenbeckplatz 2
D-65189 Wiesbaden, Germany

Dr Emma Phoebe Halmos
BNutDietet, PGradDipBiomedSc, PhD
Accredited Practising Dietitian
Walter & Eliza Hall Institute of Medical Research
1G Royal Pde Parkville, VIC 3052 Australia

Associate Professor Geoffrey Stuart Hebbard
B Med Sci, MBBS, PhD, FRACP
Director of Gastroenterology and Hepatology, The Royal Melbourne Hospital and Department of Medicine, University of Melbourne, Parkville VIC 3050 Australia

Dr Henriette Heinrich
MD
Clinical Research Fellow
Academic Surgical Unit & Neurogastroenterology Group
Centre for Neuroscience and Trauma
Blizard Institute
Barts and The London School of Medicine and Dentistry,
Queen Mary University of London
Mile End Rd, London E1 4NS UK

Professor Michael Jones
BSc (Hons), PhD, ASTAT, CSTAT
Professor & Associate Dean (Research)
Psychology Department
Faculty of Human Sciences
Macquarie University
NSW 2109 Australia

Dr Purna Kashyap
MBBS
Assistant Professor of Medicine, Mayo Clinic College of Medicine
Consultant, Division of Gastroenterology and Hepatology and Department of Physiology and Biomedical Engineering, Mayo Clinic
200 First St. S.W.
Rochester, Minnesota 55905 USA

Professor Laurie Keefer
PhD, AGAF
Health Psychologist
Division of Gastroenterology
Ichan School of Medicine at Mount Sinai
17 E. 102nd Street, 5th floor,
New York, NY 10029 USA

Dr Philip Chase Keightley
BMed, FRANZCP
Consultant Psychiatrist
Academic Unit of Psychiatry and Addiction Medicine, Australian National University Medical School
ACT 2605 Australia

Dr Simon Knowles
BA (Hons), Mpsyc (Clinical), Dip (Clin Hyp), PhD, MAPS
Senior Lecturer & Clinical Psychologist
Swinburne University of Technology
Hawthorn, VIC 3122 Australia

Dr Christopher Leung
MBBS, FRACP, DipClinEd, PhD
Consultant Gastroenterologist
Gastroenterologist
Austin Health
Level 8, Harold Stokes Building, Austin Hospital
145 Studley Road, Heidelberg, VIC 3084 Australia

Dr Perjohan Lindfors
MD, PhD, CEO
Senior Consultant in Gastroenterology and Internal Medicine
Sollentuna Specialistklinik
Malmvägen 2A-B
191 61 Sollentuna Sweden

Ecushla Linedale
BSc (Hons), Grad Dip (Sc. Comm.), Grad Dip (Psych)
PhD Candidate
The University of Adelaide
SA 5005 Australia

Associate Professor Brjánn Ljótsson
MSc, PhD
Associate Professor
Licensed Psychologist
Karolinska Institutet
Nobels väg 9
126 35 Stockholm Sweden

Ms Jenny Lövdahl
RN
Registered Nurse and Hypnotherapist
Dept of Internal Medicine
Sahlgrenska University Hospital
Mag-Tarm lab, Blå Stråket 3, 4 tr
413 45 Gothenburg Sweden

Antonina Mikocka-Walus
MA (Psych), PhD, MAPS
Senior Lecturer of Psychology
Deakin University
221 Burwood Highway
Burwood, VIC 3125 Australia

Dr Kaveh Monshat
BScMedHons, MBBS, MPsychMed, PhD, FRANCP
Consultant Psychiatrist
Pigdon St Consulting Suites
54 Pigdon St, Carlton North VIC 3054 Australia

Dr David O. Prichard
MB, BCh, PhD
Senior Associate Consultant and Assistant Professor of Medicine
Mayo Clinic Health System, La Crosse and Mayo Clinic, Rochester
700 West Ave South
La Crosse, WI 54601 USA

Dr Christopher K. Rayner
MBBS, PhD, FRACP
Consultant Gastroenterologist
Gwendolyn Michell Professor & Consultant Gastroenterologist
University of Adelaide, Australia
Royal Adelaide Hospital
Discipline of Medicine
Level 6, Eleanor Harrald Building
North Terrace, Adelaide SA 5000 Australia

Dr Anupam Rej
MRCP
Specialist Registrar
Doncaster Royal Infirmary
Armthorpe Road
Doncaster DN2 5LT UK

Dr Megan Elizabeth Riehl
MA, PsyD
Clinical Instructor & GI Psychologist
University of Michigan
1500 E. Medical Center Drive
Ann Arbor, MI 48109-5362 USA

Dr Richard J. Saad
MD, MS
Associate Clinical Professor of Medicine
Division of Gastroenterology
3912 Taubman Center
1500 E. Medical Center Drive
Ann Arbor, MI 48109 USA

Professor Magnus Simrén
MD, PhD
Professor of Gastroenterology, Senior Consultant in Gastroenterology and Internal Medicine
Dept of Internal Medicine & Clinical Nutrition
Institute of Medicine
Sahlgrenska Academy

University of Gothenburg
40530 Gothenburg Sweden

Dr Gillian Skardoon
B Phty (Hons), MBBS
Gastroenterology Fellow
Alfred Health
55 Commercial Rd,
Melbourne, VIC 3004 Australia

Professor André J.P.M. Smout
MD, PhD
Consultant Gastroenterologist &
Professor of Neurogastroenterology and Motility
Academic Medical Center, University of Amsterdam
P.O. Box 22700, 1100 DE
Amsterdam, the Netherlands

Professor Ami D. Sperber
MD, MSPH, AGAF
Emeritus Professor of Medicine
Faculty of Health Sciences
Ben-Gurion University of the Negev Beer-Sheva, Israel

Dr Julian Stern
BA, MB ChB, FRCPsych
Director of Adult and Forensic Services, and Consultant Psychiatrist in Psychotherapy
Tavistock and Portman NHS Foundation Trust
Tavistock Centre, 120 Belsize Lane
London, NW3 5BA UK

Associate Professor Miranda A.L. van Tilburg
MS in Economic Psychology, PhD
Associate Professor of Medicine
Division of Gastroenterology and Hepatology
Center for Functional GI and Motility Disorders
130 Mason Farm Road
Chapel Hill, NC 27599 USA

Dr Elizabeth J. Videlock
MD
Postdoctoral Scholar and Clinical Instructor
G Oppenheimer Center for Neurobiology of Stress and Resilience
10833 Le Conte Avenue, CHS 42-210
Los Angeles, CA 90095-7378 USA

Dr Arine Marianne Vlieger
MD, PhD
Head of Dept of Paediatrics
Dept of Paediatrics, St Antonius Hospital
PO Box 2500, 3430 EM
Nieuwegein, the Netherlands

Professor William E. Whitehead
BA, PhD
Professor of Medicine & Adjunct Professor of OB-GYN
Director, Center for Functional GI & Motility Disorders
4161-G Bioinformatics Building
130 Mason Farm Rd, CB 7080
Chapel Hill, NC 27599-7080 USA

Dr Sara E. Williams
BA (Hons), MS (Clinical Child Psychology), PhD
Paediatric Pain Psychologist
Associate Professor of Paediatrics, University of Cincinnati College of Medicine
Division of Behavioural Medicine & Clinical Psychology
3333 Burnet Ave, MLC 3015
Cincinnati, OH 45229 USA

Dr Sern Wei Yeoh
MBBS, BmedSci
Gastroenterology Fellow
Eastern Health
Level 2, 3 West, Box Hill Hospital
8 Arnold Street, Box Hill, VIC
3128, Australia

Part I

Background info and clinically oriented epidemiology topics

Chapter 1

Functional gastrointestinal disorders – disorders of brain-gut interaction in need of integrative treatment

Miranda A.L. van Tilburg
William E. Whitehead

The aim of this chapter is to review the epidemiology and aetiology of functional gastrointestinal disorders (FGIDs) and the need for integrative treatment.

Learning points

- FGIDs are prevalent in both adults and children.
- The brain and the gut interact to regulate pain perception and disability; FGIDs are disorders of brain-gut communication.
- The most important psychological factors affecting FGID symptom severity are somatization and catastrophizing about symptoms.
- Establishing a professional collaboration with a mental health provider who is familiar with FGIDs and using 'psychosocial red flag' symptom checklists to know when to refer can improve the outcome of treating FGIDs.

Introduction

FGIDS: epidemiology and aetiology

The Rome IV diagnostic criteria identify more than 40 adult and paediatric FGIDs, including well-known disorders, such as irritable bowel syndrome (IBS) and functional constipation, as well as lesser known disorders, such as functional gallbladder disorder and levator ani syndrome (rectal pain) [1]. FGIDs are common: they affect about 1 in 4 children [2, 3] and 1 in 3 adults [4]. The three most common adult FGIDs were functional dyspepsia (9.3%), functional constipation (6.3%) and irritable bowel syndrome (5.7%) [4]. Adult women were about twice as likely report FGIDs compared to men, but data on gender differences in children were inconsistent [2, 3, 5, 6]. The recent Rome III and IV prevalence data suggest there may be no gender differences for those under the age of 18. FGIDs significantly reduce quality of life [2, 3, 5] and are associated with increased disability [7, 8] and economic costs [9]. In one study, IBS patients were willing to give up 25% of their remaining lives to be symptom-free [10].

The term 'functional' was originally used to indicate that the symptoms were reflective of a different 'functioning' of the gut, such as the gut moving too slowly or being hypersensitive. Although this is still largely true, in the past decades the evidence increasingly points to the central role of the brain in these disorders [11]. Furthermore, by focusing on exclusion of organic disease in order to diagnose FGID (the gut was healthy but functioning differently), the term became stigmatizing and FGIDs were often considered as less 'real' [12]. However, FGIDs can exist in combination with organic disease, such as the well-studied IBS-IBD (inflammatory bowel disease) overlap [13]. Therefore, in Rome IV FGIDs are now characterized as *disorders of gut-brain interaction, negating the false dichotomy between functional and organic disease causes* [1]. *This definition is well rooted in the biopsychosocial model of FGIDs, which focuses on brain-gut interactions.*

The biopsychosocial model (see Figure 1.1), originally proposed by Engel [14] and expanded for FGIDs by Drossman [15, 16], postulates that disease presentation and outcomes are not driven exclusively by the disease process but based on complex interactions of various biological, psychological and social factors (see Figure 1.1). For FGIDs, this can be any combination of motility disturbances, visceral hypersensitivity, psychosocial/early life factors, altered immune functioning/gut microbiota and altered brain activity. Bidirectional interactions between the gut and the brain have long been recognized as responsible for well-known association between stress or emotions and our gut, as illustrated by the expression 'butterflies in our stomach'. Proper bowel function is expected in our society and thought to be needed for general well-being [12]. Gut disturbances and symptoms such as flatus, burping and bloating are embarrassing and shame-provoking. Given these connections between the gut and brain/emotions the role of psychological factors in FGIDs has been explored in depth.

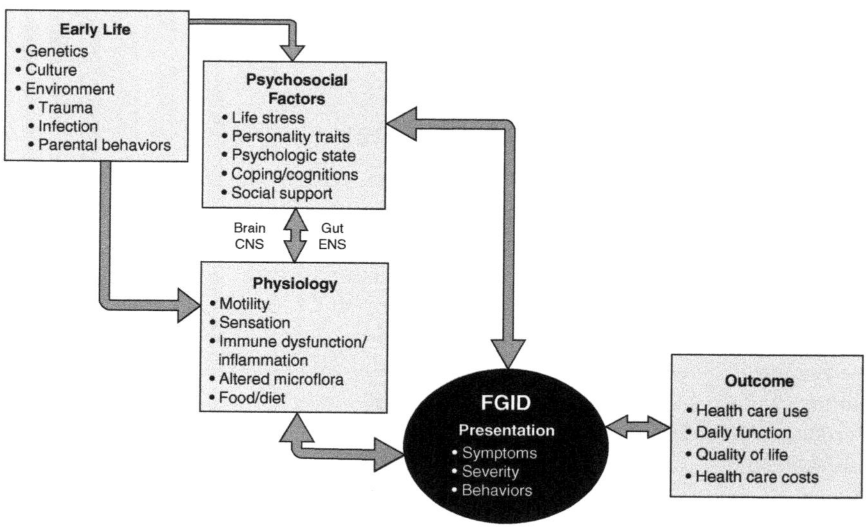

Figure 1.1 The biopsychosocial model adapted for FGIDs. It shows the interaction between brain and gut driving both symptoms and clinical outcome.

Adapted from Drossman [17].

Psychological factors in FGID

Psychiatric disorders, in particular anxiety and depression, are increased in patients with FGID [18, 19]. There is some debate about whether psychiatric disorders, such as anxiety, can cause FGIDs or are a reaction to living with a chronic illness, but in general it is well accepted that psychological factors affect the maintenance and exacerbation of the symptoms as well as disability [20, 21]. *Psychophysiological* studies have shown that descending noradrenergic pain modulation can have a powerful analgesic effect. In FGIDs anxiety-related dysregulation of the descending pain modulatory system has been reported, which facilitates pain and may partly explain why non-noxious stimuli can be perceived as painful [21].

Focusing on anxiety and depression barely scratches the surface of the myriad of psychological factors that have been tested in FGIDs. In an attempt to identify the most important psychological factors, we developed and tested a model (see Figure 1.2) [22] of psychological factors predicting FGID symptom severity. In this model catastrophizing (expecting the worst when experiencing symptoms and feeling unable to cope) and somatization (reporting many extraintestinal idiopathic symptoms) were the only factors directly related to gastrointestinal symptom severity. In another study, psychological distress also was indirectly associated with FGID symptoms through illness perceptions and maladaptive coping [23]. These data are further supported by several studies showing that the effect of psychological therapy is not through reductions in anxiety or depression but rather cognitions and coping [24–26]. Coincidentally, psychological therapy usually addresses how patients think about and cope with their disease, rather than their psychological distress, in an effort to decrease disability and increase quality of life.

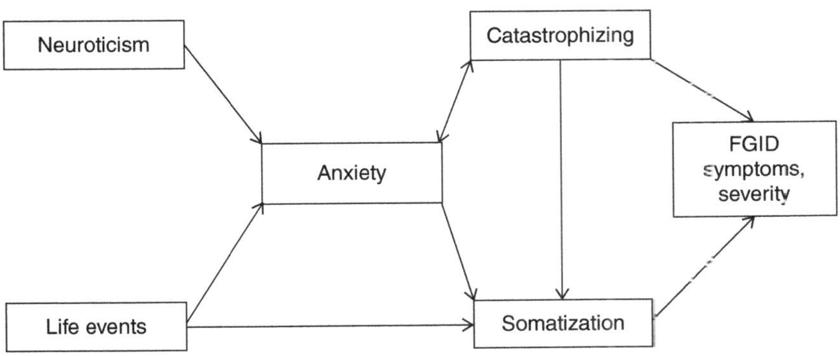

Figure 1.2 Model of psychological factors in FGID. Catastrophizing and somatization are associated with symptom severity. The effects of all other psychological variables seem to be explained by these two factors. However, anxiety has an important intermediate place in the model. The role of other psychological variables, such as neuroticism and life stressors, is limited to being associated with increases in anxiety.

Adapted from van Tilburg et *al.* [22].

Who is in need of psychological treatments?

The most commonly studied psychological therapies for FGIDs include cognitive behavioural therapy (CBT), hypnosis and biofeedback. The evidence for these treatments comes mostly from studies in IBS (CBT and hypnosis) [27] and faecal incontinence/dyssynergic defecation (biofeedback) [28], although some evidence is available for other FGIDs, such as functional dyspepsia [29] and functional chest pain [30]. The efficacy of these treatments has made them the standard of care for patients with IBS according to recommendations by the American Gastroenterology Association, the American College of Gastroenterology [31, 32] and the Rome Foundation [21]. However, not all patients are in need of referral to a mental health-care provider.

The Rome committee [33] has established a well-detailed step-wise assessment and treatment flowchart that helps physicians in determining the level of psychological care needed for their patients. Red flag symptoms, such as suicidality and substance abuse, require immediate referral to a mental health provider, but if these are absent, the following steps are recommended. Patients progress through each step when symptoms do not improve meaningfully with previous treatment. In step 1 a physician assesses the patient's symptoms, comorbidities, psychological symptoms and social support. Assessment of psychosocial factors includes key areas such as stressful life events, mood/anxiety disorders, somatization, illness cognitions/behaviours and impact on quality of life. The Rome IV committee developed a 9-item "Guidelines and Flags for Referring to a Mental Health Provider" tool to guide assessment and referral [33]. In step 1, the physician provides psychosocial support by reassuring and educating the patient and may suggest lifestyle or dietary changes. In step 2, low doses of centrally acting drugs may be prescribed. In step 3, the patient is referred to mental health practitioner after determining if the patient is a good candidate for therapy and providing a rationale for referral. In step 4, treatment is intensified and some patients may be referred to an integrative pain management program.

Implementation of psychological treatments in clinical practice

Psychological treatments for FGIDs are available to only a limited number of patients. There are several challenges to implementing these treatments in medical practice: lack of integration of care, lack of access to behavioural treatments, and reluctance of patients to follow though with treatment. Each will be discussed ahead.

Psychological treatments should ideally be offered as part of integrative care [20]. This implies a gastroenterologist and psychologist working together to create a comprehensive treatment plan. Physicians should remain involved in the medical care while the patient undergoes psychological treatment [20]. Physicians and psychologists should ideally discuss treatment goals for each patient. For most patients, integrative care is lacking and medical and psychological treatment are offered either side-by-side or consecutively without coordination of care, or not at all. Sending a 'difficult' patient to a psychologist only after medical therapy has failed or making the referral without medical guidance is unlikely to be effective. It communicates that the symptoms are all in the patient's head and the physician doesn't believe the symptoms are real. This creates resentment and resistance to future referral.

The lack of integrated care is compounded by the fact that few gastroenterologists have access to a psychologist in their medical practice. There is a lack of trained psychologists who know how to treat patients with FGIDs. Once the patient is referred to a therapist in the community, this lack of knowledge may mean the therapist will treat what he or she is familiar with. Usually this involves focusing on general anxiety or stress, rather than issues specific to FGID. As discussed before, treatment effects of CBT for IBS are mediated by changes in gastrointestinal-specific cognitions, worries and coping, but not general stress, anxiety or depression [24, 25, 34, 35]. Therefore identifying and working closely with suitable providers are important and should not be left up to the patient to arrange [36]. Furthermore, insurance does not always cover psychological treatment for patients and out-of-pocket costs can be prohibitive. Most psychologists in private practice are not covered by Medicaid/Medicare, making this type of treatment unavailable to many patients. Self-administered treatment [37, 38], electronic treatments [39], nurse delivery of treatment [40] and telemedicine may address the lack of availability of trained therapists as well as the costs of treatment. These treatment modalities are currently being developed and tested but are not yet widely available.

Lastly, a common issue is that patients are reluctant to participate in psychological treatments. Patients' expectations and reason for seeking medical care are often misunderstood; many physicians feel that patients desire medical testing to rule out organic disease [41], but even though worries about cancer are common concerns in IBS [42], patients are mostly looking for validation that they have a real gastrointestinal diagnosis and the symptoms are not simply in their heads [41]. We found that patients believe the best outcome of medical testing would be to find that they have a disease, while the worst outcome would be to find that all tests are negative [43]. The latter means continued worry about the meaning of symptoms and how to deal with them. Thus, testing does not reassure the patient. Rather studies have found that patients would like to be given information on causes and duration of FGIDs, and treatments such as diets, medications and coping strategies [44, 45]. Unfortunately few patients feel these needs are met and express frustration with care [42, 46]. Only 11% of IBS patients report positive interactions with their health-care providers [47]. Most patients do not accept the functional diagnosis [48] and this may be due to how the diagnosis is introduced and explained by physicians. Many clinicians underestimate the impact of FGIDs [48] and have a negative view of FGIDs, due to frustration with lack of effective treatments and uncertainty about causes as well as 'demanding' patient characteristics [49]. Patients pick up on this sentiment and feel stigmatized and not taken seriously by their doctors [49]. In this light, rejection of psychological treatments is understandable as it communicates the physician does not take the symptoms seriously and is trying to 'get rid' of the patient.

Addressing these concerns heads-on can help with acceptance of a referral. Palsson and Whitehead [36] offer some practical advice to physicians on how to increase acceptance of psychological treatments, including: (1) providing a positive diagnosis to validate and explain symptoms; (2) introducing the brain-gut axis as a rationale for psychological treatment of FGID; (3) establishing a therapeutic alliance with the patient and remaining available to the patient, so a referral to a mental health provider does not feel like an abandonment; (4) explaining the rationale for psychological treatment with a focus on learning to cope with the symptoms and reducing stress (as opposed to suggesting FGID is a psychological disorder); and (5) identifying and working closely with suitable local therapists (e.g., training them in FGIDs and communicating treatment goals of each specific patient).

Conclusions

FGIDs are understood in a biopsychosocial perspective, indicating the need for clinicians to attend to psychosocial factors. Clinicians should provide an in-depth psychosocial assessment that goes beyond screening for anxiety and depression, and include other factors that may influence FGID symptoms and disability. A step-wise approach is recommended by the Rome IV committee for mental health-care assessment and referral.

Acknowledgments, competing interests, and funding

Dr van Tilburg has no financial disclosures. Dr. Whitehead is on the Board of the Rome Foundation. He consults to companies on research and study design but has no conflicts of interest. The consulting companies are Ono, Ironwood, Allergan, and Takeda Pharmaceuticals. He is also supported by NIH research grants U34 DK109191, R21 DK096545, and U01 HD069031.

References

1 Drossman, D.A., Hasler, W.L.: Rome IV – functional GI disorders: Disorders of gut-brain interaction. *Gastroenterol* 2016, **150**(6): 1257–1261.
2 Lewis, M.L., Palsson, O.S., Whitehead, W.E., van Tilburg, M.A.L.: Prevalence of Functional gastrointestinal disorders in children and adolescents. *J Pediatr* 2016, **177**: 39–43. e33.
3 Van Tilburg, M.A.L, Hyman, P.E, Walker, L., Rouster, A., Palsson, O.S., Kim, S.M., Whitehead, W.E.: Prevalence of functional gastrointestinal disorders in infants and toddlers. *J Pediatr* 2015, **166**(3): 684–689.
4 Palsson, O.S., Whitehead, W.E., Van Tilburg, M.A.L., Chang, L., Chey, W., Crowell, M.D., Keefer, L., Lembo, A.J., Parkman, H.P., Rao, S.S.C., *et al.*: Development and validation of the Rome IV diagnostic questionnaire for adults. *Gastroenterol* 2016, **150**(6): 1481–1491.
5 Chang, L.: Review article: Epidemiology and quality of life in functional gastrointestinal disorders. *Aliment Pharmacol Ther,* 2004, **20**(7, Suppl): 31–39.
6 Korterink, J.J., Diederen, K., Benninga, M.A., Tabbers, M.M.: Epidemiology of pediatric functional abdominal pain disorders: A meta-analysis. *PLoS ONE* 2015, **10**(5): e0126982.

7 Ballou, S., Keefer, L.: The impact of irritable bowel syndrome on daily functioning: Characterizing and understanding daily consequences of IBS. *Neurogastroenterol Motil* 2017, **29**(4): e12982.

8 Vakil, N., Stelwagon, M., Shea, E.P., Miller, S.: Symptom burden and consulting behavior in patients with overlapping functional disorders in the US population. *UEG J* 2016, **4**(3): 413–422.

9 Herrick, L.M., Spalding, W.M., Saito, Y.A., Moriarty, J., Schleck, C.: A case-control comparison of direct healthcare-provider medical costs of chronic idiopathic constipation and irritable bowel syndrome with constipation in a community-based cohort. *J Med Econ* 2017, **20**(3): 273–279.

10 Drossman, D.A., Morris, C.B., Schneck, S., Hu, Y.J.B., Norton, N.J., Norton, W.F., Weinland, S.R., Dalton, C., Leserman, J., Bangdiwala, S.I.: International survey of patients with IBS: Symptom features and their severity, health status, treatments, and risk taking to achieve clinical benefit. *J Clin Gastroenterol* 2009, **43**(6): 541–550.

11 Rhee, S.H., Pothoulakis, C., Mayer, E.A.: Principles and clinical implications of the brain-gut-enteric microbiota axis. *Nat Rev Gastroenterol Hepatol* 2009, **6**(5): 306–314.

12 Drossman, D.A.: Functional gastrointestinal disorders: History, pathophysiology, clinical features, and Rome IV. *Gastroenterology* 2016, **150**(6): 1262–1279e1262.

13 Long, M.D., Drossman, D.A.: Editorial: Inflammatory bowel disease, irritable bowel syndrome, or what: A challenge to the functional-organic dichotomy. *Am J Gastroenterol* 2010, **105**(8): 1796–1798.

14 Engel, G.L.: The need for a new medical model: A challenge for biomedicine. *Science* 1977, **196**(4286): 129–136.

15 Drossman, D.A.: Presidential address: Gastrointestinal illness and the biopsychosocial model. *Psychosom Med* 1998, **60**(3): 258–267.

16 Drossman, D.A.: The functional gastrointestinal disorders and the Rome III process. *Gastroenterol* 2006, **130**(5): 1377–1390.

17 Drossman, D.A.: The functional gastrointestinal disorders and the Rome III process. In: *Rome III: The functional gastrointestinal disorders*, 3rd edn. Edited by Drossman, D.A., Corazziari, E., Delvaux, M., Spiller, R., Talley, N.J., Thompson, W.G., Whitehead, W.E., Committees tRI. McLean, VA: Degnon Associates, 2006: 1–30.

18 Fond, G., Loundou, A., Hamdani, N., Boukouaci, W., Dargel, A., Oliveira, J., Roger, M., Tamouza, R., Leboyer, M., Boyer, L.: Anxiety and depression comorbidities in irritable bowel syndrome (IBS): A systematic review and meta-analysis. *Eur Arch Psychiat Clin Neurosci* 2014, **264**(8): 651–660.

19 Van Oudenhove, L., Aziz, Q.: The role of psychosocial factors and psychiatric disorders in functional dyspepsia. *Nat Rev Gastroenterol Hepatol* 2013, **10**(3): 158–167.

20 Reed-Knight, B., Claar, R.L., Schurman, J.V., van Tilburg, M.A.L.: Implementing psychological therapies for functional GI disorders in children and adults. *Exp Rev Gastroenterol Hepatol* 2016, **10**(9): 981–984.

21 Van Oudenhove, L., Levy, R.L., Crowell, M.D., Drossman, D.A., Halpert, A.D., Keefer, L., Lackner, J.M., Murphy, T.B., Naliboff, B.D.: Biopsychosocial aspects of functional gastrointestinal disorders: How central and environmental processes contribute to the development and expression of functional gastrointestinal disorders. *Gastroenterology* 2016, **150**(6): 1355–1367e1352.

22 Van Tilburg, M.A.L., Palsson, O.S., Whitehead, W.E.: Which psychological factors exacerbate irritable bowel syndrome? Development of a comprehensive model. *J Psychosom Res* 2013, **74**(6): 486–492.

23 Knowles, S.R., Austin, D.W., Sivanesan, S., Tye-Din, J., Leung, C., Wilson, J., Castle, D., Kamm, M.A., Macrae, F., Hebbard, G.: Relations between symptom severity, illness perceptions, visceral sensitivity, coping strategies and well-being in irritable bowel syndrome guided by the common sense model of illness. *Psychol Health Med* 2017, **22**(5): 524–534.

24 Chilcot, J., Moss-Morris, R.: Changes in illness-related cognitions rather than distress mediate improvements in irritable bowel syndrome (IBS) symptoms and disability

following a brief cognitive behavioural therapy intervention. *Behav Res Ther* 2013, **51**(10): 690–695.

25 Lackner, J.M., Jaccard, J., Krasner, S.S., Katz, L.A., Gudleski, G.D., Blanchard, E.B.: How does cognitive behavior therapy for irritable bowel syndrome work? A mediational analysis of a randomized clinical trial. *Gastroenterology* 2007, **133**(2): 433–444.

26 Levy, R.L., Langer, S.L., Romano, J.M., Labus, J., Walker, L.S., Murphy, T.B., Van Tilburg, M.A.L., Feld, L.D., Christie, D.L., Whitehead, W.E.: Cognitive mediators of treatment outcomes in pediatric functional abdominal pain. *Clin J Pain* 2014, **30**(12): 1033–1043.

27 Ford, A.C., Quigley, E.M., Lacy, B.E., Lembo, A.J., Saito, Y.A., Schiller, L.R., Soffer, E.E., Spiegel, B.M., Moayyedi, P.: Effect of antidepressants and psychological therapies, including hypnotherapy, in irritable bowel syndrome: Systematic review and meta-analysis. *Am J Gastroenterol* 2014, **109**(9): 1350–1365, quiz 1366.

28 Chiarioni, G., Whitehead, W.E.: The role of biofeedback in the treatment of gastrointestinal disorders. *Nat Clin Pract Gastroenterol Hepatol* 2008, **5**(7): 371–382.

29 Calvert, E.L., Houghton, L.A., Cooper, P., Morris, J., Whorwell, P.J.: Long-term improvement in functional dyspepsia using hypnotherapy. *Gastroenterology* 2002, **123**(6): 1778–1785.

30 Van Peski-Oosterbaan, A.S., Spinhoven, P., Van Rood, Y., Van der Does, J.W., Bruschke, A.V., Rooijmans, H.G.: Cognitive-behavioral therapy for noncardiac chest pain: A randomized trial. *Am J Med* 1999, **106**(4): 424–429.

31 Brandt, L.J., Chey, W.D., Foxx-Orenstein, A.E., Quigley, E.M.M., Schiller, L.R., Schoenfeld, P.S., Spiegel, B.M., Talley, N.J., Moayyedi, P.: An evidence-based position statement on the management of irritable bowel syndrome. *Am J Gastroenterol* 2008, **104**(SUPPL. 1): S1–S35.

32 Drossman, D.A., Camilleri, M., Mayer, E.A., Whitehead, W.E.: AGA technical review on irritable bowel syndrome. *Gastroenterology* 2002, **123**(6): 2108–2131.

33 Levy, R.L., Crowell, M.D., Drossman, D.A., Halpert, A.D., Keefer, L., Lackner, J.M., Murphy, T.B., Naliboff, B.D., Van Oudenhove, L.: Biopsychosocial aspects of functional gastrointestinal disorders. In: *Rome IV: Functional gastrointestinal disorders: Disorders of gut-brain interaction*, Vol. I, edn. Edited by Drossman, D.A. Raleigh, NC: The Rome Foundation, 2016: 443–548.

34 Labus, J., Gupta, A., Gill, H.K., Posserud, I., Mayer, M., Raeen, H., Bolus, R., Simren, M., Naliboff, B.D., Mayer, E.A.: Randomised clinical trial: Symptoms of the irritable bowel syndrome are improved by a psycho-education group intervention. *Aliment Pharmacol Ther* 2013, **37**(3): 304–315.

35 Ljótsson, B., Hesser, H., Andersson, E., Lindfors, P., Hursti, T., Rück, C., Lindefors, N., Andersson, G., Hedman, E.: Mechanisms of change in an exposure-based treatment for irritable bowel syndrome. *J Consult Clin Psychol* 2013, **81**(6): 1113–1126.

36 Palsson, O.S., Whitehead, W.E.: Psychological treatments in functional gastrointestinal disorders: A primer for the gastroenterologist. *Clin Gastroenterol Hepatol* 2013, **11**(3): 208–216.

37 Lackner, J.M., Jaccard, J., Krasner, S.S., Katz, L.A., Gudleski, G.D., Holroyd, K.: Self-administered cognitive behavior therapy for moderate to severe irritable bowel syndrome: Clinical efficacy, tolerability, feasibility. *Clin Gastroenterol Hepatol* 2008, **6**(8): 899–906.

38 Palsson, O.S., van Tilburg, M.: Hypnosis and guided imagery Treatment for gastrointestinal disorders: Experience with scripted protocols developed at the University of North Carolina. *Am J Clin Hypn* 2015, **58**(1): 5–21.

39 Ljótsson, B., Hedman, E., Andersson, E., Hesser, H., Lindfors, P., Hursti, T., Rydh, S., Rück, C., Lindefors, N., Andersson, G.: Internet-delivered exposure-based treatment vs. Stress management for irritable bowel syndrome: A randomized trial. *Am J Gastroenterol* 2011, **106**(8): 1481–1491.

40 Dainty, A.D., Fox, M., Lewis, N., Hunt, M., Holtham, E., Timmons, S., Kinsella, P., Wragg, A., Callaghan, P.: A mixed methods feasibility study to evaluate the use of a low-intensity,

nurse-delivered cognitive behavioural therapy for the treatment of irritable bowel syndrome. *BMJ Open* 2014, **4**(6): e005262.

41 Halpert, A.: Irritable bowel syndrome: What do patients really want? *Curr Gastroenterol Rep* 2011, **13**(4): 331–335.

42 O'Sullivan, M.A., Mahmud, N., Kelleher, D.P., Lovett, E., O'Morain, C.A.: Patient knowledge and educational needs in irritable bowel syndrome. *Eur J Gastroenterol Hepatol* 2000, **12**(1): 39–43.

43 Van Tilburg, M.A.L., Chitkara, D.K., Palsson, O.S., Levy, R.L., Whitehead, W.E.: Parental worries and beliefs about abdominal pain. *J Pediatr Gastroenterol Nutr* 2009, **48**(3): 311–317.

44 Halpert, A., Dalton, C.B., Palsson, O., Morris, C., Hu, Y., Bangdiwala, S., Hankins, J., Norton, N., Drossman, D.: What patients know about Irritable Bowel Syndrome (IBS) and what they would like to know. National survey on patient educational needs in IBS and development and validation of the Patient Educational Needs Questionnaire (PEQ). *Am J Gastroenterol* 2007, **102**(9): 1972–1982.

45 Weiser, K.T., Lacy, B.E., Noddin, L., Crowell, M.D.: Patient knowledge and perspective on irritable bowel syndrome: Development of a survey instrument. *Dig Dis Sci* 2008, **53**(1): 284–295.

46 Bertram, S., Kurland, M., Lydick, E., Locke III, G.R., Yawn, B.P.: The patient's perspective of irritable bowel syndrome. *J Family Pract* 2001, **50**(6): 521–525.

47 Halpert, A., Godena, E.: Irritable bowel syndrome patients' perspectives on their relationships with healthcare providers. *Scand J Gastroenterol* 2011, **46**(7–8): 823–830.

48 Collins, J., Farrall, E., Turnbull, D.A., Hetzel, D.J., Holtmann, G., Andrews, J.M.: Do we know what patients want? The doctor-patient communication gap in functional gastrointestinal disorders. *Clin Gastroenterol Hepatol* 2009, **7**(11): 1252–1254.e1252.

49 Dixon-Woods, M., Critchley, S.: Medical and lay views of irritable bowel syndrome. *Family Pract* 2000, **17**(2): 108–113.

Chapter 2

Stress, distress and functional gastrointestinal disorders

Elizabeth J. Videlock
Lin Chang

The aim of this chapter is to review the effect of stress on gastrointestinal (GI) physiology, the evidence supporting dysregulation of stress response systems in functional gastrointestinal disorders (FGIDs), and how this informs therapeutic options.

Learning points

- Stress is associated with onset, severity and clinical outcome in FGIDs.
- There is more evidence for alteration in neural regulation of the stress response than dysfunction within the stress response systems themselves.
- Consideration of current and prior stressors is important in patient evaluation and treatment.

Introduction

The stress response system

The response to stress is an integrated and coordinated physiological process that can result in adaptation or pathologic maladaptation [1]. The term 'allostasis' describes the process by which stability is maintained in the face of stress. Systems involved in maintaining allostasis include the autonomic nervous system (ANS) and hypothalamic-pituitary-adrenal (HPA) axis, among others. 'Allostatic load' refers to the potentially damaging effects of overuse or dysregulation of allostatic systems and may cause symptoms such as fatigue and irritability, among other visceral and somatic symptoms [2], which are commonly reported in patients with IBS [3].

The autonomic nervous system (ANS) and hypothalamic-pituitary-adrenal (HPA) axis are two principal output systems of the general stress response. Activation of the HPA axis results in synthesis and release of corticotropin-releasing factor (CRF) in the paraventricular nucleus (PVN) of the hypothalamus. CRF stimulates release of adrenocorticotropin hormone (ACTH) from the anterior pituitary, leading to release of cortisol from the adrenal glands. Cortisol attenuates the response via negative feedback at the level of the hypothalamus and the pituitary. CRF also activates the ANS and mediates stress-related immune, behavioural and visceral responses [4–6].

Stress and gastrointestinal physiology

The effect of stress on gut function and sensation results from alterations in the brain-gut axis. The 'brain-gut axis' describes the bidirectional communication between the enteric, autonomic and central nervous systems [7]. The nature of this communication is complex and multidimensional (see Figure 2.1).

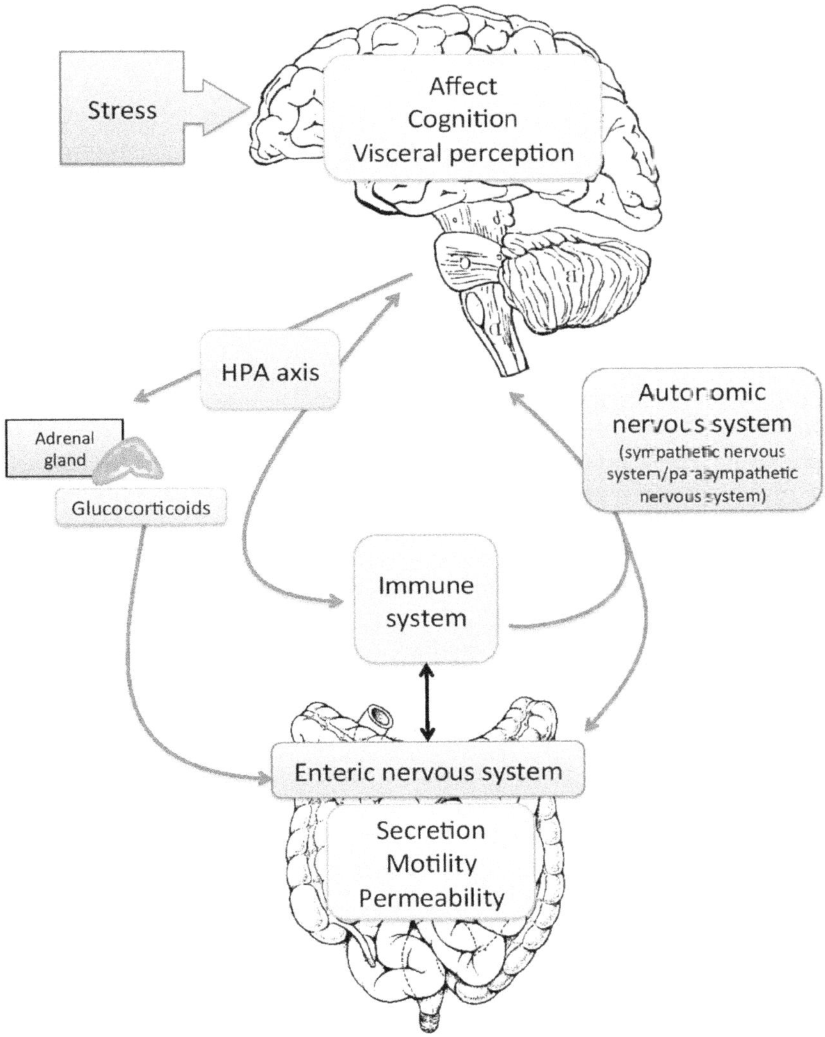

Figure 2.1 The brain-gut axis. The hypothalamic-pituitary-adrenal (HPA) axis, immune system and nervous system all participate in the complex and bidirectional communication between the gut and the central nervous system.

Source: Modified from Kennedy P.J., Clarke G., Quigley E.M., *et al. Neurosci Biobehav Rev* 2012; 36:310 [20].

Communication occurs via neurons and via humoral mediators of the HPA axis, ANS and immune system. The microbiota also participates in brain-gut interactions.

Stress can affect motility, secretion, sensation and permeability. IBS patients have higher colonic motor activity at rest compared to healthy controls as well as greater increases in response to stress [8, 9]. Abnormal response of the upper gut to stress – for example, delayed gastric emptying and decreased gastric accommodation – has also been demonstrated in IBS patients [10–13]. Stress increases sensitivity to rectal distension and paracellular permeability in animal models, which has been linked to activation of CRF receptors in the gut [14, 15]. In humans, several studies have shown that stress increases visceral perception to rectal distention [16, 17], and that stress or exogenous CRF increases permeability [18, 19]. Interestingly, stress and CRF-induced increases in permeability were inhibited by administration of a mast cell stabilizer [19].

Stressful life events are a risk factor for IBS and impact therapeutic outcome

Among functional gastrointestinal disorders (FGIDs) the role of stress has been studied most in irritable bowel syndrome (IBS); however, most FGIDs are associated with psychiatric comorbidity or increased symptoms of anxiety and depression to some extent [21]. It is important to note that many patients with IBS have anxiety symptoms related to their GI symptoms (i.e., GI symptom–specific anxiety) rather than a generalized anxiety disorder [22]. In predisposed individuals, chronic or sustained stress can be associated with enhanced responsiveness of central stress circuits and an increased vulnerability for the development of functional GI and affective disorders [23].

IBS symptom onset and exacerbation are associated with current life stress for many patients [24], and the development of post-infectious IBS (PI-IBS) is predicted by stressful life events or the presence of anxiety and depression at the time of the diarrhoeal illness [25].

Early life stress or adverse childhood experiences (ACEs), which have emerged as an important predictor of a variety of diseases and poor health outcome overall, are also associated with the development of IBS. IBS patients also have a higher prevalence of ACEs, including, but not limited to, maladjusted relationships with a parent or primary caregiver, severe illness or death of a parent, and physical, sexual or emotional abuse [26–28]. In one study, an increasing number of ACEs was associated with increased odds of having IBS and correlated with greater overall symptom and abdominal pain severity [28]. A history of abuse is also associated with increased pain reporting but increased thresholds to rectal distension [29].

In rodents, early life stress in the form of maternal separation results in stress-induced visceral hypersensitivity in adults [30–32]. This forms the basis of an important animal model for IBS. Maternally separated rats show altered visceromotor responses to stress, increased levels of plasma cortisol, an enhanced immune response to a lipopolysaccharide, and altered microbiota

[33]. Other studies have shown increased intestinal permeability in response to stress when compared to non-maternally separated rats under the same stress condition [34].

The mechanisms underlying the long-term effects of early life adversity may result from epigenetic programming, which refers to modification in gene expression resulting in a change in phenotype without a change to the genetic sequence (genotype). In an important example, decreased maternal grooming was associated with reduced expression of the glucocorticoid receptor (GR) in the hippocampus [35]. The decreased negative feedback resulting from reduced GR expression was associated with an increased and prolonged HPA response [36]. This finding was paralleled in human studies: decreased hippocampal GR expression and increased methylation of the neuron-specific GR gene promoter were seen in suicide victims with a history of childhood abuse in comparison with suicide victims without abuse and controls without abuse who died from unrelated causes [37].

In addition to affecting risk of IBS, stress affects clinical outcome. In a prospective study, the presence of at least one chronic life stressor during the first six months of the observational period was predictive of symptom intensity at 16 months. Patients who experienced symptom improvement did not report a current chronic life stressor [38].

FGID-associated changes in the central stress response

In animal models, increased responsiveness of the HPA axis is associated with increased visceral sensitivity [39], an important feature of IBS. Most studies showing an increased HPA axis response IBS have measured the response to a psychological stressor [40–43]. The HPA response to visceral stressors, such as rectal distension or flexible sigmoidoscopy, has been similar between IBS patients and healthy control subjects in most studies [16, 44–46]. Hormone challenge allows an isolated assessment of the HPA axis. The response to CRF in IBS in comparison to healthy controls was increased in two studies [47, 48] and blunted in another study, including IBS and functional dyspepsia patients [49]. The largest study evaluating the response to hormone challenge and the only one designed to account for sex and history of early adverse life events, did not find an IBS-associated difference in the cortisol and ACTH response to CRF [50]. This study also measured the cortisol response to ACTH stimulation and levels of glucocorticoid receptor (GR) mRNA in peripheral blood mononuclear cells. Interestingly, the effect of IBS on the response to ACTH was different in men and women – the response was increased in men, but blunted in women with IBS compared to healthy controls [50]. GR mRNA was decreased in IBS (primarily in men) and was inversely correlated with the ACTH response to CRF, suggesting it may be a peripheral marker of the central HPA response [50]. It was also negatively correlated with symptom severity in IBS patients [50].

It is important to consider the differences in measuring the HPA response to contextual stressors and hormone challenge. The former evaluates the inputs into the HPA axis, such as the emotional response to the stressor, while the latter begins at the level of the hypothalamus. The difference between contextual and hormonal stressors may be particularly relevant in IBS, which has been associated with changes in multiple components of the integrated response to a stressor, such as increased brain activity in emotional-arousal circuits [51] and increased cardiosympathetic tone [52], which may result in an altered HPA axis response.

One question that is commonly raised is whether there is impaired negative feedback of the HPA axis in IBS, similar to what is found in depression. While decreased peripheral GR mRNA expression could support this, it could also be a result (rather than a cause) of increased HPA activation. Results from dexamethasone suppression studies have also not supported impaired negative feedback [48, 49, 53]. Synthesis of results from different studies of the HPA axis in IBS reveals an augmented HPA axis response to psychological stress but not to stimulation with CRF, which supports increased neural regulation or 'CRF-hyperdrive' in IBS rather than impaired negative feedback.

Studies suggest that an interaction between genetic and environmental factors (including ACEs) contributes to the development of stress-sensitive conditions, such as IBS. CRH-R1 receptors are widely distributed throughout the brain-gut axis, and its role in neuroendocrinology has been intensely studied and clearly defined [54, 55]. CRH-R1 appears to play an important role in central stress circuits underlying anxiety-like sustained fear responses that are activated and modulated via the amygdala complex [56], which in turn regulates the stress response via projections to the hypothalamus and brainstem regions. An important function of the extended amygdala circuit is to modulate the threshold for defensive reflexes, such as freezing or eye blink responses. The latter response to a sudden loud sound has been termed the acoustic startle response. An enhanced threat-potentiated acoustic startle response, which likely represents amygdala-dependent central pain amplification, has been demonstrated in IBS [57]. Two studies have shown that single nucleotide polymorphisms (SNPs) in CRH-R1 are associated with the presence of IBS [58, 59]. These SNPs have also been shown to be associated with GI symptom anxiety scores and alterations in acoustic startle response [59], which supports that CRH-R1 contributes to the dysregulated stress responsiveness in IBS.

There is evidence that function of the ANS is altered in IBS, resulting in increased sympathetic tone or decreased vagal tone [60]. Alterations in ANS tone in IBS have been observed at rest [61], in response to visceral stimuli [62–65] and during mental stress [66].

FGIDs and psychiatric disorders

On the surface, there appears to be a close relationship between FGIDs and psychiatric disorders. There is a higher prevalence of psychiatric disorders in the FGID population compared to controls [67]. Mood affects visceral perception in healthy controls [68] and in IBS [69, 70], which may be mediated by the ANS [71]. Further supporting this connection, brain imaging studies have shown that improvement in symptoms and visceral sensitivity is associated with changes in emotional centres [72, 73]. It is difficult draw conclusions; however, about whether these observations are due to shared pathophysiology or common symptoms, such as anxiety, which may be GI symptom–specific in FGIDs [22]. In depression, impaired negative feedback of the HPA axis is a consistent finding, but this was not seen in IBS [50]. ACEs are common risk factors for psychiatric disorders and FGIDs, but ACEs have been associated with a wide variety of diseases and negative health outcomes [74]. Evidence also supports an association of ACEs and risk of IBS independent of current anxiety and depression [27].

Conclusions

There is increasing evidence to support that FGIDs, particularly IBS, are stress-sensitive conditions, in which stress can increase the development and/or the exacerbation of symptoms. The interactions between brain and gut appear to play a key role in the stress-induced changes of GI function, autonomic and neuroendocrine responses, and pain amplification in FGIDs. Chronic stress can affect a patient's clinical course by increasing symptom flares and maladaptive coping behaviours and decreasing health-related quality of life. Early recognition of stress-sensitive symptoms might help to proactively institute therapeutic interventions to prevent the development of IBS and/or decrease the severity of symptoms.

Acknowledgements, competing interests and funding

Dr Videlock has no financial disclosures. She receives support from the NIH training grant (T32 DK0718) and the NIH loan repayment program (L30 DK106759). D. Chang has served on scientific advisory boards for Synergy, Ironwood, Synthetics Biologics, IM Healthcare LLC and Bioamerica. She served as a speaker for Allergan and Takeda. She receives support from NIH grants P50 DK64539, R21 DK104078 and DK048351.

References

1 McEwen, B.S.: Protective and damaging effects of stress mediators: Central role of the brain. *Dialogues Clin Neurosci* 2006, **8**(4): 367–381.
2 McEwen, B.S.: Protective and damaging effects of stress mediators. *New Eng J Med* 1998, **338**(3): 171–179.
3 Whitehead, W.E., Palsson, O., Jones, K.R.: Systemic review of the comorbidity of irritable bowel syndrome with other disorders: What are the causes and implications? *Gastroenterology* 2002, **122**(4): 1140–1156.
4 Owens, M.J., Nemeroff, C.B.: Physiology and pharmacology of corticotropin-releasing factor. *Pharmacol Rev* 1991, **43**: 425–473.
5 Kiank, C., Tache, Y., Larauche, M.: Stress-related modulation of inflammation in experimental models of bowel disease and post-infectious irritable bowel syndrome: Role of corticotropin-releasing factor receptors. *Brain Behav Immun* 2010, **24**(1): 41–48.
6 Martinez, V., Tache, Y.: CRF1 receptors as a therapeutic target for irritable bowel syndrome. *Curr Pharm Des* 2006, **12**(31): 4071–4088.

7 Mayer, E.A., Tillisch, K.: The brain-gut axis in abdominal pain syndromes. *Annu Rev Med* 2011, **62**: 381–396.

8 Welgan, P., Meshkinpour, H., Beeler, M.: Effect of anger on colon motor and myoelectric activity in irritable bowel syndrome. *Gastroenterology* 1988, **94**(5 Pt 1): 1150–1156.

9 Welgan, P., Meshkinpour, H., Hoehler, F.: The effect of stress on colon motor and electrical activity in irritable bowel syndrome. *Psychosom Med* 1985, **47**: 139–149.

10 Welgan, P., Meshkinpour, H., Ma, L.: Role of anger in antral motor activity in irritable bowel syndrome. *Dig Dis Sci* 2000, **45**(2): 248–251.

11 Lind, C.D.: Motility disorders in the irritable bowel syndrome. *Gastroenterol Clin N* 1991, **20**(2): 279–295.

12 Kellow, J.E., Langeluddecke, P.M., Eckersley, G.M., Jones, M.P., Tennant, C.C.: Effects of acute psychologic stress on small-intestinal motility in health and the irritable bowel syndrome. *Scand J Gastroenterol* 1992, **27**(1): 53–58.

13 Fukudo, S., Nomura, T., Hongo, M.: Impact of corticotropin-releasing hormone on gastrointestinal motility and adrenocorticotropic hormone in normal controls and patients with irritable bowel syndrome. *Gut* 1999, **42**(6): 845–849.

14 Schwetz, I., Bradesi, S., McRoberts, J.A., Sablad, M., Miller, J.C., Zhou, H.P., Ohning, G., Mayer, E.A.: Delayed stress-induced colonic hypersensitivity in male Wistar rats: Role of neurokinin-1 and corticotropin-releasing factor-1 receptors. *Am J Physiol Gastrointest Liver Physiol* 2004, **286**: G683–G691.

15 Larauche, M., Gourcerol, G., Wang, L.X., Pambukchian, K., Brunnhuber, S., Adelson, D.W., Rivier, J., Million, M., Tache, Y.: Cortagine, a CRF1 agonist, induces stresslike alterations of colonic function and visceral hypersensitivity in rodents primarily through peripheral pathways. *Am J Physiol Gastrointest Liver Physiol* 2009, **297**: G215–G227.

16 Posserud, I., Agerforz, P., Ekman, R., Björnsson, E.S., Abrahamsson, H., Simrén, M.: Altered visceral perceptual and neuroendocrine response in patients with irritable bowel syndrome during mental stress. *Gut* 2004, **53**: 1102–1108.

17 Dickhaus, B., Mayer, E.A., Firooz, N., Stains, J., Conde, F., Olivas, T.I., Fass, R., Chang, L., Mayer, M., Naliboff, B.D.: Irritable bowel syndrome patients show enhanced modulation of visceral perception by auditory stress. *Am J Gastroenterol* 2003, **98**(1): 135–143.

18 Alonso, C., Guilarte, M., Vicario, M., Ramos, L., Ramadan, Z., Antolin, M., Martinez, C., Rezzi, S., Saperas, E., Kochhar, S., *et al.*: Maladaptive intestinal epithelial responses to life stress may predispose healthy women to gut mucosal inflammation. *Gastroenterology* 2008, **135**(1): 163–172.

19 Vanuytsel, T., van Wanrooy, S., Vanheel, H., Vanormelingen, C., Verschueren, S., Houben, E., Salim Rasoel, S., Tomicronth, J., Holvoet, L., Farre, R., *et al.*: Psychological stress and corticotropin-releasing hormone increase intestinal permeability in humans by a mast cell-dependent mechanism. *Gut* 2014, **63**(8): 1293–1299.

20 Kennedy, P.J., Clarke, G., Quigley, E.M., Groeger, J.A., Dinan, T.G., Cryan, J.F.: Gut memories: Towards a cognitive neurobiology of irritable bowel syndrome. *Neurosci Biobehav Rev* 2012, **36**(1): 310–340.

21 Koloski, N.A., Talley, N.J., Boyce, P.M.: The impact of functional gastrointestinal disorders on quality of life. *Am J Gastroenterol* 2000, **95**(1): 67–71.

22 Labus, J.S., Mayer, E.A., Chang, L., Bolus, R., Naliboff, B.D.: The central role of gastrointestinal-specific anxiety in irritable bowel syndrome: Further validation of the visceral sensitivity index. *Psychosom Med* 2007, **69**(1): 89–98.

23 Mayer, E.A., Naliboff, B.D., Chang, L., Coutinho, S.V.: V. Stress and irritable bowel syndrome. *Am J Physiol Gastrointest Liver Physiol* 2001, **280**(4): G519–G524.

24 Whitehead, W.E., Crowell, M.D., Robinson, J.C., Heller, B.R., Schuster, M.M.: Effects of stressful life events on bowel symptoms: Subjects with irritable bowel syndrome compared with subjects without bowel dysfunction. *Gut* 1992, **33**: 825–830.

25 Gwee, K.A., Leong, Y.L., Graham, C., McKendrick, M.W., Collins, S.M., Walters, S.J., Underwood, J.E., Read, N.W.: The role of psychological and biological factors in postinfective gut dysfunction. *Gut* 1999, **44**(3): 400–406.

26 Chitkara, D.K., van Tilburg, M.A., Blois-Martin, N., Whitehead, W.E.: Early life risk factors that contribute to irritable bowel syndrome in adults: A systematic review. *Am J Gastroenterol* 2008, **103**(3): 765–774.

27 Bradford, K., Shih, W., Videlock, E.J., Presson, A.P., Naliboff, B.D., Mayer, E.A., Chang, L.: Association between early adverse life events and irritable bowel syndrome. *Clin Gastroenterol Hepatol* 2012, **10**(4): 385–390.e381–383.

28 Park, S.H., Videlock, E.J., Shih, W., Presson, A.P., Mayer, E.A., Chang, L.: Adverse childhood experiences are associated with irritable bowel syndrome and gastrointestinal symptom severity. *Neuro Motil* 2016, **28**(8): 1252–1260.

29 Ringel, Y., Drossman, D.A., Leserman, J.L., Suyenobu, B.Y., Wilber, K., Lin, W., Whitehead, W.E., Naliboff, B.D., Berman, S., Mayer, E.A.: Effect of abuse history on pain reports and brain responses to aversive visceral stimulation: An fMRI study. *Gastroenterology* 2008, **134**(2): 396–404.

30 Heim, C., Nemeroff, C.B.: The role of childhood trauma in the neurobiology of mood and anxiety disorders: Preclinical and clinical studies. *Biol Psychiat* 2001, **49**(12): 1023–1039.

31 Coutinho, S.V., Plotsky, P.M., Sablad, M., Miller, J.C., Zhou, H., Bayati, A.I., McRoberts, J.A., Mayer, E.A.: Neonatal maternal separation alters stress-induced responses to viscerosomatic nociceptive stimuli in rat. *Am J Physiol Gastrointest Liver Physiol* 2002, **282**(2): G307–G316.

32 Chung, E.K.Y., Zhang, X.J., Li, Z., Zhang, H.Q., Xu, H.X., Bian, Z.X.: Neonatal maternal separation enhances central sensitivity to noxious colorectal distention in rat. *Brain Res* 2007, **1153**: 68–77.

33 O'Mahony, S.M., Marchesi, J.R., Scully, P., Codling, C., Ceolho, A.M., Quigley, E.M.M., Cryan, J.F., Dinan, T.G.: Early life stress alters behavior, immunity, and microbiota in rats: Implications for irritable bowel syndrome and psychiatric illnesses. *Biol Psychiat* 2009, **65**(3): 263–267.

34 Soderholm, J.D., Yates, D.A., Gareau, M.G., Yang, P.C., MacQueen, G., Perdue, M.H.: Neonatal maternal separation predisposes adult rats to colonic barrier dysfunction in response to mild stress. *Am J Physiol Gastrointest Liver Physiol* 2002, **283**(6): G1257–G1263.

35 Weaver, I.C., Cervoni, N., Champagne, F.A., D'Alessio, A.C., Sharma, S., Seckl, J.R., Dymov, S., Szyf, M., Meaney, M.J.: Epigenetic programming by maternal behavior. *Nat Neurosci* 2004, **7**: 847–854.

36 Rinne, T., de Kloet, E.R., Wouters, L., Goekoop, J.G., DeRijk, R.H., van den Brink, W.: Hyperresponsiveness of hypothalamic-pituitary-adrenal axis to combined dexamethasone/corticotropin-releasing hormone challenge in female borderline personality disorder subjects with a history of sustained childhood abuse. *Biol Psychiat* 2002, **52**: 1102–1112.

37 McGowan, P.O., Sasaki, A., D'Alessio, A.C., Dymov, S., Labonte, B., Szyf, M., Turecki, G., Meaney, M.J.: Epigenetic regulation of the glucocorticoid receptor in human brain associates with childhood abuse. *Nat Neurosci* 2009, **12**(3): 342–348.

38 Bennett, E.J., Tennant, C.C., Piesse, C., Badcock, C.A., Kellow, J.E.: Level of chronic life stress predicts clinical outcome in irritable bowel syndrome. *Gut* 1998, **43**(2): 256–261.

39 Myers, B., Meerveld, B.G.V.: Elevated corticosterone in the amygdala leads to persistant increases in anxiety-like behavior and pain sensitivity. *Behav Brain Res* 2010, **214**(2): 465–469.

40 Kennedy, P.J., Cryan, J.F., Quigley, E.M., Dinan, T.G., Clarke, G.: A sustained hypothalamic-pituitary-adrenal axis response to acute psychosocial stress in irritable bowel syndrome. *Psychol Med* 2014, **44**(14): 3123–3134.

41 Heitkemper, M.M., Cain, K.C., Deechakawan, W., Poppe, A., Jun, S.E., Burr, R.L., Jarrett, M.E.: Anticipation of public speaking and sleep and the hypothalamic-pituitary-adrenal axis in women with irritable bowel syndrome. *Neuro Motil* 2012, **24**: 626–631, e270–621.

42 Sugaya, N., Izawa, S., Kimura, K., Ogawa, N., Yamada, K.C., Shirotsuki, K., Mikami, I., Hirata, K., Nagano, Y., Nomura, S., *et al.*: Adrenal hormone response and psychophysiological correlates under psychosocial stress in individuals with irritable bowel syndrome. *Int J Psychophysiol* 2012, **84**: 39–44.

43 Sugaya, N., Izawa, S., Saito, K., Shirotsuki, K., Nomura, S., Shimada, H.: Effect of prolonged stress on the adrenal hormones of individuals with irritable bowel syndrome. *Biopsychosoc Med* 2015, **9**(1): 4.
44 Chang, L., Sundaresh, S., Elliott, J., Anton, P.A., Baldi, P., Licudine, A., Mayer, M., Vuong, T., Hirano, M., Naliboff, B.D., *et al.*: Dysregulation of the Hypothalamic-Pituitary-Adrenal (HPA) axis in irritable bowel syndrome. *Neuro Motil* 2009, **21**(2): 149–159.
45 Videlock, E.J., Adeyemo, M., Licudine, A., Hirano, M., Ohning, G., Mayer, M., Mayer, E.A., Chang, L.: Childhood trauma is associated with hypothalamic-pituitary-adrenal axis responsiveness in irritable bowel syndrome. *Gastroenterology* 2009, **137**(6): 1954–1962.
46 Walter, S.A., Aardal-Eriksson, E., Thorell, L.H., Bodemar, G., Hallbook, O.: Pre-experimental stress in patients with irritable bowel syndrome: High cortisol values already before symptom provocation with rectal distensions. *Neuro Motil* 2006, **18**(12): 1069–1077.
47 Fukudo, S., Nomura, T., Hongo, M.: Impact of corticotropin-releasing hormone on gastrointestinal motility and adrenocorticotropic hormone in normal controls and patients with irritable bowel syndrome. *Gut* 1998, **42**(6): 845–849.
48 Dinan, T.G., Quigley, E.M., Ahmed, S.M., Scully, P., O'Brien, S., O'Mahony, L., O'Mahony, S., Shanahan, F., Keeling, P.W.: Hypothalamic-pituitary-gut axis dysregulation in irritable bowel syndrome: Plasma cytokines as a potential biomarker? *Gastroenterology* 2006, **130**(2): 304–311.
49 Bohmelt, A.H., Nater, U.M., Franke, S., Hellhammer, D.H., Ehlert, U.: Basal and stimulated hypothalamic-pituitary-adrenal axis activity in patients with functional gastrointestinal disorders and healthy controls. *Psychosom Med* 2005, **67**(2): 288–294.
50 Videlock, E.J., Shih, W., Adeyemo, M., Mahurkar-Joshi, S., Presson, A.P., Polytarchou, C., Alberto, M., Iliopoulos, D., Mayer, E.A., Chang, L.: The effect of sex and irritable bowel syndrome on HPA axis response and peripheral glucocorticoid receptor expression. *Psychoneuroendocrinol* 2016, **69**: 67–76.
51 Stevens, J.S., Hamann, S.: Sex differences in brain activation to emotional stimuli: A meta-analysis of neuroimaging studies. *Neuropsychol* 2012, **50**(7): 1578–1593.
52 Smith, S.M., Vale, W.W.: The role of the hypothalamic-pituitary-adrenal axis in neuroendocrine responses to stress. *Dialogues Clin Neurosci* 2006, **8**(4): 383–395.
53 Videlock, E.J., Shih, W., Mayer, E.A., Chang, L.: Negative feedback of the Hypothalamic-Pituitary-Adrenal (HPA) axis as assessed by the dexamethasone-Corticotropin-Releasing Factor (CRF) test in Irritable Bowel Syndrome (IBS). *Am J Gastroenterol* 2015, **110**(S1): S755.
54 Fukudo, S.: Role of corticotropin-releasing hormone in irritable bowel syndrome and intestinal inflammation. *J Gastroenterol* 2007, **42**(Suppl 17): 48–51.
55 Tyrka, A.R., Price, L.H., Gelernter, J., Schepker, C., Anderson, G.M., Carpenter, L.L.: Interaction of childhood maltreatment with the corticotropin-releasing hormone receptor gene: Effects on hypothalamic-pituitary-adrenal axis reactivity. *Biol Psychiat* 2009, **66**(7): 681–685.
56 Walker, D.L., Davis, M.: Role of the extended amygdala in short-duration versus sustained fear: A tribute to Dr. Lennart Heimer. *Brain Struct Funct* 2008, **213**(1–2): 29–42.
57 Naliboff, B.D., Waters, A.M., Labus, J.S., Kilpatrick, L., Craske, M.G., Chang, L., Negoro, H., Ibrahimovic, H., Mayer, E.A., Ornitz, E.: Increased acoustic startle responses in IBS patients during abdominal and nonabdominal threat. *Psychosom Med* 2008, **70**(8): 920–927.
58 Sato, N., Suzuki, N., Sasaki, A., Aizawa, E., Obayashi, T., Kanazawa, M., Mizuno, T., Kano, M., Aoki, M., Fukudo, S.: Corticotropin-releasing hormone receptor 1 gene variants in irritable bowel syndrome. *PloS one* 2012, **7**(9): e42450.
59 Orand, A., Naliboff, B., Gadd, M., Shih, W., Ju, T., Presson, A.P., Mayer, E.A., Chang, L.: Corticotropin-Releasing Hormone Receptor 1 (CRH-R1) polymorphisms are associated with irritable bowel syndrome and acoustic startle response. *Psychoneuroendocrinol* 2016, **73**: 133–141.
60 Mazurak, N., Seredyuk, N., Sauer, H., Teufel, M., Enck, P.: Heart rate variability in the irritable bowel syndrome: A review of the literature. *Neuro Motil* 2012, **24**(3): 206–216.

61 Heitkemper, M., Burr, R.L., Jarrett, M., Hertig, V., Lustyk, M.K., Bond, E.F.: Evidence for autonomic nervous system imbalance in women with irritable bowel syndrome. *Dig Dis Sci* 1998, **43**(9): 2093–2098.
62 Ng, C., Malcolm, A., Hansen, R., Kellow, J.: Feeding and colonic distension provoke altered autonomic responses in irritable bowel syndrome. *Scand J Gastroenterol* 2007, **42**(4): 441–446.
63 van Orshoven, N.P., Andriesse, G.I., van Schelven, L.J., Smout, A.J., Akkermans, L.M., Oey, P.L.: Subtle involvement of the parasympathetic nervous system in patients with irritable bowel syndrome. *Clin Auton Res* 2006, **16**(1): 33–39.
64 Tillisch, K., Mayer, E.A., Labus, J.S., Stains, J., Chang, L., Naliboff, B.D.: Sex-specific alterations in autonomic function among patients with irritable bowel syndrome. *Gut* 2005, **54**: 1396–1401.
65 Cheng, P., Shih, W., Alberto, M., Presson, A.P., Licudine, A., Mayer, E.A., Naliboff, B.D., Chang, L.: Autonomic response to a visceral stressor is dysregulated in irritable bowel syndrome and correlates with duration of disease. *Neuro Motil* 2013, **25**(10): e650–e659.
66 Elsenbruch, S., Lucas, A., Holtmann, G., Haag, S., Gerken, G., Riemenschneider, N., Langhorst, J., Kavelaars, A., Heijnen, C.J., Schedlowski, M.: Public speaking stress-induced neuroendocrine responses and circulating immune cell redistribution in irritable bowel syndrome. *Am J Gastroenterol* 2006, **101**: 2300–2307.
67 Van Oudenhove, L., Crowell, M.D., Drossman, D.A., Halpert, A.D., Keefer, L., Lackner, J.M., Murphy, T.B., Naliboff, B.D., Levy, R.L.: Biopsychosocial aspects of functional gastrointestinal disorders. *Gastroenterology* 2016, **150**(6): 1355–1367e2.
68 Coen, S.J., Yaguez, L., Aziz, Q., Mitterschiffthaler, M.T., Brammer, M. Williams, S.C.R., Gregory, L.J.: Negative mood affects brain processing of visceral sensation. *Gastroenterology* 2009, **137**(1): 253–261.
69 Guthrie, E., Barlow, J., Fernandes, L., Ratcliffe, J., Read, N., Thompson, D.G., Tomenson, B., Creed, F., North England IBSRG: Changes in tolerance to rectal distension correlate with changes in psychological state in patients with severe irritable bowel syndrome. *Psychosom Med* 2004, **66**(4): 578–582.
70 Houghton, L.A., Calvert, E.L., Jackson, N.A., Cooper, P., Whorwell, P.J.: Visceral sensation and emotion: A study using hypnosis. *Gut* 2002, **51**(5): 701–704.
71 Emmanuel, A.V., Kamm, M.A.: Response to a behavioural treatment, biofeedback, in constipated patients is associated with improved gut transit and autonomic innervation. *Gut* 2001, **49**(2): 214–219.
72 Lackner, J.M., Coad, M.L., Mertz, H.R., Wack, D.S., Katz, L.A., Krasner, S.S., Firth, R., Mahl, T.C., Lockwood, A.H.: Cognitive therapy for irritable bowel syndrome is associated with reduced limbic activity, GI symptoms, and anxiety. *Behav Res Ther* 2006, **44**(5): 621–638.
73 Naliboff, B.D., Berman, S., Suyenobu, B., Labus, J.S., Chang, L., Stains, J., Mandelkern, M.A., Mayer, E.A.: Longitudinal change in perceptual and brain activation response to visceral stimuli in irritable bowel syndrome patients. *Gastroenterology* 2006, **131**(2): 352–365.
74 Anda, R.F., Felitti, V.J., Bremner, J.D., Walker, J.D., Whitfield, C., Perry, B.D., Dube, S.R., Giles, W.H.: The enduring effects of abuse and related adverse experiences in childhood: A convergence of evidence from neurobiology and epidemiology. *Eur Arch Psychiat Clin Neurosci* 2006, **256**(3): 174–186.

Chapter 3

Functional gastrointestinal disorders and the brain-gut axis

Christopher K. Rayner

The aim of this chapter is to define the elements of the brain-gut axis (BGA), how they interact, and how dysfunction of this axis may contribute to functional gastrointestinal disorders (FGIDs).

Learning points

- Communication between gut and brain is bidirectional, via autonomic and endocrine connections.
- Ascending signals arise not only from gut distension and motility but also from chemical, immune and microbiological sources.
- Processing of visceral signals in the brain is inextricably linked with emotional, affective and behavioural responses.
- Descending pathways from brain to gut not only generate autonomic and endocrine responses but also facilitate or inhibit transmission of ascending signals.

Introduction

Patients with FGIDs tend to focus on possible causes of their symptoms at the level of the gut, although many recognize a relationship between psychological stress and the onset or exacerbation of their symptoms. Indeed, common English expressions, such as 'butterflies in the stomach' or having a 'gut feeling', reflect an intuitive recognition that emotions are strongly linked to gut sensations.

The case for a central component in the aetiology of FGIDs is strengthened by the tendency for these disorders to overlap with each other and with non-gastrointestinal pain disorders, such as interstitial cystitis and fibromyalgia, rather than being distinct entities [1], and patients often transition between different functional disorders over time [2]. Moreover, patients with anxiety and depression, or a history of early adverse life events, appear more prone than others to developing FGIDs, and some of the most effective treatments are centrally targeted, such as cognitive behavioural therapy or antidepressant medications [3].

Advances in enteric neuroscience and brain imaging in recent years have yielded substantial insights into both peripheral and central mediators of gastrointestinal symptoms, and in particular how the two 'brains' of the gut – the 'big

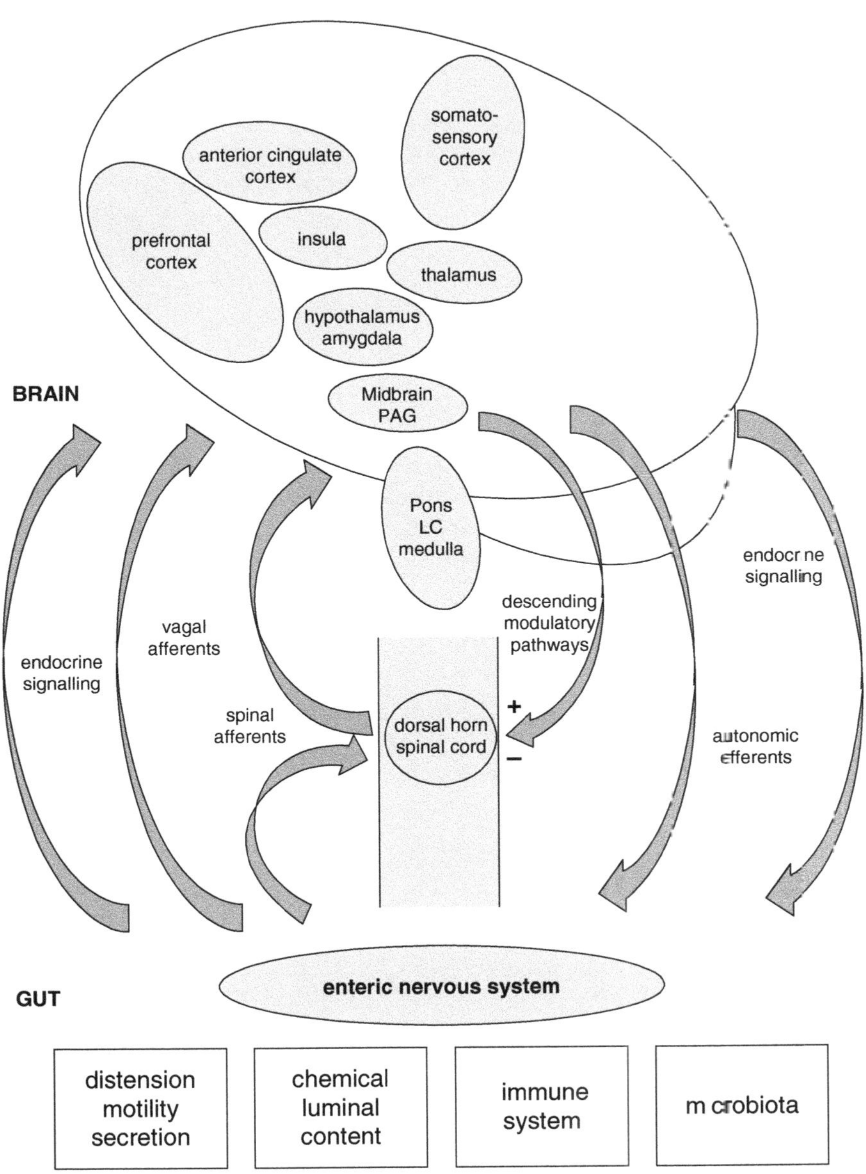

Figure 3.1 Schematic representation of the brain-gut axis. Information about gut distension and motility, the chemical composition of luminal contents, the immune system and the microbiota is conveyed to primary afferent neurons of the enteric nervous system, and via endocrine signalling to the brain. Ascending vagal and spinal afferents conduct sensory information to the CNS, the latter synapsing at the dorsal horn of the spinal cord. Both vagal and spinal pathways project via the thalamus to regions of the cortex involved in processing visceral sensation, and to subcortical structures involved in emotion, arousal and autonomic responses. The insula integrates signals from cortical and subcortical regions. Descending pathways arising from all these regions can facilitate or inhibit ascending sensory signals at the dorsal horn, and communicate with the gut via sympathetic and parasympathetic autonomic efferents, and by endocrine signalling (hypothalamo-pituitary-adrenal and sympatho-adrenal axes). PAG, periaqueductal grey; LC, locus coeruleus.

brain' of the central nervous system (CNS), and the 'little brain' of the enteric nervous system (ENS) – interact with each other in a bidirectional manner, collectively referred to as the 'brain-gut axis' (BGA) (Figure 3.1). This chapter will review the peripheral and central components of the BGA, the nature of the links between them, and how we currently understand their function to be disordered in people suffering from FGIDs. Finally, the implications for therapy and for the future direction of research will be discussed.

Structure of the BGA

The ENS consists of two nerve plexuses between layers of the gut wall that communicate with the CNS (spinal cord and brain) through multiple neural and endocrine pathways [4]. In this manner, many elements of gut function (distension and motility, luminal content, immune function and even the microbiota) can influence, and be influenced by, higher centres, in both 'bottom-up' and 'top-down' directions [5].

Enteric nervous system

The ENS is distributed between layers of the gut wall, forming both a submucous and a myenteric plexus, and containing a similar number of neurons to the spinal cord (~10^8). Though connected to the CNS, the ENS can operate independently – for example, in co-ordinating the peristaltic reflex.

Ascending pathways

Signals from gut to brain arise from mechanical and chemical stimuli in the gut, as well as immune cells and the microbiota [6]. They are conveyed via primary afferent neurons which are both intrinsic and extrinsic (vagal and spinal), resulting in input to reflex loops both within the gut and at multiple levels in the spinal cord, medulla and midbrain.

Vagal afferent fibres project to the nucleus of the solitary tract, and from there to subcortical structures involved in emotion, arousal and autonomic responses (hypothalamus, locus coeruleus, amygdala and periaqueductal grey [PAG]), and via the thalamus to cortical areas involved in processing visceral sensation [7].

Spinal afferents synapse in the dorsal horn of the cord, with projections to the reticular formation, midbrain and hypothalamus again mediating emotional, behavioural and autonomic responses, and via the thalamus to viscerosensory regions of the cortex [7]. Although only a fraction of ascending signals from the gut is consciously perceived, such as those related to swallowing or defaecation, the remainder can influence emotions, arousal and memory formation at a subconscious level.

Central processing of visceral sensation

The somatosensory cortices ('lateral pain system') can discriminate the location and intensity of a stimulus [7], while the anterior cingulate cortex (ACC) ('medial pain system') generates autonomic, affective and behavioural responses, and is involved in the anticipation of aversive stimuli [8]. The insula ('interoceptive cortex') integrates visceral sensation with emotional inputs, to generate autonomic responses that in turn influence visceral activity. Even in the absence of any neural input from the gut, subjects who image feelings of disgust can experience nausea-like sensations, associated with activation of the anterior insula and ACC. Such processing of sensations is potentially influenced by developmental events, such as aversive memories, and provides the basis for intuitive decision-making (acting on 'gut feelings') [6]. No single brain region is responsible for processing visceral pain; rather, the experience of uncomfortable gut sensations and associated emotions represents the net result of an integrated network of neural activity [1].

Descending pathways

Every level of the BGA gives rise to descending pathways that influence gut function, acting via the autonomic nervous system, the hypothalamic-pituitary-adrenal axis, the sympatho-adrenal axis and descending neural pathways that modulate ascending visceral signals at the level of the dorsal horn of the spinal cord [9].

The PFC and ACC, subcortical structures including hypothalamus and amygdala, and medullary vagal complex and PAG, form a cortico-limbo-pontine network referred to as the 'emotional motor system' (EMS). The EMS gives rise to descending pathways that influence (i) pain sensitivity at the dorsal horn level, via neurotransmitters that include serotonin, noradrenaline and endogenous opioids, and (ii) visceral motor activity via the sympathetic and parasympathetic nerves [6].

Sympathetic input inhibits gut transit and secretion, stimulates contractile activity of the sphincters, induces vasoconstriction and can even modulate the mucosal immune system and microbiota [10]. Parasympathetic input, transmitted through the vagus nerve, drives vago-vagal motor reflexes and the cephalic phase of gastric acid secretion, stimulates secretion of gastrin, somatostatin and serotonin and can also modulate the function of immune cells in the gut [11].

Mechanisms of visceral hypersensitivity

'Visceral hypersensitivity' refers to painful perceptions arising from gastrointestinal stimuli at a lower threshold than that observed in health [4], and is commonly observed in patients with FGIDs [12]. Visceral hypersensitivity could potentially arise from sensitization of (i) afferent neurons in the gut (peripheral sensitization), (ii) neurons in the dorsal horn of the spinal cord (central sensitization) or (iii) altered processing of sensory inputs in the brain [4]. These mechanisms are not mutually exclusive, and the relative contribution of each may differ in different subsets of patients with FGIDs.

Peripheral sensitization

In some patients with IBS or other FGIDs, the onset of symptoms follows an episode of gastroenteritis ('post-infectious IBS') or abdominal/pelvic surgery, suggesting the role of inflammation or damage to visceral afferent nerves. Inflammatory mediators (e.g., potassium or hydrogen ions, ATP, histamine, serotonin, bradykinin and prostaglandins) can reduce the activation threshold of primary afferent neurons, and recruit nociceptors [13], while cytokines derived from macrophages and mast cells induce production of cyclo-oxygenase metabolites [14].

Peripheral sensitization tends to be transient, so that further changes would be required to perpetuate the hypersensitivity in chronic illness, such as an increase in mast cells and inflammatory mediators (e.g., substance P or interleukin-4) [9].

Central sensitization in the spinal cord

Responses to both noxious and innocuous stimuli can be enhanced at the level of the dorsal horn by the presynaptic release of glutamate, substance P, brain-derived neurotrophic factor and prostaglandins. This can result, for example, from immune activation of the glia, which produce pro-inflammatory cytokines and undergo downregulation of glutamate transport, elevating glutamate at the synapse [6]. A phenotypic shift can be induced in otherwise non-nociceptive afferents, so that previously innocuous stimuli now induce pain ('allodynia') [15].

Descending pathways play a key role in facilitating or inhibiting pain at the level of the dorsal horn. These originate from the EMS, and those that inhibit pain transmission utilize serotonergic and opioidergic signalling [16]. Inhibitory phenomena within the cord can also modulate pain – for example, noxious somatic stimuli can attenuate visceral pain perception ('counter-irritation'), while conversely, inhibition of inputs from other sources can accentuate perception of a visceral signal [4]. Inhibitory phenomena can be time-limited – for example, pain signals from the viscera may cause transient inhibition, resulting in the phenomenon of intermittent, colicky pain.

Pain processing in the brain

Advances in neuroimaging over the past 1–2 decades have provided insights into changes in brain function and structure in patients with FGIDs, and how these relate to emotions, cognition and even genetics [3].

During rectal balloon distension in humans, brain activation can be observed with functional magnetic resonance imaging (fMRI). While similar brain regions are activated by a given stimulus in both health and disease (a 'salience network', responsible for processing sensory information related to a stimulus), chronic visceral pain states are associated with modifications in both degree of response and connectivity, so as to attribute greater weight to the visceral stimulus, particularly in terms of generating emotional arousal [17].

Cognitive factors, particularly expectations, can have a major impact on sensory processing. The 'central executive network' (dorsolateral PFC and posterior parietal cortex), together with the salience network, is involved in states of increased attention to gut stimuli [18], and associated with reduced engagement of regions of the cortex that give rise to inhibitory pathways [17]. The concept of 'prediction error', proposed by Paulus and Stein, refers to a mismatch in the anterior insula between the predicated interoceptive state (arising from aversive memories or a perception of threat) and the actual interoceptive state (generated by sensory signals from the gut) [6]. Prediction error results in activation of the ACC, generates feelings of anxiety and increases autonomic activity, which in turn modifies the motor and secretory activity of the gut to alter actual interoceptive feedback. Failure to correct prediction error (as in the state of 'catastrophizing') can lead to perpetuation of gut symptoms.

As well as functional changes in brain processing, imaging studies have revealed structural differences in both grey and white matter in regions associated with viscero-sensory processing, including the somatosensory cortex, subcortical structures and the salience network (ACC and insula) [3]. Variations in these brain regions are observed even between healthy volunteers, and correlate with symptom intensity, suggesting that these differences may predispose to visceral hypersensitivity.

A number of factors are associated with modifications in the processing of pain by the brain. Single nucleotide polymorphisms for receptors related to serotonin, corticotrophin releasing hormone, catecholamines, glucocorticoids and progesterone provide evidence for a genetic influence [1], while sex differences include an increased engagement of emotional brain networks in women, and prefrontal circuits in men [3]. The immune system can influence pain processing through trafficking of primed monocytes between gut and brain, which can alter both ENS and CNS plasticity [19, 20]. The microbiota have been shown to influence the processing of pain and emotions in rodent models, particularly during brain development, through endocrine pathways and vagal and sympathetic afferents (e.g., by release of cytokines and bacterial metabolites); similar mechanisms are likely to apply in humans, but the evidence is currently less clear-cut [21].

Implications for therapy

The nature of the BGA suggests that control of gut symptoms such as chronic pain could be targeted to either peripheral or central sites. However, the relative contribution of each site to symptoms is likely to vary substantially between individuals and between subsets of patients [4].

Modulation of peripheral sensitization

A focus of recent drug development for FGIDs has been at the level of peripheral pain mechanisms [1]. Targets include TRPV1 and voltage-gated sodium channels, Nav 1.8 and Nav 1.9, but much of this work remains in the preclinical phase.

Modulation of visceral pain at the dorsal horn

The experimental model of acid-induced hypersensitivity of the oesophagus has yielded insights into the modulation of visceral pain at the dorsal horn of the spinal cord in humans [22]. Acid-induced hypersensitivity can be prevented by either the NMDA receptor antagonist ketamine [23] or by prostaglandin E2 receptor antagonism [24]. COX-2 inhibition is ineffective, however, supporting the hypothesis that the oesophageal hypersensitivity is a central rather than peripheral phenomenon [25]. Nevertheless, NK-1 receptor antagonists have not been effective in preventing proximal oesophageal hypersensitivity induced by distal oesophageal acid exposure (allodynia) in the laboratory, and have been clinically disappointing in the treatment of somatic pain [4].

Modulation of pain processing in the brain

Pharmacological treatments with potential to modify central pain processing include tricyclic antidepressants [26] and drugs acting on serotonin pathways, including selective serotonin reuptake inhibitors or 5HT3 antagonists (e.g., alosetron) [1]; the latter reduce blood flow to limbic, paralimbic and central autonomic circuits during anticipation of rectal distension in IBS patients during PET imaging [27]. The kappa and mu opioid agonist/delta antagonist eluxadoline can relieve pain as well as improve stool form in diarrhoea-predominant IBS patients [28]. CRF1 receptor antagonists, on the other hand, have been disappointing [29]. Agonists of the endogenous cannabinoid system, acting on descending pain inhibitory pathways, represent another target, although they may be less efficacious for visceral than somatic pain [30].

Non-pharmacological treatments, including cognitive behavioural therapy, mindfulness [31] and hypnosis [32], are some of the more consistently effective approaches in FGID therapy. They potentially act by augmenting inhibitory pathways from the PFC that control stress and arousal networks, and by modifying deleterious interoceptive memories [5].

Practical recommendations

Attempts to modulate peripheral and/or central pain pathways need further development to enhance the management options for people with FGIDs. More evidence is needed as to the clinical significance of peripheral and dorsal horn targets identified in preclinical studies. Stronger support should be gathered for pharmacological interventions that modify central pain processing, while non-pharmacological approaches appear rewarding.

Practical recommendations

- Potential targets for pain modulation at the perphery, dorsal horn and in the brain need further development to establish clinical utility.
- Facilitating access to non-pharmacological techniques for modulating central pain processing is likely to benefit patients with FGIDs.

Current limitations/future considerations

- Despite recent advances in understanding the broad contribution of the BGA to the pathogenesis of FGIDs, through animal models and clinical association studies, our knowledge of which abnormalities drive specific symptoms is limited, and human data have tended to be cross-sectional, so that cause and effect are difficult to distinguish.

- Future studies should characterize patient phenotypes in more detail, and follow groups of patients in longitudinal fashion, as well as examining the roles of genetic variation and developmental influences, and the effects of interventions.

Acknowledgements, competing interests and funding

The author has received research funding from AstraZeneca, Merck Sharp & Dohme, Novartis and Sanofi, and from the National Health and Medical Research Council of Australia.

References

1 Mayer, E.A., Labus, J.S., Tillisch, K., Cole, S.W., Baldi, P.: Towards a systems view of IBS. *Nat Rev Gastroenterol Hepatol* 2015, **12**(10): 592–605.

2 Wilder-Smith, C.H.: The balancing act: Endogenous modulation of pain in functional gastrointestinal disorders. *Gut* 2011, **60**(11): 1589–1599.

3 Mayer, E.A., Gupta, A., Kilpatrick, L.A., Hong, J.Y.: Imaging brain mechanisms in chronic visceral pain. *Pain* 2015, **156**(Suppl 1): S50–S63.

4 Anand, P., Aziz, Q., Willert, R., van Oudenhove, L.: Peripheral and central mechanisms of visceral sensitization in man. *Neurogastroenterol Motil* 2007, **19**(1 Suppl): 29–46.

5 Mayer, E.A., Tillisch, K.: The brain-gut axis in abdominal pain syndromes. *Annu Rev Med* 2011, **62**: 381–396.

6 Mayer, E.A.: Gut feelings: The emerging biology of gut-brain communication. *Nat Rev Neurosci* 2011, **12**(8): 453–466.

7 Van Oudenhove, L., Demyttenaere, K., Tack, J., Aziz, Q.: Central nervous system involvement in functional gastrointestinal disorders. *Best Pract Res Clin Gastroenterol* 2004, **18**(4): 663–680.

8 Naliboff, B.D., Mayer, E.A.: Brain imaging in IBS: Drawing the line between cognitive and non-cognitive processes. *Gastroenterology* 2006, **130**(1): 267–270.

9 Mayer, E.A.: The neurobiology of stress and gastrointestinal disease. *Gut* 2000, **47**(6): 861–869.

10 Mayer, E.A., Savidge, T., Shulman, R.J.: Brain-gut microbiome interactions and functional bowel disorders. *Gastroenterology* 2014, **146**(6): 1500–1512.

11 Pavlov, V.A., Tracey, K.J.: The cholinergic anti-inflammatory pathway. *Brain Behav Immun* 2005, **19**(6): 493–499.

12 Mayer, E.A., Gebhart, G.F.: Basic and clinical aspects of visceral hyperalgesia. *Gastroenterology* 1994, **107**(1): 271–293.

13 Costigan, M., Woolf, C.J.: Pain: Molecular mechanisms. *J Pain* 2000, **1**(3 Suppl): 35–44.

14 Seibert, K., Zhang, Y., Leahy, K., Hauser, S., Masferrer, J., Perkins, W., Lee, L., Isakson, P.: Pharmacological and biochemical demonstration of the role of cyclooxygenase 2 in inflammation and pain. *Proc Natl Acad Sci U S A* 1994, **91**(25): 12013–12017.

15 Neumann, S., Doubell, T.P., Leslie, T., Woolf, C.J.: Inflammatory pain hypersensitivity mediated by phenotypic switch in myelinated primary sensory neurons. *Nature* 1996, **384**(6607): 360–364.

16 Millan, M.J.: Descending control of pain. *Prog Neurobiol* 2002, **66**(6): 355–474.

17 Tillisch, K., Mayer, E.A., Labus, J.S.: Quantitative meta-analysis identifies brain regions activated during rectal distension in irritable bowel syndrome. *Gastroenterology* 2011, **140**(1): 91–100.

18 Mayer, E.A., Bradesi, S., Chang, L., Spiegel, B.M., Bueller, J.A., Naliboff, B.D.: Functional GI disorders: From animal models to drug development. *Gut* 2008, **57**(3): 384–404.
19 Hughes, P.A., Zola, H., Penttila, I.A., Blackshaw, L.A., Andrews, J.M., Krumbiegel, D.: Immune activation in irritable bowel syndrome: Can neuroimmune interactions explain symptoms? *Am J Gastroenterol* 2013, **108**(7): 1066–1074.
20 Ohman, L., Simren, M.: Pathogenesis of IBS: Role of inflammation, immunity and neuroimmune interactions. *Nat Rev Gastroenterol Hepatol* 2010, **7**(3): 163–173.
21 Mayer, E.A., Tillisch, K., Gupta, A.: Gut/brain axis and the microbiota. *J Clin Invest* 2015, **125**(3): 926–938.
22 Sarkar, S., Aziz, Q., Woolf, C.J., Hobson, A.R., Thompson, D.G.: Contribution of central sensitisation to the development of non-cardiac chest pain. *Lancet* 2000, **356**(9236): 1154–1159.
23 Willert, R.P., Woolf, C.J., Hobson, A.R., Delaney, C., Thompson, D.G., Aziz, Q.: The development and maintenance of human visceral pain hypersensitivity is dependent on the N-methyl-D-aspartate receptor. *Gastroenterology* 2004, **126**(3): 683–692.
24 Sarkar, S., Hobson, A.R., Hughes, A., Growcott, J., Woolf, C.J., Thompson, D.G., Aziz, Q.: The prostaglandin E2 receptor-1 (EP-1) mediates acid-induced visceral pain hypersensitivity in humans. *Gastroenterology* 2003, **124**(1): 18–25.
25 Willert, R.P., Delaney, C., Hobson, A.R., Thompson, D.G., Woolf, C.J., Aziz, Q.: Constitutive cyclo-oxygenase-2 does not contribute to the development of human visceral pain hypersensitivity. *Eur J Pain (London, England)* 2006, **10**(6): 487–494.
26 Drossman, D.A., Toner, B.B., Whitehead, W.E., Diamant, N.E., Dalton, C.B., Duncan, S., Emmott, S., Proffitt, V., Akman, D., Frusciante, K., *et al.*: Cognitive-behavioral therapy versus education and desipramine versus placebo for moderate to severe functional bowel disorders. *Gastroenterology* 2003, **125**(1): 19–31.
27 Berman, S.M., Chang, L., Suyenobu, B., Derbyshire, S.W., Stains, J., Fitzgerald, L., Mandelkern, M., Hamm, L., Vogt, B., Naliboff, B.D., *et al.*: Condition-specific deactivation of brain regions by 5-HT3 receptor antagonist Alosetron. *Gastroenterology* 2002, **123**(4): 969–977.
28 Lembo, A.J., Lacy, B.E., Zuckerman, M.J., Schey, R., Dove, L.S., Andrae, D.A., Davenport, J.M., McIntyre, G., Lopez, R., Turner, L., *et al.*: Eluxadoline for irritable bowel syndrome with diarrhea. *N Engl J Med* 2016, **374**(3): 242–253.
29 Sweetser, S., Camilleri, M., Linker Nord, S.J., Burton, D.D., Castenada, L., Croop, R., Tong, G., Dockens, R., Zinsmeister, A.R.: Do corticotropin releasing factor-1 receptors influence colonic transit and bowel function in women with irritable bowel syndrome? *Am J Physiol Gastrointest Liver Physiol* 2009, **296**(6): G1299–G1306.
30 Klooker, T.K., Leliefeld, K.E., Van Den Wijngaard, R.M., Boeckxstaens, G.E.: The cannabinoid receptor agonist delta-9-tetrahydrocannabinol does not affect visceral sensitivity to rectal distension in healthy volunteers and IBS patients. *Neurogastroenterol Motil* 2011, **23**(1): 30–35, e32.
31 Kim, S., Chang, L.: A mindful way through IBS: Reducing abdominal pain and improving quality of life. *Gastroenterology* 2012, **142**(5): 1247–1250, author reply 1250.
32 Miller, V., Carruthers, H.R., Morris, J., Hasan, S.S., Archbold, S., Whorwell, P.J.: Hypnotherapy for irritable bowel syndrome: An audit of one thousand adult patients. *Aliment Pharmacol Ther* 2015, **41**(9): 844–855.

Chapter 4

Psychosocial and individual aspects of functional gastrointestinal disorders

Anton Emmanuel

The aim of this chapter is to review the psychosocial and individual aspects of functional gastrointestinal disorders (FGIDs), including evidence for the biopsychosocial model and how it underpins the brain-gut axis, specifically in relation to sexual (and other forms of) abuse, personality factors and environmental factors on FGIDs. The chapter also provides practical recommendations in relation to applying a holistic integrative biopsychosocial approach in clinical practice.

Learning points

- The biopsychosocial model is the standard framework for understanding the brain-gut axis as it operates in FGIDs, providing both an explanatory model and a focus for treatments
- Family clustering of irritable bowel syndrome cases does not necessarily imply abuse: it can reflect maladaptive coping and abnormal learned behaviours.
- Recognition of the role of psychological traits and states is important both as part of the formulation and because it reflects on FGID symptom severity and treatment response.
- The hypersensitive response of the gut to stress in FGIDs is in part related to psychological factors, especially anxiety and neuroticism.

Introduction

The relationship between emotions and function of the gastrointestinal (GI) tract is well recognized. Almost all individuals will be able to identify an experience of stress- or emotion-induced alterations of gut movement or sensation – such as urgency or loose stools before a stressful event or the 'butterflies in my stomach' sensation during times of arousal. In healthy individuals, these are not a cause of presentation to medical care, since the degree of arousal required to precipitate these feelings is in keeping with the experience of the majority. In individuals with FGIDs the intensity of feelings is severe and/or the degree of provocation relatively minor. Such individuals are considered, in contemporary psychological practice, to suffer from a psychosomatic condition [1]. This relationship between mind and body is not uni-directional; rather, it is reciprocal. In other words, it is as much somatopsychic as it is psychosomatic [1, 2]. It is little surprise, therefore, that there is often much overlap in the epidemiology and nature of symptoms between FGIDs and other functional somatic syndromes, such as chronic fatigue syndrome and fibromyalgia [2, 3]. This is embedded in the new *Diagnostic and Statistical Manual of Mental Disorders* (DSM-5) classification system with the new diagnosis of 'somatic symptom disorder' [4].

The current aetio-pathological model of FGIDs is biopsychosocially focused; see Figure 4.1 [5]. As such, there are potentially predisposing factors (e.g., personality or early life experience), precipitating ones (e.g., following infection or at times of stress) and perpetuating factors (e.g., chronic stressors, mood or attenuated coping mechanisms). This has contributed to the notion of a 'brain-gut axis', which can be both a focus for understanding of the conditions and a framework for therapy [6]. It is evident from Figure 4.1 that much of what is described is part of the normal make-up of an individual: it is part of the lived experience of individuals, emphasizing the all-encompassing nature of these somatoform disorders, at the intersection of disease and psychosocial trait.

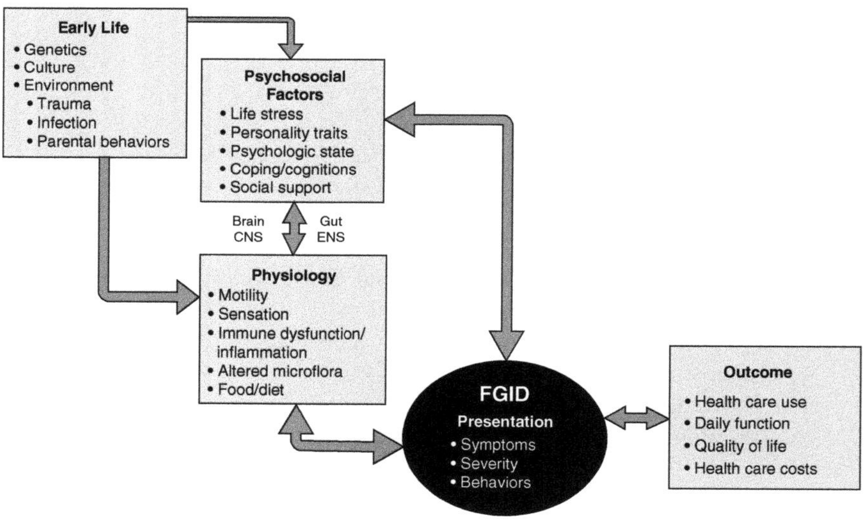

Figure 4.1 A biopsychosocial conceptualization of the pathogenesis, clinical experience and effects of functional GI disorders. There is a relationship between early life factors that can influence the psychosocial milieu of the individual, the individual's physiological functioning and his or her mutual interaction (brain-gut axis). These factors influence the clinical presentation of the disorder and the clinical outcome. Consistent with this biopsychosocial conceptualization is that the influences on these factors are bidirectional and mutually interactive. Figure and text description are taken from D.A. Drossman [7] Functional Gastrointestinal Disorders and the Rome IV Process, Chapter 1, page 15 of the *Rome IV Functional Gastrointestinal Disorders: Disorders of Gut-Brain Interaction*. Reproduction approved by Professor Douglas Drossman 23/10/2016.

Environmental factors

Among potentially important aetiological factors in FGIDs, there are a range of environmental factors – infection, alterations of the gut microbiome, diet and lifestyle. They are the focus of other chapters in this book. This section will briefly outline the individual, social and psychological factors that have been studied in IBS and other FGIDs.

Early life experience

The traumatic early life events that are prevalent in FGIDs are best described in the irritable bowel syndrome (IBS) [8–10]. Typically, such early adverse life events are classified under four domains (general, emotional, physical and sexual), and there is a two- to three-fold greater likelihood of such experiences in IBS patients compared to controls [9], with almost half IBS patients in tertiary settings having an abuse history. Such events are also associated with increased symptom severity and health-care utilization [8, 11].

It is unsurprising then that there are family clusters of IBS patients [12]. These seem to have less a genetic basis and more a behavioural one. Such clustering is compounded by positive reinforcement of aberrant illness behaviour when a parent 'rewards' subjective complaints with school absence and health-care visits [13]. In short, the cycle of having IBS, and/or of having been the victim of abuse, often perpetuates the condition in future generations. This perpetuating pattern may be facilitated by several factors, including intrapersonal beliefs, developmental and social learning experiences. The treating clinician should be aware of these factors, but care needs to be taken in directly addressing them unless there is an appropriate staff and environment, given the risk of further traumatizing the patient [3, 6]. Parental influences extend beyond the social. There is evidence for the contributory effect of parental psychological status (notably somatization trait, anxiety and depression) on presentations with abdominal complaints [14]. This could arise from parental rewarding of illness behaviour (as earlier), or reflect child modelling of observed parental patterns and reflected beliefs. Both the rewarding of illness behaviour and modelling observed parental patterns are likely to have an enduring impact on illness perceptions. Several studies have demonstrated the adverse impact of particular illness beliefs (e.g., seeing the illness as uncontrollable, untreatable, chronic and causing significant adverse impacts upon physical and mental health) in IBS [15–18].

Lifestyle, life events and intrapersonal processes

The presence of recent life stressors (especially those of a traumatic nature) is a common precipitant to the onset or exacerbation of symptoms, with the degree of perceived stress being the chief predictor of the intensity of IBS symptoms [19]. Therefore, an individual's lifestyle and how he or she comes to terms with both intrapersonal and interpersonal stressors play key roles in both the genesis and expression of FGIDs. This finding is irrespective of personality traits, such as neuroticism (a personality trait characterized by anxiety, low mood, worry, fear), suggesting a true effect of stress on the gut [20]. This is a rather oversimplified view, however, and there is evidence that personal attitudes (in particular the tendency to catastrophize in response to pain) interact with life stressors in terms of generating gut symptoms and health-care utilization [21, 22]. The effect of stress on the gut seems to be related to abnormal autonomically mediated hypersensitivity and enteric dysmotility [20].

Coping is a key component of the healthy response to stress. Coping has internal components (based on the individual's psychological make-up) as well as external ones (to do with support systems). Patients with FGIDs have reduced quality and number of social supports, and this correlates to symptom severity [23]. It is a hallmark of successful therapy for patients with IBS that there is a supportive patient-professional relationship, which helps the patient cope with a chronic illness characterized by recurrent symptom episodes [24]. Examples of maladaptive coping include catastrophizing, the cognitive process in which an individual magnifies the seriousness of symptoms and consequences while feeling helpless in him- or herself. This is different to hypervigilance, in which there is increased attention paid to bodily symptoms and reminder of symptoms. Several studies provide strong evidence for the adverse impact of heightened visceral sensitivity (gastrointestinal-specific anxiety) on increasing GI symptoms, especially thoughts associated with IBS [17, 25–28] although not explored, it is likely that similar heightened visceral sensitivity processes occur in other FGIDs.

Psychological factors

The central nervous part of the brain-gut axis that has been most studied is the brain, and a combination of functional imaging studies and epidemiology has been used to derive the biopsychosocial model. Psychological disorders are key perpetuators of IBS symptoms [2]. A classic system to assess the interplay between brain and gut in FGIDs is the post-infectious functional dyspepsia or IBS-model [29]. Psychological traits present at the time of infection can be identified at baseline, and their influence on the subsequent course of the FGID explored.

Depression

The presence of a mood disorder predisposes to the development of IBS symptoms following enteric infection [30]. A clinical conundrum facing practitioners, however, is the 'chicken-and-egg' issue – that chronic FGIDs will provoke low mood. Depression is associated with worse symptoms, greater health-care spending, poorer engagement with treatment and worse quality of life [23]. Another clinical challenge for the non-psychiatrist physician looking after patients with FGIDs is knowing when there is a psychiatric severity depressive disorder present as opposed to the low mood that accompanies the gut condition [6]. Notwithstanding, it appears that about one third of FGID patients in primary care have comorbid depression and up to 38% in a tertiary care setting have a sense of hopelessness and suicidal ideation due to their FGID [31].

Anxiety

Anxiety disorders are the commonest psychiatric comorbidity in FGIDs. As many as 67% have trait anxiety and 84% state anxiety in a large series of FGID outpatients [32]. Two forms of anxiety in particular have been studied. The first is 'illness anxiety', a global tendency to worry about current and future bodily symptoms (previously referred to as hypochondriasis), and the second is 'symptom-specific anxiety' (as in aerophagia) and describes hypervigilance around the presence of specific symptoms and the contexts in which they occur [33]. Both types are associated with increased health-care costs due to lack of insight or acceptance that there may be a non-organic contributor to symptom burden [34]. The effects of anxiety on the gut stress response in both acute and chronic stress form a core part of the understanding of the pathophysiology of FGIDs, whereby anxiety can result in abnormal autonomically mediated gut motor and sensory change through altered stress responses [20, 33].

Somatization and medically unexplained symptoms

The frequently observed overlap between FGIDs and medically unexplained symptoms (whereby IBS patients reported an average of four physical comorbidities [35]) has led to the popularity of the term 'somatization' among many gastroenterologists. However, this is a contentious label, from both the classification and the therapeutic perspectives. Current classification focuses on the distress caused by the patient's perceived symptoms and the disproportionate cognitions and behaviours that are associated with that [36]. This change of paradigm allows for the cause-and-effect aspect of symptoms causing worry about physical function and in turn offers the potential for the efficacy of cognitive behavioural therapy in this setting. The relationship between somatization scores and gut sensori-motor function has been proposed as possibly reflecting a distinct pathology from other functional somatic syndromes, but it remains possible that the different symptom presentations are no more than different manifestations of a common underlying pathophysiological process [37].

Personality

The five-factor model accounting for the trait structure of personality has been one of the developments in personality research [38]. This model comprises five broad personality dimensions which demonstrate stability across cultures and over time [38] and which are held to have a biological basis. 'Neuroticism' is the factor identified as the key personality dimension associated with IBS, even when controlling for psychiatric comorbidity [27]. The neuroticism trait may represent a link between childhood abuse and bowel symptoms in FGIDs. Data from a longitudinal study showed that early life abuse was significantly associated with neuroticism, which in turn was strongly associated with baseline prevalence of bowel disturbance [39]. There are discrepant data about whether any particular subtype is particularly associated with neuroticism [40]. In a recent review of the literature, Muscatello and colleagues [34] suggest that along with neuroticism, conscientiousness is also linked to IBS. Individuals reporting greater levels of conscientiousness (e.g., achievement striving) are more likely to report IBS symptoms and symptom exacerbation. Another personality factor that has shown a consistent association with FGIDs is 'alexithymia' [41]. This personality trait, characterized by the inability to recognize or describe emotions and their nuances, is found in two thirds of IBS patients [41]. Compared to non-alexithymic IBS patients, alexythymic IBS patients have heightened pain sensitivity to rectal distension [42], raising the possibility that the latter group misinterprets somatic sensations triggered by states of emotional arousal.

Thus, there are a number of psychological factors, including psychological comorbidity, personality and intrapersonal and interpersonal coping patterns, that have been demonstrated to impact upon FGIDs. Therefore for clinicians, it is important to explore and listen to patient language, emotions and nonverbal cues and consider how these may pertain to personal attitudes, personality structure and coping patterns.

Conclusion

The patient with a FGID needs to have a formulation made. This comprises, initially, an understanding of the symptoms reported (reflecting the enteric and central physiological disturbances). Secondly, it requires an understanding of the reasons for the current presentation (in terms of the current and recent social stresses, the patient's lifestyle and his or her coping strategies). Finally, an exploration of the patient's background and personality, using an approach that is collaborative and respectful of the patient's defences and fears, may identify some of the predisposing and perpetuating factors contributing to their presentation. Such an approach allows for the patient to be gently led through a history, rather than being treated like a zoo animal with an unusual background and strange current circumstance. Psychological distress is common in FGID patients and needs considering regarding whether it is symptom-specific or more global, as the former may require physical correlates to aid treatment alongside consideration of the psychological ones. Personality factors do have an impact on FGIDs, but personality is a nuanced consideration and should not be assessed in a hasty and pejorative way.

Acknowledgements, competing interests and funding

Anton Emmanuel is supported by the UCL Biomedical Research Centre. There are no competing interests.

References

1 Wessely, S., Nimnuan, C., Sharpe, M.: Functional somatic syndromes: One or many? *Lancet* 1999, **354**(9182): 936–939.

2 Mayou, R., Kirmayer, L.J., Simon, G., Kroenke, K., Sharpe, M.: Somatoform disorders: Time for a new approach in DSM-V. *Am J Psychiat* 2005, **162**(5): 847–855.

3 Whitehead, W.E., Palsson, O., Jones, K.R.: Systematic review of the comorbidity of irritable bowel syndrome with other disorders: What are the causes and implications? *Gastroenterology* 2002, **122**(4): 1140–1156.

4 American Psychiatric Association: *Diagnostic and statistical manual of mental disorders*, 5th edn. Washington, DC: Author, 2013.

5 Van Oudenhove, L., Levy, R.L., Crowell, M.D., Drossman, D.A., Halpert, A.D., Keefer, L., Lackner, J.M., Murphy, T.B., Naliboff, B.D.: Biopsychosocial aspects of functional gastrointestinal disorders: How central and environmental processes contribute to the development and expression of functional gastrointestinal disorders. *Gastroenterology* 2016, **150**(6): 1355–1367e1352.

6 Stern, J.M.: Review article: Psychiatry, psychotherapy and gastroenterology – Bringing it all together. *Aliment Pharmacol Ther* 2003, **17**(2): 175–184.

7 Drossman, D.A.: *Rome IV functional gastrointestinal disorders: Disorders of gut-brain interaction*, 4th edn. Raleigh, NC: Rome Foundation, 2016.

8 Bradford, K., Shih, W., Videlock, E.J., Presson, A.P., Naliboff, B.D., Mayer, E.A., Chang, L.: Association between early adverse life events and irritable bowel syndrome. *Clin Gastroenterol Hepatol* 2012, **10**(4): 385–390.

9 Chitkara, D.K., Van Tilburg, M.A.L., Blois-Martin, N., Whitehead, W.E.: Early life risk factors that contribute to irritable bowel syndrome in adults: A systematic review. *Am J Gastroenterol* 2008, **103**(3): 765–774.

10 Park, S.H., Videlock, E.J., Shih, W., Presson, A.P., Mayer, E.A., Chang, L.: Adverse childhood experiences are associated with irritable bowel syndrome and gastrointestinal symptom severity. *Neurogastroenterol Motil* 2016, **28**(8): 1252–1260.

11 Drossman, D.A.: Abuse, trauma, and GI illness: Is there a link. *Am J Gastroenterol* 2011, **106**(1): 14–25.

12 Levy, R.L., Jones, K.R., Whitehead, W.E., Feld, S.I., Talley, N.J., Corey, L.A.: Irritable bowel syndrome in twins: Heredity and social learning both contribute to etiology. *Gastroenterology* 2001, **121**(4): 799–804.

13 Levy, R.L., Whitehead, W.E., Walker, L.S., Von Korff, M., Feld, A.D., Garner, M., Christie, D.: Increased somatic complaints and health-care utilization in children: Effects of parent IBS status and parent response to gastrointestinal symptoms. *Am J Gastroenterol* 2004, **99**(12): 2442–2451.

14 Walker, L.S., Garber, J., Greene, J.W.: Somatic complaints in pediatric patients: A prospective study of the role of negative life events, child social and academic competence, and parental somatic symptoms. *J Consult Clin Psychol* 1994, **62**(6): 1213–1221.

15 Spence, M.J., Moss-Morris, R.: The cognitive behavioural model of irritable bowel syndrome: A prospective investigation of patients with gastroenteritis. *Gut* 2007, **56**(8): 1066–1071.

16 De Gucht, V.: Illness perceptions mediate the relationship between bowel symptom severity and health-related quality of life in IBS patients. *Qual Life Res* 2015, **24**(8): 1845–1856.

17 Knowles, S.R., Austin, D.W., Sivanesan, S., Tye-Din, J., Leung, C., Wilson, J., Castle, D., Kamm, M.A., Macrae, F., Hebbard, G.: Relations between symptom severity, illness perceptions, visceral sensitivity, coping strategies and well-being in irritable bowel syndrome guided by the common sense model of illness. *Psychol Health Med* 2017, **22**(5): 524–534.

18 Sherwin, L.B., Leary, E., Henderson, W.A.: Effect of illness representations and catastrophizing on quality of life in adults with irritable bowel syndrome. *J Psych Nurs Mental Health Serv* 2016, **54**(9): 44–53.

19 Whitehead, W.E., Crowell, M.D., Robinson, J.C., Heller, B.R., Schuster, M.M.: Effects of stressful life events on bowel symptoms: Subjects with irritable bowel syndrome compared with subjects without bowel dysfunction. *Gut* 1992, **33**(6): 825–830.
20 Murray, C.D.R., Flynn, J., Ratcliffe, L., Jacyna, M.R., Kamm, M.A., Emmanuel, A.V.: Effect of acute physical and psychological stress on gut autonomic innervation in irritable bowel syndrome. *Gastroenterology* 2004, **127**(6): 1695–1703.
21 Bennett, E.J., Tennant, C.C., Piesse, C., Badcock, C.A., Kellow, J.E.: Level of chronic life stress predicts clinical outcome in irritable bowel syndrome. *Gut* 1998, **43**(2): 256–261.
22 Lackner, J.M., Gurtman, M.B.: Pain catastrophizing and interpersonal problems: A circumplex analysis of the communal coping model. *Pain* 2004, **110**(3): 597–604.
23 Lackner, J.M., Brasel, A.M., Quigley, B.M., Keefer, L., Krasner, S.S., Powell, C., Katz, L.A., Sitrin, M.D.: The ties that bind: Perceived social support, stress, and IBS in severely affected patients. *Neurogastroenterol Motil* 2010, **22**(8): 893–900.
24 Conboy, L.A., Macklin, E., Kelley, J., Kokkotou, E., Lembo, A., Kaptchuk, T.: Which patients improve: Characteristics increasing sensitivity to a supportive patient-practitioner relationship. *Soc Sci Med* 2010, **70**(3): 479–484.
25 Ng, S.M., Chow, K.W.: Symptoms catastrophizing versus social hypervigilance in irritable bowel syndrome patients. *Soc Work Health Care* 2012, **51**(8): 743–756.
26 Labus, J.S., Bolus, R., Chang, L., Wiklund, I., Naesdal, J., Mayer, E.A., Naliboff, B.D.: The visceral sensitivity index: Development and validation of a gastrointestinal symptom-specific anxiety scale. *Aliment Pharmacol Ther* 2004, **20**(1): 89–97.
27 Labus, J.S., Mayer, E.A., Chang, L., Bolus, R., Naliboff, B.D.: The central role of gastrointestinal-specific anxiety in irritable bowel syndrome: Further validation of the visceral sensitivity index. *Psychosom Med* 2007, **69**(1): 89–98.
28 Saigo, T., Tayama, J., Hamaguchi, T., Nakaya, N., Tomiie, T., Bernick, P.J., Kanazawa, M., Labus, J.S., Naliboff, B.D., Shirabe, S., *et al.*: Gastrointestinal specific anxiety in irritable bowel syndrome: Validation of the Japanese version of the visceral sensitivity index for university students. *BioPsychoSocial Med* 2014, **8**(1): 10.
29 Gwee, K.A., Leong, Y.L., Graham, C., McKendrick, M.W., Collins, S.M., Walters, S.J., Underwood, J.E., Read, N.W.: The role of psychological and biological factors in postinfective gut dysfunction. *Gut* 1999, **44**(3): 400–406.
30 Dunlop, S.P., Jenkins, D., Spiller, R.C.: Distinctive clinical, psychological, and histological features of postinfective irritable bowel syndrome. *Am J Gastroenterol* 2003, **98**(7): 1578–1583.
31 Miller, V., Hopkins, L., Whorwell, P.J.: Suicidal ideation in patients with irritable bowel syndrome. *Clin Gastroenterol Hepatol* 2004, **2**(12): 1064–1068.
32 Addolorato, G., Mirijello, A., D'Angelo, C., Leggio, L., Ferrulli, A., Abenavoli, L., Vonghia, L., Cardone, S., Leso, V., Cossari, A., *et al.*: State and trait anxiety and depression in patients affected by gastrointestinal diseases: Psychometric evaluation of 1641 patients referred to an internal medicine outpatient setting. *Int J Clin Pract* 2008, **62**(7): 1063–1069.
33 Sibelli, A., Chalder, T., Everitt, H., Workman, P., Windgassen, S., Moss-Morris, R.: A systematic review with meta-analysis of the role of anxiety and depression in irritable bowel syndrome onset. *Psychol Med* 2016, **46**(15): 3065–3080.
34 Muscatello, M.R.A., Bruno, A., Mento, C., Pandolfo, G., Zoccali, R.A.: Personality traits and emotional patterns in irritable bowel Syndrome. *WJG* 2016, **22**(28): 6402–6415.
35 Lackner, J.M., Ma, C., Keefer, L., Brenner, D.M., Gudleski, G.D., Satchidanand, N., Firth, R., Sitrin, M.D., Katz, L., Krasner, S.S., *et al.*: Type, rather than number, of mental and physical comorbidities increases the severity of symptoms in patients with irritable bowel syndrome. *Clin Gastroenterol Hepatol* 2013, **11**(9): 1147–1157.
36 Dimsdale, J.E., Creed, F., Escobar, J., Sharpe, M., Wulsin, L., Barsky, A., Lee, S., Irwin, M.R., Levenson, J.: Somatic symptom disorder: An important change in DSM. *J Psychosom Res* 2013, **75**(3): 223–228.
37 Duddu, V., Isaac, M.K., Chaturvedi, S.K.: Somatization, somatosensory amplification, attribution styles and illness behaviour: A review. *Int Rev Psychiat* 2006, **18**(1): 25–33.

38 Costa Jr., P.T., McCrae, R.R.: Stability and change in personality assessment: The revised NEO personality inventory in the year 2000. *J Pers Asses* 1997, **68**(1): 86–94.
39 Jones, M.P., Van Oudenhove, L., Koloski, N., Tack, J., Talley, N.J.: Early life factors initiate a 'vicious circle' of affective and gastrointestinal symptoms: A longitudinal study. *United European Gastroenterol J* 2013, **1**(5): 394–402.
40 Tayama, J., Nakaya, N., Hamaguchi, T., Tomiie, T., Shinozaki, M., Saigo, T., Shirabe, S., Fukudo, S.: Effects of personality traits on the manifestations of irritable bowel syndrome. *BioPsychoSocial Med* 2012, 6: 20.
41 Portincasa, P., Moschetta, A., Baldassare, G., Altomare, D.F., Palasciano, G.: Pan-enteric dysmotility, impaired quality of life and alexithymia in a large group of patients meeting ROMEII criteria for irritable bowel syndrome. *WJG* 2003, **9**(10): 2293–2299.
42 Kano, M., Hamaguchi, T., Itoh, M., Yanai, K., Fukudo, S.: Correlation between alexithymia and hypersensitivity to visceral stimulation in human. *Pain* 2007, **132**(3): 252–263.

Chapter 5

Cross-cultural aspects of functional gastrointestinal disorders

Sern Wei Yeoh
Christopher Leung

The aim of this chapter is to review the implications of approaching functional gastrointestinal disorders (FGIDs) from a cross-cultural perspective. The chapter reviews the epidemiology of FGIDs and outlines how cultural factors affect the complex interplay between patient, health provider and disorder. Moreover, FGID management recommendations, including both variations and shared themes between cultural groups, are identified.

Learning points

- Culture denotes a learned set of beliefs that interacts with patients' social environments. It influences symptom perceptions, relationships with health providers and therapeutic strategies.
- FGIDs have been described among patients from different global cultures in the last two decades.
- While culture can impact upon FGID presentation and management, it should not be over-emphasized, as there are many similarities between FGID patients from different cultures.
- Variations in study methodologies and limited multinational research make it difficult to make conclusions about cross-cultural differences in FGID, though the field is expanding rapidly.

Introduction

In 2011, the Rome Foundation and the World Gastroenterology Organisation convened a global symposium of over 100 participants from multidisciplinary and multinational backgrounds on cross-cultural understanding and research [1]. They published a comprehensive report in 2014 [2], followed by an entire chapter in the latest Rome IV guidelines [3] devoted to cross-cultural aspects of FGIDs. With technology surmounting barriers of geographic and linguistic distance, capacity for multinational research is growing exponentially.

Definitions

'Culture' is a learned set of beliefs influencing individuals' behaviours and decisions [4] which are shaped by social and physical environments, and economic and political experiences [5]. 'Race', in contrast, arises from outdated categories of 'subspecies' of humans [6] distinguishable by appearance and separated by distinct, fixed biological profiles, and the term is best avoided. 'Ethnicity' is a more sophisticated concept that encompasses shared characteristics of a group, including ancestral geographic origins and traditions [7]. Due to the influence of geography, people within an ethnic group share genetic characteristics (e.g., external appearance), but are not defined exclusively by them. This chapter will use the term 'culture' in a similar manner to 'ethnicity', shaped by geographical parameters.

Epidemiology of FGIDs

Irritable bowel syndrome (IBS) predominates in the FGID literature. A 2012 meta-analysis [8] of 81 cross-sectional studies from 1947–2011 found a pooled community IBS prevalence of 11.2%. IBS was less frequent in South-East Asian (7.0%) and Middle Eastern (7.5%) cohorts than in South Asian (17%) and South American (21%) cohorts. In 2016, Sperber *et al.* [9] reviewed 83 studies from 1999 to 2013 and found that compared to 'Western' regions with a prevalence of 8.1%, rates were lower in the Middle East (5.8%) and higher in Central America (17.5%).

In 45 studies, Suares *et al.* [10] found a global pooled prevalence of chronic idiopathic constipation of 14%, higher in South America (18%) and lower in South-East Asia (11%). In 103 studies, Ford *et al.* [11] reported a global pooled prevalence of functional dyspepsia of 21%, higher in South America (37.7%) and lower in South-East Asia (14.6%). African data are scarce, with small studies from Kenya and Nigeria recruited from patients in private hospitals and a small rural province, respectively. Thus, their generalizability is limited [12, 13]. Prevalence rates are highly variable in various regions due to methodological heterogeneity (mail questionnaires, telephone or face-to-face interviews) and diagnostic criteria (Manning, Rome I, Rome II, Rome III).

Studies on incidence rates of FGIDs are sparse, with none comparing incidence across cultures [14]. Incidence studies have methodological difficulties, as illustrated by a study of paired mail questionnaires in the Olmsted County, Minnesota. Over 12–20 months, IBS incidence was 67 per 1,000 person-years. However, during this interval, many patients' symptoms disappeared such that they no longer fulfilled diagnostic criteria [15]. Furthermore, there was a discrepancy between the onset of FGID symptoms (often insidious and long-standing prior to diagnosis) and formal diagnosis [14]. Therefore, in another study in the same Olmsted County population, the incidence of physician-diagnosed IBS was only 2 per 1,000 person-years [16].

Within countries, FGID rates between countries do not appear to differ significantly. For example, when adjusting for age, gender and socioeconomic status, Zuckerman found no significant differences in IBS prevalence between American Hispanics and whites [17]. A similarly adjusted study from Singapore [18] and two smaller unadjusted studies from Singapore [19] and Malaysia [20] showed no difference in FGID symptom rates between three common ethnic groups (Malay, Indian and Chinese).

Thus, epidemiological studies are fraught with methodological biases with prevalence and incidence rates not well established. Moreover, similarities of epidemiologies between ethnic groups within countries highlight more similarities than differences in ethnic experiences.

The impact of culture on patient experience of FGIDs

Cultural differences in health perceptions between patients and health-care providers may limit the efficacy of cross-cultural consultation [21, 22]. Patients may have idiosyncratic ways of expressing symptoms [23], coping with illness and uncertainty [24], accepting treatments [25], utilizing complementary medicine [23] or manipulating diet [26]. The perceived influence of diet on health is central to many traditional complementary medical systems. For example, some Chinese and Hispanic traditions divide food into 'cold' and 'hot' categories, with varying effects on the body during times of health and illness [27]. Ayurvedic traditions from the Indian subcontinent prescribe a balance of food across six tastes depending on one's mind-body type [28]. Such beliefs may alter how FGID patients approach their management.

Health-seeking behaviours are influenced by cultural determinants. Family networks are defined differently between cultures: some (urban, Western cultures) may emphasize a small family of first-degree relatives, while others (rural, Asian and African) may include large groups spanning many generations [29]. This may lead to different levels of social support and willingness to seek health advice from professional, non-family sources. Child-rearing practices, particularly parental attentiveness to children's health complaints, may also influence future health-seeking behaviours in adulthood [30]. Cultural groups may be economically underprivileged or have poor health literacy [31], limiting health access and treatment adherence. Those having experienced political repression may develop distrust of health-care services or increased psychiatric distress [32]. Socially marginalized cultures, such as women in rural India, may have restricted awareness of their own health-care needs, leading them to disregard FGID symptoms [33]. Culturally mediated stigmas, such as mental disability in migrants, may also hinder health-care-seeking behaviour [34].

Potential determinants of cultural differences

Linguistic challenges are pertinent in cross-cultural FGID experiences. Ghoshal *et al.* described their experience in translating Rome III questionnaires into several Asian languages (Chinese, Hindi-Telugu, Indonesian, Korean and Thai) [35]. English words with ambiguous meanings included 'constipation' (can be interpreted as hard stool consistency or decreased stool frequency) and 'bloating' (often synonymous with postprandial fullness, pain or distension). Gerson *et al.* [36] found bloating to be negatively correlated with pain among Chinese IBS patients, perhaps because bloating and pain are considered part of a spectrum rather than separate entities [26]. There is also no specific term for 'bloating' in many languages, including Farsi and Spanish [26].

From an economical viewpoint, Schmulson *et al.* [37] found that South Korea and Italy had government-subsidized health-care systems while patients often had significant out-of-pocket costs in Mexico and India. Thus, patients in countries with easier access to health-care resources may have heightened awareness of FGID symptoms, as interventions may be more readily sought [38]. Conversely, those in countries with limited resources may be conditioned to disregard FGID symptoms in the absence of easy or affordable interventions. Similarly, clinicians in limited resourced countries may be more willing to trial therapies for longer before ordering endoscopy. Both clinicians and patients in such countries may be more willing to use complementary medications if they are more affordable.

Physiological differences between cultural groups are also important. Baseline exposures to gastrointestinal pathogens vary according to geographical region, potentially altering the symptomatology of FGIDs [2]. Lactose intolerance has been shown to be more common in Asian and Hispanic populations compared to whites [39]. Other studies have described a shorter colonic transit time in Indians [40] and Chinese [41] compared to Western cohorts. Yet others have reported differences in subjective pain sensations between Hispanic, black and white subgroups [42]. They also have different serotonin receptor genetic polymorphisms [43], interleukin-10 and tumour necrosis factor-alpha [44] levels. More research, however, needs to be performed.

Figure 5.1 summarizes the interaction between cultural factors and patient experience of FGIDs within a biopsychosocial context.

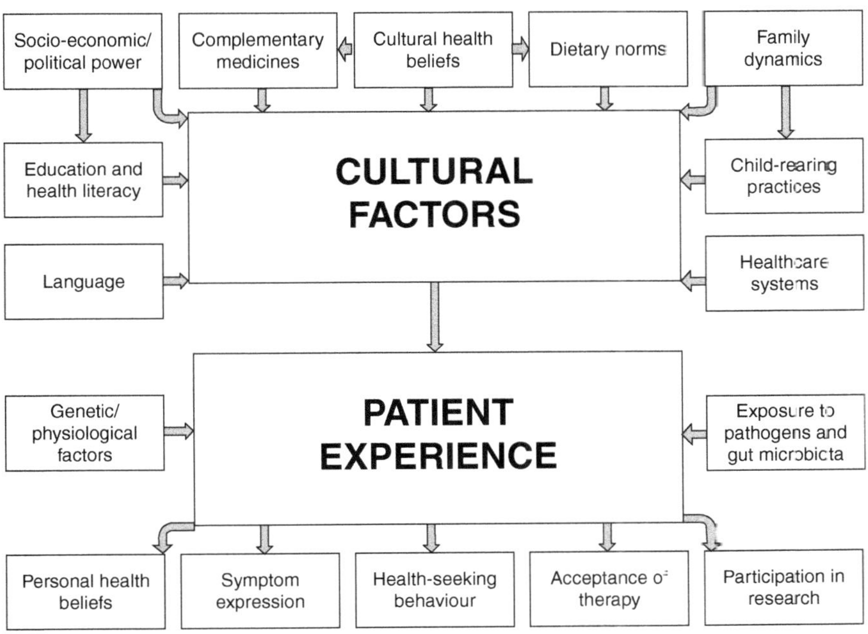

Figure 5.1 Interaction between cultural factors and patient experience in FGIDs.

Cultural differences and similarities described in research

Empirical observations have been made about different FGID experiences between cultures, mostly between Asian and Western cohorts. Notably, studies are non-uniform [2], but some conclusions can be drawn:

- Female predominance is less marked among ethnically Chinese IBS patients in China, Singapore, Malaysia and Taiwan [45].
- IBS patients from these regions are less concerned with bowel frequency than postprandial discomfort, limiting the diagnostic accuracy of the Rome criteria which doesn't consider the relationship of symptoms with meals [33].
- Chinese and Korean patients describe less effect of IBS on social, sexual and relationship domains in quality-of-life surveys [46].
- IBS-related discomfort is labelled more often as bloating than pain [47] in Chinese cohorts, and Indian cohorts report less pain or bloating than Western cohorts [48].
- Indian [38] and Chinese [18] IBS cohorts localize pain more to the upper than the lower abdomen, which complicates the differentiation of IBS and functional dyspepsia.

Robust studies involving different cultures, countries and standardized study criteria are limited. Gerson *et al.* [36] surveyed 239 IBS patients in eight countries (USA, Mexico, Canada, United Kingdom, Italy, Israel, India and China). Pain and bloating scores were particularly high in Italy. Constipation was particularly high and diarrhoea low in Mexico and vice versa in China. These findings may relate to different diets of starches and legumes, and different rates of intestinal infections.

Another study by Gerson [49] recruited 463 IBS patients from seven countries (USA, Mexico, Italy, Romania, Iran, India and China) and found increased avoidance, catastrophizing and negative pain beliefs among Romanian patients and increased anxiety in Chinese patients. These findings may reflect disrupted family structures and childhood nurturing associated with significant political upheaval.

Studies of different cultural groups in the same country have also been performed. Zuckerman *et al.* [17, 50] surveyed 580 Hispanic and 325 non-Hispanic Texan health-care employees. Hispanics were less likely to consult doctors and more likely to use herbal remedies and be concerned about their gastrointestinal health independent of symptom rates. Another survey found that Americans self-identifying as 'black' were more likely to self-report constipation, despite having higher stool frequencies than 'white' participants [51].

Indeed, globally, IBS symptom scores correlated with greater family conflict, poorer mental well-being, catastrophizing, negative beliefs and somatization. In another study [49, 52], these similarities unite FGID patients across the globe and cross ethno-cultural boundaries so that truly multinational studies have found unifying rather than dividing themes [43, 53].

Conclusion

While culture can impact upon FGID presentation and management, it should not be over-emphasized, as there are many similarities between FGID patients from different cultures. Variations in study methodologies and limited multinational research make it difficult to make conclusions about cross-cultural differences in FGID, though the field is expanding rapidly. With that being said, health professionals should seek to understand patient backgrounds and how they may impact upon both investigations and treatments in FGID cohorts.

References

1 Sperber, A.D., Drossman, D.A., Quigley, E.M.: The global perspective on irritable bowel syndrome: A Rome Foundation-World Gastroenterology Organisation symposium. *Am J Gastroenterol* 2012, **107**(11): 1602–1609.

2 Sperber, A.D., Gwee, K.A., Hungin, A.P., Corazziari, E., Fukudo, S., Gerson, C., Ghoshal, U.C., Kang, J.Y., Levy, R.L., Schmulson, M., *et al.*: Conducting multinational, cross-cultural research in the functional gastrointestinal disorders: Issues and recommendations. A Rome Foundation working team report. *Aliment Pharmacol Ther* 2014, **40**(9): 1094–1102.

3 Drossman, D.A.: Functional gastrointestinal disorders: History, pathophysiology, clinical features, and Rome IV. *Gastroenterology* 2016, **150**(6): 1262–1279e2.

4 Saha, S.: The relevance of cultural distance between patients and physicians to racial disparities in health care. *J Gen Intern Med* 2006, **21**(2): 203–205.

5 Taylor, J.S.: The story catches you and you fall down: Tragedy, ethnography, and "cultural competence". *Med Anthropol Q* 2003, **17**(2): 159–181.

6 Huth, E.J.: Identifying ethnicity in medical papers. *Ann Intern Med* 1995, **122**(8): 619–621.

7 Bhopal, R.: Is research into ethnicity and health racist, unsound, or important science? *BMJ* 1997, **314**(7096): 1751–1756.

8 Lovell, R.M., Ford, A.C.: Global prevalence of and risk factors for irritable bowel syndrome: A meta-analysis. *Clin Gastroenterol Hepatol* 2012, **10**(7): 712–721 e714.

9 Sperber, A.D., Dumitrascu, D., Fukudo, S., Gerson, C., Ghoshal, U.C., Gwee, K.A., Hungin, A.P., Kang, J.Y., Minhu, C., Schmulson, M., *et al.*: The global prevalence of IBS in adults remains elusive due to the heterogeneity of studies: A Rome Foundation working team literature review. *Gut* 2017, **66**(6): 1075–1082.

10 Suares, N.C., Ford, A.C.: Prevalence of, and risk factors for, chronic idiopathic constipation in the community: Systematic review and meta-analysis. *Am J Gastroenterol* 2011, **106**(9): 1582–1591, quiz 1581, 1592.

11 Ford, A.C., Marwaha, A., Sood, R., Moayyedi, P.: Global prevalence of, and risk factors for, uninvestigated dyspepsia: A meta-analysis. *Gut* 2015, **64**(7): 1049–1057.

12 Lule, G.N., Amayo, E.O.: Irritable bowel syndrome in Kenyans. *East Afr Med J* 2002, **79**(7): 360–363.

13 Okeke, E.N., Ladep, N.G., Adah, S., Bupwatda, P.W., Agaba, E.I., Malu, A.O.: Prevalence of irritable bowel syndrome: A community survey in an African population. *Ann Afr Med* 2009, **8**(3): 177–180.

14 Hungin, A.P., Chang, L., Locke, G.R., Dennis, E.H., Barghout, V.: Irritable bowel syndrome in the United States: Prevalence, symptom patterns and impact. *Aliment Pharmacol Ther* 2005, **21**(11): 1365–1375.

15 Talley, N.J., Weaver, A.L., Zinsmeister, A.R., Melton III, L.J.: Onset and disappearance of gastrointestinal symptoms and functional gastrointestinal disorders. *Am J Epidemiol* 1992, **136**(2): 165–177.

16 Locke III, G.R., Yawn, B.P., Wollan, P.C., Melton III, L.J., Lydick, E., Talley, N.J.: Incidence of a clinical diagnosis of the irritable bowel syndrome in a United States population. *Aliment Pharmacol Ther* 2004, **19**(9): 1025–1031.
17 Zuckerman, M.J., Guerra, L.G., Drossman, D.A., Foland, J.A., Gregory, G.G.: Comparison of bowel patterns in Hispanics and non-Hispanic whites. *Dig Dis Sci* 1995, **40**(8): 1763–1769.
18 Gwee, K.A., Wee, S., Wong, M.L., Png, D.J.: The prevalence, symptom characteristics, and impact of irritable bowel syndrome in an asian urban community. *Am J Gastroenterol* 2004, **99**(5): 924–931.
19 Ho, K.Y., Kang, J.Y., Seow, A.: Prevalence of gastrointestinal symptoms in a multiracial Asian population, with particular reference to reflux-type symptoms. *Am J Gastroenterol* 1998, **93**(10): 1816–1822.
20 Rajendra, S., Alahuddin, S.: Prevalence of irritable bowel syndrome in a multi-ethnic Asian population. *Aliment Pharmacol Ther* 2004, **19**(6): 704–706.
21 Bates, M.S., Rankin-Hill, L., Sanchez-Ayendez, M.: The effects of the cultural context of health care on treatment of and response to chronic pain and illness. *Soc Sci Med* 1997, **45**(9): 1433–1447.
22 Carrillo, J.E., Green, A.R., Betancourt, J.R.: Cross-cultural primary care: A patient-based approach. *Ann Intern Med* 1999, **130**(10): 829–834.
23 Gerson, C.D., Gerson, M.J.: A cross-cultural perspective on irritable bowel syndrome. *Mt Sinai J Med* 2010, **77**(6): 707–712.
24 Lackner, J.M., Gudleski, G.D., Thakur, E.R., Stewart, T.J., Iacobucci, G.J., Spiegel, B.M.: The impact of physical complaints, social environment, and psychological functioning on IBS patients' health perceptions: Looking beyond GI symptom severity. *Am J Gastroenterol* 2014, **109**(2): 224–233.
25 Dimsdale, J.E.: Stalked by the past: The influence of ethnicity on health. *Psychosom Med* 2000, **62**(2): 161–170.
26 Francisconi, C.F., Sperber, A.D., Fang, X., Fukudo, S., Gerson, M.J., Kang, J.Y., Schmulson, W.M.: Multicultural aspects in Functional Gastrointestinal Disorders (FGIDs). *Gastroenterology* 2016, **150**: 1344–1354.
27 Drossman, D.A., Weinland, S.R.: Commentary: Sociocultural factors in medicine and gastrointestinal research. *Eur J Gastroenterol Hepatol* 2008, **20**(7): 593–595.
28 Payyappallimana, U., Venkatasubramanian, P.: Exploring ayurvedic knowledge on food and health for providing innovative solutions to contemporary healthcare. *Front Public Health* 2016, **4**: 57.
29 McGoldrick, M., Rohrbaugh, M.: Researching ethnic family stereotypes. *Fam Process* 1987, **26**(1): 89–99.
30 Rothbaum, F., Pott, M., Azuma, H., Miyake, K., Weisz, J.: The development of close relationships in Japan and the United States: Paths of symbiotic harmony and generative tension. *Child Dev* 2000, **71**(5): 1121–1142.
31 Baker, D.W., Parker, R.M., Williams, M.V., Pitkin, K., Parikh, N.S., Coates, W., Imara, M.: The health care experience of patients with low literacy. *Arch Fam Med* 1996, **5**(6): 329–334.
32 Burnett, A., Peel, M.: Health needs of asylum seekers and refugees. *BMJ* 2001, **322**(7285): 544–547.
33 Gwee, K.A., Lu, C.L., Ghoshal, U.C.: Epidemiology of irritable bowel syndrome in Asia: Something old, something new, something borrowed. *J Gastroenterol Hepatol* 2009, **24**(10): 1601–1607.
34 Selkirk, M., Quayle, E., Rothwell, N.: A systematic review of factors affecting migrant attitudes towards seeking psychological help. *J Health Care Poor Underserved* 2014, **25**(1): 94–127.
35 Ghoshal, U.C., Gwee, K.A., Chen, M., Gong, X.R., Pratap, N., Hou, X., Syam, A.F., Abdullah, M., Bak, Y.T., Choi, M.G., *et al.*: Development, translation and validation of enhanced Asian Rome III questionnaires for diagnosis of functional bowel diseases in

major Asian languages: A Rome Foundation-Asian neurogastroenterology and motility association working team report. *J Neurogastroenterol Motil* 2015, **21**(1): 85–92.

36 Gerson, C.D., Gerson, M.J., Awad, R.A., Chowdhury, A., Dancey, C., Poitras, P., Porcelli, P., Sperber, A., Wang, W.A.: Irritable bowel syndrome: An international study of symptoms in eight countries. *Eur J Gastroenterol Hepatol* 2008, **20**(7): 659–667.

37 Schmulson, M., Corazziari, E., Ghoshal, U.C., Myung, S.J., Gerson, C.D., Quigley, E.M., Gwee, K.A., Sperber, A.D.: A four-country comparison of healthcare systems, implementation of diagnostic criteria, and treatment availability for functional gastrointestinal disorders: A report of the Rome Foundation Working Team on cross-cultural, multinational research. *Neurogastroenterol Motil* 2014, **26**(10): 1368–1385.

38 Ghoshal, U.C., Abraham, P., Bhatt, C., Choudhuri, G., Bhatia, S.J., Shenoy, K.T., Banka, N.H., Bose, K., Bohidar, N.P., Chakravartty, K., *et al.*: Epidemiological and clinical profile of irritable bowel syndrome in India: Report of the Indian Society of Gastroenterology Task Force. *Indian J Gastroenterol* 2008, **27**(1): 22–28.

39 Jackson, K.A., Savaiano, D.A.: Lactose maldigestion, calcium intake and osteoporosis in African-, Asian-, and Hispanic-Americans. *J Am Coll Nutr* 2001, **20**(2 Suppl): 198S–207S.

40 Ghoshal, U.C., Gupta, D., Kumar, A., Misra, A.: Colonic transit study by radio-opaque markers to investigate constipation: Validation of a new protocol for a population with rapid gut transit. *Natl Med J India* 2007, **20**(5): 225–229.

41 Chan, Y.K., Kwan, A.C., Yuen, H., Yeung, Y.W., Lai, K.C., Wu, J., Wong, G.S., Leung, C.M., Cheung, W.C., Wong, C.K.: Normal colon transit time in healthy Chinese adults in Hong Kong. *J Gastroenterol Hepatol* 2004, **19**(11): 1270–1275.

42 Edwards, R.R., Moric, M., Husfeldt, B., Buvanendran, A., Ivankovich, O.: Ethnic similarities and differences in the chronic pain experience: A comparison of african american, Hispanic, and white patients. *Pain Med* 2005, **6**(1): 88–98.

43 Wagner, G.J., Maguen, S., Rabkin, J.G.: Ethnic differences in response to fluoxetine in a controlled trial with depressed HIV-positive patients. *Psychiatr Serv* 1998, **49**(2): 239–240.

44 Schmulson, M., Pulido-London, D., Rodriguez, O., Morales-Rochlin, N., Martinez-Garcia, R., Gutierrez-Ruiz, M.C., Lopez-Alvarenga, J.C., Gutierrez-Reyes, G.: IL-10 and TNF-alpha polymorphisms in subjects with irritable bowel syndrome in Mexico. *Rev Esp Enferm Dig* 2013, **105**(7): 392–399.

45 Chang, F.Y., Lu, C.L.: Irritable bowel syndrome in the 21st century: Perspectives from Asia or South-east Asia. *J Gastroenterol Hepatol* 2007, **22**(1): 4–12.

46 Choi, M.G., Jung, H.K.: Health related quality of life in functional gastrointestinal disorders in Asia. *J Neurogastroenterol Motil* 2011, **17**(3): 245–251.

47 Kwan, A.C., Hu, W.H., Chan, Y.K., Yeung, Y.W., Lai, T.S., Yuen, H.: Prevalence of irritable bowel syndrome in Hong Kong. *J Gastroenterol Hepatol* 2002, **17**(11): 1180–1186.

48 Ghoshal, U.C., Abraham, P., Bhatia, S.J., Misra, S.P., Choudhuri, G. Biswas, K.D., Chakravartty, K., Dadhich, S., Goswami, B.D., Jayanthi, V., *et al.*: Comparison of Manning, Rome I, II, and III, and Asian diagnostic criteria: Report of the Multicentric Indian Irritable Bowel Syndrome (MIIBS) study. *Indian J Gastroenterol* 2013, **32**(6): 369–375.

49 Gerson, C.D., Gerson, M.J., Chang, L., Corazziari, E.S., Dumitrascu, D. Ghoshal, U.C., Porcelli, P., Schmulson, M., Wang, W.A., Zali, M.: A cross-cultural investigation of attachment style, catastrophizing, negative pain beliefs, and symptom severity in irritable bowel syndrome. *Neurogastroenterol Motil* 2015, **27**(4): 490–500.

50 Zuckerman, M.J., Guerra, L.G., Drossman, D.A., Foland, J.A., Gregory G.G.: Health-care-seeking behaviors related to bowel complaints: Hispanics versus non-Hispanic whites. *Dig Dis Sci* 1996, **41**(1): 77–82.

51 Everhart, J.E., Go, V.L., Johannes, R.S., Fitzsimmons, S.C., Roth, H.P., White, L.R.: A longitudinal survey of self-reported bowel habits in the United States. *Dig Dis Sci* 1989, **34**(8): 1153–1162.

52 Gerson, M.J., Gerson, C.D., Awad, R.A., Dancey, C., Poitras, P., Porcelli, P., Sperber, A.D.: An international study of irritable bowel syndrome: Family relationships and mind-body attributions. *Soc Sci Med* 2006, **62**(11): 2838–2847.

53 Brach, C., Fraser, I.: Can cultural competency reduce racial and ethnic health disparities? A review and conceptual model. *Med Care Res Rev* 2000, **57**(Suppl 1): 181–217.
54 Hahn, E.A., Cella, D.: Health outcomes assessment in vulnerable populations: Measurement challenges and recommendations. *Arch Phys Med Rehabil* 2003, **84**(4 Suppl 2): S35–S42.

Part II

Diagnostic procedures, assessment and biopsychosocial methods in functional gastrointestinal disorders

Chapter 6

Diagnostic procedures in functional gastrointestinal disorders – addressing patient concerns

Geoffrey Stuart Hebbard

The aim of this chapter is to review the role of diagnostic testing in functional gastrointestinal disorders (FGIDs), the importance of collaborative discussions with patient as to the role and expected outcomes of testing and how they relate to a holistic treatment approach.

Learning points

- Individualize tests to the patient based on risk factors, symptoms and previous investigations.
- Patients need to understand that the results of routine investigations are likely to be 'normal' and that this does not invalidate their illness experience.
- Normal investigations should not be repeated.
- Underlying anxiety and/or a previous history of abuse are common and may increase the morbidity of investigations.
- Patients need to be reviewed soon after investigations have been performed in order to discuss the results in the context of their symptoms and the expected outcomes of testing, and to reduce anxiety.
- Utilize discussions of investigations and their results to strengthen the physician-patient therapeutic relationship.

Diagnostic testing in FGIDs

Philosophy of diagnostic testing in FGIDs

FGIDs comprise a heterogeneous group of conditions defined on the basis of symptomatology. The underlying cause of these conditions has not been fully defined, and a diagnosis is therefore made on the basis of a constellation of symptoms, with appropriate investigations to exclude other 'organic' disorders that may result in a similar presentation. The costs of FGIDs – for example, IBS – are considerable to the patient in terms of both quality of life and lost productivity and health-care expenditures [1]. A significant component of the health-care expenditure in FGIDs relates to the cost of investigation, and physicians who practise a greater degree of patient-centred communication have a lower diagnostic testing expenditure [2, 3]. Unfortunately, detailing physicians in patient-centred counselling does not appear to reduce the ordering of low-value diagnostic tests [4], and many primary care physicians, although confident in the recognition of IBS, still refer frequently for endoscopic investigation [5]. In contrast, experts are more confident in positively diagnosing IBS with minimal testing and consequent lower expenditure on testing [6].

The extent of diagnostic testing should be minimized and, in the absence of alarm features, patients with typical features of IBS have equivalent outcomes utilizing a positive diagnostic strategy with few screening tests compared to a strategy of 'exclusion' involving more extensive testing [7]. This may not, however, be true for all FGIDs as alarm features do not appear to discriminate as effectively between functional dyspepsia and diseases of the upper GI tract [8], and 'red flags' are common, occurring in up to 84% of patients with IBS [9]. Patient with high levels of somatization appear to be more likely to have high levels of health-care costs [10], likely driven by patient requests for low-value investigations, which physicians may find difficult to resist. Nevertheless, standardization of approach and reduction in variation between practitioners is possible; the institution of a clinical pathway involving defined investigation and management for patients with suspected IBS reduced health-care utilization and costs [11].

In the Western model of medical practice, many patients have an expectation that they will be offered diagnostic tests [12], and FGIDs are no exception, with just over 40% of patients believing that IBS can be diagnosed on a colonoscopy, [13] and when presented with a scenario of IBS, 97% of laypersons believed that investigation was required [14].

In only a minority of FGIDs (largely anorectal disorders) is measurement of a physiological parameter required in order to make a diagnosis, and investigations are performed to exclude other conditions that may present with similar symptoms. It is important that patients are aware of the role of investigation in FGIDs – specifically that, apart from the few conditions where physiological measurement contributes to the diagnosis, the expected outcome of routine testing is that no abnormality will be found. This will avoid the negative consequences of being informed that 'everything is okay', a statement that patients may interpret as being dismissive of their symptoms or invalidating of their illness. Rather if the patient understands that negative tests are expected, testing can be minimized (as it will not contribute to management), and the results are seen as confirming the diagnosis, rather than posing new questions. It is therefore important to ensure (as for any chronic condition) that patient expectations of the diagnostic (as well as the treatment) process are realistic and this is ideally done at the point of referral [15]. The alternative may be a self-perpetuating cycle of troublesome interactions in the health-care system with negative outcomes [16].

The parameters for the interpretation of the results of any diagnostic testing therefore need to be set in the first consultation, where the role of the routine tests in excluding underlying conditions, such as cancers and inflammatory conditions, is discussed. It is often helpful to explain that the underlying pathophysiology of FGIDs is poorly understood and that testing of specific physiological parameters (e.g., sensory threshold), although potentially abnormal, will not contribute to a diagnosis or change management. In certain centres research into biomarkers may generate specific tests and, although these markers are not yet established diagnostic criteria, they may inform a local approach to management or contribute to research studies [17].

Testing should therefore be individualized; indeed as the criteria for diagnosing FGIDs are symptom-based, the main 'diagnostic test' is the interview and examination. The physician-patient relationship is formed and many of its important components are defined at the initial consultation, which is usually where diagnostic testing and an overall approach to management are discussed, so this is a pivotal point in the interaction. If the role of the diagnostic testing is not explicitly discussed and the biopsychosocial nature of the patient's illness is not emphasized, this can be very difficult to undo at a later consultation without damaging the therapeutic relationship ('The tests were negative, so the doctor sent me to a psychiatrist'). The core components of the collaborative relationship – that is, empathy through listening, validation of the patient's symptoms, an agreed model of the illness and a plan of treatment – are all formed in the first few consultations and are determinants of outcome and patient satisfaction. Patients with FGIDs often report that clinicians offer insufficient empathy and validation of their symptoms [18], and interviews with patients who expressed dissatisfaction with omissions of care related to examination or investigation revealed that they attached both pragmatic and symbolic value to the testing. Pragmatic values included diagnosis, prognosis and therapy, symbolic values related to the physician-patient relationship [19].

An important factor that must be taken into account when performing diagnostic testing is the high prevalence of psychological and psychiatric comorbidity in the population of patients with FGIDs (see Table 6.1), and patients at the more severe end of the spectrum of FGIDs are very likely to have had previous negative experiences with testing. In general, these are the patients least likely to benefit from testing in terms of diagnosis or to guide therapy, and invasive diagnostic testing is best avoided in this group unless the suspicion of 'organic' disease is particularly strong (patients with FGIDs can of course have intercurrent illnesses) and less invasive tests are not available.

In order to reduce the anxiety and morbidity related to the procedure, patients should be carefully educated as to:

- the preparation required for the procedure,
- what will happen on the day,
- the likely effect of the procedure on their symptoms, and
- when the results will be discussed with them (preferably some indication on the day of testing, with rapid follow-up to discuss in more detail).

Table 6.1 Prevalence of anxiety and depression among patients with FGIDs.

Authors/country	*FGID condition*	*Number of participants*	*Anxiety/depression*
V Gül, G Geschwindt and C Şen [20], Germany	Functional dyspepsia and IBS	423	60% Psychiatric comorbidity
ST Hosseinzadeh, S Poorsaadati, B Radkani and M Forootan [21], Iran	Chronic functional constipation	54	33.3% Clinical anxiety 22.2% Clinical depression
NK Ibrahim, WF Battarjee and SA Almehmadi [22], Saudi Arabia	Irritable bowel syndrome	190	36.1% Morbid anxiety 31.1% Borderline anxiety 15.4% Morbid depression 27.1% Borderline depression
E Jonsbu, T Dammen, G Morken and EW Martinsen [23], Norway	Non-cardiac chest pain (FCP)	107	14.9% Panic disorder 31.8% Any anxiety disorder 4.7% Major depression 38.3% Any psychiatric disorder
Y Li, Y Nie, W Sha and H Su [24], China	Functional dyspepsia	239	10.9% Depression 2.1% Anxiety 2.5% Depression with anxiety 15.5% Depression or anxiety
S Mahadeva and KL Goh [25], Malaysia	Functional dyspepsia	472	28.5% Mod./severe anxiety 10.9% Mod./severe depression
V Miller, HR Carruthers, J Morris, SS Hasan, S Archbold and PJ Whorwell [26], UK	Irritable bowel syndrome	1000	63% Anxious 25% Depressed
K Mine, F Kanazawa, M Hosoi, N Kinukawa and C Kubo [27], Japan	Non-ulcer dyspepsia	66	25.8% Major depression 1.5% Generalized anxiety

G Moser, TA Wenzel-Abatzi, M Stelzeneder, T Wenzel, U Weber, S Wiesnagrotzki, C Schneider, W Schima, G Stacher-Janotta, GV Vacariu-Granser, *et al.* [28], USA	Globus	58	19.0% Major depression 10.3% Generalized anxiety 8.6% Panic disorder 63.8% Any psychiatric disorder
NX Ortiz-Olvera, M Gonzalez-Martinez, LG Ruiz-Flores, JM Blancas-Valencia, S Moran-Villota and M Dehesa-Violante [29], Mexico	Non-cardiac chest pain (FCP)	31	52% Any psychiatric disorder
C Prakash and RE Clouse [30], USA	Cyclic vomiting syndrome	17	23% Anxiety or affective disorder
EA Walker, AN Gelfand, MD Gelfand and WJ Katon [31], USA	Irritable bowel syndrome	71	76% Depression (15% lifetime) 28% Panic (41% lifetime) 58% Generalized anxiety
EA Walker, WJ Katon, PP Jemelka and PP Roy-Byrne [32], USA	Irritable bowel syndrome	1134	13.4% Major depression 5.2% Panic

Types of diagnostic testing and patient concerns

As the symptoms of FGIDs are protean and commonly involve extraintestinal systems, testing needs to be tailored to the patient and to the symptom pattern; indeed if adequate previous investigations have been performed, further testing may not be required. In this situation, however, the results of the previous tests should be carefully reviewed and discussed with the patient to emphasize that adequate information has been gathered and that the negative tests so far do not invalidate the patient's illness experience.

Patient concerns at this stage of the interaction are likely to include the following.

> *Should the tests that have already been done be repeated?* It is common for patients to request the repetition of previously negative tests, often based on the belief that 'something must have been missed.' If the tests have been performed by a reputable provider and the index of suspicion for other conditions is low, there is no reason to repeat them. Indeed even an initial colonoscopy has a very limited effect in reducing patient anxiety [33].

Are there more tests that can/need to be done? This needs to be discussed in the context of the patient's symptoms and the investigations that have been performed to date to avoid repeated or over-investigation with attendant cost and risk. There may be specific physiological investigations (e.g., anorectal physiology studies) required in order to make a more refined diagnosis. In addition, some centres may have specific tests may have specific tests that are the subject of research studies and which the investigators feel may be of value in diagnosis or defining the most effective therapy. In general, however, these tests are not mainstream and are not required for the diagnosis of a FGID [17].

Why have the tests not shown any abnormality? This question leads naturally to a discussion as to what the tests that have been performed so far are able to detect and their role in management. Some patients may be emotionally invested in finding an abnormal test result that they feel validates their symptoms with a specific diagnosis and have clear expectations as to what the consultation will provide – for example, in patients with back pain, expectations include a clear diagnosis, further tests and referral/therapy [12]. As discussed earlier, considerable education may be required to provide a perspective on the role of diagnostic testing in FGIDs.

If an abnormality has been found, what is the relevance of that to the symptoms? By definition standard diagnostic tests will have been negative; however, minor abnormalities are common. The significance of these for the patient's health needs to be assessed, and tests occasionally repeated to determine whether the abnormality represents a finding requiring further investigation or management.

As a result of the tendency of patient with FGIDs to consult multiple practitioners and often alternative medicine practitioners in parallel, it is common for patients to bring along results of nonstandard tests for the practitioner to 'interpret'. This can be a challenge and needs to be handled in a sensitive manner. The requests vary from the results of tests that may one day become more mainstream, but which are currently not sufficiently sensitive/specific/understood (e.g., faecal microbiota analysis), to those which are unlikely ever to have any relevance (e.g., Vega machine testing). The motivation of the patient in seeking the test should be explored as this may provide insights into the patient's beliefs as to the cause of his or her symptoms; however, it is usually unwise to directly confront the patient's beliefs directly, regardless of the views of the practitioner with regard to the specific test. However, the result may be able to be incorporated into an overall management plan.

Specific investigations

FGIDs cause non-specific symptoms that overlap with those of 'organic' disease, and in order to engage patients with an explanation for their symptoms that emphasizes the biopsychosocial aspects it is important that the both the physician and the patient recognize and accept that underlying 'organic' and 'serious' conditions have been appropriately excluded. The conditions that need to be considered are determined by the age and sex of the and his or her past medical history and symptoms. It should be ensured that relevant age- and sex-appropriate screening investigations are up-to-date according to local guidelines.

Diagnostic algorithms have been developed for specific symptoms [34] and non-invasive testing is available for many conditions. Initial investigation will often involve routine blood testing, including a full blood count, assessment of liver, thyroid and renal function, inflammatory markers, nutritional status, serology for coeliac disease, and stool testing for inflammation and occult blood. Normal blood/serum parameters with normal faecal calprotectin have a high negative predictive value in excluding IBD [35], and combining a positive diagnosis based on Rome III criteria with psychological factors and limited blood investigations results in a high likelihood ratio for the diagnosis of IBS [36]. If further investigation is required, relevant considerations include risk, cost, diagnostic accuracy and potential for incidental findings. Imaging investigations may include cross-sectional imaging or more targeted investigations depending on symptoms; endoscopic investigation may include upper and/or lower GI endoscopy. A therapeutic trial of medication can be of value in the diagnostic process – for example, a trial of bile salt binding agent in patients presenting with diarrhoea as part of their symptom complex. A therapeutic trial, while not perfect in terms of diagnostic accuracy, is cheap and has the added advantage of defining the efficacy of the intervention.

Endoscopic investigations are performed worldwide, with varying degrees of sedation; issues may include the introduction of tubes into regions of the body that have been previously violated and discomfort during and following the procedure, with the risk of exacerbating symptoms, or even causing new symptoms that may be subsequently referred to the procedure. Non-invasive tests are preferred, particularly if the likelihood of pathology is low, as the rate of abnormality on colonoscopy in patients with IBS is no different to the general population [37].

Physiological investigations may include studies of motor or sensory function, and transit. Motility is traditionally assessed using luminal manometry, with pressure sensors placed into the region of the GI tract to be assessed. The placement of the sensors (via the nose or anus) is associated with some discomfort and may occasionally be very confronting for patients, particularly those with a history of sexual abuse. Gastrointestinal transit is commonly assessed using nuclear medicine markers which are non-invasive and have a relatively low radiation burden (especially compared to CT cross-sectional imaging). Other methods of measurement include breath testing and ingestion of a capsule.

Assessment of sensory function is less well standardized than motor function, and may be carried out using nutrient or mechanical/electrical stimuli delivered directly to the region of the gut. In principle this is similar from the patient perspective to luminal manometry, although the added stimuli are generally designed to be increased until the patient experiences discomfort. A more physiological assessment may be carried out with the ingestion of a standardized meal (e.g., a nutrient drink); however, this may involve the ingestion of substances that the patient does not usually take and is generally continued until the patient experiences discomfort or pain.

Breath testing involves the ingestion of a particular substance (labelled and/or metabolized by luminal bacteria), followed by the collection of breath samples over a period of several hours. The taste of the substances is relatively inoffensive, but (particularly with sugar malabsorption tests) symptoms may be induced.

Collection of stool samples for faecal analysis may present some logistical problems and patients may not like to handle stool, but it is generally well tolerated, as are most radiological procedures.

Discussing the results of diagnostic testing

Once diagnostic testing has been completed it is vital that the patient is informed of the result as soon as possible. As noted earlier the prevalence of psychiatric and psychological comorbidity, particularly anxiety, is considerable and waiting for the results of a test may increase symptoms. The results of any investigations need to be interpreted in light of the patient's symptoms and appropriate reassurance provided for negative investigations. Incidental findings may be made and will need to be discussed with a plan of action, either observation or occasionally further investigation or referral (this is one of the toxicities of diagnostic testing). Diagnostic testing then needs to be firmly put into the background and a management plan developed to address the patient's symptoms. Positive outcomes are most likely when the patient recognizes and accepts that he or she needs to take an active part within the treatment team.

Conclusion

A major role of the physician is to recognize the patient's concerns and expectations [38] as well as to listen and provide validation, empathy and education [39, 40]. The role of education, particularly in allaying anxiety, is demonstrated by the prevalence of misconceptions with regard to the role of diagnostic testing in IBS held by patients [13], and it should be emphasized that once the diagnosis of IBS has been made, the likelihood of an alternative subsequent diagnosis being made is very low [41]. The diagnostic process, with emphasis on making a positive diagnosis using the symptom-based criteria for FGIDs, exclusion of alarm symptoms, discussion of the role of diagnostic tests and limited, directed testing, if required, with the results of the testing 'confirming the diagnosis', forms the basis for the subsequent therapeutic relationship and is a determinant of outcome [42, 43].

Acknowledgments, competing interests, and funding

The author is unaware of any competing interests in relation to this chapter. No external funding was received for this chapter.

References

1 Agarwal, N., Spiegel, B.M.: The effect of irritable bowel syndrome on health-related quality of life and health care expenditures. *Gastroenterol Clin North Am* 2011, **40**(1): 11–19.
2 Stewart, M., Brown, J.B., Donner, A., McWhinney, I.R., Oates, J., Weston, W.W., Jordan, J.: The impact of patient-centered care on outcomes. *J Fam Pract* 2000, **49**(9): 796–804.
3 Epstein, R.M., Franks, P., Shields, C.G., Meldrum, S.C., Miller, K.N., Campbell, T.L., Fiscella, K.: Patient-centered communication and diagnostic testing. *Ann Fam Med* 2005, **3**(5): 415–421.
4 Fenton, J.J., Kravitz, R.L., Jerant, A., Paterniti, D.A., Bang, H., Williams, D., Epstein, R.M., Franks, P.: Promoting patient-centered counseling to reduce use of low-value diagnostic tests: A randomized clinical trial. *JAMA Intern Med* 2016, **176**(2): 191–197.
5 Hungin, A.P., Molloy-Bland, M., Claes, R., Heidelbaugh, J., Cayley, W.E., Jr., Muris, J., Seifert, B., Rubin, G., de Wit, N.: Systematic review: The perceptions diagnosis and management of irritable bowel syndrome in primary care – a Rome Foundation working team report. *Aliment Pharmacol Ther* 2014, **40**(10): 1133–1145.
6 Spiegel, B.M., Farid, M., Esrailian, E., Talley, J., Chang, L.: Is irritable bowel syndrome a diagnosis of exclusion? A survey of primary care providers, gastroenterologists, and IBS experts. *Am J Gastroenterol* 2010, **105**(4): 848–858.
7 Begtrup, L.M., Engsbro, A.L., Kjeldsen, J., Larsen, P.V., Schaffalitzky de Muckadell, O., Bytzer, P., Jarbol, D.E.: A positive diagnostic strategy is noninferior to a strategy of exclusion for patients with irritable bowel syndrome. *Clin Gastroenterol Hepatol* 2013, **11**(8): 956–962 e951.

8 Hammer, J., Eslick, G.D., Howell, S.C., Altiparmak, E., Talley, N.J.: Diagnostic yield of alarm features in irritable bowel syndrome and functional dyspepsia. *Gut* 2004, **53**(5): 666–672.

9 Whitehead, W.E., Palsson, O.S., Feld, A.D., Levy, R.L., Vonk, M., Turner, M.J., Drossman, D.A.: Utility of red flag symptom exclusions in the diagnosis of irritable bowel syndrome. *Aliment Pharmacol Ther* 2006, **24**(1): 137–146.

10 Spiegel, B.M., Kanwal, F., Naliboff, B., Mayer, E.: The impact of somatization on the use of gastrointestinal health-care resources in patients with irritable bowel syndrome. *Am J Gastroenterol* 2005, **100**(10): 2262–2273.

11 Williams, M., Barclay, Y., Benneyworth, R., Gore, S., Hamilton, Z., Matull, R., Phillips, I., Seamark, L., Staveley, K., Thole, S., *et al.*: Using best practice to create a pathway to improve management of irritable bowel syndrome: Aiming for timely diagnosis, effective treatment and equitable care. *Frontline Gastroenterol* 2016, **7**(4): 323–330.

12 Verbeek, J., Sengers, M.J., Riemens, L., Haafkens, J.: Patient expectations of treatment for back pain: A systematic review of qualitative and quantitative studies. *Spine (Phila Pa 1976)* 2004, **29**(20): 2309–2318.

13 Lacy, B.E., Weiser, K., Noddin, L., Robertson, D.J., Crowell, M.D., Parratt-Engstrom C, Grau, M.V.: Irritable bowel syndrome: Patients' attitudes, concerns and level of knowledge. *Aliment Pharmacol Ther* 2007, **25**(11): 1329–1341.

14 Ahn, E., Son, K.Y., Shin, D.W., Han, M.K., Lee, H., An, A.R., Kim, E.H., Cho, B.: Perceived risk as a barrier to appropriate diagnosis of irritable bowel syndrome. *World J Gastroenterol* 2014, **20**(48): 18360–18366.

15 Bhana, N., Thompson, L., Alchin, J., Thompson, B.: Patient expectations for chronic pain management. *J Prim Health Care* 2015, **7**(2): 130–136.

16 Olden, K.W.: Approach to the patient with severe, refractory irritable bowel syndrome. *Curr Treat Options Gastroenterol* 2003, **6**(4): 311–317.

17 Sood, R., Ford, A.C.: Use of biomarkers in irritable bowel syndrome: To predict the future, look at the past. *Clin Transl Gastroenterol* 2015, **6**: e116.

18 Kuritzky, L.: Hot topics in primary care: Individualizing pharmacologic management of irritable bowel syndrome. *J Fam Pract* 2015, **64**(12 Suppl): S16–S21.

19 Kravitz, R.L., Callahan, E.J.: Patients' perceptions of omitted examinations and tests: A qualitative analysis. *J Gen Intern Med* 2000, **15**(1): 38–45.

20 Gül, V., Geschwindt, G., Şen, C.: Functional gastrointestinal disorders and psychiatric morbidity in Turkish patients in Germany. *Internistische Praxis* 2011, **51**(1): 107–114.

21 Hosseinzadeh, S.T., Poorsaadati, S., Radkani, B., Forootan, M.: Psychological disorders in patients with chronic constipation. *Gastroenterol Hepatol Bed Bench* 2011, **4**(3): 159–163.

22 Ibrahim, N.K., Battarjee, W.F., Almehmadi, S.A.: Prevalence and predictors of irritable bowel syndrome among medical students and interns in King Abdulaziz University, Jeddah. *Lib J Med* 2013, **8**: 21287.

23 Jonsbu, E., Dammen, T., Morken, G., Martinsen, E.W.: Patients with noncardiac chest pain and benign palpitations referred for cardiac outpatient investigation: A 6-month follow-up. *Gen Hosp Psychiat* 2010, **32**(4): 406–412.

24 Li, Y., Nie, Y., Sha, W., Su, H.: The link between psychosocial factors and functional dyspepsia: An epidemiological study. *Chin Med J* 2002, **115**(7): 1082–1084.

25 Mahadeva, S., Goh, K.L.: Anxiety, depression and quality of life differences between functional and organic dyspepsia. *J Gastroenterol Hepatol* 2011, **26**: 49–52.

26 Miller, V., Carruthers, H.R., Morris, J., Hasan, S.S., Archbold, S., Whorwell, P.J.: Hypnotherapy for irritable bowel syndrome: An audit of one thousand adult patients. *Aliment Pharm Ther* 2015, **41**(9): 844–855.

27 Mine, K., Kanazawa, F., Hosoi, M., Kinukawa, N., Kubo, C.: Treating nonulcer dyspepsia considering both functional disorders of the digestive system and psychiatric conditions. *Dig Dis Sci* 1998, **43**(6): 1241–1247.

28 Moser, G., Wenzel-Abatzi, T.A., Stelzeneder, M., Wenzel, T., Weber, U., Wiesnagrotzki, S., Schneider, C., Schima, W., Stacher-Janotta, G., Vacariu-Granser, G.V., *et al.*: Globus

sensation: Pharyngoesophageal function, psychometric and psychiatric findings, and follow-up in 88 patients. *Arch Inter Med* 1998, **158**(12): 1365–1373.

29 Ortiz-Olvera, N.X., Gonzalez-Martinez, M., Ruiz-Flores, L.G., Blancas-Valencia, J.M., Moran-Villota, S., Dehesa-Violante, M.: Causes of non-cardiac chest pain: Multidisciplinary perspective. *Revista de gastroenterologia de Mexico* 2007, **72**(2): 92–99.

30 Prakash, C., Clouse, R.E.: Cyclic vomiting syndrome in adults: Clinical features and response to tricyclic antidepressants. *Am J Gastroenterol* 1999, **94**(10): 2855–2860.

31 Walker, E.A., Gelfand, A.N., Gelfand, M.D., Katon, W.J.: Psychiatric diagnoses, sexual and physical victimization, and disability in patients with irritable bowel syndrome or inflammatory bowel disease. *Psychol Med* 1995, **25**(6): 1259–1267.

32 Walker, E.A., Katon, W.J., Jemelka, P.P., Roy-Byrne, P.P.: Co- morbidity of gastrointestinal complaints, depression, and anxiety in the epidemiologic catchment area (ECA) study. *Am J Med* 1992, **92**: 26S–30S.

33 Spiegel, B.M., Gralnek, I.M., Bolus, R., Chang, L., Dulai, G.S., Naliboff, B., Mayer, E.A.: Is a negative colonoscopy associated with reassurance or improved health-related quality of life in irritable bowel syndrome? *Gastrointest Endosc* 2005, **62**(6): 892–899.

34 Kellow, J.E., Drossman, D.A., Chang, A.S., Chey, W.D., Tack, J., Whitehead, W.E.: *Rome IV diagnostic algorithms for common GI symptoms*, 2nd edn. Raleigh, NC: Rome Foundation, 2016.

35 Menees, S.B., Powell, C., Kurlander, J., Goel, A., Chey, W.D.: A meta-analysis of the utility of C-reactive protein, erythrocyte sedimentation rate, fecal calprotectin, and fecal lactoferrin to exclude inflammatory bowel disease in adults with IBS. *Am J Gastroenterol* 2015, **110**(3): 444–454.

36 Sood, R., Camilleri, M., Gracie, D.J., Gold, M.J., To, N., Law, G.R., Ford, A.C.: Enhancing diagnostic performance of symptom-based criteria for irritable bowel syndrome by additional history and limited diagnostic evaluation. *Am J Gastroenterol* 2016, **111**(10): 1446–1454.

37 Chey, W.D., Nojkov, B., Rubenstein, J.H., Dobhan, R.R., Greenson, J.K., Cash, B.D.: The yield of colonoscopy in patients with non-constipated irritable bowel syndrome: Results from a prospective, controlled US trial. *Am J Gastroenterol* 2010, **105**(4): 859–865.

38 Marple, R.L., Kroenke, K., Lucey, C.R., Wilder, J., Lucas, C.A.: Concerns and expectations in patients presenting with physical complaints: Frequency, physician perceptions and actions, and 2-week outcome. *Arch Intern Med* 1997, **157**(13): 1482–1488.

39 Halpert, A., Godena, E.: Irritable bowel syndrome patients' perspectives on their relationships with healthcare providers. *Scand J Gastroenterol* 2011, **46**(7–8): 823–830.

40 Dhaliwal, S.K., Hunt, R.H.: Doctor-patient interaction for irritable bowel syndrome in primary care: A systematic perspective. *Eur J Gastroenterol Hepatol* 2004, **16**(11): 1161–1166.

41 Carter, D., Beer-Gabel, M., Derazne, E., Tzur, D., Bardan, E.: The severity of symptoms related to irritable bowel syndrome is a risk factor for the misclassification of significant organic disease. *J Clin Gastroenterol* 2017, **51**(5): 421–425.

42 Thompson, W.G.: Irritable bowel syndrome: A management strategy. *Baillieres Best Pract Res Clin Gastroenterol* 1999, **13**(3): 453–460.

43 Kelley, J.M., Kraft-Todd, G., Schapira, L., Kossowsky, J., Riess, H.: The influence of the patient-clinician relationship on healthcare outcomes: A systematic review and meta-analysis of randomized controlled trials. *PLoS One* 2014, **9**(4): e94207.

Chapter 7

Psychological assessment and questionnaires in functional gastrointestinal disorders

Philip Chase Keightley
Simon Knowles

The aim of this chapter is to provide a guide to assessing individuals with functional gastrointestinal disorders (FGIDs) from a psychological perspective. In addition to summarizing the standard psychological assessment, recommendations in relation to FGID-specific questions are provided. The chapter also presents currently available questionnaires that can be utilized in FGIDs to assess multiple domains (e.g., symptom activity, anxiety, depression and quality of life).

Learning points

- A patient's ability to understand, better manage and/or reduce FGID symptoms requires the successful combination of physiological and psychological approaches.
- The success of a psychological approach is underpinned by a collaborative approach that undertakes a comprehensive psychological assessment, utilizing multiple sources of information to assess both current symptoms and changes over time.

Introduction

Psychological interventions and psychotropic medications are effective treatments for functional gastrointestinal disorders [1, 2]. However, this effectiveness is underpinned by a comprehensive psychological assessment and related formulation which are used to direct and assess an intervention. While many individuals with FGIDs are motivated to seek and utilize psychological approaches, a subset are wary of this approach, searching instead for an exclusively physiological explanation for their symptoms. For this subset, psychological referrals may be seen as an attempt to dismiss their symptoms. Even among the most psychologically motivated, beginning a conversation about embarrassing problems is awkward.

Clinicians must be sensitive to avoid provoking shame, or the patient will not return, and the condition may deteriorate further. Therefore, honoring a patient's current situation, concerns and/or ambivalence is essential. The use of questionnaires can be helpful for engagement, particularly as a normalization

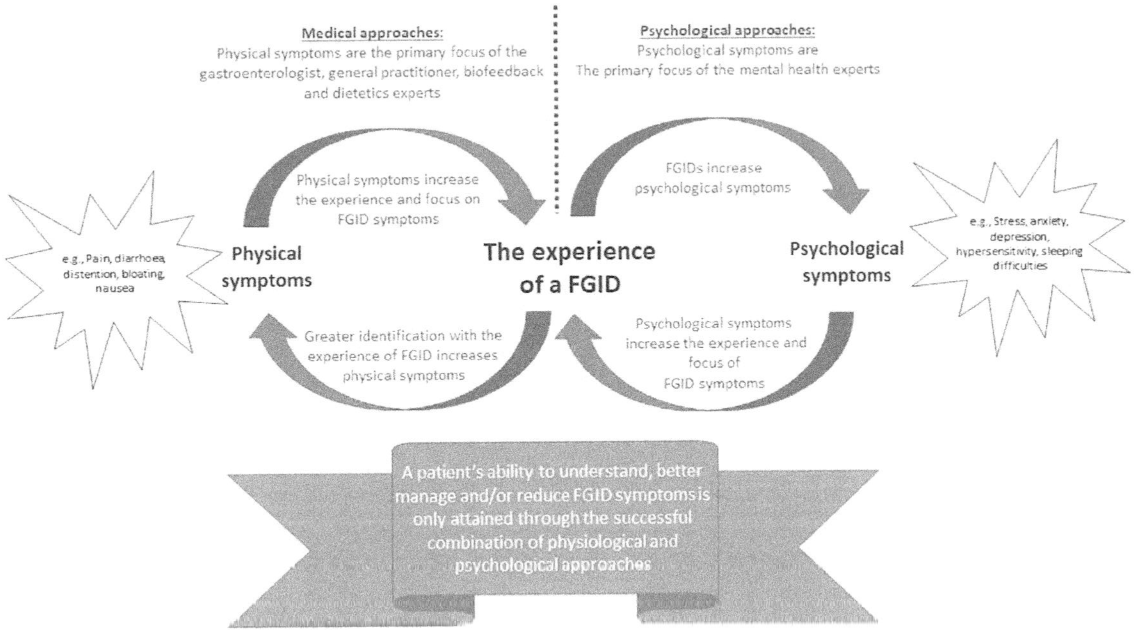

Figure 7.1 The experience of a FGID is due to the interplay between psychological and physiological processes.

device, as can having a joint assessment with the treating gastroenterologist. Throughout the assessment and treatment, education and promotion of health literacy play an important role in helping patients understand the important interplay between physical and psychological aspects of their FGID. See Figure 7.1 for a visual depiction of the experience of an individual's FGID. Therefore, psychological assessment has a dual role: diagnosis and treatment planning, but often more importantly, therapeutic engagement and education about the role of psychological processes in FGIDs.

Assessment, formulation and diagnosis of psychopathology

A psychological assessment should be undertaken only after a formal FGID diagnosis is made by a medical professional due to the multiple medical conditions which may cause FGID-like symptoms (e.g., inflammatory bowel disease, thyroid dysfunction, diabetes, substance abuse and dependence issues); see [3] for an example of the usual medical workup for irritable bowel syndrome.

Given the significant interplay between patient mind/gut experiences and treatment outcomes, a collaborative approach to the assessment, formulation and treatment plan is essential. One goal will be to obtain a comprehensive history and mental state examination [4], including basic demographic details, primary and secondary concerns and present and past history relating to medications, mental and physical history, drug and alcohol use, family and personal history (including education, friendships, social interactions), and premorbid personality. Exploration of trauma (both personal and generational), family health history and how the individual and family cope with problems (especially health-related) is important to understand. Based on the assessment, a patient-focused formulation should be derived. This formulation (see the example matrix in Table 7.1) should represent the cumulative, interrelated and concise summary of the key features of the patient's underlying concerns and symptoms.

If patient symptoms warrant it, a working diagnosis should also be developed based upon a review of symptoms in relation to standardized diagnostic criteria (e.g., Diagnostic and Statistical Manual of Mental Disorders 5 [DSM-5] [5] or the International Statistical Classification of Diseases and Related Health Problems [ICD-10] [6]). Finally, with the aim of developing a collaborative approach

Table 7.1 Standard formulation matrix (taken from [8]).

		Biopsychosocial factors		
		Biological	*Psychological*	*Social*
The 4 P'S of formulation	Predisposing factors			
	Precipitating factors			
	Perpetuating factors			
	Protective factors			

to treatment, the working diagnosis and formulation should be discussed with the patient and linked to the recommended intervention options.

Diagnostic considerations in relation to FGIDs

While anxiety- and depression-related disorders are most commonly identified in FGID cohorts, clinicians also need to be aware of other differential diagnoses. As an aside, one diagnostic challenge is that the DSM-5 does not offer a fully integrated view of mind-body problems [5]. The choice is between limited possibilities: the patient is overreacting to a somatic symptom (somatic symptom disorder or illness anxiety), anxiety or depression is worsening the somatic problem (psychological factors affecting other medical conditions) or the patient is making it up (factitious disorder). The diagnosis of conversion disorder rests on symptoms being inconsistent with known medical causes, but this ignores the known complex signalling pathways between gut and brain.

The ICD-10 [6] gives the option of 'somatoform autonomic dysfunction'. The explanatory text advises that this may apply to 'nervous diarrhoea', and that although a psychological stressor is often present, it is not a necessary criterion nor universally present. This seems much closer to the clinical reality of a functional gut disorder. This diagnosis may be replaced with 'bodily distress syndrome' in ICD-11 [7].

Issues where specialist psychiatric consultation can be helpful include: diagnostic uncertainty; advanced age; complicated medication regimes; before prescribing psychiatric medications for a child or adolescent; inadequate treatment of a psychiatric condition, such as a mood, psychotic or anxiety disorder; non-responsiveness to current prescribed psychiatric medication (a psychiatrist may be able to change a medication rather than adding another one); and concerns around addiction.

FGID-specific patient questions to consider

- What are the gastrointestinal symptoms that you experience? (including frequency, intensity, duration)
- Are there any non-gastrointestinal symptoms that you experience? (including frequency, intensity, duration)
- Are there any patterns you are aware of between your symptoms, and also with regard to other aspects of your life, such as stressors and eating patterns?
- What are the primary concerns or worries you have in relation to the symptoms you experience?
- Are there ways you have found that help you manage the physical and psychological impact of FGID on your life? If so, what are they?
- What do you believe helps best manage your FGID?
- What are the warning signs in relation to your FGID and/or psychological symptoms that suggest you need to get help? Has this happened before, and if so what did you do?

- How do your family/partner/friends/co-workers communicate with you (or react) when you talk about having a FGID and/or experience symptoms and/or associated difficulties?
- Do you feel you have enough information and support to help manage your symptoms?
- Do you use, or have you thought about, getting in contact with your local FGID organization/association, support groups?
- Do you have any questions about your FGID?

Self-report questionnaires

A brief summary of the most common questionnaires available for the assessment of non-specific and specific FGID symptoms, anxiety, depression, stress, illness perceptions and quality of life is provided in Table 7.2. Selection of questionnaires should be based upon assessment rationale and any time-dependent issues. Copyright, permission and cost-to-use issues also need to be considered. Several books are available which identify and review developed questionnaires (including their psychometric properties); these include health status measures [9] and quality of life [10].

Table 7.2 Summary of questionnaires that can be utilized in FGID cohorts to assess multiple psychosocial domains (e.g., symptom activity, anxiety, depression, stress, disease activity, illness perceptions and quality of life).

FGID activity: *Non-specific FGID activity measures:* Gastrointestinal Symptom Diary (GISD) [11]
FGID-specific activity measures: Structured Interview for Bowel Symptoms (SIBS)[a] [12]; Short Form Nepean Dyspepsia Index (SF-NDI)[b] [13]; Bristol Stool Scale (BSS) [14]; Irritable Bowel Syndrome Symptom Severity Scale (IBS-SSS)[a,b] [15]; Irritable Bowel Syndrome Questionnaire (SIBSQ)[b] [16]; Bowel Symptom Severity Scale (BSSS)[a] [12]; Functional Bowel Disorder Severity Index (FBDSI)[a,b] [17]; Bowel Symptom Severity and Frequency Scale (BSS-FS)[b] [18]; Patient Assessment of Constipation Symptoms (PAC-SYM)[b] [19]; Gastrointestinal Symptom Rating Scale modified for IBS patients (GSRS-IBS)[a,b] [20]

General psychological well-being: K10 or K6[b,c] [21]; General Health Questionnaire (GHQ; 28-item or 12-item)[b,c] [22]

Anxiety, depression, stress: Beck Depression Inventory (BDI-II) (1996 revision)[b,d] [23]; Beck Anxiety Inventory (BAI)[b] [24]; Hospital Anxiety and Depression Scale (HADS)[b] [25]; State-Trait Anxiety Inventory (STAI)[b] [26]; Depression, Anxiety and Stress Scale (DASS)[b] [27]; Perceived Stress scale (PSS)[b] [28]

Illness perceptions: Illness Perception Questionnaire (IPQ)[b] [29]; Illness Perception Questionnaire-Revised (IPQ-R)[b] [30]; Brief Illness Perception Questionnaire (Brief-IPQ)[b] [31]

Coping: Brief COPE (COPE)[b] [32]; Ways of Coping Questionnaire (WOCQ)[b] [33]; Coping strategies Inventory (CSI)[b] [34]; Coping Inventory for Stressful Situations (CISS)[b] [35]

Quality of life: Fecal Incontinence Quality of Life Scale (FIQLS) [36]; Gastrointestinal Quality of Life Index (GIQLI) [37]; Irritable Bowel Syndrome Quality of Life (IBS-QOL)[a,b] [38]; Patient Assessment of Constipation Quality of Life (PAC-QOL) [39]; Quality of Life Index for patients with Functional Gastrointestinal Disorders (QOLI-FGID) [40]; Quality of Life in Reflux and Dyspepsia (QOLRAD)[a,b] [41]; World Health Organization Quality of Life (WHOQoL) 100 item[b,c] [42], WhoQoL BREF 26-item[b,c] [43], EUROHISQOL-8[b,c] [44]; Medical Outcomes Study Short-Form: SF-36 (36-item)[b,c] [45], SF-12 (12-item)[b,c] [46]

Pain severity: Chest Pain Questionnaire CPQ [47, 48]; Chronic Widespread Pain Questionnaire (CWPQ) [49]; McGill Pain Questionnaire (MPQ)[a] [50]; Short Form McGill Pain Questionnaire (SF-MPQ) [51]; Pain Catastrophising Scale (PCS) [52]

Visceral Sensitivity: Visceral Sensitivity Index (VSI)[a,b] [53]

Personality: Eysenck Personality Questionnaire (EPQ) b,c [54], Minnesota Multiphasic Personality Inventory (MMPI)[a,b,c] [55], Minnesota Multiple Personality Inventory-2 (MMPI-2)[b,c] [56], NEO Five-Factor Inventory (NEO-FFI)[b,c] [57]

Structures psychological assessments: Mini-International Neuropsychiatric Interview (M.I.N.I.) SCID-5-RV [58]; Structured Clinical Interview for DSM-IV-TR Axis I Disorders, Patient Edition. (SCID-I/P) [59]

Notes: [a]Utilized and published in three or more FGID research studies; [b]strong psychometric properties; [c]population data; [d]may not be useful in GI populations as it assumes bowel symptoms are signs of depression.

Conclusions

A collaborative comprehensive psychological assessment is essential to attain a valid formulation of a patient's mental health status and the factors that relate to it. Collaboration between a clinician and treating the gastroenterologist can and does promote client understanding and engagement with psychologically based interventions. Clinicians should explore patient concerns and perceptions in relation to both their FGID and mental health. To facilitate assessment, diagnosis, formulation and treatment plan and monitor treatment progress, clinicians should consider using standardized questionnaires.

References

1 Ford, A.C., Talley, N.J., Schoenfeld, P.S., Quigley, E.M., Moayyedi, P.: Efficacy of antidepressants and psychological therapies in irritable bowel syndrome: Systematic review and meta-analysis. *Gut* 2009, **58**(3): 367–378.

2 Talley, N.J., Richard, Locke, G., Saito, Y.A., Almazar, A.E., Bouras, E.P., Howden, C.W., Lacy, B.E., Dibaise, J.K., Prather, C.M., Abraham, B.P., *et al.*: Effect of amitriptyline and escitalopram on functional dyspepsia: A multicenter, randomized controlled study. *Gastroenterology* 2015, **149**(2): 340–349.e342.

3 Keightley, P., Pavli, P., Platten, J., Looi, J.C.: Gut feelings 1. Mind, mood and gut in irritable bowel syndrome: Approaches to psychiatric care. *Aus Psychiat* 2015, **23**(4): 403–406.

4 Castle, D., Bassett, D.: *A primer of clinical psychiatry*, 2nd edn. Marrickville, NSW: Churchill Livingstone, 2013: 1 online resource (416 p.).

5 American Psychiatric Association, DSM-5 Task Force: *Diagnostic and statistical manual of mental disorders: DSM-5*, 5th edn. Washington, DC: American Psychiatric Association, 2013.

6 National Centre for Classification in Health (Australia): The international statistical classification of diseases and related health problems, tenth revision, Australian modification (ICD-10-AM), 7th edn. Lidcombe, NSW: National Centre for Classification in Health, 2010.
7 Lam, T., Goldberg, D., Dowell, A., Fortes, S., Mbatia, J., Minhas, F., Klinkman, M.: Proposed new diagnoses of anxious depression and bodily stress syndrome in ICD-11-PHC: An international focus group study. *Family Pract* 2013, **30**(1): 76–87.
8 Knowles, S.R.: Psychological assessment and the use of questionnaires in IBD cohorts. In: *Psychological aspects of inflammatory bowel disease: A biopsychosocial approach*. Edited by Knowles, S.R., Mikocka-Walus, A.A. London: Routledge Press, 2014: 150–163.
9 McDowell, I: *Measuring health a guide to rating scales and questionnaires*, 3rd edn. New York; Oxford: Oxford University Press, 2006: xvi, 748 p.
10 Bowling, A: *Measuring health: A review of quality of life measurement scales*, 3rd edn. Maidenhead, Berks: Open University Press, 2005.
11 Neff, D.F., Blachard, E.B.: A multi-component treatment for irritable bowel syndrome. *Behav Ther* 1987, **18**(1): 70–83.
12 Boyce, P., Gilchrist, J., Talley, N.J., Rose, D.: Cognitive-behaviour therapy as a treatment for irritable bowel syndrome: A pilot study. *Aus NZ J Psychiat* 2000, **34**(2): 300–309.
13 Talley, N., Verlinden, M., Jones, M.: Quality of life in functional dyspepsia: Responsiveness of the Nepean Dyspepsia Index and development of a new 10-item short form. *Aliment Pharm Ther* 2001, **15**(2): 207–216.
14 Lewis, S., Heaton, K.: Stool form scale as a useful guide to intestinal transit time. *Scand J Gastroentero* 1997, **32**(9): 920–924.
15 Francis, C., Morris, J., Whorwell, P.: The irritable bowel severity scoring system: A simple method of monitoring irritable bowel syndrome and its progress. *Aliment Pharm Ther* 1997, **11**(2): 395–402.
16 遠藤由香, 吉澤正彦, 福土審, 佐々木雅之, 本郷通夫: 過敏性腸症候群におけるパニック障害. 心身医学 2000, **40**(5): 339–346.
17 Drossman, D.A., Li, Z., Toner, B.B., Diamant, N.E., Creed, F.H., Thompson, D., Read, N.W., Babbs, C., Barreiro, M., Bank, L., *et al.*: Functional bowel disorders: A multicenter comparison of health status and development of illness severity index. *Dig Dis Sci* 1995, **40**(5): 986–995.
18 Solati, D.K., Adibi, P., Ghamarani, A.: The effects of cognitive – behavior therapy and drug therapy on quality of life and symptoms of patients with irritable bowel syndrome. *J Kerm Univ Med Sci* 2012, **19**(1): 94–103.
19 Frank, L., Farup, C., Jones, R., Miner, P., Taylor, L., Kleinman, L.: Evaluation of a patient symptom measure for constipation. *Gastroenterology* 1998, **114**: A14.
20 Wiklund, I.K., Fullerton, S., Hawkey, C.J., Jones, R.H., Longstreth, G.F., Mayer, E.A., Peacock, R.A., Wilson, I.K., Naesdal, J.: An irritable bowel syndrome-specific symptom questionnaire: Development and validation. *Scand J Gastroenterol* 2003, **38**(9): 947–954.
21 Kessler, R.C., Andrews, G., Colpe, L.J., Hiripi, E., Mroczek, D.K., Normand, S.L., Walters, E.E., Zaslavsky, A.M.: Short screening scales to monitor population prevalences and trends in non-specific psychological distress. *Psychol Med* 2002, **32**(6): 959–976.
22 Goldberg, D.P.: *The detection of psychiatric illness by questionnaire*. London: Oxford University Press, 1972.
23 Beck, A.T., Steer, R.A., Brown, G.K.: *Manual for the beck depression inventory-II*. San Antonio, TX: Psychological Corporation, 1996.
24 Beck, A.T., Steer, R.A.: *Beck anxiety inventory manual*. San Antonio, TX: Psychological Corporation, 1993.
25 Zigmond, A.S., Snaith, R.P.: The hospital anxiety and depression scale. *Acta psychiatrica Scandinavica* 1983, **67**(6): 361–370.
26 Spielberger, C.D., Gorssuch, R.L., Lushene, P.R., Vagg, P.R., Jacobs, G.A.: *Manual for the state-trait anxiety inventory*. Palo Alto, CA: Consulting Psychologists Press, Inc., 1983.
27 Lovibond, S.H., Lovibond, P.F.: *Manual for the depression anxiety stress scales*, 2nd edn. Sydney: Psychology Foundation, 1995.

28 Cohen, S., Kamarck, T., Mermelstein, R.: A global measure of perceived stress. *J Health Soc Behav* 1983, **24**(4): 385–396.

29 Weinman, J., Petrie, K.J., Moss-Morris, R., Horne, R.: The illness perception questionnaire: A new method for assessing the cognitive representation of illness. *Psychol Health* 1996, **11**(3): 431–445.

30 Moss-Morris, R., Weinman, J., Petrie, K.J., Horne, R., Cameron, L.D., Buick, D.: The Revised Illness Perception Questionnaire (IPQ-R). *Psychol Health* 2002, **17**(1): 1–16.

31 Broadbent, E., Petrie, K.J., Main, J., Weinman, J.: The brief illness perception questionnaire. *J Psychosom Res* 2006, **60**(6): 631–637.

32 Carver, C.S., Scheier, M.F., Weintraub, J.K.: Assessing coping strategies: A theoretically based approach. *J Person Soc Psychol* 1989, **56**(2): 267–283.

33 Folkman, S., Lazarus, R.S.: If it changes it must be a process: Study of emotion and coping during three stages of a college examination. *J Person Soc Psychol* 1985, **48**(1): 150–170.

34 Moos, L.H.: *The coping response inventory manual.* Palo Alto, CA: Social Ecology Laboratory, Stanford University and Department ofVeterans Affairs Medical Centers, 1988.

35 Endler, N.S., Parker, J.D.A.: *Coping inventory for stressful situations.* Toronto: Multi-Health Systems, 1990.

36 Naimy, N., Lindam, A.T., Bakka, A., Faerden, A.E., Wiik, P., Carlsen, E., Nesheim, B.I.: Biofeedback vs. electrostimulation in the treatment of postdelivery anal incontinence: A randomized, clinical trial. *Dis Colon Rectum* 2007, **50**(12): 2040–2046

37 Heymann-Monnikes, I., Arnold, R., Florin, I., Herda, C., Melfsen, S.: The combination of medical treatment plus multicomponent behavioral therapy is superior to medical treatment alone in the therapy of irritable bowel syndrome. *Am J Gastroenterol* 2000, **95**(4): 981–994.

38 Patrick, D.L., Drossman, D.A., Frederick, I.O., Dicesare, J., Puder, K.L.: Quality of life in persons with irritable bowel syndrome (development and validation of a new measure). *Dig Dis Sci* 1998, **43**(2): 400–411.

39 Marquis, P., De La Loge, C., Dubois, D., McDermott, A., Chassany, O. Development and validation of the Patient Assessment of Constipation Quality of Life questionnaire. *Scand J Gastroenterol* 2005, **40**(5): 540–51.

40 Poitras, M.R., Verrier, P., So, C., Pâquet, S., Bouin, M., Poitras, P.: Group counseling psychotherapy for patients with functional gastrointestinal disorders: Development of new measures for symptom severity and quality of life. *Dig Dis Sci* 2002, **47**(6): 1297–1307.

41 Bredenoord, A.J., Weusten, B.L.A.M., Timmer, R., Smout, A.J.P.M.: Psychological factors affect the frequency of belching in patients with aerophagia. *Am J Gastroenterol* 2006, **101**(12): 2777–2781.

42 Power, M., Harper, A., Bullinger, M.: The World Health Organization WHOQOL-100: Tests of the universality of Quality of Life in 15 different cultural groups worldwide. *Health Psychol* 1999, **18**(5): 495–505.

43 Skevington, S.M., Lotfy, M., O'Connell, K.A., Group, W.: The World Health Organization's WHOQOL-BREF quality of life assessment: Psychometric properties and results of the international field trial. A report from the WHOQOL group. *Qual Life Res* 2004, **13**(2): 299–310.

44 Schmidt, S., Muhlan, H., Power, M.: The EUROHIS-QOL 8-item index: Psychometric results of a cross-cultural field study. *Eur J Public Health* 2006, **16**(4): 420–428.

45 Ware, J.E., Kosinski, M., Bjorner, J.B., Turner-Bowker, D.M., Gandek, B., Maruish, M.E.: *User's manual for the SF-36v2TM health survey*, 2nd edn. Lincoln, RI: QualityMetric Inc, 2007.

46 Ware, J.E., Kosinski, M., Turner-Bowker, D.M., Gandek, B.: *How to score version 2 of the SF-12v2® health survey.* Lincoln, RI: QualityMetric Inc., 2002.

47 Eslick, G.D., Jones, M.P., Talley, N.J.: Non-cardiac chest pain: Prevalence, risk factors, impact and consulting – a population-based study. *Aliment Pharm Ther* 2003, **17**(9): 1115–1124.

48 Locke, G., Talley, N., Weaver, A., Zinsmeister, A.: A new questionnaire for gastroesophageal reflux disease. *Mayo Clin Proc* 1994, **69**(6): 539–547.
49 Wolfe, F., Ross, K., Anderson, J., Russell, I.J., Hebert, L.: The prevalence and characteristics of fibromyalgia in the general population. *Arthritis Rheum* 1995, **38**(1): 19–28.
50 Melzack, R.: The McGill Pain Questionnaire: Major properties and scoring methods. *Pain* 1975, **1**(3): 277–299.
51 Melzack, R.: The short-form McGill pain questionnaire. *Pain* 1987, **30**(2): 191–197.
52 Sullivan, M.J., Bishop, S.R., Pivik, J.: The pain catastrophizing scale: Development and validation. *Psychol Assess* 1995, **7**(4): 524.
53 Labus, J., Bolus, R., Chang, L., Wiklund, I., Naesdal, J., Mayer, E., Naliboff, B.: The Visceral Sensitivity Index: Development and validation of a gastrointestinal symptom-specific anxiety scale. *Aliment Pharm Ther* 2004, **20**(1): 89–97.
54 Grayson, D.A.: Latent trait analysis of the Eysenck personality questionnaire. *J Psychiat Res* 1986, **20**(3): 217–235.
55 Hathaway, S.R., McKinley, J.C.: *Minnesota multiphasic personality inventory*; manual (Revised), 1951. San Antonio, TX: Psychological Corporation.
56 Butcher, J.N.: Minnesota multiphasic personality inventory-2: Manual for administration, scoring, and interpretation. Minnesota: University of Minnesota Press, 2001.
57 Costa, P.T., MacCrae, R.R.: Revised NEO personality inventory (NEO PI-R) and NEO five-factor inventory (NEO FFI): Professional manual: Psychological Assessment Resources, 1992. Lutz, Florida.
58 Sheehan, D.V., Lecrubier, Y., Sheehan, K.H., Amorim, P., Janavs, J., Weiller, E., Hergueta, T., Baker, R., Dunbar, G.C.: The Mini-International Neuropsychiatric Interview (MINI): The development and validation of a structured diagnostic psychiatric interview for DSM-IV and ICD-10. *J Clin Psychiat* 1998, **59**(Suppl 20): 22–33;quiz 34–57.
59 First, M.B., Spitzer, R.L.: *Structured clinical interview for DSM-IV-TR axis I disorders, research version (SCID-I/P)*, Patient edn. New York: Biometrics Research, New York State Psychiatric Institute, 2002.

Chapter 8

Diet in functional gastrointestinal disorders

Emma Phoebe Halmos

The aim of this chapter is to review the current practice and evidence for dietary therapy of functional gastrointestinal disorders (FGIDs) and possible negative consequences of treatment.

Learning points

- Dietary treatments are gaining popularity among the FGID community and it is essential to stay up-to-date with knowledge of their efficacy and application.
- A low FODMAP (fermentable oligosaccharides, disaccharides, monosaccharides and polyols) diet works well to reduce symptoms in approximately 75% of IBS sufferers.
- Application of a low FODMAP diet should be supervised by a dietitian to ensure appropriate application and nutritional adequacy.
- Optimal long-term application of a low FODMAP diet is individual and should be aimed to apply the minimal restriction for maximal symptomatic benefit.
- Other dietary therapies have limited evidence of efficacy for IBS and evidence for diet to target other FGIDs is largely anecdotal.

Introduction

Functional gastrointestinal disorders (FGIDs) are extremely common, affecting up to one third of the Australian population [1]. The three modes of treatments targeting FGIDs are dietary, psychological and pharmacological, and this chapter will review dietary therapy. Dietary interventions that describe supplementation of one single food component, often in supra-physiological doses taken in isolation of their natural context (e.g., fibre or prebiotic supplementation), are more akin to pharmacological therapy than diet. In reality, diet is about food choice rather than dietary supplementation and will be the focus of this chapter.

There is an increasing interest in the use of diet as a therapy among patients and health professionals. Diet is perceived to be a major contributing factor to symptoms among patients with FGID, with 60% of patients with IBS trialling an empirical exclusion [2]. With a growing focus in the community, it is vital that the relationship between diet and FGID is clearly and accurately represented and that careful interpretation of literature guides practice. As the majority of research into dietary therapy has been targeted to IBS, the following chapter will mainly focus on this subgroup of FGID, but the general principles are relevant to other functional bowel disorders.

Dietary therapies

Dietary therapies are often very appealing to IBS sufferers and have included reduction of fat to influence motility, avoidance of caffeine because of its bioactive nature, alteration of dietary fibre to improve the quality of colonic contents and reduce constipation, and elimination of suspected dietary triggers with a purely trial-and-error approach [3]. There have also been many complex dietary strategies based on unsubstantiated concepts published via books or online, such as the 'paleo diet' or 'GAPS diet'. While these diets may have anecdotal reports of benefit in a proportion of people with IBS, evidence supporting their efficacy is lacking and their philosophy behind mechanism of action is based on pseudoscience. The most concerning aspect of these diets is often the extremely restrictive and inflexible structure of the diet that may lead to adherence difficulties and likely promote nutritional inadequacies. The dietary strategy that has had the greatest impact in the management of IBS symptoms has been the low FODMAP (fermentable oligosaccharides, disaccharides, monosaccharides and polyols) diet.

Low FODMAP diet

FODMAPs refer to fermentable, poorly absorbed, short-chain carbohydrates widely present in the food supply. The mechanism by which FODMAPs induce symptoms relates to the physiological effects of luminal distension, which emerges through three characteristics of FODMAPs: (1) poor and slow intestinal absorption, (2) osmotic effect and (3) rapid colonic fermentation, producing gas. In the small bowel, distension will be contributed particularly by osmotic load, as demonstrated in magnetic resonance imaging studies in which monosaccharide but not oligosaccharide FODMAPs increased small bowel water content [4]. An ileostomy model has demonstrated the increased water content yielded by unabsorbed FODMAPs in the distal small bowel and colon applies a natural laxative effect [5] and the rapid fermentability of FODMAPs leads to gas production. These characteristics of FODMAPs can lead to laxation and distension of the bowel that result in symptoms of bloating, pain and motility disturbances. Such effects are exaggerated in patients with IBS because of the presence of visceral hypersensitivity and abnormal motility responses.

Dietary FODMAPs include the oligosaccharides fructans and galacto-oligosaccharides, the disaccharide lactose, the monosaccharide fructose (found in excess of glucose) and polyols, such as sorbitol and mannitol. The symptomatic benefit of restricting more than one FODMAP concurrently was first examined in the form of a 'fructose malabsorption diet' assessed in a retrospective study of selected patients with both IBS and fructose malabsorption, in which 74% of subjects reported a positive symptomatic response [6]. The first implementation of the low FODMAP diet in unselected IBS subjects was a crossover trial where low FODMAP and high FODMAP diets were provided for two days each [7]. This evidence base, however, still lacked a blinded randomized controlled trial with all food-related confounders minimized and that compared symptom measures to healthy controls. To fill the evidence gap, a closely controlled interventional trial followed, proving efficacy of a low FODMAP diet in the management of IBS symptoms [8]. This randomized crossover trial in unselected IBS subjects indicated that a provided low FODMAP diet significantly reduced gastrointestinal symptoms in 70% of IBS subjects compared to a provided diet matched for all nutrients except for dietary FODMAPs. A healthy control comparator showed that the results were specific to IBS. Since then, many Level II trials around the world have been published confirming the efficacy of a low FODMAP diet in managing symptoms of IBS [9–11].

The low FODMAP diet is also now supported by an extensive database of FODMAP composition of food, which enables further manipulation of FODMAPs. Common food sources of FODMAPs are listed in Table 8.1. Level I formal systematic review of trials has not yet been undertaken, but all randomized controlled trials have had positive outcomes and have consistently indicated

Table 8.1 Common food sources of FODMAPs and suitable food alternatives.

FODMAP	*Dietary form*	*Common sources*	*Suitable low FODMAP alternatives*
Fructose	Free monosaccharide (fructose in excess of glucose)	Apple, pear, honey	Banana, citrus, most berries, sucrose
Lactose	Disaccharide	Milk, yoghurt	Lactose-free milk, lactose-free yoghurt, ripened cheese
Polyols	Sorbitol, mannitol, xylitol, maltitol, lactitol, isomalt	Apple, pear, apricot, plum, mushroom, cauliflower, low-joule sweeteners	Kiwifruit, pineapple, grapes, capsicum, zucchini, sucrose
Fructans	Fructo-oligosaccharides, inulin	Wheat, rye, onion, garlic, inulin fibre supplement	Spelt, rice, greens of spring onion, sterculia fibre supplement
Galacto-oligosaccharides	Raffinose, stachyose	Lentils, chick peas, kidney beans, navy beans	Tofu, meat, chicken fish, eggs

that approximately 75% of patients with IBS benefit symptomatically from a low FODMAP diet.

Application of a low FODMAP diet

With growing awareness of a low FODMAP diet come mis-use and over-prescription of the treatment. Sources of lay information include the Internet, cookbooks and smartphone apps; however, this information usually provides only estimations of the FODMAP content of food. This creates problems with proper diagnosis of IBS and appropriate application of the diet. Manipulation of FODMAPs is best done in conjunction with a dietitian well versed in IBS and dietary treatments so that detailed explanation of IBS and individualized dietary therapy are applied while nutritional adequacy is maintained.

The two main approaches that a dietitian may take in applying a FODMAP restriction is the *top-down* or the *bottom-up* approach. The more traditional top-down approach involves over-restriction of all or most dietary FODMAPs above an arbitrary dose for a period of time. If symptomatic benefit is seen, dietary liberalization may be undertaken via structured food 'challenges' or by general recommendations describing FODMAP dosing of food. Alternatively,

Table 8.2 Top-down and bottom-up approaches to implementation of a low FODMAP diet (adapted from Halmos EP. 2016 [12]).

Dietary approach	*Top-down*	*Bottom-up*
Description	Over-restriction of all/most FODMAPs, and then liberalization of diet to tolerance level	Reduction of foods with large amount of/specific FODMAPs, then further restriction to tolerance level as required
Usual duration	4–8 weeks	4–8 weeks
Suitable IBS population	Patients in whom the success of the low FODMAP diet or type/amount of tolerance is uncertain Patients who do not normally eat a lot of FODMAPs Patients who are very symptomatic Patients who prefer this approach	Patients who eat a lot of FODMAPs Patients who are mildly symptomatic Patients in whom prebiotics are particularly important Patients who prefer this approach
Possible contraindications	Patients who are nutritionally compromised Patients with eating disorders Children Patients with other dietary restrictions	

the bottom-up approach describes the reduction of a few foods that are very concentrated in FODMAPs or only specific FODMAPs are targeted, and then further restriction if indicated. Descriptions of the top-down and bottom-up approaches of implementing a low FODMAP diet are detailed in Table 8.2 [12].

Potential negative consequences of a low FODMAP diet

Although never formally investigated, it appears that a low FODMAP diet, if well designed under the guidance of a dietitian, is nutritionally adequate as there are suitable food alternatives for all restricted foods. Nonetheless, any dietary restriction has the potential to lead to nutritional inadequacies. Fibre is the most at risk of being decreased if not replaced by fibre-rich low FODMAP food alternatives. As wheat, legumes and many FODMAP-containing fruits are high in fibre, alternatives such as oats, gluten-free grains (which are often incidentally low FODMAP), such as quinoa, brown rice and buckwheat, and low FODMAP fruits and vegetables are encouraged. Additionally, methods of reducing FODMAP content within foods may be applied, such as using canned or soaked and drained legumes to reduce the content of these water-soluble nutrients. This is particularly useful for vegetarians and vegans, who rely on legumes as meat and dairy alternatives. Caution should be exercised in restricting FODMAPs in this population in addition to those at high risk of malnutrition. Allowance may need to be made in such scenarios and a modified approach (or the 'bottom-up approach') to a low FODMAP diet should be instructed.

The best documented consequence of a low FODMAP diet is its potential to impact negatively on the gut microbiome. The first trial to investigate effects on the microbiome of FODMAP restriction in an IBS population was a randomized parallel group study, where the effects of a dietitian-taught low FODMAP diet reduced the proportion and concentration of *Bifidobacteria* spp. compared to that seen with those of a habitual diet [13]. A diet-controlled crossover trial in IBS and healthy subjects showed that a low FODMAP diet reduced total bacterial abundance and relative abundance of short-chain fatty acid-producing bacteria [14]. While the functional significance of these findings is not yet known, they provide evidence for potentially unfavourable effects of the low FODMAP diet on the microbiome by promoting a potentially pro-inflammatory luminal environment. Application of a low FODMAP diet long-term should be exercised with caution and should not be recommended for asymptomatic subjects or in IBS subjects who do not see symptomatic benefit from the diet.

Other dietary treatments for IBS

Before the low FODMAP diet, the diet that had been the most thoroughly researched to manage symptoms of IBS was a high-fibre diet. Level I systematic review of literature has shown that overall, a high-fibre diet has poor efficacy in reducing symptoms of IBS [15], although it may be that types of fibre should be considered individually as supplementation with some soluble fibre, such as psyllium and linseeds, may reduce overall symptoms and ease stool passage. These effects have not been seen with insoluble fibre, such as bran, which may even worsen IBS symptoms [15, 16].

Another diet with widespread application in Australia is termed the low food chemical diet, which restricts dietary food chemicals naturally occurring (salicylates, amines and glutamate) and/or food additives (colours, preservatives and flavour enhancers) [17]. These bioactive molecules are hypothesized to induce gastrointestinal symptoms in some IBS patients by acting on specific gut receptors or directly on mast cells, leading to increased sensation [18, 19]. Anecdotally, there is symptomatic benefit in a proportion of those with gastrointestinal and extra-gastrointestinal symptoms. Unfortunately, no patient-outcome trials have been published and the developed protocols using strict restrictions and fixed rechallenges are labour-intensive. Most concerning is the consequence of the nutritional inadequacy of these diets, as has been highlighted in children [20] but is likely true for an adult population too.

The diet that has gained the most amount of global popularity in the community for targeting symptoms of IBS is a gluten-free diet. Literature on the role of a gluten-free diet in patients with IBS symptoms has mainly focused on patients with self-reported non-coeliac gluten sensitivity (NCGS). NCGS is defined as a condition whereby gluten leads to intestinal or extraintestinal symptoms. The existence and prevalence of this condition are controversial and the evidence is conflicting [21, 22]. Furthermore, the lines are often blurred between IBS and NCGS as to whether they are separate entities; however, data on using a gluten-free diet to reduce symptoms in an unselected IBS population indicate good clinical response [23]. Although a gluten-free diet is effective in reducing symptoms of IBS, dietary gluten co-exists with FODMAPs and amylase trypsin inhibitors, both of which have been shown to contribute to gastrointestinal symptoms [21, 22, 24]. Indeed, a controlled double-blinded, placebo-controlled dietary trial using carbohydrate-depleted gluten in patients with both NCGS and IBS showed high nocebo responses, but no specific induction of symptoms from gluten. Furthermore, all subjects had more predictable beneficial symptom response to restricting FODMAPs compared to gluten [21]. It would seem that response to a gluten-free diet does not necessarily mean that gluten is the cause of symptoms.

Dietary treatments for other FGIDs

There is limited evidence for the use of diet as treatment for upper gastrointestinal symptoms. Patient-reported influences on symptoms of heartburn and dyspepsia are more related to larger meal volumes, time of eating and posture [25]. Anecdotally, in addition to promoting small and frequent meals, reducing foods that delay gastric emptying, such as foods high in fat and fibre, may also provide some symptomatic benefit. Mechanism studies on dietary FODMAPs have indicated that possible restriction specifically of monosaccharides and disaccharides, which have a greater impact on proximal small bowel luminal distension than oligosaccharides, may have symptomatic benefit for those with functional heartburn or dyspepsia. However, patient-outcome trials have not been completed.

Implementation of dietary treatments

Before implementation of any dietary therapy is completed, assessment of patients' clinical situation, including nutrition, is needed to lessen the risk of negatively impacting health and well-being. Dietary and nutritional assessment requires understanding of each patient's individual pattern of eating, food intake and current nutritional status. By definition, FGIDs are not associated with intestinal injury; therefore, patients with FGIDs will not have any altered or increased nutritional requirements compared to the general population. However, self-restriction of diet is common [2], due to either associated symptoms with specific foods or non-specific reduction of intake because of feeling unwell. Altered eating behaviour, such as skipping meals, inappropriate eating times (e.g., overnight), extreme dietary restriction due to philosophy, religion or cultural beliefs and general lack of food variety would indicate referral to a dietitian and/or even psychologist in the case of disordered eating. Extreme dietary alterations may contraindicate application of any dietary treatment – for example, in someone with an overt eating disorder. Dietary therapy has potential to impact not only nutritionally but also psychologically and psychosocially. Survey data in patients with IBS have indicated that a higher number of food items reported to trigger abdominal symptoms was associated with a lower quality of life [26]. Additionally, subsequent unnecessary caution and over-restriction of food can lead to psychosocial implications and even anxiety [27]. Ideally, management of patients with FGIDs is multidisciplinary, with involvement from primary care physicians, gastroenterologists, dietitians and psychologists.

Conclusions

Dietary therapies for FGIDs have mainly targeted IBS. A low FODMAP diet is a well-established treatment and now has good evidence of efficacy worldwide for the management of IBS symptoms. Ideally, management of treatment should be under the guidance of a dietitian together with other health professionals well experienced in the area of IBS. If ineffective in reducing IBS symptoms, other dietary therapies with less evidence base may be trialled with caution.

Acknowledgments, competing interests, and funding

The author is unaware of any competing interests in relation to this chapter. No external funding was received for this chapter.

References

1 Boyce, P.M., Talley, N.J., Burke, C., Koloski, N.A.: Epidemiology of the functional gastrointestinal disorders diagnosed according to Rome II criteria: An Australian population-based study. *Intern Med J* 2006, **36**(1): 28–36.
2 Brandt, L.J., Chey, W.D., Foxx-Orenstein, A.E., Schiller, L.R., Schoenfeld, P.S., Spiegel, B.M., Talley, N.J., Quigley, E.M.M., Moayyedi, P.: An evidence-based systematic review on the management of irritable bowel syndrome American College of Gastroenterology Task Force on IBS. *Am J Gastroenterol* 2009, **104**(Supp 1): S1–S35.
3 Ford, A.C., Talley, N.J., Spiegel, B.M., Foxx-Orenstein, A.E., Schiller, L., Quigley, E.M., Moayyedi, P.: Effect of fibre, antispasmodics, and peppermint oil in the treatment of irritable bowel syndrome: Systematic review and meta-analysis. *Br Med J (Clin Res Ed)* 2008, **337**: a2313.
4 Murray, K., Wilkinson-Smith, V., Hoad, C., Costigan, C., Cox, E., Lam, C., Marciani, L., Gowland, P., Spiller, R.C.: Differential effects of FODMAPs (Fermentable Oligo-, Di-, Mono-Saccharides and Polyols) on small and large intestinal contents in healthy subjects shown by MRI. *Am J Gastroenterol* 2014, **109**(1): 110–119.
5 Barrett, J.S., Gearry, R.B., Muir, J.G., Irving, P.M., Rose, R., Rosella, O., Haines, M.L., Shepherd, S.J., Gibson, P.R.: Dietary poorly absorbed, short-chain carbohydrates increase delivery of water and fermentable substrates to the proximal colon. *Aliment Pharmacol Ther* 2010, **31**(8): 874–882.
6 Shepherd, S.J., Gibson, P.R.: Fructose malabsorption and symptoms of irritable bowel syndrome: Guidelines for effective dietary management. *J Am Diet Assoc* 2006, **106**(10): 1631–1639.
7 Ong, D.K., Mitchell, S.B., Barrett, J.S., Shepherd, S.J., Irving, P.M., Biesiekierski, J.R., Smith, S., Gibson, P.R., Muir, J.G.: Manipulation of dietary short chain carbohydrates alters the pattern of gas production and genesis of symptoms in irritable bowel syndrome. *J Gastroenterol Hepatol* 2010, **25**(8): 1366–1373.
8 Halmos, E.P., Power, V.A., Shepherd, S.J., Gibson, P.R., Muir, J.G.: A diet low in FODMAPs reduces symptoms of irritable bowel syndrome. *Gastroenterol* 2014, **146**(1): 67–75.
9 Eswaran, S.L., Chey, W.D., Han-Markey, T., Ball, S., Jackson, K.: A randomized controlled trial comparing the low FODMAP diet vs. modified NICE guidelines in US adults with IBS-D. *Am J Gastroenterol* 2016, **111**(12): 1824–1832.
10 McIntosh, K., Reed, D.E., Schneider, T., Dang, F., Keshteli, A.H., De Palma, G., Madsen, K., Bercik, P., Vanner, S.: FODMAPs alter symptoms and the metabolome of patients with IBS: A randomised controlled trial. *Gut* 2017, **66**(7): 1241–1251.
11 Peters, S.L., Yao, C.K., Philpott, H., Yelland, G.W., Muir, J.G., Gibson, P.R.: Randomised clinical trial: The efficacy of gut-directed hypnotherapy is similar to that of the low FODMAP diet for the treatment of irritable bowel syndrome. *Aliment Pharmacol Ther* 2016, **44**(5): 447–459.
12 Halmos, E.P.: When the low FODMAP diet does not work. *J Gastroenterol Hepatol* (Australia) 2017, **32**: 69–72.
13 Staudacher, H., Lomer, M.C.E., Anderson, J., Barrett, J., Muir, J., Irving, P., Whelan, K.: Fermentable carbohydrate restriction reduces luminal bifidobacteria and gastrointestinal symptoms in patients with irritable bowel syndrome. *J Nutr* 2012, **142**(8): 1510–1518.
14 Halmos, E.P., Christophersen, C.T., Bird, A.R., Shepherd, S.J., Gibson, P.R., Muir, J.G.: Diets that differ in their FODMAP content alter the colonic luminal microenvironment. *Gut* 2015, **64**: 93–100.
15 Bijkerk, C.J., Muris, J.W.M., Knottnerus, J.A., Hoes, A.W., De Wit, N.J.: Systematic review: The role of different types of fibre in the treatment of irritable bowel syndrome. *Aliment Pharmacol Ther* 2004, **19**(3): 245–251.
16 Moayyedi, P., Quigley, E.M., Lacy, B.E., Lembo, A.J., Saito, Y.A., Schiller, L.R., Soffer, E.E., Spiegel, B.M., Ford, A.C.: The effect of fiber supplementation on irritable bowel syndrome: A systematic review and meta-analysis. *Am J Gastroenterol* 2014, **109**(9): 1367–1374.

17 Gibson, A.R., Clancy, R.L.: An Australian exclusion diet. *Med J Aus* 1978, **1**: 290–292.
18 Depoortere, I.: Taste receptors of the gut: Emerging roles in health and disease. *Gut* 2014, **63**(1): 179–190.
19 Suzuki, Y., Ra, C.: Analysis of the mechanism for the development of allergic skin inflammation and the application for its treatment: Aspirin modulation of IgE-dependent mast cell activation: Role of aspirin-induced exacerbation of immediate allergy. *J Pharmacol Sci* 2009, **110**(3): 237–244.
20 Gray, P.E.A., Mehr, S., Katelaris, C.H., Wainstein, B.K., Star, A., Campbell, D., Joshi, P., Wong, M., Frankum, B., Keat, K., *et al.*: Salicylate elimination diets in children: Is food restriction supported by the evidence? *Med J Aus* 2013, **198**(11): 600–602.
21 Biesiekierski, J.R., Peters, S.L., Newnham, E.D., Rosella, O., Muir, J.G., Gibson, P.R.: No effects of gluten in patients with self-reported non-celiac gluten sensitivity after dietary reduction of fermentable, poorly absorbed, short-chain carbohydrates. *Gastroenterol* 2013, **145**(2): 320–328.
22 Carroccio, A., Mansueto, P., Iacono, G., Soresi, M., D'Alcamo, A., Cavataio, F., Brusca, I., Florena, A.M., Ambrosiano, G., Seidita, A., *et al.*: Non-celiac wheat sensitivity diagnosed by double-blind placebo-controlled challenge: Exploring a new clinical entity. *Am J Gastroenterol* 2012, **107**(12): 1898–1906.
23 Aziz, I., Trott, N., Briggs, R., North, J.R., Hadjivassiliou, M., Sanders, D.S.: Efficacy of a gluten-free diet in subjects with irritable bowel syndrome-diarrhea unaware of their HLA-DQ2/8 genotype. *Clin Gastroenterol Hepatol* 2016, **14**(5): 696–703.
24 Elli, L., Tomba, C., Branchi, F., Roncoroni, L., Lombardo, V., Bardella, M.T., Ferretti, F., Conte, D., Valiante, F., Fini, L., *et al.*: Evidence for the presence of non-celiac gluten sensitivity in patients with functional gastrointestinal symptoms: Results from a multicenter randomized double-blind placebo-controlled gluten challenge. *Nutrients* 2016, **8**(2): 84.
25 Oliver, K., Davies, G., Dettmar, P.: Diet and lifestyle as trigger factors for the onset of heartburn. *Nurs Stand* 2011, **25**(36): 44–48.
26 Bohn, L., Storsrud, S., Tornblom, H., Bengtsson, U., Simren, M. Self-reported food-related gastrointestinal symptoms in IBS are common and associated with more severe symptoms and reduced quality of life. *Am J Gastroenterol* 2013, **108**(5): 634–641.
27 Addolorato, G., Mirijello, A., D'Angelo, C., Leggio, L., Ferrulli, A., Vonghia, L., Cardone, S., Leso, V., Miceli, A., Gasbarrini, G.: Social phobia in coeliac disease. *Scand J Gastroenterol* 2008, **43**(4): 410–415.

Chapter 9

The role of biofeedback in functional gastrointestinal disorders

Rebecca E. Burgell
Gillian Skardoon

The aim of this chapter is to discuss the practical use of biofeedback, including the instruments utilized and its evidence base, in functional gastrointestinal disorders (FGIDs).

Learning points

- Biofeedback is a behavioural therapy based on operant conditioning techniques.
- Biofeedback therapy has an established role in dyssynergic defaecation and should also be considered in other FGIDs.
- Further research into the mechanism of action of biofeedback and the development of standardized protocols for management of functional gastrointestinal disorders are urgently required.

Introduction

Biofeedback therapy for functional gastrointestinal disorders has gathered increased momentum as its evidence base expands. Biofeedback is a behavioural therapy using 'operant conditioning' techniques, including reinforcement with verbal instruction and instrumental stimuli, to modify breathing, intraabdominal pressure and/or pelvic floor muscle strength and coordination [1].

Biofeedback has an established role in a number of functional bowel disorders (FGIDs), including dyssynergic defaecation, slow transit constipation and faecal incontinence, and limited evidence in irritable bowel syndrome (IBS), levator ani syndrome and upper FGIDs, although biofeedback therapy is contraindicated in pregnancy, active infection or inflammation, active anal fissures, acute postoperative period, severe anal sphincter injuries, dementia and uncontrolled psychosis.

Practical aspects of biofeedback therapy

The role of the biofeedback practitioner is fundamental in providing accurate instruction and modification for optimization of function. With respect to anorectal disorders, biofeedback is ideally undertaken in the defaecation position

Table 9.1 Behavioural training programme and biofeedback protocol defaecation (adapted with permission from Khera, A. [5]).

Session	*Description of session*
First session	Full history and examination Education – anatomy and function Establish realistic goals Regular timed toileting Correct toileting posture Cessation of straining/digitation – suppositories permitted Diaphragmatic breathing Biofeedback guided skills Pelvic floor contraction and relaxation Effective expulsive effort Simulated defaecation Laxative reduction/cessation regime Emotional and psychological support Home programme prescriptionw Duration of session: 60 minutes
Subsequent sessions	Reassessment of symptoms Practice and reinforcement Revision of home programme – address barriers to adherence Duration: 30 minutes

(seated, leaning forward at 45 degree angle, legs apart) with the instrument correctly placed as described ahead [2]. An example of a biofeedback protocol is detailed in Table 9.1. Biofeedback training is individually tailored; however, traditionally it requires 5–6 training sessions lasting 30–60 minutes on a weekly to fortnightly basis [1].

Furthermore, the presence of concurrent psychological morbidity in patients with FGIDs has been recognized in the literature and may directly and indirectly influence management [3]. Biofeedback has been shown to improve the psychological state and quality of life in patients with FGIDs [3]. Routine supervision for biofeedback therapists has been recommended for optimal management of patients with psychological comorbidities and to ensure ongoing support for biofeedback practitioners [4].

Instrument modalities

Instruments utilized for biofeedback include manometry, EMG, rectal balloons, ultrasound (intrarectal, intravaginal, perineal), digital guidance or visual feedback techniques. Anorectal manometry records anal and rectal pressures via a probe embedded with microtransducers. This is presented as either auditory and/or visual information on a display unit to the patient. EMG biofeedback systems include a sensor placed on the surface of the external anal sphincter, which again provides real-time visual and auditory feedback of the activation of the anal musculature. In addition, balloon biofeedback comprises a catheter with a balloon attached, which is inserted 10 cm into the rectum and inflated with either water or air to create sensory awareness. Ultrasound is a relatively new biofeedback modality and allows real-time feedback to assist in teaching and reinforcing the correct defaecation technique.

Comparison of biofeedback modalities

Head-to-head trials between biofeedback treatment techniques are limited and a recent Cochrane review was unable to form a significant conclusion regarding the most efficacious modality [6].

The role of biofeedback in individual FGIDs

Dyssynergic defaecation

Introduction

Dyssynergic defaecation is defined as a paradoxical contraction or failure of pelvic floor muscle relaxation during defaecation (Figure 9.1) [1]. Dyssynergic defaecation is suggested to be an acquired condition predominantly associated with functional constipation; however, it has been observed in other disorders, including slow transit constipation, IBS, inflammatory bowel disease and neurological conditions [1]. The pelvic floor muscles ('levator ani') include puborectalis, iliococcygeus, ischiococcygeus and pubococcygeus. They are linked both anatomically and physiologically with the internal and external anal sphincter to provide support for continence. The use of biofeedback in dyssynergic defaecation has a substantial evidence base, consisting predominantly of uncontrolled trials and small randomized controlled trials (Level of Evidence II).

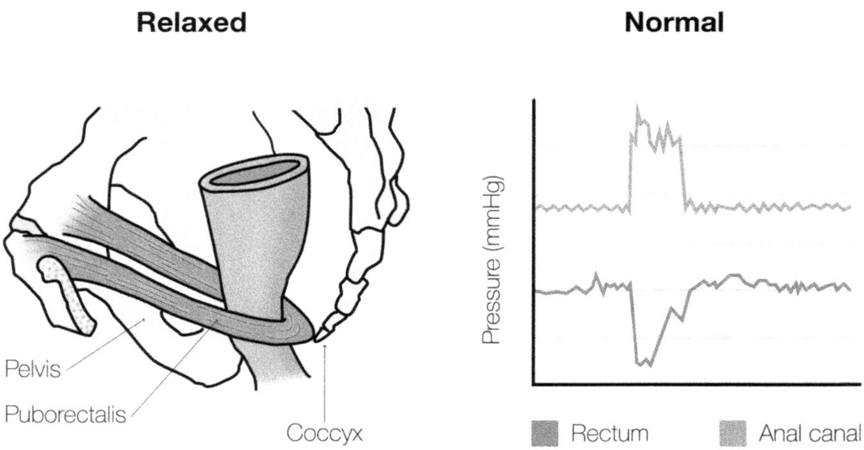

Figure 9.1 Manometric and anatomical representation of dyssynergic defaecation (adapted from [7] with permission, acknowledgement Dane Robertson).

Mechanism of action

The exact mechanism of biofeedback therapy in dyssynergic defaecation is unclear, with evidence conflicting as to its primary effect on local structures or central processing. Biofeedback may act locally by relaxing the puborectalis muscle, allowing the anorectal angle to widen and thereby removing the mechanical barrier to defaecation [8]. Alternatively, biofeedback may act via modulation of the autonomic nervous system as there is evidence that biofeedback results in enhanced gut microcirculation in patients with chronic constipation, resulting in decreased stool transit time [9]. Furthermore, bidirectional brain-gut dysfunction has been established in patients with dyssynergic defecation, although the role of biofeedback in improving central processing in bowel conditions is yet to be determined [2].

Efficacy of biofeedback

Biofeedback therapy has achieved a symptom response rate of up to 80% in patients with dyssynergic defaecation, with results maintained at 44 months [10, 11]. Symptom improvement in patients with good compliance can be demonstrated within 4–6 sessions and reinforcement sessions may provide additional benefit [2].

Six of the nine randomized controlled trials that have been performed comparing biofeedback and non-biofeedback modalities [10, 12–19] in patients who have failed conservative medical therapy have demonstrated significant improvement in subjective scores of symptoms, quality of life or objective scores, including resting anal sphincter pressure, complete spontaneous bowel movement (CSBM) per week scores or correction of the dyssynergic pattern.

Nevertheless, interpreting the literature is inherently difficult due to inconsistencies in both the diagnosis of dyssynergia and variations in study design and treatment protocols. This was recognized in a recent Cochrane review [6] that concluded the efficacy and safety of biofeedback could not be established due to inadequacies in study methodology and bias [6]. Despite these reservations, biofeedback is recommended as first-line therapy for patients with dyssynergic defaecation who have failed conservative management, in part because it is efficacious, cost-effective and low-risk, particularly when compared with other treatment strategies, such as *Botulinum toxin* injection and surgical procedures [1].

Biofeedback therapy has also been proven in patients with slow transit constipation and dyssynergia, with 63% reporting subjective improvement [9]. Biofeedback may also improve whole gut transit in slow transit constipation without dyssynergia, although treatment effects appear less durable [9, 21, 22].

Predictors of response to therapy

Patients who have an increased likelihood of clinical success convey symptoms of harder stool consistency, shorter duration of laxative use and willingness to comply with treatment protocols [23]. Conversely, those who described a long history of constipation, history of an eating disorder or poor compliance are more likely to have a poor response to biofeedback therapy [24].

Faecal incontinence

Introduction

Faecal incontinence is defined as the involuntary loss of liquid or solid stool leading to social or hygiene problems [25]. It has a prevalence of 2%–9% in the Australian community and is the second most common cause for institutionalization [26, 27]. Symptoms of faecal incontinence include urgency (associated with weakness of the external anal sphincter), passive soiling without an urge for defaecation (may indicate internal anal sphincter dysfunction) and incomplete evacuation with consequent overflow diarrhoea (associated with pelvic floor dyssynergia) [25]. Rectal sensory dysfunction is also well documented in faecal incontinence, with 7%–50% of patients displaying evidence of rectal hypersensitivity [28, 29], and 7%–24% hyposensitivity [29].

The goals of biofeedback in faecal incontinence are twofold: (1) promote abdominal and pelvic floor muscle strength and coordination, and (2) improve sensation and perception of rectal distention to recover urge control [30]. This is optimally undertaken with a regimen of twice-weekly 60-minute sessions, for a total of six sessions with a comprehensive home exercise plan [30].

Mechanism of action

The mechanism of action of biofeedback in patients with faecal incontinence is yet to be established; however, it predominantly trains the striated muscle of the external anal sphincter, and puborectalis by its anatomical association, to co-ordinate and strengthen anal contraction [25]. Sensory and perception retraining is also an important component of biofeedback therapy, although the mechanism by which improvement is achieved is unknown.

Process of biofeedback therapy

Muscular strengthening, muscle coordination and, if relevant, rectal sensitivity training are key components of biofeedback therapy in patients with faecal incontinence [30]. Muscular strengthening is undertaken by teaching anal squeeze with hold for 30 seconds without activating the abdominal or gluteal muscles [30]. Anal squeeze pressure has been demonstrated to improve following biofeedback training [31]. Sensory-motor coordination is assessed as the maximum voluntary squeeze in less than 1 second after inflation of the rectal balloon [30]. Sensory training for patients with hyposensitivity is undertaken by inflating the balloon to the volume that the patient has the urge to defecate and gradually decreasing this volume by 5–10 millilitres in order to detect smaller volumes of stool to prompt defaecation and improve evacuation [30]. Conversely, in patients with hypersensitivity and urgency, the balloon is inflated to incrementally larger volumes. Urge control management is encouraged by teaching relaxation techniques, including deep breathing exercises, while at the urge threshold [30].

Efficacy of biofeedback in faecal incontinence

The role of biofeedback therapy in patients with faecal incontinence is largely based on a small number of randomized controlled trials (detailed in Table 9.2), uncontrolled prospective trials and case reports (Level of Evidence II). Studies indicate that approximately 65%–75% of patients with faecal incontinence may benefit from biofeedback [30] which is maintained for at least two years [32].

Table 9.2 Comparison between randomized controlled trials of biofeedback and non-biofeedback modalities for faecal incontinence.

Authors (date)	*Study description*	*Response rates*	*Limitations/ bias*
Faecal incontinence			
Norton *et al.* (2003) [34]	Compared (a) standard care (advice), (b) advice plus instruction on sphincter exercises, (c) hospital-based computer-assisted sphincter pressure biofeedback, (d) biofeedback plus home EMG biofeedback. N=171.	Neither pelvic floor exercises nor biofeedback was superior to standard care supplemented by advice and education.	
Solomon *et al.* (2003) [35]	Compared: (a) biofeedback with anal manometry, (b) biofeedback with transanal ultrasound, (c) pelvic floor exercises with digital examination feedback. N=120.	70% of patients improved symptom severity. No difference between treatment groups in quality of life or clinical measures.	
Davis *et al.* (2004) [36]	Compared sphincter repair or sphincter repair plus biofeedback 3 months post surgery. N=38.	QOL measures showed greater improvement and were sustained over time within biofeedback group but no difference between groups.	Most data discussed as before-after analysis
Ilnyckyj *et al.* (2005) [37]	Education and pelvic exercise vs education and BF therapy. N=23.	No difference in response rate between treatment arms	Not powered sufficiently

(*Continued*)

Table 9.2 (Continued)

Authors (date)	*Study description*	*Response rates*	*Limitations/ bias*
Heymen *et al.* (2009) [31]	Compared pelvic floor exercises alone or manometric biofeedback plus pelvic floor exercises	Biofeedback group had significantly greater reduction in FISI (P= 0.01); this was maintained at 12 months, and fewer days with faecal incontinence (P= 0.083) 3 months after treatment. 76% of patients treated with biofeedback vs 41% of patients treated with pelvic floor exercises reported relief.	High risk of blinding bias
Bols *et al.* (2012) [38]	Compared rectal balloon training (RBT) and pelvic floor muscle training (PFMT) versus PFMT alone in patients with faecal incontinence. N=80.	RBT equally effective as PFMT alone. The addition of RBT did not improve Vaizey score. Secondary outcomes that favoured RBT included: urgency control, global perceived effect and lifestyle adaptations.	

Unfortunately, similar to biofeedback in dyssynergic defaecation, a Cochrane review found that due to heterogeneous patient populations (21 studies including 1525 patients) and methodological weaknesses overall no definite response to therapy was able to be concluded, although there was a suggestion of therapeutic effect [25].

Predictors of response to therapy

Patient characteristics that predict a favourable outcome include the use of constipating medications, obstetric factors and minor embarrassment regarding their condition in addition to physiological parameters, including first rectal sensation threshold of 50 mL or less and urge of 100 mL or less [33]. A longer duration of symptoms and younger age of onset predict an unfavourable response [33].

Irritable bowel syndrome

Introduction

Markedly different biofeedback modalities have been utilized in managing IBS, ranging from a physiological approach, including pelvic floor muscle biofeedback, to therapies targeting vagal tone/autonomic function (i.e., diaphragmatic breathing exercises) and psychological rehabilitation. The use of physiological biofeedback therapy in patients with IBS has a very limited evidence base, comprising predominantly uncontrolled trials (Level of Evidence III-2). Multiple uncontrolled trials and one randomized controlled trial have been undertaken directed at psychological and autonomic biofeedback therapy for IBS (Level of Evidence II) albeit with poor clinical applicability.

Efficacy of biofeedback therapy

Physiological biofeedback rehabilitation aimed at correcting anorectal function is an emerging therapy for managing patients with IBS, in particular those with dyssynergic overlap. Patients with non-diarrhoea-predominant IBS with symptoms of pelvic floor dyssynergia may demonstrate overall pelvic floor dyssynergic physiology similar to that of patients with functional constipation [39]. Studies have shown that the presence of IBS symptoms in dyssynergic defaecation did not affect the outcome of biofeedback therapy. Furthermore, treating dyssynergic defaecation in patients with IBS using biofeedback therapy improved both constipation and IBS symptoms [39]. Therefore, dyssynergia and in turn biofeedback therapy should be considered in all patients with constipation-predominant IBS.

There has also been limited work targeting colonic motility in patients with diarrhoea-predominant IBS using sound-based biofeedback (electronic stethoscope) or step-wise rectal balloon distension; however, they proved to have poor clinical application and replication [40].

Biofeedback directed at psychological relaxation training and autonomic nervous system modification using forehead EMG, thermal biofeedback, heart-rate variability or a gut-directed computer biofeedback game has been undertaken with overall positive results but limited clinical applicability [40].

Additional anorectal disorders

Levator ani syndrome has been described as a vague ache or pressure sensation high in the rectum, which worsens with sitting compared with standing or lying down and may demonstrate tenderness on palpation and spasm of the levator ani muscles on examination [41]. Levator ani syndrome is difficult to manage as it has a variable response to many therapies, including electrogalvanic stimulation, massage therapy, sacral nerve stimulation, and steroid and *Botulinum toxin* injections [30]. Chiarioni *et al.* performed a rigorous randomized controlled trial comparing biofeedback therapy with electrogalvanic stimulation (EGS) or digital massage [42]. The intent-to-treat analysis demonstrated that 59.6% of biofeedback-treated patients reported adequate relief compared with 32.7% of patients undergoing EGS and 28.3% of patients who underwent massage (Level of Evidence II). The mechanism that biofeedback improves pain in levator ani syndrome was postulated to be similar to dyssynergic defaecation with actions on relaxing pelvic floor muscles and thereby muscle tension with additional effects on rectal sensitivity and smooth muscle tone [42]. Patients who reported tenderness on palpation were more likely to benefit from all three of the treatments.

Upper gastrointestinal functional disorders

Biofeedback therapy has been utilized in conditions of the upper gastrointestinal tract, including functional dyspepsia, belching disorders and rumination syndrome.

Functional dyspepsia

Defined as one or more of postprandial fullness, early satiety, epigastric pain or burning that are not explained by routine clinical investigation [44], it is a common disorder affecting 10%–30% of patients worldwide [44]. Biofeedback has been found to alter gastric motility in healthy subjects [40], and biofeedback training targeting the autonomic nervous system has been shown to be efficacious in improving symptoms and quality of life, although no effects were noted on vagal tone (Level of Evidence II) [40].

Supragastric belching

Patients presenting with symptoms of frequent, repetitive belching may also benefit from biofeedback therapy [44]. Symptomatic improvement and reduction in swallowing rate following biofeedback therapy have been demonstrated by using diaphragmatic breathing biofeedback techniques to encourage habit reversal (Level of Evidence III-1) [44].

Rumination syndrome

Behavioural therapy, such as biofeedback, has been shown to diminish the urge to ruminate using breathing techniques and abdominal muscle relaxation (Level of Evidence II) [44].

Conclusions

The effectiveness of biofeedback therapy is practitioner-dependent. Consideration of the increased prevalence of psychological morbidity patients with FGIDs should be recognized, in addition to support and routine supervision for biofeedback therapists. Biofeedback should be considered for all patients with evidence of dyssynergic defaecation and in selected patients with other FGIDs based on clinical or diagnostic testing.

Acknowledgments, competing interests, and funding

The authors are unaware of any competing interests in relation to this chapter. No external funding was received for this chapter.

References

1 Rao, S.S.C., Patcharatrakul, T.: Diagnosis and treatment of dyssynergic defecation. *J Neurogastroenterol Motil* 2016, **22**: 423–435.
2 Rao, S.S.C.: Biofeedback therapy for constipation in adults. *Best Pract Res Clin Gastroenterol* 2011, **25**: 159–166.
3 Mason, H.J., Serrano-Ikkos, E., Kamm, M.A.: Psychological state and quality of life in patients having behavioral treatment (biofeedback) for intractable constipation. *Am J Gastroenterol* 2002, **97**: 3154–3159.
4 Stern, J.: Making the case for psychological supervision. *Gastrointest Nurs* 2011, **9**: 42–46.
5 Yang, L.S., Khera, A., Kamm, M.A.: Outcome of behavioural treatment for idiopathic chronic constipation. *Intern Med J* 2014, **44**: 858–864.
6 Woodward, S., Norton, C., Chiarelli, P.: Biofeedback for treatment of chronic idiopathic constipation in adults. *Cochrane Database Syst Rev* 2014, **3**: CD008486.
7 Rao, S.S., Welcher, K.D., Leistikow, J.S.: Obstructive defecation: A failure of rectoanal coordination. *Am J Gastroenterol* 1998, **93**: 1042–1050.
8 Papachrysostomou, M., Smith, A.N.: Effects of biofeedback on obstructive defecation – reconditioning of the defecation reflex? *Gut* 1994, **35**: 252–256.
9 Emmanuel, A.V, Kamm, M.A.: Response to a behavioural treatment, biofeedback, in constipated patients is associated with improved gut transit and autonomic innervation. *Gut* 2001, **49**: 214–219.
10 Rao, S.S.C., Seaton, K., Miller, M., *et al.*: Randomized controlled trial of biofeedback, sham feedback, and standard therapy for dyssynergic defecation. *Clin Gastroenterol Hepatol* 2007, **5**: 331–338.
11 Lee, H.J., Boo, S-J, Jung, K.W., *et al.*: Long-term efficacy of biofeedback therapy in patients with dyssynergic defecation: Results of a median 44 months follow-up. *Neurogastroenterol Motil* 2015, **27**: 787–795.
12 Chang, H-S., Myung, S-J., Yang, S-K., *et al.*: Effect of electrical stimulation in constipated patients with impaired rectal sensation. *Int J Colorectal Dis* 2003, **18**: 433–438.
13 Chiarioni, G., Whitehead, W.E., Pezza, V., *et al.*: Biofeedback is superior to laxatives for normal transit constipation due to pelvic floor dyssynergia. *Gastroenterology* 2006, **130**: 657–664.
14 Heymen, S., Scarlett, Y., Jones, K., *et al.*: Randomized, controlled trial shows biofeedback to be superior to alternative treatments for patients with pelvic floor dyssynergia-type constipation. *Dis Colon Rectum* 2007, **50**: 428–441.

15 Rao, S.S., Valestin, J., Kice Brown, C., *et al.*: Long-term efficacy of biofeedback therapy for dyssynergic defecation: Randomized controlled trial. *Am J Gastroenterol* 2010, **105**(4): 890–896.
16 Jung, K.W., Myung, S.J., Byeon, J.S., *et al.*: Electrical stimulation therapy in pelvic floor dyssynergia: Prospective, randomized study combined with biofeedback. *J Gastroenterol Hepatol* 2007, **22**: A 209.
17 Simón, M.A., Bueno, A.M.: Behavioural treatment of the dyssynergic defecation in chronically constipated elderly patients: A randomized controlled trial. *Appl Psychophysiol Biofeedback* 2009, **34**: 273–277.
18 Hart, S.L., Lee, J.W., Berian, J., *et al.*: A randomized controlled trial of anorectal biofeedback for constipation. *Int J Colorectal Dis* 2012, **27**: 459–466.
19 Ba-Bai-Ke-Re, M.M.T.J.A., Wen, N.R., Hu, Y.L., *et al.*: Biofeedback-guided pelvic floor exercise therapy for obstructive defecation: An effective alternative. *World J Gastroenterol* 2014, **20**: 9162–9169.
20 Chang, H-S., Myung, S-J., Yang, S-K., *et al.*: Effect of electrical stimulation in constipated patients with impaired rectal sensation. *Int J Colorectal Dis* 2003, **18**: 433–438.
21 Chiarioni, G., Salandini, L., Whitehead, W.E.: Biofeedback benefits only patients with outlet dysfunction, not patients with isolated slow transit constipation. *Gastroenterology* 2005, **129**: 86–97.
22 Battaglia, E., Serra, A.M., Buonafede, G., *et al.*: Long-term study on the effects of visual biofeedback and muscle training as a therapeutic modality in pelvic floor dyssynergia and slow-transit constipation. *Dis Colon Rectum* 2004, **47**: 90–95.
23 Shim, L.S.E., Jones, M., Prott, G.M., *et al.*: Predictors of outcome of anorectal biofeedback therapy in patients with constipation. *Aliment Pharmacol Ther* 2011, **33**: 1245–1251.
24 Lembo, A., Camilleri, M.: Chronic constipation. *N Engl J Med* 2003, **349**: 1360–1368.
25 Norton, C., Cody, J.D.: Biofeedback and/or sphincter exercises for the treatment of faecal incontinence in adults. *Cochrane Database Syst Rev* 2012, **7**: CD002111.
26 Kalantar, J.S., Howell, S., Talley, N.J.: Prevalence of faecal incontinence and associated risk factors; an underdiagnosed problem in the Australian community? *Med J Aust* 2002, **176**: 54–57.
27 Lahr, C.J.: Evaluation and treatment of incontinence. *Pract Gastroenterol* 1988, **12**: 27–35.
28 Chan, C.L.H., Scott, M.S., Williams, N.S., *et al.*: Rectal hypersensitivity worsens stool frequency, urgency, and lifestyle in patients with urge fecal incontinence. *Dis Colon Rectum* 2005, **48**: 134–140.
29 Townsend, D.C., Carrington, E.V., Grossi, U., *et al.*: Pathophysiology of fecal incontinence differs between men and women: A case-matched study in 200 patients. *Neurogastroenterol Motil* 2016, **28**: 1580–1588.
30 Rao, S.S.C., Benninga, M.A., Bharucha, A.E., *et al.*: ANMS-ESNM position paper and consensus guidelines on biofeedback therapy for anorectal disorders HHS public access. *Neurogastroenterol Motil* 2015, **27**: 594–609.
31 Heymen, S., Scarlett, Y., Jones, K., *et al.*: Randomized controlled trial shows biofeedback to be superior to pelvic floor exercises for fecal incontinence. *Dis Colon Rectum* 2009, **52**: 1730–1737.
32 Enck, P., Däublin, G., Lübke, H.J., *et al.*: Long-term efficacy of biofeedback training for fecal incontinence. *Dis Colon Rectum* 1994, **37**: 997–1001.
33 Bols, E., Hendriks, E., de Bie, R., *et al.*: Predictors of a favorable outcome of physiotherapy in fecal incontinence: Secondary analysis of a randomized trial. *Neurourol Urodyn* 2012, **31**: 1156–1160.
34 Norton, C., Chelvanayagam, S., Wilson-Barnett, J., *et al.*: Randomized controlled trial of biofeedback for fecal incontinence. *Gastroenterology* 2003, **125**: 1320–1329.
35 Solomon, M.J., Pager, C.K., Rex, J., *et al.*: Randomized, controlled trial of biofeedback with anal manometry, transanal ultrasound, or pelvic floor retraining with digital guidance alone in the treatment of mild to moderate fecal incontinence. *Dis Colon Rectum* 2003, **46**: 703–710.
36 Davis, K.J., Kumar, D., Poloniecki, J.: Adjuvant biofeedback following anal sphincter repair: A randomized study. *Aliment Pharmacol Ther* 2004, **20**: 539–549.

37 Ilnyckyj, A., Fachnie, E., Tougas, G.: A randomized-controlled trial comparing an educational intervention alone vs education and biofeedback in the management of faecal incontinence in women. *Neurogastroenterol Motil* 2005, **17**: 58–63.
38 Bols, E., Berghmans, B., de Bie, R., *et al.*: Rectal balloon training as add-on therapy to pelvic floor muscle training in adults with fecal incontinence: A randomized controlled trial. *Neurourol Urodyn* 2012, **31**: 132–138.
39 Patcharatrakul, T., Gonlachanvit, S.: Outcome of biofeedback therapy in dyssynergic defecation patients with and without irritable bowel syndrome. *J Clin Gastroenterol* 2011, **45**: 593–598.
40 Chiarioni, G., Whitehead, W.E.: The role of biofeedback in the treatment of gastrointestinal disorders. *Nat Clin Pract Gastroenterol Hepatol* 2008, **5**: 371–382.
41 Rao, S.S.C., Bharucha, A.E., Chiarioni, G., *et al.*: Anorectal disorders. *Gastroenterology* 2016, **150**: 1430–1442.e4.
42 Chiarioni, G., Nardo, A., Vantini, I., *et al.*: Biofeedback is superior to electrogalvanic stimulation and massage for treatment of levator ani syndrome. *Gastroenterology* 2010, **138**: 1321–1329.
43 Rao, S.S.C., Ozturk, R., De Ocampo, S., *et al.*: Pathophysiology and role of biofeedback therapy in solitary rectal ulcer syndrome. *Am J Gastroenterol* 2006, **101**: 613–618.
44 Stanghellini, V., Chan, F.K.L.L., Hasler, W.L., *et al.*: Gastroduodenal disorders. *Gastroenterology* 2016, **150**: 1380–1392.

Part III

Functional gastrointestinal disorders and biopsychosocial approaches across the age range

Chapter 10

Diagnostic and treatment approaches associated with functional oesophageal disorders

Megan Elizabeth Riehl
André J.P.M. Smout

The aim of this chapter is to review these disorders from a biopsychosocial perspective and discuss current research findings relating to the aetiology, physiology and diagnostic considerations and review of current psychological and medical interventions. Practical recommendations regarding comprehensive treatment approaches to manage these conditions are provided.

Learning points

- Visceral hypersensitivity and hypervigilance provide a logical explanation of the pathophysiology of functional oesophageal disorders.
- For all functional oesophageal disorders, symptoms must be present for at least three months with an onset at least six months before each diagnosis is applied to establish chronicity.
- Treatment for functional oesophageal disorders includes a holistic approach that incorporates the use of neuromodulation, pain modulation, medical therapy and psychological intervention.

Introduction

Patients with upper gastrointestinal complaints account for a significant proportion of health-care utilization in adult populations throughout the United States [1]. The prevalence of oesophageal disorders (functional and organic combined) is estimated at 17.5% of all digestive system diagnoses [2]. Most patients with oesophageal symptoms first present in a primary care setting, where diagnostic possibilities are limited. However, it is important that the first health-care provider in the chain considers a functional oesophageal disorder as a differential diagnosis. Gastroesophageal reflux disease (GERD) represents the most common upper GI disorder in the outpatient setting with nearly 7 million visits for GERD-related symptoms in 2010 [3]. Historically, emphasis was placed on prescribing a trial of proton pump inhibitor (PPI) therapy to determine whether acid was contributing to the presentation. If patients reported symptom improvement, they traditionally were encouraged to remain on their daily dose of PPI and were loosely defined as having GERD. The attempt to define

GERD and exclude a functional oesophageal diagnosis with the use of PPI has been found to have limited predictive value and low specificity [4]. Therefore, Rome IV guidelines have moved away from this model, as the understanding of the role of visceral hypersensitivity and hypervigilance provides a more logical explanation of the pathophysiology of functional oesophageal disorders [5].

To properly diagnose and determine an appropriate treatment plan, a patient presenting with oesophageal symptoms should undergo a thorough clinical history in addition to any necessary procedures (e.g., upper endoscopy, pH monitoring, manometry). Some patients also have access to a consultation with a gastrointestinal-focused psychologist; therefore, more comprehensive assessments include consideration for potential psychological management [6]. Functional oesophageal disorders compose a disease category with symptoms not explained by an oesophageal motility abnormality, mechanical obstruction, GERD or oesophageal inflammation by other causes. This group of disorders tends to be difficult to treat given the often-unexplained mechanisms responsible for the burdensome symptoms. Patients are often presenting for evaluation due to the physical discomfort related to symptoms, but it is also common to hear significant complaints of the impact of the symptoms on their quality of life (QoL) and daily functioning [1]. The importance of conceptualizing patients with these disorders from a biopsychosocial perspective is highlighted as our understanding extends far past monocausal aetiopathogenetic processes to now acknowledge the complex interplay of one's environment, psychology and biological components.

Diagnostic criteria for functional oesophageal disorders

For all functional oesophageal disorders, symptoms must be present for at least three months with an onset at least six months before each diagnosis is applied to establish chronicity. The Rome IV diagnostic criteria for the five functional oesophageal disorders are listed in Table 10.1.

Table 10.1 Diagnostic criteria for functional oesophageal disorders.

A1. Functional chest pain[1]

Diagnostic criteria* Must include **all** of the following:

1. Retrosternal chest pain or discomfort**
2. Absence of associated oesophageal symptoms, such as heartburn and dysphagia
3. Absence of evidence that gastroesophageal reflux or eosinophilic woesophagitis is the cause of the symptom
4. Absence of major oesophageal motor disorders†

* Criteria fulfilled for the last three months with symptom onset at least six months prior to diagnosis with a frequency of at least once a week

** Cardiac causes should be ruled out.

† Achalasia/EGJ outflow obstruction, diffuse oesophageal spasm, jackhammer oesophagus, absent peristalsis

A2. Functional heartburn[2]

Diagnostic criteria* Must include **all** of the following:

1. Burning retrosternal discomfort or pain
2. No symptom relief despite optimal antisecretory therapy
3. Absence of evidence that gastroesophageal reflux** or eosinophilic oesophagitis is the cause of the symptom
4. Absence of major oesophageal motor disorders†

* Criteria fulfilled for the last three months with symptom onset at least six months prior to diagnosis with a frequency of at least twice a week

** Elevated acid exposure time and/or symptom reflux association

† Achalasia/EGJ outflow obstruction, diffuse oesophageal spasm, jackhammer oesophagus, absent peristalsis

A3. Reflux hypersensitivity[3]

Diagnostic criteria* Must include **all** of the following:

1. Retrosternal symptoms, including heartburn and chest pain
2. Normal endoscopy and absence of evidence that eosinophilic oesophagitis is the cause of the symptoms
3. Absence of major oesophageal motor disorders**
4. Evidence of triggering of symptoms by reflux events despite normal acid exposure on pH or pH-impedance monitoring†

* Criteria fulfilled for the last three months with symptom onset at least six months prior to diagnosis with a frequency of at least twice a week

** Achalasia/EGJ outflow obstruction, diffuse oesophageal spasm, jackhammer oesophagus, absent peristalsis

† Response to antisecretory therapy does not exclude the diagnosis.

A4. Globus[4]

Diagnostic criteria* Must include **all** of the following:

1. Persistent or intermittent, nonpainful sensation of a lump or foreign body in the throat with no structural lesion identified on physical examination, laryngoscopy or endoscopy
   a. Occurrence of the sensation between meals
   b. Absence of dysphagia or odynophagia
   c. Absence of a gastric inlet patch in the proximal oesophagus
2. Absence of evidence that gastroesophageal reflux or eosinophilic oesophagitis is the cause of the symptom
3. Absence of major oesophageal motor disorders**

* Criteria fulfilled for the last three months with symptom onset at least six months prior to diagnosis with a frequency of at least once a week

** Achalasia/EGJ outflow obstruction, diffuse oesophageal spasm, jackhammer oesophagus, absent peristalsis

A5. Functional dysphagia[5]

Diagnostic criteria* Must include **all** of the following:

1. Sense of solid and/or liquid foods sticking, lodging or passing abnormally through the oesophagus
2. Absence of evidence that oesophageal mucosal or structural abnormality is the cause of the symptom
3. Absence of evidence that gastroesophageal reflux or eosinophilic oesophagitis is the cause of the symptom
4. Absence of major oesophageal motor disorders**

* Criteria fulfilled for the last three months with symptom onset at least six months prior to diagnosis with a frequency of at least once a week

** Achalasia/EGJ outflow obstruction, diffuse oesophageal spasm, jackhammer oesophagus, absent peristalsis

Diagnostic criteria taken from R. Fass, J.E. Pandolfino, Q. Aziz, C.P. Gyawali, H. Miwa and F. Zerbib [8], Esophageal Disorders, Chapter 9, pages [1]840, [2]854, [3]863, [4]870, [5]879 of the *Rome IV Functional Gastrointestinal Disorders: Disorders of Gut-Brain Interaction*. Reproduction approved by Professor Douglas Drossman 23/10/2016.

Functional chest pain

The cardinal symptom in functional chest pain is retrosternal chest discomfort or pain. Typically, the pain is described as a pressure sensation in the mid-chest with radiation to the mid-back, arms and jaw. Patients presenting with chest pain to a gastroenterologist have usually been seen in an emergency room or by a cardiologist where they have undergone necessary evaluations to rule out a cardiac cause. It is understandable that anxiety is commonly comorbid at the onset of chest pain. However, even after diagnosis, fear, ruminating thoughts and anticipatory anxiety may drive continued health-care utilization with impacts on QoL and ability to attend to day-to-day activities [9].

Functional heartburn

Given that heartburn is the most frequently reported symptom within the oesophageal region [10], functional heartburn must be carefully defined and now serves as a model for understanding oesophageal hypersensitivity, as well as for comprehending the role of sustained stress and psychological processes, such as catastrophizing, oesophageal hypervigilance and somatization [11, 12]. Oesophageal hypervigilance happens in the context of a learned behaviour, reinforced over time by an individual's sustained focus on interoceptive and environmental cues which can result in a cognitive-affective shift, where those cues become comparable to heartburn [13].

Reflux hypersensitivity

In Rome IV, reflux hypersensitivity has been added to the functional oesophageal conditions, whereas in Rome III the entity was part of the reflux disease spectrum. In reflux hypersensitivity similar pathophysiologic properties (peripheral and central sensitization, autonomic dysregulation and psychological abnormalities) play a role as in functional chest pain and functional heartburn. The only difference is that in reflux hypersensitivity the trigger (gastroesophageal reflux) can be identified using reflux monitoring [5].

Globus

Globus sensation is a common symptom typically described as a 'lump' or tightness in the throat which is nonpainful but persistent or intermittent. Usually the patient has been seen by an ear nose and throat (ENT) specialist before the diagnosis of functional globus is made and local causes have been excluded.

Functional dysphagia

Functional dysphagia is characterized by a "sensation of abnormal bolus transit" down the oesophagus, in the absence of obstruction or a severe oesophageal motor disorder. Its prevalence is relatively low, accounting for 7%–8%

of dysphagia [14]. However, one episode of dysphagia can lead to significant emotional distress, which is perpetuated by avoidance behaviours and fears of eating, choking or the inability to swallow. Classic emergency room descriptions include the feeling of food "sticking or lodging" in the oesophagus or chest after a swallow [7].

Differential diagnosis

There is a high prevalence of GERD within patients with chest pain and heartburn; therefore high-dose PPI therapy may be initially used to determine whether a diagnosis of GERD should be considered. It must be noted, however, that the ability of the PPI test to identify patients with GERD is limited [15]. PPI non-responders should be considered for endoscopy with mucosal biopsy to rule out eosinophilic oesophagitis (EoE). An ambulatory pH study (off PPI) can be performed to identify reflux. A motility study will rule out achalasia or diffuse oesophageal spasm. Given the high prevalence of globus sensation reported in the general population, possible causes include GERD, visceral hypersensitivity and upper oesophageal sphincter dysfunction [16]. Dysphagia can occur in a variety of diseases, the most feared of which is a malignancy. Therefore, upper endoscopy usually is the mandatory first step. Other differential diagnoses include GERD, EoE, major oesophageal motor disorders (diagnosed on motility studies) and oropharyngeal diseases.

Common patient concerns and issues associated with functional oesophageal disorders

Receiving a diagnosis of a functional oesophageal disorder can bring about feelings of frustration driven by misunderstanding (i.e., 'the doctor thinks this is all in my head'). A patient may also feel invalidated, hopeless or upset due to a perceived lack of treatment options. Doctors and other health professionals should provide clear explanations in non-stigmatizing language to describe the functional diagnosis, as well as information about the medical, pharmaceutical or psychological treatment options available to ensure that a patient is not left feeling helpless. Empathic communication can aid in ensuring that patients feel validated and cared for, and not passed along to another provider. This is especially true if the treatment plan will include a health psychologist [6]. Basic psychoeducation pertaining to oesophageal hypersensitivity, gastrointestinal-specific anxiety and the perception of sensory experiences can aid in validating the patient's experience, while also helping him or her to understand the manner in which a comprehensive treatment plan can be effective [13].

Given the sensitivity and fear that some functional oesophageal symptoms can cause, patients develop GI-specific anxieties which begin to impact their day-to-day functioning. In particular, fear of choking or not being able to breathe drives symptom-specific anxiety.

Despite this, many patients function well despite their symptoms, and fear that they will be labelled with a mental health diagnosis if they work with a psychologist or mental health professional to address their GI condition. Therefore, working with a psychologist with specific training in the treatment of GI disorders can aid patients in decreasing stigmatization, getting them adequate treatment and ultimately improving their quality of life. In a similar way, when GI patients are prescribed neuromodulators to aid with symptom management, careful explanation by the prescribing provider is essential. The likelihood of non-compliance will be reduced when the patient understands that the medication is given to improve physical symptoms rather than for emotional reasons.

Medical and allied health standard care treatment approaches for functional oesophageal disorders

Treatment for functional oesophageal disorders includes a holistic approach that incorporates the use of neuromodulation, pain modulation, medical therapy and psychological intervention. For most patients with functional oesophageal disorders who have attempted a PPI trial with no symptom alleviation, it is helpful to use reassurance and explanation as to why they should not continue with PPI use. While treatment for reflux hypersensitivity remains empiric, some patients with acid-sensitivity may respond well to single- or double-dose PPI [17], while those with symptoms triggered by weakly acidic or non-acid reflux remain PPI non-responders and should be encouraged to use other treatment options [18]. With the exception of dysphagia, where a bougie dilation may offer symptom relief for patients with intermittent food-related symptoms, medical procedures are typically not of benefit [5].

Patients can implement lifestyle modifications for most oesophageal conditions. Dietary changes (eliminating spicy, fatty or acidic foods), elevating the head of the bed, smoking cessation and increasing activities to aid with stress management (i.e., exercise) may offer symptom relief, especially for patients with functional heartburn or reflux hypersensitivity [12, 19]. Behavioural modifications for patients with dysphagia include instruction on eating more slowly in an upright position, chewing food well, drinking liquid with meals and avoiding stress while having a meal [20].

Since oesophageal hypersensitivity seems to play a role in functional chest pain, heartburn and reflux hypersensitivity, the use of a neuromodulator in the form of a low-dose antidepressant may be considered. Tricyclic antidepressants (TCAs), selective serotonin reuptake inhibitors (SSRIs) and serotonin and norepinephrine reuptake inhibitors (SNRIs) have all been recommended [21–23]. Gabapentinoids have also been mentioned for use in reflux hypersensitivity but there is a need for clinical trials to prove efficacy [5].

Psychological interventions are indicated for patients with no treatment response while on medication or who are interested in a non-pharmaceutical approach. The use of psychological interventions for functional oesophageal conditions can be focused on the reduction of oesophageal symptom catastrophizing and perseveration on the symptom, distress tolerance and improvement in the use of adaptive coping skills [6]. Cognitive behavioural therapy (CBT) can be implemented to aid patients in gaining insight into how stressful events, thought patterns, emotions and physiological responses interact together.

While most evidence of use is empirical, treatment models have been adapted from the use of CBT for irritable bowel syndrome (IBS) [24]. CBT in the form of relaxation training, cognitive restructuring and behavioural modification has been adapted for use with each of the functional oesophageal conditions [6]. CBT for functional chest pain has been well studied in seven randomized controlled trials, all showing better pain reduction with CBT than with usual care [22]. More robust research is needed in the area of psychological intervention for these conditions, as published studies had small sample sizes and contained bias, control groups were lacking and follow-up after treatment has been difficult. A recent review of the use of oesophageal-directed hypnotherapy highlights the use in functional oesophageal conditions (heartburn, chest pain, globus, dysphagia) to promote a state of deep relaxation with focused attention while allowing the patient to learn how to modulate physiological sensations and symptoms [25]. Finally, acupuncture has demonstrated effects on gastrointestinal motility, neurohormonal levels, acid secretion and sensory perception of pain thresholds, indicating that with more research it could offer a viable treatment alternative in this patient population [26, 27]. It is likely that psychological and complementary and alternative medicine alternatives are underutilized and should be considered for patients with oesophageal complaints [28].

Summary of the current evidence regarding standard care for functional oesophageal disorders

With a growing body of literature pertaining to standard care practices for functional oesophageal disorders, proper diagnosis, medical evaluation and treatment planning remain the first step. In addition to how a patient presents with an oesophageal symptom, a practitioner should consider an individual's lifestyle, stress level, mental health and level of physiological distress when developing a treatment plan (see Table 10.2).

Table 10.2 Summary of the current evidence base regarding medical and allied health approaches.

Treatment approach	*Level of evidence*	*Comments*
Medical/pharmaceutical	I	PPI therapy [4, 18, 21, 23]; neuromodulation/pain modulators [7, 21, 22]; smooth muscle relaxants [22]; botulin toxin injection [7, 22]; bougie dilation [22]
Psychological	I	Cognitive behavioural therapy [24]; oesophageal-directed hypnotherapy [16, 25]
Behavioural	IV	Behavioural modification of dietary choices and lifestyle activities [19, 28]; speech and language therapy [7, 11], 22]
Other	IV	Acupuncture [26, 27]

Practical recommendations

- Patients should have comprehensive medical evaluation with clinical interview to determine appropriate diagnosis.
- Medical and pharmaceutical interventions at present have the most efficacy and sound research backing, and should be considered early in terms of treatment planning; however, patients should be informed of treatment alternatives.
- Physicians should consider the use of a gastrointestinal-focused psychologist or other alternative treatment interventions for patients with functional oesophageal disorders.
- Patients with insight, acceptance and understanding about the role of psychosocial factors in their illness tend to be more open to integrative treatment plans that include medical and mental health interventions in their treatment plan.

Current limitations/future considerations

- Studies of the use of psychological intervention require replication with randomized controlled trials to improve the evidence base of the literature.
- Optimal treatment planning can require close collaboration of a gastroenterologist and gastrointestinal-focused psychologist.
- Psychological clinical trials are difficult to complete and require large amounts of time and follow-up that can be difficult to accomplish in this patient population.

Acknowledgments, competing interests, and funding

The authors are unaware of any competing interests in relation to this chapter. No external funding was received for this chapter.

References

1 Camilleri, M., Dubois, D., Coulie, B., Jones, M., Kahrilas, P.J., Rentz, A.M., Sonnenberg, A., Stanghellini, V., Stewart, W.F., Tack, J., *et al.*: Prevalence and socioeconomic impact of upper gastrointestinal disorders in the United States: Results of the US upper gastrointestinal study. *Clin Gastroenterol Hepatol* 2005, **3**(6): 543–552.
2 Everhart, J.E., Ruhl, C.E.: Burden of digestive diseases in the United States Part I.: Overall and upper gastrointestinal diseases. *Gastroenterology* 2009, **136**(2): 376–386.
3 Peery, A.F., Crockett, S.D., Barritt, A.S., Dellon, E.S., Eluri, S., Gangarosa, L.M., Jensen, E.T., Lund, J.L., Pasricha, S., Runge, T., *et al.*: Burden of gastrointestinal, liver, and pancreatic diseases in the United States. *Gastroenterology* 2015, **149**(7): 1731–1741e1733.
4 De Bortoli, N., Martinucci, I., Savarino, E., Bellini, M., Bredenoord, A.J., Franchi, R., Bertani, L., Furnari, M., Savarino, V., Blandizzi, C., *et al.*: Proton pump inhibitor responders who are not confirmed as GERD patients with impedance and pH monitoring: Who are they? *Neurogastroenterol Motil* 2014, **26**(1): 28–35.
5 Aziz, Q., Fass, R., Gyawali, C.P., Miwa, H., Pandolfino, J.E., Zerbib, F.: Esophageal disorders. *Gastroenterology* 2016, **150**(6): 1368–1379.
6 Riehl, M.E., Kinsinger, S., Kahrilas, P.J., Pandolfino, J.E., Keefer, L.: Role of a health psychologist in the management of functional esophageal complaints. *Dis Esophag* 2015, **28**(5): 428–436.

7 Kumar, A.R., Katz, P.O.: Functional esophageal disorders: A review of diagnosis and management. *Exp Rev Gastroenterol Hepatol* 2013, **7**(5): 453–461.

8 Fass, R., Pandolfino, J.E., Aziz, Q., Gyawali, C.P., Miwa, H., Zerbib, F.: Esophageal Disorders. In: *Rome IV functional gastrointestinal disorders: Disorders of gut-brain interaction*, 4th edn. Edited by Chang, L., Chey, W.D., Kellow, J., Tack, J., Whitehead W.E., The Rome IV Committees. Raleigh, NC: Rome Foundation, 2016: 833–902.

9 Nasr, I., Attaluri, A., Hashmi, S., Gregersen, H., Rao, S.S.C.: Investigation of esophageal sensation and biomechanical properties in functional chest pain. *Neurogastroenterol Motil* 2010, **22**(5): 520–526+e116.

10 Kahrilas, P.J., Smout, A.J.P.M.: Esophageal disorders. *Am J Gastroenterol* 2010, **105**(4): 747–756.

11 McDonald-Haile, J., Bradley, L.A., Bailey, M.A., Schan, C.A., Richter, J.E.: Relaxation training reduces symptom reports and acid exposure in patients with gastroesophageal reflux disease. *Gastroenterology* 1994, **107**(1): 61–69.

12 Naliboff, B.D., Mayer, M., Fass, R., Fitzgerald, L.Z., Chang, L., Bolus, R., Mayer, E.A.: The effect of life stress on symptoms of heartburn. *Psychosom Med* 2004, **66**(3): 426–434.

13 Taft, T., Riehl, M.: Gastrointestinal disorders. In: *Handbook of clinical psychology in medical settings: Evidence based assessment and intervention*, 1st edn. Edited by Hunter, C.M., Hunter, C.L., Kessler, R. New York: Springer, 2014: 459–493.

14 Drossman, D.A., Li, Z., Andruzzi, E., Temple, R.D., Talley, N.J., Grant Thompson, W., Whitehead, W.E., Janssens, J., Funch-Jensen, P., Corazziari, E., *et al.*: U. S. Householder survey of functional gastrointestinal disorders – Prevalence, sociodemography, and health impact. *Dig Dis Sci* 1993, **38**(9): 1569–1580.

15 Bytzer, P., Jones, R., Vakil, N., Junghard, O., Lind, T., Wernersson, B., Dent, J.: Limited ability of the proton-pump inhibitor test to identify patients with gastroesophageal reflux disease. *Clin Gastroenterol Hepatol* 2012, **10**(12): 1360–1366.

16 Kiebles, J.L., Kwiatek, M.A., Pandolfino, J.E., Kahrilas, P.J., Keefer, L.: Do patients with globus sensation respond to hypnotically assisted relaxation therapy? A case series report. *Dis Esophag* 2010, **23**(7): 545–553.

17 Savarino, E., Zentilin, P., Savarino, V.: NERD: An umbrella term including heterogeneous subpopulations. *Nat Rev Gastroenterol Hepatol* 2013, **10**(6): 371–380.

18 Weijenborg, P.W., Cremonini, F., Smout, A.J.P.M., Bredenoord, A.J.: PPI therapy is equally effective in well-defined non-erosive reflux disease and in reflux esophagitis: A meta-analysis. *Neurogastroenterol Motil* 2012, **24**(8): 747–e350.

19 Kaltenbach, T., Crockett, S., Gerson, L.B.: Are lifestyle measures effective in patients with gastroesophageal reflux disease? An evidence-based approach. *Arch Inter Med* 2006, **166**(9): 965–971.

20 Smout, A., Fox, M.: Weak and absent peristalsis. *Neurogastroenterol Motil* 2012, **24**(Suppl 1): 40–47.

21 Dickman, R., Maradey-Romero, C., Fass, R.: The role of pain modulators in esophageal disorders – no pain no gain. *Neurogastroenterol Motil* 2014, **26**(5): 603–610.

22 George, N., Abdallah, J., Maradey-Romero, C., Gerson, L., Fass, R.: Review article: The current treatment of non-cardiac chest pain. *Aliment Pharm Ther* 2016, **43**(2): 213–239.

23 Quigley, E.M.M., Lacy, B.E.: Overlap of functional dyspepsia and GERD – Diagnostic and treatment implications. *Nat Rev Gastroenterol Hepatol* 2013, **10**(3): 175–186.

24 Li, L., Xiong, L., Zhang, S., Yu, Q., Chen, M.: Cognitive-behavioral therapy for irritable bowel syndrome: A meta-analysis. *J Psychosom Res* 2014, **77**(1): 1–12.

25 Riehl, M.E., Keefer, L.: Hypnotherapy for esophageal disorders. *Am J Clin Hypn* 2015, **58**(1): 22–33.

26 Diehl, D.L.: Acupuncture for gastrointestinal and hepatobiliary disorders. *J Alter Complement Med* 1999, **5**(1): 27–45.

27 Samuels, N.: Acupuncture for nausea: How does it work? *Harefuah* 2003, **142**(4): 297–300+316.

28 Maradey-Romero, C., Kale, H., Fass, R.: Nonmedical therapeutic strategies for Nonerosive reflux disease. *J Clin Gastroenterol* 2014, **48**(7): 584–589.

Chapter 11

Diagnostic and treatment approaches associated with functional gastroduodenal disorders

Sebastian Haag

The aim of this chapter is to review the current research findings relating to functional gastroduodenal disorders (FGDs). Current interventions, including dietary, pharmacological and psychological treatments, are reviewed in relation to their efficacy in FGDs.

Learning points

- FGDs include functional dyspepsia, belching disorders, nausea and vomiting disorders (all of which have subclassifications) and rumination.
- FGDs are heterogeneous with respect to symptoms, aetiology and response to treatments, so management should be individualized.
- Treatments include dietary manipulation, pharmacological and psychological therapies.
- Evidence for most therapies is not as strong in FGDs as irritable bowel syndrome, largely due to a small literature base.

Introduction

In the Rome IV [1] classification, FGDs are classified into (i) functional dyspepsia (FD), (ii) belching disorders, (iii) nausea and vomiting disorders and (iv) rumination syndrome [2]. FD is the most prevalent FGD and has therefore attracted the most study.

The biopsychosocial model: underlying mechanisms

Central processing of gastrointestinal symptoms

Both irritable bowel syndrome (IBS) and FD patients demonstrate greater activation of homeostatic-afferent and sensory brain regions to visceral stimuli, such as rectal distension or painful gastric distention, than healthy subjects. Additionally, FD patients both have increased activity in emotional-arousal regions compared to healthy subjects as well as diminished involvement of key cortical-modulatory regions [3, 4]. This response pattern is consistent with the increased sympathetic arousal, anxiety and vigilance often associated with FGID demonstrated on neuroimaging studies [5]. These abnormalities seem to be at least partly related to comorbid anxiety and depression, with evidence of bidirectional effects (brain-gut and gut-brain) in the pathophysiology of FD [6] and premorbid anxiety both increasing severity of concurrent dyspepsia and predicting onset of new dyspepsia at ten-year follow-up [7].

Influences of stress, immune functions and inflammation on the upper gastrointestinal tract

Evidence on the influence of stress on gastric function is mixed, although most older studies point towards a stress-induced reduction in antral motility and/or gastric emptying [8]. More recent studies demonstrated impairment of gastric accommodation during experimentally induced anxiety in healthy subjects, as well as an association between both state anxiety and comorbid anxiety disorders and impaired accommodation in FD [9]. A subset of both IBS and FD patients (not limited to post-infectious FGID) is characterized by impaired mucosal integrity and low-grade mucosal and even systemic inflammation. These alterations, although not confirmed in all studies, may be related to rectal hypersensitivity and pain symptom levels [10].

Psychosocial influences on perception of gastrointestinal distension

In functional dyspepsia, psychological comorbidity ranged between 15.5% and 70% [11–15], significantly higher than controls [11, 16]. More specifically, individuals with functional dyspepsia have 10.9%–42.1% comorbid mild to severe depression symptoms [15, 17–19, and 6%–28.5% have comorbid mild to severe anxiety [18, 19]. Depression was 28.9% more prevalent in serious functional dyspepsia as compared to mild [15], and other comorbidity includes 13.2% conversion disorder symptoms and 11.8% panic disorder symptoms [15]. In regard to non-dyspepsia FGDs, 50.0% have depression [17] and 19% have anxiety [18]. In functional vomiting, 30.0% have depression [17, 20], and in cyclic vomiting, 23% have an anxiety or affective disorder [20]. Individuals with rumination syndrome in adults have 75.0% depression [17], and also 17% of females have a history of bulimia [21], and 20% of individuals with bulimia ruminate [22].

Diagnosis of functional gastrointestinal disorders

Clinical assessment

The criteria for diagnosis of FGDs are given in Table 11.1; however, in keeping with the multidimensional clinical profile, it is important to assess the individual psychological distress as an important risk factor for the development and, when present, perpetuation and exacerbation of symptoms in FGID, as well as a consequence of disease burden.

Table 11.1 Diagnostic criteria for gastroduodenal disorders.

B1. Functional dyspepsia* (FD)[1]
Diagnostic criteria**
1. ***One or more*** of the following:
   a. Bothersome postprandial fullness
   b. Bothersome early satiation
   c. Bothersome epigastric pain
   d. Bothersome epigastric burning

AND

2. No evidence of structural disease (including at upper endoscopy) that is likely to explain the symptoms

* Must fulfil criteria for B1a. PDS and/or B1b. EPS
** Criteria fulfilled for the last three months with symptom onset at least six months prior to diagnosis

B1a. Postprandial distress syndrome (PDS)[2]
Diagnostic criteria* Must include **one or both** of the following at least three days a week:
1. Bothersome postprandial fullness (i.e., severe enough to impact on usual activities)
2. Bothersome early satiation (i.e., severe enough to prevent finishing a regular-size meal)

No evidence of organic, systemic or metabolic disease that is likely to explain the symptoms on routine investigations (including at upper endoscopy)
* Criteria fulfilled for the last three months with symptom onset at least six months prior to diagnosis

Supportive criteria
1. Postprandial epigastric pain or burning, epigastric bloating, excessive belching, and nausea can also be present.
2. Vomiting warrants consideration of another disorder.
3. Heartburn is not a dyspeptic symptom but may often co-exist.
4. Symptoms that are relieved by evacuation of faeces or gas should generally not be considered as part of dyspepsia.
5. Other individual digestive symptoms or groups of symptoms (e.g., from GERD and IBS) may co-exist with PDS.

B1b. Epigastric pain syndrome (EPS)[3]
Diagnostic criteria* Must include **one or both** of the following symptoms at least one day a week:
1. Bothersome epigastric pain (i.e., severe enough to impact on usual activities)
2. Bothersome epigastric burning (i.e., severe enough to impact on usual activities)

No evidence of organic, systemic or metabolic disease that is likely to explain the symptoms on routine investigations (including at upper endoscopy)
* Criteria fulfilled for the last three months with symptom onset at least six months prior to diagnosis

Supportive criteria
1. Pain may be induced by ingestion of a meal, relieved by ingestion of a meal, or may occur while fasting.
2. Postprandial epigastric bloating, belching and nausea can also be present.
3. Persistent vomiting likely suggests another disorder.
4. Heartburn is not a dyspeptic symptom but may often co-exist.
5. The pain does not fulfil biliary pain criteria.

6. Symptoms that are relieved by evacuation of faeces or gas generally should not be considered as part of dyspepsia.

Other digestive symptoms (e.g., from GERD and IBS) may co-exist with EPS.

B2. Belching disorders[4]

Diagnostic criteria*

Bothersome (i.e., severe enough to impact on usual activities) belching from the oesophagus or stomach more than three days a week

B2a. Excessive supragastric belching (from oesophagus)

B2b. Excessive gastric belching (from stomach)

Supportive criteria

1. Supragastric belching is supported by observing frequent, repetitive belching.
2. Gastric belching has no established clinical correlate.
3. Objective intraluminal impedance measurement is required to distinguish supragastric from gastric belching.

*Criteria fulfilled for the last three months with symptom onset at least six months prior to diagnosis

B3. Nausea and vomiting disorders

B3a. Chronic nausea vomiting syndrome[5]

Diagnostic criteria* Must include all of the following:

1. Bothersome (i.e., severe enough to impact on usual activities) nausea, occurring at least one day per week and/or one or more vomiting episodes per week
2. Self-induced vomiting, eating disorders, regurgitation or rumination are excluded.
3. No evidence of organic, systemic or metabolic diseases likely to explain the symptoms on routine investigations (including at upper endoscopy)

* Criteria fulfilled for the last three months with symptom onset at least six months prior to diagnosis

B3b. Cyclic vomiting syndrome (CVS)[6]

Diagnostic criteria* Must include all of the following:

1. Stereotypical episodes of vomiting regarding onset (acute) and duration (less than one week)
2. At least three discrete episodes in the prior year and two episodes in the past six months occurring at least one week apart
3. Absence of vomiting between episodes, but other milder symptoms can be present between cycles

* Criteria fulfilled for the last three months with symptom onset at least six months prior to diagnosis

Supportive remark

History or family history of migraine headaches

B3c. Cannabinoid hyperemesis syndrome[7]

Diagnostic criteria* Must include all of the following:

1. Stereotypical episodic vomiting resembling cyclic vomiting syndrome (CVS) in terms of onset, duration and frequency
2. Presentation after prolonged use of cannabis
3. Relief of vomiting episodes by sustained cessation of cannabis use

* Criteria fulfilled for the last three months with symptom onset at least six months prior to diagnosis

(Continued)

Table 11.1 (Continued)

Supportive remark
May be associated with pathologic bathing behaviour (prolonged hot baths or showers)

B4. Rumination syndrome[8]
Diagnostic criteria* Must include all of the following:
1. Persistent or recurrent regurgitation of recently ingested food into the mouth with subsequent spitting or remastication and swallowing
2. Regurgitation is not preceded by retching.

* Criteria fulfilled for the last three months with symptom onset at least six months prior to diagnosis

Supportive criteria
1. Effortless regurgitation events are usually not preceded by nausea.
2. Regurgitant contains recognizable food which may have a pleasant taste.
3. The process tends to cease when the regurgitated material becomes acidic.

Diagnostic criteria taken from N.J. Talley, V. Stanghellini, F.K.L. Chan, W.L. Hasler, J.-R. Malagelada, H. Suzuki and J. Tack [1], Gastroduodenal Disorders, Chapter 10, pages [1]907, [2,3]912, [4]934, [5]937, [6,7]938, [8]946 of the *Rome IV Functional Gastrointestinal Disorders: Disorders of Gut-Brain Interaction*. Reproduction approved by Professor Douglas Drossman 23/10/2016.

Many other disorders can present with symptoms similar to those of FGDs [23] and appropriate assessment with blood, endoscopy and imaging investigations may need to be performed depending on the clinical profile (see Chapter 6).

Medical and allied health standard care treatment approaches for functional gastroduodenal disorders

Dietary approaches

FD symptoms commonly occur following the consumption of food, which is a significant sensory stimulus to the upper GI tract [24]. Only a limited literature is available to guide dietary therapy for FD; however, general advice includes avoiding foods that cause symptoms (likely to include fatty and spicy foods) [25, 26], eating smaller, more frequent meals and maintaining overall nutritional balance. Individuals with functional vomiting may also benefit from smaller particle-sized meals [27]. Fad diets should be avoided, as should over-restriction.

Medical and pharmaceutical approaches

Given the lack of evidence in terms of predictive factors, therapy is likely to be empirical, based on the dominant symptom. Approaches include acid suppression, prokinetics, antiemetics, herbal medications, including traditional Chinese medicines [28], Helicobacter pylori eradication, medications that relax the fundus, antidepressants [29, 30] and neuromodulators. This is an active area of research with a number of novel medications under development [31, 32].

Psychological approaches

Functional dyspepsia has received the most research in regards to psychological interventions (see Table 11.2 for summary). Several RCTs have been done that focus on CBT interventions [33–35]. In an RCT of cognitive therapy, the therapy group experienced a significantly greater reduction in symptoms, including pain, nausea, heartburn, diarrhoea and constipation, at one-year follow-up [34]. Using applied relaxation in a behaviour therapy RCT, the therapy group experienced a significantly greater reduction in self-reported pain. However, the effect was not seen at one-year follow-up [35]. CBT also has been shown in an RCT to be effective in treating comorbid anxiety and depression [33].

Table 11.2 Summary of evidence regarding psychological interventions for FGDs.

Treatment approach	*Level of evidence*	*Comments*
Medical/ pharmaceutical	I	Functional dyspepsia has the most evidence for medical and allied health treatment approaches for FGDs. Meta-analyses have found dyspeptic symptoms can be reduced by Mosapride [40], antianxiety and antidepressants [41], prokinetics, H2 receptor antagonists, proton pump inhibitors [42] and *H pylori* eradication therapy [43]. Transcutaneous electrical stimulation [44] and complementary and alternative medicine [45, 46] have been found helpful. Balcofen has been found to significantly reduce the frequency of aerophagia and rumination [47] Tricyclic antidepressant therapy and gastric electrical stimulation are helpful in functional vomiting [20, 48]– [50].
Psychological	II	The majority of research on psychological interventions is RCTs aimed at functional dyspepsia. Symptoms of pain [34, 35], nausea, heartburn, diarrhoea and constipation [34] as well as anxiety and depression can be reduced by CBT [33]. Psychodynamic interpersonal can improve well-being and perception of health [36]. Biofeedback with breathing exercises can improve quality of life and drinking capacity [38]. There is also evidence that subjective improvement can be achieved with biofeedback for rumination syndrome [39].
Dietary	III-2	Dyspeptic symptoms often occur following the consumption of food [24]. Avoiding trigger foods [25, 26] and eating smaller meals [51] can help. Smaller meals are also helpful for functional vomiting [27].

Psychodynamic interpersonal therapy was found in an RCT to have significantly greater subjective symptom scores for both patients and gastroenterologists that were persistent at the one-year follow-up when heartburn symptoms were excluded [36]. Hypnotherapy in an RCT was shown to significantly improve symptoms and quality of life at one-year follow-up compared with standard medical treatment and also to consume less medication [37]. Biofeedback for functional dyspepsia aimed at improving vagal tone through breathing exercises was found in an RCT to improve drinking capacity and quality of life more than controls [38]. Biofeedback with relaxation has also shown subjective improvement in a sample of individuals with rumination syndrome [39].

Practical recommendations

- Commence dietary treatment concentrating on avoidance of foods exacerbating symptoms, smaller and more frequent meals and a nutritionally adequate diet.
- Pharmacological options include prokinetics, antiemetics, analgesics and antidepressants.
- Be aware of the complex biopsychosocial mechanisms associated with FGDs, set up a satisfactory patient-doctor relationship and integrate a brief psychological assessment into routine visits to identify potential psychosocial comorbidities.
- If stress or psychological factors are likely to be exacerbating or contributing to symptoms, consider psychological therapy.

Current limitations/future considerations

- The pathophysiological mechanisms underlying the impact of psychological therapies in FGDs are still unclear and treatments are symptomatic rather than based on underlying pathophysiology.
- Identification of patients who may benefit from psychological therapy is often not routinely undertaken, and access to mental health professionals trained in FGDs is limited.
- More controlled trials of psychological treatments are required.

Acknowledgements, competing interests and funding

Thank you to Drs Hebbard and Knowles for their comments and contributions, and Ms Sarina Cook for her help finalizing this chapter.

References

1 Talley, N.J., Stanghellini,V., Chan, F.K.L., Hasler,W.L., Malagelada, J-R., Suzuki, H., Tack, J.: Gastroduodenal disorders. In: *Rome IV functional gastrointestinal disorders: Disorders of gut-brain interaction*. Edited by Chang, L., Chey,W.D., Kellow, J., Tack, J., Whitehead, W.E., The Rome IV Committees. Raleigh, NC: Rome Foundation, 2016: 903–966.

2 Stanghellini, V., Chan, F.K., Hasler, W.L., Malagelada, J.R., Suzuki, H., Tack, J., Talley, N.J.: Gastroduodenal disorders. *Gastroenterology* 2016, **150**(6): 1380–1392.

3 Tillisch, K., Mayer, E.A., Labus, J.S.: Quantitative meta-analysis identifies brain regions activated during rectal distension in irritable bowel syndrome. *Gastroenterology*, **140**(1): 91–100.

4 Van Oudenhove, L., Vandenberghe, J., Dupont, P., Geeraerts, B., Vos, R., Dirix, S., Bormans, G., Vanderghinste, D., Van Laere, K., Demyttenaere, K., *et al.*: Abnormal regional brain activity during rest and (anticipated) gastric distension in functional dyspepsia and the role of anxiety: A H(2)(15)O-PET study. *Am J Gastroenterol* 2010, **105**(4): 913–924.

5 Lee, I.S., Wang, H., Chae, Y., Preissl, H., Enck, P.: Functional neuroimaging studies in functional dyspepsia patients: A systematic review. *Neurogastroenterol Motil* 2016, **28**(6): 793–805.

6 Koloski, N.A., Jones, M., Talley, N.J.: Evidence that independent gut-to-brain and brain-to-gut pathways operate in the irritable bowel syndrome and functional dyspepsia: A 1-year population-based prospective study. *Aliment Pharmacol Ther* 2016, **44**(6): 592–600.

7 Aro, P., Talley, N.J., Johansson, S.E., Agreus, L., Ronkainen, J.: Anxiety is linked to new-onset dyspepsia in the Swedish population: A 10-year follow-up study. *Gastroenterology* 2015, **148**(5): 928–937.

8 Geeraerts, B., Vandenberghe, J., Van Oudenhove, L., Gregory, L.J., Aziz, Q., Dupont, P., Demyttenaere, K., Janssens, J., Tack, J.: Influence of experimentally induced anxiety on gastric sensorimotor function in humans. *Gastroenterology* 2005, **129**(5): 1437–1444.

9 Van Oudenhove, L., Aziz, Q.: The role of psychosocial factors and psychiatric disorders in functional dyspepsia. *Nat Rev Gastroenterol Hepatol* 2013, **10**(3): 158–167.

10 Matricon, J., Meleine, M., Gelot, A., Piche, T., Dapoigny, M., Muller, E., Ardid, D.: Review article: Associations between immune activation, intestinal permeability and the irritable bowel syndrome. *Aliment Pharm Ther* 2012, **36**(11–12): 1009–1031.

11 Brook, R.A., Kleinman, N.L., Choung, R.S., Smeeding, J.E., Talley, N.J.: Excess comorbidity prevalence and cost associated with functional dyspepsia in an employed population. *Dig Dis Sci* 2012, **57**(1): 109–118.

12 Gül, V., Geschwindt, G., Şen, C.: Functional gastrointestinal disorders and psychiatric morbidity in Turkish patients in Germany. *Internistische Praxis* 2011, **51**(1): 107–114.

13 Madhubhashini, M., Vyas, N., Navaneethan, U., Jayanthi, V.: Functional gastrointestinal disorders: Is there a link to psychological factors? A prospective study. *Minerva Psichiatrica* 2008, **49**(4): 249–253.

14 Li, Y., Nie, Y., Sha, W., Su, H.: The link between psychosocial factors and functional dyspepsia: An epidemiological study. *Chin Med J* 2002, **115**(7): 1082–1084

15 Mine, K., Kanazawa, F., Hosoi, M., Kinukawa, N., Kubo, C.: Treating nonulcer dyspepsia considering both functional disorders of the digestive system and psychiatric conditions. *Dig Dis Sci* 1998, **43**(6): 1241–1247.

16 Koloski, N.A., Talley, N.J., Boyce, P.M.: The impact of functional gastrointestinal disorders on quality of life. *Am J Gastroenterol* 2000, **95**(1): 67–71.

17 Lopez-Colombo, A., Morgan, D., Bravo-Gonzalez, D., Montiel-Jarquin, A., Mendez-Martinez, S., Schmulson, M.: The epidemiology of functional gastrointestinal disorders in Mexico: A population-based study. *Gastroenterol Res Pract* 2012, 606174.

18 Chitkara, D.K., Bredenoord, A.J., Rucker, M.J., Talley, N.J.: Aerophagia in adults: A comparison with functional dyspepsia. *Aliment Pharm Ther* 2005, **22**(9): 855–858.

19 Mahadeva, S., Goh, K.L.: Anxiety, depression and quality of life differences between functional and organic dyspepsia. *J Gastroenterol Hepatol* 2011, **26**: 49–52.

20 Prakash, C., Clouse, R.E.: Cyclic vomiting syndrome in adults: Clinical features and response to tricyclic antidepressants. *Am J Gastroenterol* 1999, **94**(10): 2855–2860.

21 O'Brien, M.D., Bruce, B.K., Camilleri, M.: The rumination syndrome: Clinical features rather than manometric diagnosis. *Gastroenterology* 1995, **108**(4): 1024–1029.

22 Fairburn, C.G., Cooper, P.J.: Rumination in bulimia nervosa. *Br Med J (Clin Res Ed)* 1984, **288**(6420): 826–827.

23 Camilleri, M.: Functional dyspepsia and gastroparesis. *Dig Dis* 2016, **34**(5): 491–499.
24 Feinle-Bisset, C.: Upper gastrointestinal sensitivity to meal-related signals in adult humans – relevance to appetite regulation and gut symptoms in health, obesity and functional dyspepsia. *Physiol Behav* 2016, **162**: 69–82.
25 Goktas, Z., Koklu, S., Dikmen, D., Ozturk, O., Yilmaz, B., Asil, M., Korkmaz, H., Tuna, Y., Kekilli, M., Karamanoglu Aksoy, E., *et al.*: Nutritional habits in functional dyspepsia and its subgroups: A comparative study. *Scand J Gastroenterol* 2016, **51**(8): 903–907.
26 Akhondi-Meybodi, M., Aghaei, M.A., Hashemian, Z.: The role of diet in the management of non-ulcer dyspepsia. *Middle East J Dig Dis* 2015, **7**(1): 19–24.
27 Olausson, E.A., Storsrud, S., Grundin, H., Isaksson, M., Attvall, S., Simren, M.: A small particle size diet reduces upper gastrointestinal symptoms in patients with diabetic gastroparesis: A randomized controlled trial. *Am J Gastroenterol* 2014, **109**(3): 375–385.
28 Holtmann, G., Talley, N.J.: Herbal medicines for the treatment of functional and inflammatory bowel disorders. *Clin Gastroenterol Hepatol* 2015, **13**(3): 422–432.
29 Lu, Y., Chen, M., Huang, Z., Tang, C.: Antidepressants in the treatment of functional dyspepsia: A systematic review and meta-analysis. *PLoS One* 2016, **11**(6): e0157798.
30 Ford, A.C., Luthra, P., Tack, J., Boeckxstaens, G.E., Moayyedi, P., Talley, N.J.: Efficacy of psychotropic drugs in functional dyspepsia: Systematic review and meta-analysis. *Gut* 2017, **66**(3): 411–420.
31 Camilleri, M., Bueno, L., Andresen, V., De Ponti, F., Choi, M.G., Lembo, A.: Pharmacological, Pharmacokinetic, and Pharmacogenomic Aspects of Functional Gastrointestinal Disorders. *Gastroenterology* 2016, **150**(6): 1319–1331.
32 Zala, A.V., Walker, M.M., Talley, N.J.: Emerging drugs for functional dyspepsia. *Exp Opin Emerg Drugs* 2015, **20**(2): 221–233.
33 Haag, S., Senf, W., Tagay, S., Langkafel, M., Braun-Lang, U., Pietsch, A., Heuft, G., Talley, N.J., Holtmann, G.: Is there a benefit from intensified medical and psychological interventions in patients with functional dyspepsia not responding to conventional therapy? *Aliment Pharmacol Ther* 2007, **25**(8): 973–986.
34 Haug, T.T., Wilhelmsen, I., Svebak, S., Berstad, A., Ursin, H.: Psychotherapy in functional dyspepsia. *J Psychosom Res*1994, **38**(7): 735–744.
35 Bates, S., Sjoden, P.O., Nyren, O.: Behavioral treatment of non-ulcer dyspepsia. *Scand J Behav Ther*1988, **17**(2): 155–166.
36 Hamilton, J., Guthrie, E., Creed, F., Thompson, D., Tomenson, B., Bennett, R., Moriarty, K., Stephens, W., Liston, R.: A randomized controlled trial of psychotherapy in patients with chronic functional dyspepsia. *Gastroenterology* 2000, **119**(3): 661–669.
37 Calvert, E.L., Houghton, L.A., Cooper, P., Morris, J., Whorwell, P.J.: Long-term improvement in functional dyspepsia using hypnotherapy. *Gastroenterology* 2002, **123**(6): 1778–1785.
38 Hjelland, I.E., Svebak, S., Berstad, A., Flatabo, G., Hausken, T.: Breathing exercises with vagal biofeedback may benefit patients with functional dyspepsia. *Scand J Gastroenterol* 2007, **42**: 1054–1062.
39 Soykan, I., Chen, J., Kendall, B.J., McCallum, R.W.: The rumination syndrome: Clinical and manometric profile, therapy, and long-term outcome. *Dig Dis Sci* 1997, **42**(9): 1866–1872.
40 Wu, Z., Wang, Y., Chao, Z.: Mosapride for functional dyspepsia: A systematic review. *Chin J Evid Med* 2006, **6**(11): 790–803.
41 Hojo, M., Miwa, H., Yokoyama, T., Ohkusa, T., Nagahara, A., Kawabe, M., Asaoka, D., Izumi, Y., Sato, N.: Treatment of functional dyspepsia with antianxiety or antidepressive agents: Systematic review. *J Gastroenterol* 2005, **40**(11): 1036–1042.
42 Moayyedi, P., Shelly, S., Deeks, J.J., Delaney, B., Innes, M., Forman, D.: WITHDRAWN: Pharmacological interventions for non-ulcer dyspepsia. *Cochrane Database Syst Rev* 2011, **2**: CD001960.
43 Moayyedi, P., Soo, S., Deeks, J., Delaney, B., Harris, A., Innes, M., Oakes, R., Wilson, S., Roalfe, A., Bennett, C., *et al.*: Eradication of Helicobacter pylori for non-ulcer dyspepsia. *Cochrane Database Syst Rev* 2003, **1**: CD002096.

44 Koklu, S., Koklu, G., Ozguclu, E., Kayani, G.U., Akbal, E., Hascelik, Z.: Clinical trial: Interferential electric stimulation in functional dyspepsia patients – a prospective randomized study. *Aliment Pharm Ther* 2010, **31**(9): 961–968.
45 Dabos, K.J., Sfika, E., Vlatta, L.J., Frantzi, D., Amygdalos, G.I., Giannikopoulos, G.: Is Chios mastic gum effective in the treatment of functional dyspepsia? A prospective randomised double-blind placebo controlled trial. *J Ethnopharmacol* 2010, **127**(2): 205–209.
46 Sheng, J., Chen, Z., Wu, A., Tian, G., Zhang, Y., Wang, H., Li, S.: Observation on the therapeutic efficacy of Jinghua Weikang capsule for functional dyspepsia. *Chin J Gastroenterol* 2007, **12**(7): 408–410.
47 Blondeau, K., Boecxstaens, V., Rommel, N., Farre, R., Depeyper, S., Holvoet, L., Boeckxstaens, G., Tack, J.F.: Baclofen improves symptoms and reduces postprandial flow events in patients with rumination and supragastric belching. *Clin Gastroenterol Hepatol* 2012, **10**(4): 379–384.
48 Andersson, S., Ringstrom, G., Elfvin, A., Simren, M., Lonroth, H., Abrahamsson, H.: Temporary percutaneous gastric electrical stimulation: A novel technique tested in patients with non-established indications for gastric electrical stimulation. *Digestion* 2011, **83**(1–2): 3–12.
49 Gourcerol, G., Huet, E., Vandaele, N., Chaput, U., Leblanc, I., Bridoux, V., Michot, F., Leroi, A.M., Ducrotte, P.: Long term efficacy of gastric electrical stimulation in intractable nausea and vomiting. *Dig Liver Dis* 2012, **44**(7): 563–568.
50 McCallum, R.W., Lin, Z., Forster, J., Roeser, K., Hou, Q., Sarosiek, I.: Gastric electrical stimulation improves outcomes of patients with gastroparesis for up to 10 years. *Clin Gastroenterol Hepatol* 2011, **9**(4): 314–319 e311.
51 Pilichiewicz, A.N., Horowitz, M., Holtmann, G.J., Talley, N.J., Feinle-Bisset, C.: Relationship between symptoms and dietary patterns in patients with functional dyspepsia. *Clin Gastroenterol Hepatol* 2009, **7**(3): 317–322.

Chapter 12

Functional bowel disorder (irritable bowel syndrome; IBS)

Diagnoses and current treatment options

Rebecca E. Burgell
Peter R. Gibson

The aim of this chapter is to review current research related to the aetiopathology of irritable bowel syndrome (IBS). Diagnostic considerations will be explored, particularly related to commonly associated conditions that may contribute towards the disorder and represent therapeutic targets.

Learning points

- IBS is a heterogeneous disorder and likely encompasses many pathological processes.
- Diagnosis relies on the presence of specific symptoms as defined by the Rome criteria in the absence of alarm features.
- A number of physiological abnormalities are associated with IBS, including visceral hypersensitivity, altered gut motility/secretion and altered intestinal permeability.
- Potential aetiopathological mechanisms include: genetic predisposition, centrally mediated neuro-immune mechanisms, altered gut microbiota and mast cell activation.
- Small intestinal bacterial overgrowth (SIBO), bile acid malabsorption, pancreatic exocrine insufficiency and food intolerances may precipitate symptoms in IBS and represent targets for therapy.

Introduction

Irritable bowel syndrome (IBS) is not a disease per se but a syndrome, diagnosed in the presence of specific symptoms as defined by the Rome Foundation (Table 12.1). IBS is divided into subtypes as determined by stool form (Figure 12.1, 12.2) [1]. IBS is a heterogeneous disorder and likely encompasses many pathogenic processes. While research in the field has been impacted by the diverse nature of the condition, clear physiological differences have been determined between sufferers and healthy individuals that likely explain symptomatology. In addition, a number of recognized conditions are more frequently observed in patients with IBS and have been postulated to be contributing factors.

Table 12.1 Diagnostic criteria for irritable bowel syndrome.

C1. Irritable bowel syndrome (IBS)[1]
Diagnostic criteria*
Recurrent abdominal pain on average at least one day/week in the last three months, associated with **two or more** of the following criteria:
1. Related to defecation
2. Associated with a change in frequency of stool
3. Associated with a change in form (appearance) of stool

* Criteria fulfilled for the last three months with symptom onset at least six months prior to diagnosis

Diagnostic criteria for IBS subtypes[2] (see Figures 12.1 **and** 12.2**)**
Predominant bowel habits are based on stool form on days with at least one abnormal bowel movement.

IBS with predominant constipation (IBS-C): > ¼ (25%) of bowel movements with Bristol stool types 1 or 2 and >¼ (25%) of bowel movements with Bristol stool types 6 or 7. Alternative for epidemiology or clinical practice: patient reports that abnormal bowel movements are usually constipation (like Type 1 or 2 in the picture of BSF; see Figure 12.1).

IBS with predominant diarrhoea (IBS-D): > ¼ (25%) of bowel movements with Bristol stool types 6 or 7 and < ¼ (25%) of bowel movements with Bristol stool types 1 or 2. Alternative for epidemiology or clinical practice: patient reports that abnormal bowel movements are usually diarrhoea (like Type 6 or 7 in the picture of BSF; see Figure 12.1).

IBS with mixed bowel habits (IBS-M): > ¼ (25%) of bowel movements with Bristol stool types 1 or 2 and > ¼ (25%) of bowel movements with Bristol stool types 6 or 7.
Alternative for epidemiology or clinical practice: patient reports that abnormal bowel movements are usually both constipation and diarrhoea (more than ¼ of all the abnormal bowel movements were constipation and more than ¼ were diarrhoea, using picture of BSF; see Figure 12.1).

IBS unclassified (IBS-U): Patients who meet diagnostic criteria for IBS but whose bowel habits cannot be accurately categorized into one of the three foregoing groups should be categorized as having IBS-U. *Alternative for epidemiology or clinical practice: patient reports that abnormal stools (both diarrhoea and constipation) are rare.*
For clinical trials, subtyping based on at least two weeks of daily diary data is recommended, using the '25%-rule.'
* IBS subtypes related to bowel habit abnormalities (IBS-C, IBS-D and IBS-M) can be confidently established only when the patient is evaluated off medications used to treat bowel habit abnormalities.
Diagnostic criteria taken from F. Mearin, B.E. Lacy, L. Chang, W.D. Chey, A.J. Lembo, M. Simrén and R. Spiller [2], Bowel Disorders, Chapter 11, pages [1]973, [2]976 of the *Rome IV Functional Gastrointestinal Disorders: Disorders of Gut-Brain Interaction*. Reproduction approved by Professor Douglas Drossman 23/10/2016.

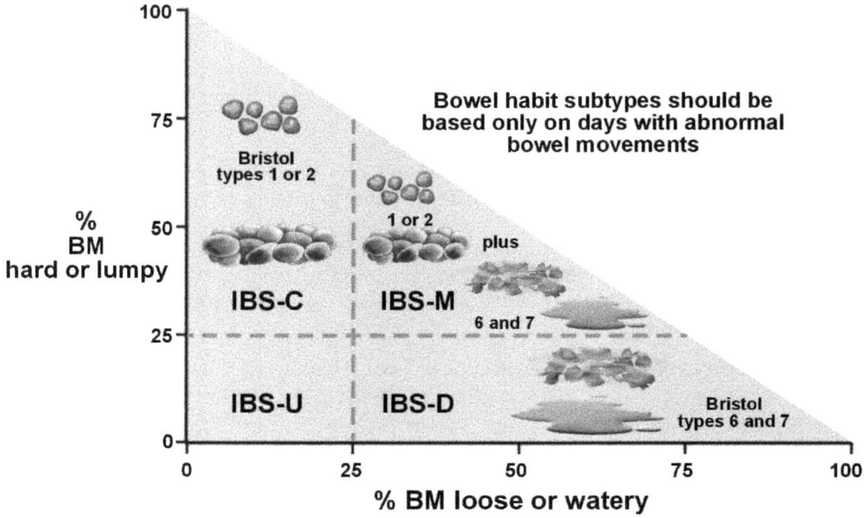

Figure 12.1 IBS subtypes.*

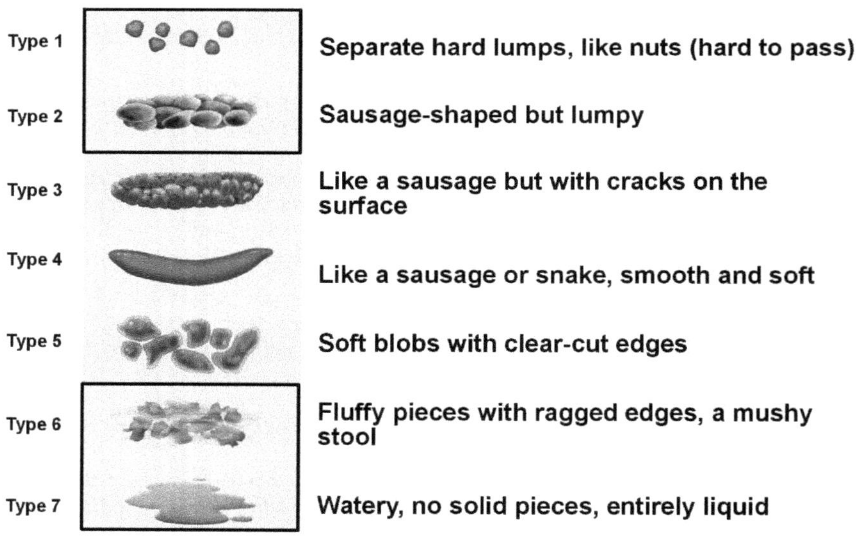

Figure 12.2 Bristol Stool Form Scale*

*Images for Figures 12.1 and 12.2 taken from F. Mearin, B.E. Lacy, L. Chang, W.D. Chey, A.J. Lembo, M. Simrén and R. Spiller [2], Bowel Disorders, Chapter 11, pages 973–976 of the *Rome IV Functional Gastrointestinal Disorders: Disorders of Gut-Brain Interaction*. Reproduction approved by Professor Douglas Drossman 04/11/2016). Original source: Lewis S.J., Heaton K.W. Stool form Scale as a Useful Guide to Intestinal Transit Time. *Scand J Gastroenterol*, 1997(32), 920–924.

Pathophysiology of irritable bowel syndrome

Altered visceral sensitivity

Visceral hypersensitivity to rectal distension is considered a hallmark for IBS and is found in 30%–90% patients with IBS [3], where it is associated with more severe symptomatology [3]. Indeed, some authors have suggested that pain perception during colonoscopy can be a useful adjunctive method for the diagnosis of IBS [4]. Patients with IBS have reduced rectal sensory thresholds, rectal compliance and increased viscerosensory referral areas [5]. The presence of visceral hypersensitivity is associated with increased somatization, indicating the importance of both peripheral and central mechanisms.

Altered gut motility

Reflecting the heterogeneous nature of the disorder, no unifying motility patterns have been identified in patients with IBS. Colonic transit is abnormal in about one third of patients and is associated with clinical subtype [6]. Patients have higher rectal basal tone, increased colonic contractility and an exaggerated response to corticotropin-releasing hormone (CRH) and gastrointestinal reflexes than healthy individuals [5, 7, 8].

Altered intestinal fluid secretion

Intestinal secretion is regulated by epithelial enteroendocrine cells that release peptides and amines in response to luminal factors. The predominant neurotransmitter is serotonin, which influences the enteric nervous system (ENS) and impacts upon intestinal motility, vasodilatation and secretion. Circulating serotonin is increased in IBS-D and reduced/normal in IBS-C [9]. The importance of serotonin signalling in IBS is highlighted by the efficacy of serotonin receptor (5-HT_3) antagonists in patients with IBS-D. Other neurotransmitters (VIP, somatostatin, neuropeptide Y) that are also increased in IBS [10] and histamine (released during mast cell degranulation) are integral to intestinal fluid handling. H_1 antagonists (e.g., ketotifen) result in symptomatic improvement [11], indicating a potential therapeutic target and/or pathogenic mechanism.

Altered intestinal permeability (the 'leaky gut')

The role that the intestinal epithelial barrier plays in disease is a new frontier in understanding IBS [12]. Increased intestinal permeability has been found in patients with post-infective IBS and IBS-D by both in vivo studies and ex vivo testing with biopsy samples. This appears to be secondary to altered expression of tight junction proteins, influenced by enteric nerve signalling and surrounding inflammatory mediators. Altered intestinal permeability has been postulated to be an early event that allows development of low-grade intestinal inflammation [12].

There is increasing interest in the influence that environmental exposures, particularly dietary substrates, have on intestinal permeability. For instance, in patients who report food sensitivities, direct exposure of duodenal mucosa to potential antigenic proteins (e.g., cow's milk, wheat, soy) resulted in rapid increase in epithelial tight junction spaces, intervillous space and intra-epithelial lymphocytes, and these reactions correlate with therapeutic response to specific dietary exclusion [13].

Postulated aetiological mechanisms

1. Genetic variations

Up to one third of patients with IBS report a relative with IBS [14] and twin studies suggest the genetic heritability is 22%–57% [15]. Despite this, few reproducible positive genetic associations have been detected. The majority of genetic research has focused on candidate genes within the serotonergic system which have been associated with higher IBS symptom scores, anxiety and central processing of emotions [16]. Polymorphisms have also been found in genes encoding important proteins for the regulation of visceral sensitivity, the immune system and tight junction proteins that may lead to increased intestinal permeability [16] and altered neuroimmune cytokine signalling.

2. Altered neuroimmune function

Physical and psychological stresses have long been known to impact upon the gastrointestinal tract. One in two healthy individuals describes a change in bowel habit with stress and over two thirds describe abdominal pain [17]. Physical stress results in increased contraction of the gut, likely mediated via autonomic pathways, which resolves when stress is removed. Psychological stress, in contrast, results in slowed gastric emptying, altered small bowel motility and accelerated colonic transit. Psychological stress is likely mediated via the hypothalamic-pituitary-adrenal (HPA) axis and its effects generally persist beyond the period of stress itself. It is not surprising, therefore, that stress plays a role in IBS. A stressful event preceding a gastrointestinal infection predicts the development of post-infectious IBS [18] and stressful life events are associated with escalation of symptoms [19]. Chronic stress is the main predictor of symptom severity in patients with IBS [20]. It has been postulated that symptoms of IBS are secondary to an abnormal stress response (reviewed previously [18]), perhaps driven by altered stress-responsive neurobiology as a result of early life trauma, the severity of which predicts the development of psychological (anxiety, depression and somatization) and somatic disorders, such as IBS [21]. It is recognized that patients with IBS have greater prevalence of physical, emotional and sexual abuse than healthy controls [18].

3. Mast cell activation

Mast cells are emerging as a critical 'hot spot' in the pathogenic mechanism in IBS [22]. Mast cells are intimately co-located with enteric neurons with an increased density in patients with IBS. Their degranulation releases mediators critically involved in the regulation of blood flow, intestinal fluid secretion, epithelial permeability, bacterial defence, innate and adaptive immunity, inflammation, motility and visceral sensation. Mast cells interact with lumen contents via stimulation of entero-endocrine cells, receive descending control through the autonomic nerves and are stimulated indirectly via the HPA.

4. Gut microbiome

Numerous studies have found altered gut microbiota in patients with IBS compared with healthy controls, although, to date, a 'normal' bacterial profile has not yet been adequately defined [23]. Gut bacteria interact with the host's immune system at the gut epithelium, where they influence the release of neurotransmitters, resulting in changes in gut physiology. Colonic hypersensitivity [24], altered transit time and intestinal permeability can be 'transferred' to rats from patients with IBS through their microbiota [12], suggesting an aetiopathogenic role of intestinal bacterial in the IBS.

Fermentation by gut microbiota of dietary and/or endogenous carbohydrates or protein also lead to the production of gases and other metabolites. These distend the lumen, which activates the ENS. Short-chain fatty acids and gaseous products of fermentation (methane, hydrogen sulphide) may also act as transmitters to alter motility and visceral sensitivity. The role of these and their contribution to symptom generation and physiological changes are dependent upon dietary intake, but dysbiosis of the gut microbiota may also play a role.

Conditions known to contribute to IBS symptoms

A number of clinical conditions have been found with higher prevalence in patients who meet the symptomatic criteria for IBS. Whether these are causative, an epiphenomenon or simply unmasked by the physiological changes seen in IBS is unclear. However, if present, such conditions represent a target for treatment with resultant symptomatic improvement.

Small intestinal bacterial overgrowth

Bacterial overgrowth in the proximal small intestine unequivocally occurs in disorders of motility or following anatomic alteration of the gut, and is associated with functional-like symptoms as well as malabsorption. However, small intestinal bacterial growth (SIBO) has been postulated to be present in anatomically normal patients with IBS, presumably as a distal or diffuse phenomenon.

Evidence for this has predominantly been the symptomatic response to antibiotics [25], which is not necessarily specific to SIBO. Unfortunately, tests purported to detect SIBO, especially hydrogen breath tests, have been poorly validated with low sensitivity (17%–68%) and specificity (44%–86%) [26]. Culture of small bowel aspirates is the closest to a gold standard for detection, but these suffer from problems of contamination and uncertain normative values. Such studies have found SIBO in as low as 2%–4% of patients with IBS, which equates with that seen in healthy individuals [27], and as high as 60% [28], with an odds ratio of up to 6.28 [29]. The notion that SIBO is a cause of IBS rather than a physiological situation representing a therapeutic opportunity is poorly established.

Bile acid malabsorption

Bile acids are produced by the liver and stored in the gall bladder. They are released into the bowel when required and reabsorbed in the terminal ileum, with a small quantity spilling over into the colon, and following cholecystectomy or small resection, greater spillage of bile acids may occur. Bile acids promote secretion from the colonic epithelium, stimulate propagating pressure waves in the colon and result in a reduction in visceral sensory thresholds [30], physiological changes which are commonly seen in IBS. A recent meta-analysis indicated that bile acid malabsorption occurs in more than one quarter of patients with IBS-D [31]. Colesevelam, a bile acid binder, has been shown to improve stool form and possibly reduce stool frequency in patients with IBS-D [32].

Pancreatic exocrine insufficiency

Post mortem studies suggest a prevalence of chronic pancreatitis of 6%–13%, the majority of which is undiagnosed [33]. Reduced faecal elastase concentrations are found in up to 6% of patients with IBS [35]. In such patients, pancreatic enzyme replacement therapy results in significant symptomatic improvement [35].

Dietary intolerances

In more than 60% of patients with IBS, ingestion of food is associated with induction of or worsening of symptoms. While this can be non-specific, there are several candidate food components that might underlie this association [36]. The majority of work has involved studying indigestible or poorly absorbed short-chain carbohydrates (FODMAPs) and proteins, especially associated with wheat (Chapter 8). Bioactive food chemicals that include salicylates, amines, glutamates, capsaicin and caffeine have also been implicated [36].

Gluten-free diets are often used with benefit in patients with IBS in whom coeliac disease has been excluded (so-called non-coeliac gluten sensitivity), but the evidence that gluten is the inciting agent is poor, as reviewed in [39]. The absence of a convincing biological mechanism of action for gluten is also an issue. Food proteins can be pathogenically associated with functional gastrointestinal symptoms by inciting immune reactions via uncertain mechanisms. The best evidence for this is altered tight junction processes and increased density of intra-epithelial lymphocytes following positive blinded challenge test results to milk protein or wheat protein [13].

Conclusions

As IBS is a heterogenous, symptom-defined condition, the aetiopathologic mechanisms remain poorly delineated. While there are clear physiological changes seen in individuals with IBS, no single unifying pathophysiology has been identified. It is likely that altered gut microbiota, altered mast cell function and altered neuroimmune and central processing, either secondary to genetic predisposition or acquired as a result of early life trauma or stress, are significant contributors in specific individuals. While there is increasing interest in developing treatments that target these potential aetiologic mechanisms, at present the majority of therapies achieve symptom reduction by treating either physiological (i.e., FODMAP intolerance) or pathological (i.e., SIBO, pancreatic insufficiency, bile acid malabsorption) conditions commonly seen concurrently in patients with IBS.

Current limitations/future considerations

- The heterogenous nature of the disorder limits conclusions which may be drawn regarding aetiopathology.
- Further research focused on improved phenotyping of patients is urgently needed to better understand the pathophysiology of the disorder. This will lead to the development of more targeted therapies and improved clinical outcomes.
- Most studies highlight pathology associated with IBS, but are unable to establish causation.
- In many cases, more than one pathology may contribute to the development of symptoms (i.e., visceral hypersensitivity and food intolerance).
- Ongoing research examining neuroimmune and microbiota interactions within the gut are critical to improve our understanding of the disorder.

Acknowledgments, competing interests, and funding

The authors are unaware of any competing interests in relation to this chapter. No external funding was received for this chapter.

References

1 Lacy, B.E., Mearin, F., Chang, L., Chey, W.D., Lembo, A.J., Simren, M., Spiller, R.: Bowel disorders. *Gastroenterology* 2016, **150**(6): 1393–1407e1395.

2 Mearin, F., Lacy, B.E., Chang, L., Chey, W.D., Lembo, A.J., Simrén, M., Spiller, R.: Bowel disorders. In: *Rome IV functional gastrointestinal disorders: Disorders of gut-brain interaction*, 1st edn. Edited by Chang, L., Chey, W.D., Kellow, J., Tack, J., Whitehead, W.E., Committees tRI. Raleigh, NC: Rome Foundation, 2016: 967–1058.

3 van der Veek, P.P.J., Van Rood, Y.R., Masclee, A.A.M.: Symptom severity but not psychopathology predicts visceral hypersensitivity in irritable bowel syndrome. *Clin Gastroenterol Hepatol* 2008, **6**(3): 321–328.

4 Kim, E.S., Cheon, J.H., Park, J.J., Moon, C.M., Hong, S.P., Kim, T.I., Kim, W.H.: Colonoscopy as an adjunctive method for the diagnosis of irritable bowel syndrome: Focus on pain perception. *J Gastroenterol Hepatol (Australia)* 2010, **25**(7): 1232–1238.

5 Törnblom, H., Van Oudenhove, L., Tack, J., Simrén, M.: Interaction between preprandial and postprandial rectal sensory and motor abnormalities in IBS. *Gut* 2014, **63**(9): 1441–1449.

6 Camilleri, M., McKinzie, S., Busciglio, I., Low, P.A., Sweetser, S., Burton, D., Baxter, K., Ryks, M., Zinsmeister, A.R.: Prospective study of motor, sensory, psychologic, and

autonomic functions in patients with irritable bowel syndrome. *Clin Gastroenterol Hepatol* 2008, **6**(7): 772–781.e775.
7 Fukudo, S., Nomura, T., Hongo, M.: Impact of corticotropin-releasing hormone on gastrointestinal motility and adrenocorticotropic hormone in normal controls and patients with irritable bowel syndrome. *Gut* 1998, **42**(6): 845–849.
8 Bassotti, G., Sietchiping-Nzepa, F., De Roberto, G., Chistolini, F., Morelli, A.: Colonic regular contractile frequency patterns in irritable bowel syndrome: The 'spastic colon' revisited. *Eur J Gastroenterol Hepatol* 2004, **16**(6): 613–617.
9 Atkinson, W., Lockhart, S., Whorwell, P.J., Keevil, B., Houghton, L.A.: Altered 5-hydroxytryptamine signaling in patients with constipation- and diarrhea-predominant irritable bowel syndrome. *Gastroenterology* 2006, **130**(1): 34–43.
10 Camilleri, M.: Intestinal secretory mechanisms in irritable bowel syndrome-diarrhea. *Clin Gastroenterol Hepatol* 2015, **13**(6): 1051–1057.
11 Klooker, T.K., Braak, B., Koopman, K.E., Welting, O., Wouters, M.M., Van Der Heide, S., Schemann, M., Bischoff, S.C., Van Den Wijngaard, R.M., Boeckxstaens, G.E.: The mast cell stabiliser ketotifen decreases visceral hypersensitivity and improves intestinal symptoms in patients with irritable bowel syndrome. *Gut* 2010, **59**(9): 1213–1221.
12 Enck, P., Aziz, Q., Barbara, G., Farmer, A.D., Fukudo, S., Mayer, E.A., Niesler, B., Quigley, E.M., Rajilic-Stojanovic, M., Schemann, M., *et al.*: Irritable bowel syndrome. *Nat Rev Dis Prim* 2016, **2**: 16014.
13 Fritscher-Ravens, A., Schuppan, D., Ellrichmann, M., Schoch, S., Röcken, C., Brasch, J., Bethge, J., Böttner, M., Klose, J., Milla, P.J.: Confocal endomicroscopy shows food-associated changes in the intestinal mucosa of patients with irritable bowel syndrome. *Gastroenterology* 2014, **147**(5): 1012–1020.e1013.
14 Saito, Y.A., Petersen, G.M., Larson, J.J., Atkinson, E.J., Fridley, B.L., De Andrade, M., Locke III, G.R., Zimmerman, J.M., Almazar-Elder, A.E., Talley, N.J.: Familial aggregation of irritable bowel syndrome: A family case-control study. *Am J Gastroenterol* 2010, **105**(4): 833–841.
15 Saito, Y.A.: The role of genetics in IBS. *Gastroenterol Clin N Am* 2011, **40**(1): 45–67.
16 Gazouli, M., Wouters, M.M., Kapur-Pojskić, L., Bengtson, M.B., Friedman, E., Nikčević, G., Demetriou, C.A., Mulak, A., Santos, J., Niesler, B.: Lessons learned-resolving the enigma of genetic factors in IBS. *Nat Rev Gastroenterol Hepatol* 2016, **13**(2): 77–87.
17 Drossman, D.A., Sandler, R.S., McKee, D.C., Lovitz, A.J.: Bowel patterns among subjects not seeking health care: Use of a questionnaire to identify a population with bowel dysfunction. *Gastroenterology* 1982, **83**(3): 529–534.
18 Chang, L.: The role of stress on physiologic responses and clinical symptoms in irritable bowel syndrome. *Gastroenterology* 2011, **140**(3): 761–765.e765.
19 Whitehead, W.E., Crowell, M.D., Robinson, J.C., Heller, B.R., Schuster, M.M.: Effects of stressful life events on bowel symptoms: Subjects with irritable bowel syndrome compared with subjects without bowel dysfunction. *Gut* 1993, **33**(6): 825–830.
20 Bennett, E.J., Piesse, C., Palmer, K., Badcock, C.A., Tennant, C.C., Kellow, J.E.: Functional gastrointestinal disorders: Psychological, social, and somatic features. *Gut* 1998, **42**(3): 414–420.
21 Park, S.H., Videlock, E.J., Shih, W., Presson, A.P., Mayer, E.A., Chang, L.: Adverse childhood experiences are associated with irritable bowel syndrome and gastrointestinal symptom severity. *Neurogastroenterol Motil* 2016, **28**(8): 1252–1260.
22 Wouters, M.M., Van Wanrooy, S., Nguyen, A., Dooley, J., Aguilera-Lizarraga, J., Van Brabant, W., Garcia-Perez, J.E., Van Oudenhove, L., Van Ranst, M., Verhaegen, J., *et al.*: Psychological comorbidity increases the risk for postinfectious IBS partly by enhanced susceptibility to develop infectious gastroenteritis. *Gut* 2016, **65**(8): 1279–1288.
23 Collins, S.M.: A role for the gut microbiota in IBS. *Nat Rev Gastroenterol Hepatol* 2014, **11**(8): 497–505.
24 Crouzet, L., Gaultier, E., Del'Homme, C., Cartier, C., Delmas, E., Dapoigny, M., Fioramonti, J., Bernalier-Donadille, A.: The hypersensitivity to colonic distension of IBS

patients can be transferred to rats through their fecal microbiota. *Neurogastroenterol Motil* 2013, **25**(4): e272–e282.

25 Pimentel, M., Lembo, A., Chey, W.D., Zakko, S., Ringel, Y., Yu, J., Mareya, S.M., Shaw, A.L., Bortey, E., Forbes, W.P.: Rifaximin therapy for patients with irritable bowel syndrome without constipation. *N Engl J Med* 2011, **364**(1): 22–32.

26 Saad, R.J., Chey, W.D.: Breath testing for small intestinal bacterial overgrowth: Maximizing test accuracy. *Clin Gastroenterol Hepatol* 2014, **12**(12): 1964–1972.

27 Posserud, I., Stotzer, P.O., Björnsson, E.S., Abrahamsson, H., Simrén, M. Small intestinal bacterial overgrowth in patients with irritable bowel syndrome. *Gut* 2007 **56**(6): 802–808.

28 Pyleris, E., Tzivras, D., Barbatzas, C., Giamarellos-Bourboulis, E.J., Koussoulas, V., Pimentel, M.: The prevalence of overgrowth by aerobic bacteria in the small intestine by small bowel culture: Relationship with irritable bowel syndrome. *Dig Dis Sci* 2012, **57**(5): 1321–1329.

29 Giamarellos-Bourboulis, E.J., Pyleris, E., Barbatzas, C., Pistiki, A., Pimentel, M.: Small intestinal bacterial overgrowth is associated with irritable bowel syndrome and is independent of proton pump inhibitor usage. *BMC Gastroenterol* 2016, **16**(1): 67.

30 Bampton, P.A., Dinning, P.G., Kennedy, M.L., Lubowski, D.Z., Cook, I.J.: The proximal colonic motor response to rectal mechanical and chemical stimulation. *Am J Physiol Gastrointest Liver Physiol* 2002, **282**(3 45–3): G443–G449.

31 Slattery, S.A., Niaz, O., Aziz, Q., Ford, A.C., Farmer, A.D.: Systematic review with meta-analysis: The prevalence of bile acid malabsorption in the irritable bowel syndrome with diarrhoea. *Aliment Pharmacol Ther* 2015, **42**(1): 3–11.

32 Camilleri, M., Acosta, A., Busciglio, I., Boldingh, A., Dyer, R.B., Zinsmeister, A.R., Lueke, A., Gray, A., Donato, L.J.: Effect of colesevelam on faecal bile acids and bowel functions in diarrhoea-predominant irritable bowel syndrome. *Aliment Pharm Ther* 2015, **41**(5): 438–448.

33 Olsen, R.S.: The incidence and clinical relevance of chronic inflammation in the pancreas in autopsy material. *Acta Pathol Microbiol Scand* 1978, **86 A**(5): 361–365.

34 Campbell, J.A., Sanders, D.S., Francis, K.A., Kurien, M., Lee, S., Taha, H., Ramadas, A., Joy, D., Hopper, A.D.: Should we investigate gastroenterology patients for pancreatic exocrine insufficiency? A dual centre UK study. *J Gastrointest Liver Dis* 2016, **25**(3): 303–309.

35 Leeds, J.S., Hopper, A.D., Sidhu, R., Simmonette, A., Azadbakht, N., Hoggard, N., Morley, S., Sanders, D.S.: Some patients with irritable bowel syndrome may have exocrine pancreatic insufficiency. *Clin Gastroenterol Hepatol* 2010, **8**(5): 433–438.

36 Gibson, P.R., Varney, J., Malakar, S., Muir, J.G.: Food components and irritable bowel syndrome. *Gastroenterology* 2015, **148**(6): 1158–1174.

37 Halmos, E.P., Power, V.A., Shepherd, S.J., Gibson, P.R., Muir, J.G.: A diet low in FODMAPs reduces symptoms of irritable bowel syndrome. *Gastroenterology* 2014, **146**(1): 67–75.e65.

38 Tuck, C.J., Muir, J.G., Barrett, J.S., Gibson, P.R.: Fermentable oligosaccharides, disaccharides, monosaccharides and polyols: Role in irritable bowel syndrome. *Exp Rev Gastroenterol Hepatol* 2014, **8**(7): 819–834.

39 De Giorgio, R., Volta, U., Gibson, P.R.: Sensitivity to wheat, gluten and FODMAPs in IBS: Facts or fiction? *Gut* 2016, **65**(1): 169–178.

Chapter 13

Functional bowel disorders (non-IBS)

Diagnosis and current treatment options

Anupam Rej
Anurag Agrawal

This aim of this chapter is to review the assessment and management of non-irritable bowel syndrome (IBS) functional bowel disorders (FBDs) – functional bloating, functional constipation and functional diarrhoea.

Learning points

- Non-IBS FBDs are common.
- Rome IV acknowledges that patients may have a multitude of symptoms, with FBDs forming a continuous spectrum.
- The evidence base for management is variable, based on extrapolation of data from IBS.
- Management is likely to change in future with further awareness of pathophysiology of these conditions.

Introduction

Non-IBS functional disorders, as defined by Rome IV [1], include functional abdominal bloating/distension, functional constipation, functional diarrhoea and unspecified bowel disorders. Symptoms associated with FBDs are common, with variable prevalence rates [2], and with bloating being recorded in 10%–30% of healthy volunteers [3]. Ranked as one of the most debilitating symptoms by sufferers, many potential mechanisms can lead to the symptom of bloating and the objective abdominal distension, including impaired gas handling, altered viscero-somatic reflex with abnormal diaphragmatic descent, visceral hyper- and hyposensitivity, alterations in small bowel and colonic motility and changes in bacterial flora [4].

Functional constipation is a common and troublesome symptom, with pooled prevalence being recorded at 14%, and a greater preponderance for women than men worldwide [5]. Broadly, functional constipation can be divided into primary and secondary, with drug-induced constipation accounting for the majority of secondary constipation. Mechanistically, primary constipation can be subdivided into altered motility–related and outflow tract problems, such as rectocele or pelvic floor dyssynergia or anorectal dysfunction [6].

Functional diarrhoea is recorded at 7% prevalence [2, 7]. This is thought to be secondary to rapid intestinal transit, which can be increased by stress or affected by post-infectious gastroenteritis [8].

Diagnostic criteria for functional bowel disorder (non-IBS)

Before diagnosing FBDs (see Table 13.1 for diagnostic criteria for functional bowel disorders – non-IBS), organic disease must be excluded by appropriate history and investigation.

Functional abdominal bloating/distension

To confirm a diagnosis of functional abdominal bloating/distension, the symptoms of abdominal bloating and/or distension must outweigh any other symptom. The Rome IV criteria highlight the differences between functional abdominal bloating, a subjective assessment, and functional abdominal distension, an objective measure [1]. This is an important differentiation, as even though these are interrelated, they seem to be distinct physiological processes [4, 9], which do not necessarily correlate [4, 10]. Furthermore, the Rome IV criteria acknowledge that the symptoms of abdominal pain and altered bowel habit may also co-exist with this diagnosis, albeit to a minor degree, highlighting the overlap with IBS [1].

Functional constipation

The diagnosis of functional constipation encompasses symptoms of reduction in stool frequency, difficulty in defaecation and incomplete evacuation, with loose stools rarely being present [7]. The Rome IV criteria acknowledge that abdominal pain and bloating may be present in functional constipation, albeit to a lesser extent than IBS [1], and this has been supported by more recent studies comparing Rome III criteria of IBS-C and functional constipation [11]. Interestingly this study seemed to suggest meal ingestion worsened symptoms in patients with IBS-C but not functional constipation, thereby lending further credence to the inclusion of meal ingestion as a diagnostic criteria for IBS [11].

Functional diarrhoea

Functional diarrhoea is defined as the passage of loose or watery stools [1]. As for functional constipation, symptoms of abdominal pain and bloating are now included in the Rome IV criteria, although should not be predominant.

Unspecified bowel disorders and opioid-induced constipation

Unspecified functional bowel disorder is defined as patients who have no organic pathology but fail to meet the diagnostic criteria for any of the other functional bowel disorders.

Opioid-induced constipation (OIC) is a change in bowel frequency, worsening straining, a feeling of incomplete bowel emptying or distress associated with bowel habits upon initiation of opioids [1]. Population-based studies have reported that up to 57% of patients taking opioids for a non-malignant indication report constipation as a side effect [12]. The incidence is even higher in those taking opioids for a malignant indication. [13].

Table 13.1 Diagnostic criteria for functional bowel disorders (non-IBS).

C2. Functional constipation (FC)[1]
Diagnostic criteria*
1. Must include ***two or more*** of the following:**
a. Straining during more than ¼ (25%) of defecations
b. Lumpy or hard stools (Bristol Stool Form Scale 1–2) more than ¼ (25%) of defecations
c. Sensation of incomplete evacuation more than ¼ (25%) of defecations
d. Sensation of anorectal obstruction/blockage more than ¼ (25%) of defecations
e. Manual manoeuvres to facilitate more than ¼ (25%) of defecations (e.g., digital evacuation, support of the pelvic floor)
f. Fewer than three SBM per week
2. Loose stools are rarely present without the use of laxatives
3. Insufficient criteria for irritable bowel syndrome
* Criteria fulfilled for the last three months with symptom onset at least six months prior to diagnosis
** For research studies, patients meeting criteria for opioid-induced constipation (OIC) should not be given a diagnosis of FC because it is difficult to distinguish between opioid side effects and other causes of constipation. However, clinicians recognize that these two conditions may overlap.

C3. Functional diarrhoea[2]
Diagnostic criterion*
Loose or watery stools, without predominant abdominal pain or bothersome bloating, occurring in more than 25% of stools**
* Criterion fulfilled for the last three months with symptom onset at least six months prior to diagnosis
** Patients meeting criteria for IBS-D (diarrhoea-predominant IBS) should be excluded.

C4. Functional abdominal bloating/distension[3]
Diagnostic criteria* Must include **both** of the following:
1. Recurrent bloating and/or distension occurring on average at least 1 day/week; abdominal bloating and/or distension predominates over other symptoms**
2. There are insufficient criteria for a diagnosis of irritable bowel syndrome, functional constipation, functional diarrhoea or postprandial distress syndrome.
* Criteria fulfilled for the last three months with symptom onset at least six months prior to diagnosis
** Mild pain related to bloating may be present as well as minor bowel movement abnormalities.

C5. Unspecified functional bowel disorder[4]
Diagnostic criterion*
Bowel symptoms not attributable to an organic aetiology that do not meet criteria for IBS, or functional constipation, diarrhoea or abdominal bloating/ distension disorders
* Criterion fulfilled for the last three months with symptom onset at least six months prior to diagnosis

C6. Opioid-induced constipation (OIC)[5]
Diagnostic criteria
1. New, or worsening, symptoms of constipation when initiating, changing or increasing opioid therapy, that must include two or more of the following:
a. Straining during more than ¼ (25%) of defecations
b. Lumpy or hard stools (Bristol Stool Form Scale 1–2) more than ¼ (25%) of defecations
c. Sensation of incomplete evacuation more than ¼ (25%) of defecations
d. Sensation of anorectal obstruction/blockage more than ¼ (25%) of defecations
e. Manual manoeuvres to facilitate more than ¼ (25%) of defecations (e.g., digital evacuation, support of the pelvic floor)
f. Fewer than three SBM per week
2. Loose stools are rarely present without the use of laxatives.
* Diagnostic criteria taken from N.J. Talley, V. Stanghellini, F.K.L. Chan, W.L. Hasler, J.-R. Malagelada, H. Suzuki and J. Tack [14], Bowel Disorders, Chapter 11, pages [1]840, [2]854, [3]863, [4]870, [5]879 of the *Rome IV Functional Gastrointestinal Disorders: Disorders of Gut-Brain Interaction*. Reproduction approved by Professor Douglas Drossman 23/10/2016.

Differential diagnosis

Functional abdominal bloating/distension

While evaluating functional abdominal bloating/distension, it is important to ensure other diagnoses are not overlooked as there is considerable overlap between other functional GI disorders – for example, IBS with constipation (IBS-C) [15].

Functional constipation

A good history and clinical examination, including a rectal examination, is needed to exclude secondary, neurological and metabolic disorders, establish a diagnosis and rule out any complications of constipation, such as haemorrhoids and rectal prolapse. It is also important to consider a diagnosis of IBS-C, which may be more likely if abdominal pain and bloating predominate.

Functional diarrhoea

The causes for diarrhoea are numerous, and therefore the history and physical examination remain crucial in differentiating between functional diarrhoea and other pathology (Chapter 6). IBS with diarrhoea (IBS-D) can present similarly and therefore needs to be considered. In addition to considering IBS-D, it is also worthwhile excluding bile acid malabsorption, with a study identifying this in up to 30% of patients who actually met the criteria for IBS-D [16].

Common patient concerns and issues associated with functional bowel disorders (non-IBS)

Patients with FBDs can become dissatisfied by the way information is communicated and provided [17], making effective communication paramount in helping to address patient concerns. Somatization symptoms can also be present in these patients, which are often extra-colonic in nature, such as headaches, dysuria, back pain, palpitations and muscle aches [18]. There may be overlap with other conditions, such as fibromyalgia, and it is therefore important that symptoms are addressed as a whole [18]. Presence of these symptoms can lead to inappropriate clinical referrals, with unnecessary procedures leading to a further erosion of the patient's quality of life [19].

Even though FBDs are not associated with reduced life expectancy, there is often patient concern with regards to other diagnoses, including malignancy. It is therefore important that a positive diagnosis is made early, without the need for invasive investigations unless indicated. Patients may also have concern about medication overuse and harm, with a study suggesting that this correlated with greater psychiatric comorbidity [20]. Therefore, it is paramount to give the patient a good explanation for their use and effects to improve compliance. Another common concern for patients is the role of stress. Anxiety [21] and high psychological distress [22] have been noted to be associated with these disorders, with studies showing stress having an effect on intestinal sensitivity and motility [23]. Therefore, it is important that management strategies are also directed at managing this effectively. Even though there is no convincing evidence of food allergies in patients with functional bowel disorders, like IBS [24], dietary advice is normally a concern.

Medical and allied health standard care treatment approaches for functional bowel disorders (non-IBS)

For a summary of the current evidence base regarding medical and allied health approaches, see Table 13.2.

Functional abdominal bloating/distension

The evidence base for treatment of functional abdominal bloating/distension tends to be extrapolated from other functional bowel disorders – namely, IBS [1] – with few studies using abdominal bloating/distension as a primary endpoint. Dietary changes, including low FODMAPs (fermentable oligosaccharides, disaccharides, monosaccharides and polyols) for bloating, have shown some benefit [25], while limiting the use of high fibre may be beneficial [26]. Antispasmodics, such as otilinium bromide [27], could also be trialled with some evidence for benefit for bloating. Antifoaming agents, such as simethicone, have conflicting evidence and therefore cannot be recommended [28, 29]. Agents such as polyethylene glycol (PEG) have been used to improve the symptoms of constipation and thereby may improve symptoms of abdominal bloating [30]. As postulated for its prokinetic effects, neostigmine has been studied and shown to improve abdominal symptoms and distension [31]. In one study, EMG-guided respiratory targeted biofeedback therapy showed a reduction in abdominal distension with associated relaxation of the diaphragmatic and internal oblique musculature. However, this was a non-controlled study and included patients predominantly with IBS and constipation who also suffered from abdominal distension [32].

Functional constipation

Lifestyle modifications include change in diet. The use of soluble fibre appears to be beneficial in certain patients with functional constipation, although this benefit does not appear to be present with insoluble fibre [33]. Secretagogues, such as linaclotide and lubiprostone, as well as the prokinetic prucalopride, have also been shown to be effective therapies [34, 35]. Non-medical therapy in the form of biofeedback has been shown to be effective in pelvic floor dyssynergia constipation [36, 37]. Surgical options, such as colectomy for slow transit constipation, repair of the rectocele for obstructed defaecation and rectopexy for rectal prolapse, are rarely required.

Functional diarrhoea

The opioid receptor agonist loperamide has been shown to improve stool consistency in patients with IBS and diarrhoea and the results could be extrapolated to the patient with functional diarrhoea [38]. As functional diarrhoea is on the spectrum of IBS-D, management strategies have focused on data gained from IBS patients, rather than functional diarrhoea solely. Antidepressants have been suggested, as they have been shown to be effective in patients with IBS [39]. Dietary changes, such as a low FODMAP diet, have been shown to increase patient satisfaction with regards to stool consistency [23] and therefore are also likely to be beneficial in this subgroup of patients. There has been some role for probiotics in reducing bowel frequency but further evaluation is needed in its efficacy for these patients [40]. Psychological therapies also remain a treatment option, but the evidence for this is less robust [39].

Opioid-induced constipation (OIC)

Initial treatment and prophylaxis for OIC are along similar lines to functional constipation, with laxatives the initial mainstay of management [1]. Lubiprostone is approved by FDA when opioids are taken for a noncancer painful indication. Subsequent management involves use of partial antagonists. These could be central, such as naloxone, or peripheral antagonists, such as methylnaltroxone and Naloxegol, an oral PEGylated derivative of naloxone [41–43].

Summary of current evidence base regarding medical and allied health-care standard treatment approaches for functional bowel disorders (non-IBS)

Table 13.2 Summary of the current evidence base regarding medical and allied health approaches.

Condition	*Evidence*	*Management strategies*
Functional bloating/ distension	II	Antispasmodics [44], Antifoaming [45], Diet [25], Rifaximin [46], Hypnotherapy [47], Probiotics [48]
Functional constipation	I	Linaclotide [48], Lubiprostone [50]
	II	Fibre, PEG, Na Picosulfate, Bisacodyl [33], Prucalopride [33]
	III	Lactulose, Biofeedback [33, 35] Probiotics [51]
Functional diarrhoea	II	Lopermaide [40], Probiotics [48]
	III	Rifaximin [46], 5-HT3 antagonists [52]
Unspecified functional bowel disorder		No available studies
Opioid-induced constipation (OIC)	III	Naloxone, Methylnaltreoxonem [40, 42]

Practical recommendations

The key to managing patients with non-IBS functional bowel disorders is to make a firm diagnosis. The Rome IV [1] guidelines have been updated to highlight the spectrum of functional bowel disorders and to acknowledge symptoms may overlap. Once a firm diagnosis is made, after excluding red flag signs, patients should be empowered to understand and manage their condition, with a clear explanation of their diagnosis. Patients at risk of psychological distress and poor quality of life as a result of their condition should be identified, as well as assessing extra-colonic manifestations. Clinicians should aim to work with patients to help manage their condition, using both non-pharmacological and pharmacological management, tailoring management to symptoms and response.

Summary of practical recommendations

- Make a firm diagnosis.
- Exclude organic pathology and other functional GI tract disorders.
- Empower patients to take ownership of their symptoms.

- Give dietary and pharmacological advice, working with patients.
- Assess response and aim to identify patients at risk of psychological distress.

Current limitations/future considerations

- Pathophysiology of functional bowel disorders is still not fully understood with a focus on symptom reduction.
- As patients with IBS are on the same spectrum as non-IBS functional disorders, a lot of the evidence base is derived from these patients, which limits the evidence base.
- Further research is required in this area to elucidate the underlying pathophysiology of these conditions.

Acknowledgments, competing interests, and funding

The authors are unaware of any competing interests in relation to this chapter. No external funding was received for this chapter.

References

1 Lacy, B.E., Mearin, F., Chang, L., Chey, W.D., Lembo, A.J., Simren, M., Spiller, R.: Bowel disorders. *Gastroenterology* 2016, **150**(6): 1393–1407e1395.

2 Talley, N.J., Weaver, A.L., Zinsmeister, A.R., Melton, L.J.: Onset and disappearance of gastrointestinal symptoms and functional gastrointestinal disorders. *Am J Epidemiol* 1992, **136**(2): 165–177.

3 Sullivan, S.N.: Functional abdominal bloating with distention. *ISRN Gastroenterol* 2012, **2012:** 721820.

4 Agrawal, A., Whorwell, P.J.: Review article: Abdominal bloating and distension in functional gastrointestinal disorders – epidemiology and exploration of possible mechanisms. *Aliment Phar Ther* 2008, **27**(1): 2–10.

5 Suares, N.C., Ford, A.C.: Prevalence of, and risk factors for, chronic idiopathic constipation in the community: Systematic review and meta-analysis. *Am J Gastroenterol* 2011, **106**(9): 1582–1591.

6 Basilisco, G., Coletta, M.: Chronic constipation: A critical review. *Dig Liver Dis* 2013, **45**(11): 886–893.

7 Tack, J.: Functional diarrhea. *Gastroenterol Clin N Am* 2012, **41**(3): 629–637.

8 Long, Y., Huang, Z., Deng, Y., Chu, H., Zheng, X., Yang, J., Zhu, Y., Fried, M., Fox, M., Dai, N.: Prevalence and risk factors for functional bowel disorders in South China: A population based study using the Rome III criteria. *Neurogastroenterol Motil* 2017 **29**(1): e12897.

9 Chang, L., Lee, O.Y., Naliboff, B., Schmulson, M., Mayer, E.A.: Sensation of bloating and visible abdominal distension in patients with irritable bowel syndrome. *Am J Gastroenterol* 2001, **96**(12): 3341–3347.

10 Houghton, L.A., Whorwell, P.J.: Towards a better understanding of abdominal bloating and distension in functional gastrointestinal disorders. *Neurogastroenterol Motil* 2005, **17**(4): 500–511.

11 Shekhar, C., Monaghan, P.J., Morris, J., Issa, B., Whorwell, P.J., Keevil, B., Houghton, L.A.: Rome III functional constipation and irritable bowel syndrome with constipation are similar disorders within a spectrum of sensitization, regulated by serotonin. *Gastroenterology* 2013, **145**(4): 749–757.

12 Cook, S.F., Lanza, L., Zhou, X., Sweeney, C.T., Goss, D., Hollis, K., Mangel, A.W., Fehnel, S.E.: Gastrointestinal side effects in chronic opioid users: Results from a population-based survey. *Aliment Pharmacol Ther* 2008, **27**(12): 1224–1232.

13 Sykes, N.P.: The relationship between opioid use and laxative use in terminally ill cancer patients. *Palliative Med* 1998, **12**(5): 375–382.

14 Talley, N.J., Stanghellini, V., Chan, F.K.L., Hasler, W.L., Malagelada, J-R., Suzuki, H., Tack, J.: Gastroduodenal disorders. In: *Rome IV functional gastrointestinal disorders: Disorders of gut-brain interaction*. Edited by Chang, L., Chey, W.D., Kellow, J., Tack, J., Whitehead, W.E., The Rome IV Committees. Raleigh, NC: Rome Foundation, 2016: 903–966.

15 Talley, N.J., Dennis, E.H., Schettler-Duncan, V.A., Lacy, B.E., Olden, K.W., Crowell, M.D.: Overlapping upper and lower gastrointestinal symptoms in irritable bowel syndrome patients with constipation or diarrhea. *Am J Gastroenterol* 2003, **98**(11): 2454–2459.

16 Gracie, D.J., Kane, J.S., Mumtaz, S., Scarsbrook, A.F., Chowdhury, F.U., Ford, A.C.: Prevalence of, and predictors of, bile acid malabsorption in outpatients with chronic diarrhea. *Neurogastroenterol Motil* 2012, **24**(11): 983–e538.

17 Dhaliwal, S.K., Hunt, R.H.: Doctor-patient interaction for irritable bowel syndrome in primary care: A systematic perspective. *Eur J Gastroenterol Hepatol* 2004, **16**(11): 1161–1166.

18 Häuser, W., Layer, P., Henningsen, P., Kruis, W.: Functional bowel disorders in adults. *Deutsches Arzteblatt Int* 2012, **109**(5): 83–94.

19 Agrawal, A., Whorwell, P.J.: Irritable bowel syndrome: Diagnosis and management. *Br Med J* 2006, **332**(7536): 280–283.

20 Cassell, B., Gyawali, C.P., Kushnir, V.M., Gott, B.M., Nix, B.D., Sayuk, G.S.: Beliefs about GI medications and adherence to pharmacotherapy in functional GI disorder outpatients. *Am J Gastroenterol* 2015, **110**(10): 1382–1387.

21 Song, J.Y., Merskey, H., Sullivan, S., Noh, S.: Anxiety and depression in patients with abdominal bloating. *Can J Psychiat* 1993, **38**(7): 475–479.

22 Wald, A., Hinds, J.P., Caruana, B.J.: Psychological and physiological characteristics of patients with severe idiopathic constipation. *Gastroenterology* 1989, **97**(4): 932–937.

23 Qin, H.Y., Cheng, C.W., Tang, X.D., Bian, Z.X.: Impact of psychological stress on irritable bowel syndrome. *WJG* 2014, **20**(39): 14126–14131.

24 El-Salhy, M., Gundersen, D.: Diet in irritable bowel syndrome. *Nut J* 2015, **14**(1): 36.

25 Halmos, E.P., Power, V.A., Shepherd, S.J., Gibson, P.R., Muir, J.G.: A diet low in FODMAPs reduces symptoms of irritable bowel syndrome. *Gastroenterology* 2014, **146**(1): 67–75.e65.

26 Francis, C.Y., Whorwell, P.J.: Bran and irritable bowel syndrome: Time for reappraisal. *Lancet* 1994, **344**(8914): 39–40.

27 Clavé, P., Acalovschi, M., Triantafillidis, J.K., Uspensky, Y.P., Kalayci, C., Shee, V., Tack, J.: Randomised clinical trial: Otilonium bromide improves frequency of abdominal pain, severity of distention and time to relapse in patients with irritable bowel syndrome. *Aliment Pharm Ther* 2011, **34**(4): 432–442.

28 Ducrotte, P., Grimaud, J.C., Dapoigny, M., Personnic, S., O'Mahony, V., Andro-Delestrain, M.C.: On-demand treatment with alverine citrate/simeticone compared with standard treatments for irritable bowel syndrome: Results of a randomised pragmatic study. *Int J Clin Pract* 2014, **68**(2): 245–254.

29 Friis, H., Bodé, S., Rumessen, J.J., Gudmand-Høyer, E.: Effect of simethicone on lactulose-induced H2 production and gastrointestinal symptoms. *Digestion* 1991, **49**(4): 227–230.

30 Schmulson, M., Chang, L.: Review article: The treatment of functional abdominal bloating and distension. *Aliment Pharm Ther* 2011, **33**(10): 1071–1086.

31 Caldarella, M.P., Serra, J., Azpiroz, F., Malagelada, J.: Prokinetic effects in patients with intestinal gas retention. *Gastroenterology* 2002, **122**(7): 1748–1755.

32 Barba, E., Burri, E., Accarino, A., Cisternas, D., Quiroga, S., Monclus, E., Navazo, I., Malagelada, J.R., Azpiroz, F.: Abdominothoracic mechanisms of functional abdominal distension and correction by biofeedback. *Gastroenterology* 2015, **148**(4): 732–739.

33 Suares, N.C., Ford, A.C.: Systematic review: The effects of fibre in the management of chronic idiopathic constipation. *Aliment Phar Ther* 2011, **33**(8): 895–901.

34 Ford, A.C., Suares, N.C.: Effect of laxatives and pharmacological therapies in chronic idiopathic constipation: Systematic review and meta-analysis. *Gut* 2011, **60**(2): 209–218.

35 Quigley, E.M.M., Vandeplassche, L., Kerstens, R., Ausma, J.: Clinical trial: The efficacy, impact on quality of life, and safety and tolerability of prucalopride in severe chronic constipation – A 12-week, randomized, double-blind, placebo-controlled study. *Aliment Pharm Ther* 2009, **29**(3): 315–328.

36 Heymen, S., Scarlett, Y., Jones, K., Ringel, Y., Drossman, D., Whitehead, W.E.: Randomized, controlled trial shows biofeedback to be superior to alternative treatments for patients with pelvic floor dyssynergia-type constipation. *Dis Colon Rectum* 2007, **50**(4): 428–441.

37 Rao, S.S.C., Seaton, K., Miller, M., Brown, K., Nygaard, I., Stumbo, P., Zimmerman, B., Schulze, K.: Randomized controlled trial of biofeedback, sham feedback, and standard therapy for dyssynergic defecation. *Clin Gastroenterol Hepatol* 2007, **5**(3): 331–338.

38 Lävo, B., Stenstam, M., Nielsen, A.L.: Loperamide in treatment of irritable bowel syndrome – a double-blind placebo controlled study. *Scand J Gastroenterol* 1987, **22**(S130): 77–80.

39 Ford, A.C., Talley, N.J., Schoenfeld, P.S., Quigley, E.M.M., Moayyedi, P.: Efficacy of antidepressants and psychological therapies in irritable bowel syndrome: Systematic review and meta-analysis. *Gut* 2009, **58**(3): 367–378.

40 Brenner, D.M., Moeller, M.J., Chey, W.D., Schoenfeld, P.S.: The utility of probiotics in the treatment of irritable bowel syndrome: A systematic review. *Am J Gastroenterol* 2009, **104**(4): 1033–1049.

41 Liu, M., Wittbrodt, E.: Low-dose oral naloxone reverses opioid-induced constipation and analgesia. *J Pain Symp Manag* 2002, **23**(1): 48–53.

42 Sykes, N.P.: An investigation of the ability of oral naloxone to correct opioid-related constipation in patients with advanced cancer. *Palliative Med* 1996, **10**(2): 135–144.

43 Thomas, J., Karver, S., Cooney, G.A., Chamberlain, B.H., Watt, C.K., Slatkin, N.E., Stambler, N., Kremer, A.B., Israel, R.J.: Methylnaltrexone for opioid-induced constipation in advanced illness. *N Engl J Med* 2008, **358**(22): 2332–2343.

44 Seo, A.Y., Kim, N., Oh, D.H.: Abdominal bloating: Pathophysiology and treatment. *J Neurogastroenterol Motil* 2013, **19**(4): 433–453.

45 Kimura, K.K., Treon, J.F., Benson, F.R.: Therapeutic use of methylpolysiloxane. *Curr Ther Res Clin Exp* 1964, **6**: 202–216.

46 Pimentel, M., Lembo, A., Chey, W.D., Zakko, S., Ringel, Y., Yu, J., Mareya, S.M., Shaw, A.L., Bortey, E., Forbes, W.P.: Rifaximin therapy for patients with irritable bowel syndrome without constipation. *N Engl J Med* 2011, **364**(1): 22–32.

47 Miller, V., Whorwell, P.J.: Hypnotherapy for functional gastrointestinal disorders: a review. *Int J Clin Exp Hypn* 2009, **57**(3): 279–292.

48 Hungin, A.P.S., Mulligan, C., Pot, B., Whorwell, P., Agréus, L., Fracasso, P., Lionis, C., Mendive, J., Philippart De Foy, J.M., Rubin, G., *et al.*: Systematic review: Probiotics in the management of lower gastrointestinal symptoms in clinical practice – An evidence-based international guide. *Aliment Pharmacol Ther* 2013, **38**(8): 864–886.

49 Lembo, A.J., Kurtz, C.B., MacDougall, J.E., Lavins, B.J., Currie, M.G., Fitch, D.A., Jeglinski, B.I., Johnston, J.M.: Efficacy of linaclotide for patients with chronic constipation. *Gastroenterology* 2010, **138**(3): 886–895.e881.

50 Johanson, J.F., Ueno, R.: Lubiprostone, a locally acting chloride channel activator, in adult patients with chronic constipation: A double-blind, placebo-controlled, dose-ranging study to evaluate efficacy and safety. *Aliment Pharmacol Ther* 2007, **25**(11): 1351–1361.

51 Ford, A.C., Moayyedi, P., Lacy, B.E., Lembo, A.J., Saito, Y.A., Schiller, L.R., Soffer, E.E., Spiegel, B.M.R., Quigley, E.M.M.: American college of gastroenterology monograph on the management of irritable bowel syndrome and chronic idiopathic constipation. *Am J Gastroenterol* 2014, **109**(Suppl 1): S2–S26.

52 Garsed, K., Chernova, J., Hastings, M., Lam, C., Marciani, L., Singh, G., Henry, A., Hall, I., Whorwell, P., Spiller, R.: A randomised trial of ondansetron for the treatment of irritable bowel syndrome with diarrhoea. *Gut* 2014, **63**(10): 1617–1625.

Chapter 14

Functional bowel disorders (IBS and non-IBS)

Psychodynamic therapy

Gareth Drake
Rebecca Ellis
Julian Stern

The aims of this chapter are to trace the origins of psychodynamic thinking about somatic symptoms through to contemporary psychodynamic thinking about functional bowel disorders (FBDs), before reviewing the current evidence and examining the role of psychodynamic approaches beyond individual treatment.

Learning points

- Understanding the unique contributions of a psychodynamic approach to FBDs when working with individual patients
- How psychodynamic thinking can offer support at the level of teams and systems around the patient
- A critical appreciation of the current evidence for psychodynamic models and interventions for FBDs
- An understanding of 'transference' and 'counter-transference', and why such phenomena are important for clinicians working with this group of patients
- An awareness of limitations and ways forward in psychodynamic thinking about FBDs

Introduction

Current thinking about FBDs is influenced by a biopsychosocial model of gastrointestinal illness [1], in which psychological and social stressors reciprocally influence biological changes to gut motility and visceral sensitivity within the brain-gut axis. Homeostatic afferents from the GI tract that make possible communication between the brain and gut ascend into autonomic reflex arcs in subcortical areas, usually operating below the level of conscious awareness. However, with input from the prefrontal cortex and hypothalamus, which regulate the activity of descending pathways [2], the influence of stress, memories of early adverse GI experiences and beliefs about gastrointestinal function can manifest in alterations to processes along the GI tract.

Within the complexity of the brain-gut axis, there is thus room for the influence of multiple complex contextual and psychological stressors [3]. Stressful life events often precede the onset of FBD symptoms and patients report that stress exacerbates their symptoms [4]. A review of ten studies found patients with IBS had significantly higher anxiety and depression levels than healthy controls [5], and psychosocial factors, rather than intensity of IBS symptoms, have been shown to differentiate those patients who sought help and those who did not [6]. Further, participants who believed symptoms were associated with serious pathology reported more intense pain [6] and patients with IBS have been shown to experience greater interpersonal stress related to a distinctive interpersonal style [7]. Thus the aetiology and course of FBDs are inextricably linked with patients' emotional life, their responses to stress and their relationships.

Origins of psychodynamic thinking about somatic symptoms

The psychodynamic approach to understanding and treating symptoms and illnesses is based on the work of Sigmund Freud. Like all pioneers, he had forerunners in many fields, including philosophers and authors who recognized the importance of unconscious wishes, symbolism and dreams. Yet Freud managed to systematically study unconscious processes – one of his many achievements was to address these ideas in a medical context. Among Freud's patients were those with 'hysterical symptoms' whose treatment he described in *Studies on Hysteria* [8], leading to the birth of the 'talking cure'. Freud himself was preoccupied with the relationship between body and mind throughout his life and was deeply rooted in the methodology of medical research and in the practice of medicine.

Subsequently, gastroenterology has attracted much attention from psychodynamic psychotherapists. Feeding (drinking and eating), expulsion (urine and faeces) and feelings of hunger or thirst – all these states and associated relationships to crucial individuals (e.g., mothers, fathers and caregivers) are central to psychoanalytic thinking and practice. Substantial attention has been directed to the disorders of the GI tract by clinicians who use psychodynamic approaches [9–13].

Psychodynamic theories and models of FBDs

Early psychodynamic theories of functional somatic disorders tended to view symptoms as either the symbolic manifestation of repressed psychic content or due to chronic physiological arousal of an organ because of a struggle with repressed unconscious material [14]. Therapy aimed to unearth the root of such conflicts in order to alleviate symptoms. Though the focus of recent psychodynamic theories of FBDs has shifted towards patients' own understanding of their symptoms, the importance of relationships remains central to a psychodynamic understanding of FBDs.

Recent psychodynamic thinking has considered the evidence for comorbidity of FBDs with psychological disorders and other functional somatic disorders [15] so that a person-centred rather than symptom-centred approach is taken. A recent evidence-based psychodynamic model of functional somatic disorders posits the importance of patients' early experiences with caregivers in facilitating the ability 'think about thinking'/'mentalize' in relation to their own and others' minds [16]. Individuals with 'good enough' early experiences with caregivers respond to current stressors by seeking comfort in others, which helps regulate the stress system, promoting the development of neural pathways associated with further 'mentalization'. In contrast, patients with functional somatic disorders have been found to have had early adverse experiences, a relational style characterized by insecure attachments and unhelpful interpersonal responses to stress – either denying reliance on others or exhibiting overly demanding styles of relating – that lead to increased isolation. Such patients also struggle to link bodily sensations to emotions so that sensations are felt as foreign attacks from within [16].

Though a promising model, the direction of causality between interpersonal difficulties, physical symptoms and impairments in mentalization remains unclear – namely, whether patients experience impairments in mentalization that lead them to misinterpret sensations from their body and struggle interpersonally, or whether distressing symptoms disrupt their ability to mentalize, in turn affecting relationships.

A psychodynamic approach to therapy for FBDs

Central to psychodynamic therapies are relationships: between the patient and others; the patient, their symptoms and their emotional life; and, importantly, between patient and therapist. Indeed, the latter relationship functions as a vehicle through which interpersonal responses to stress as well emotions, urges and wishes from other important relationships are experienced and thought about in therapy. This therapeutic phenomenon, the 'transference', is key in psychodynamic therapies and, though psychodynamic therapists aim to deliberately distil and explore the patient's transference and the therapist's 'counter-transferential' feelings, any clinician who has experienced a strong emotional reaction to or from a patient will recognize that the phenomena operate in all clinician-patient relationships, regardless of whether utilized as a tool.

In most studies reviewed ahead, the treatment protocol begins with an extended first session not only to foster the therapeutic relationship but also to try to prevent the patient feeling that a psychological explanation is being forced onto them or that the referral means that their symptoms are 'all in their head'. Instead, the therapist creates a climate in which emotional factors might be thought of as relevant to symptoms, employing the language used by the patient to bridge the gap between the way in which they think about their body and symptoms and the way they think about themselves in relation to others. This is in keeping with research attempting to identify specific therapy techniques associated with improvements in IBS symptoms and in psychological distress which has emphasized the importance of reflectiveness and working with the patients' own beliefs, particularly for patients who begin with purely somatic illness attributions [17]. Guthrie and colleagues [18] give the example of a patient's use of the phrase 'a wound that has never healed' when describing a seeping sore inside her that continually oozed, which was used as a bridge to thinking about repeated abuse from her father. Simultaneously, transference phenomena are utilized throughout the course of therapy to explore how, for example, a patient's feelings about becoming close to a therapist or ending therapy might elicit overwhelming feelings related to early experiences of loss or neglect, which might affect FBD symptoms and relationships outside of therapy.

Evidence for the effectiveness of psychodynamic therapy for FBDs

Evidence for psychodynamic therapies is summarized in Table 14.1. An early trial of psychodynamic therapy found that patients responded better to psychotherapy plus pharmacological interventions than the latter alone after a three-month intervention and at one-year follow-up. However, patients with a mental health diagnosis were excluded and no independent assessment of bowel function was performed [19]. Guthrie [20] addressed these shortcomings in a larger (n>100) randomised control trial, giving independent ratings of bowel symptoms made by a gastroenterologist blind to the study design, using a 12-week psychotherapy protocol for patients with chronic, refractory IBS. Compared to an equal number of 'supportive listening' sessions, psychodynamic psychotherapy led to significant improvements of both psychological and physical symptoms. After one year, individuals who received psychotherapy remained well, whereas those who dropped out or did not receive psychotherapy experienced severe symptoms. The authors concluded that "psychotherapy

Table 14.1 Summary of the current evidence regarding psychodynamic approaches for FBDs.

Condition	*Level of evidence*	*Comments*
IBS	Level I	One meta-analysis found equivalent outcomes on various domains relating to symptom severity and psychological distress for psychodynamic therapies compared to other psychological therapies [26].
	Level II	Three RCTs have shown: improvements in symptom scores compared to care as usual [19]; improvements in psychological distress and symptoms compared to supportive listening sessions [20]; and no improvements in symptoms but improvements in health-related quality of life equal to that of an SSRI compared to care as usual [21]. The quality of randomization in studies by Svedlund *et al.* [19] and Guthrie *et al.* [20] has been questioned [27]. The mediating role of psychological distress, explored through post hoc analysis or follow-up, remains uncertain [22–24].

is feasible and effective in the majority of irritable bowel syndrome patients with chronic symptoms unresponsive to medical treatment" [20, p. 315]. Further analysis suggested that improvement in bowel symptoms was mediated by improvement of psychological distress [20]. Furthermore, a recent review of psychological therapies suggests psychological treatment might ameliorate IBS symptoms through changes in mood, anxiety and depressive symptoms [17].

In another study, the authors used the same protocol and compared psychotherapy to treatment with a selective serotonin reuptake inhibiter (SSRI) or treatment as usual, no significant changes in abdominal pain were observed, but both the psychotherapy and SSRI groups showed significant improvement in health-related quality of life [21]. Of 257 patients recruited to this study, 107 met criteria for a concurrent psychiatric disorder. Although improvements in psychiatric domains were correlated with improvements in health-related quality of life, they could not account for all improvements, suggesting that symptom relief was not specific to a reduction in psychological symptoms solely among the subgroup of patients with a psychiatric disorder [22]. The same cohort was followed up at 15 months, with emphasis on the role of interpersonal problems in mediating psychological distress and health status. The authors concluded that specific help with interpersonal problems can improve health status, particularly in patients with chronic IBS, but the precise mechanisms remain unclear [23]. This tallies with the finding that abdominal and psychological symptoms independently relate to quality of life and the recommendation that a holistic approach to treatment be taken [24, 25].

Psychodynamic therapies and best practice guidelines for FBDs

In the UK, National Institute of Clinical Excellence (NICE) guidance recommends referral for psychological interventions for people with refractory IBS after 12 months of non-responsiveness to pharmacological treatment [25]. A recent review found equivalent outcomes for psychodynamic therapy compared to other psychological interventions for IBS [26]. Specifically, psychodynamic psychotherapy can effectively reduce abdominal pain, bowel dysfunction, depression and anxiety in different subsets of patients with IBS [28]. The American Gastroenterologist Association does not mention psychological therapies in its current guidance on IBS but suggests psychological support broadly for defecatory disorders [29]. The Gastroenterological Society of Australia (GESA) does not mention psychodynamic therapy in its guidelines for IBS, but includes a suggestion for CBT, relaxation therapy or hypnotherapy [30].

Applications for psychodynamic approaches beyond individual therapy: working with the team

St Mark's Hospital offers an example from the UK of the impact of applied psychodynamic thinking within gastroenterology [31]. At St Mark's, the fundamental premise is of a psychodynamic understanding of patients, and of working with staff members in dealing with their own emotional responses (counter-transference), boundaries and the propensity for acting out – that is, the clinician's tendency to become involved in an unhelpful clinical encounter or course of investigation, due to the feelings stirred up in them by the patient – for example, feeling guilty that they have not done enough, or being 'pushed' into prescribing a medication or recommending a procedure by an insistent patient, even in the absence of clear clinical indications.

The occurrence of notable 'splitting' among staff members, where one (or a group of staff) is more sympathetic towards a patient and another member (or group) is less so, might also suggest the need for further reflection. A detailed description of this work this described how "Many patients . . . have no obvious disease, yet move from one doctor to another, demanding more investigations and sometimes surgery to cut out a part of the bowel which is causing offence. The counter-transference evoked in the medical and nursing staff is often intense. Counter-transference phenomena of sadism, disgust, sexual excitement, rescue fantasies and identification with such patients are omnipresent, as is the tendency to 'act out'" – in other words, there can be feelings evoked in this area of work that need managing, be they a wish to punish a particular patient, an unexplained desire to end a consultation abruptly with a particular patient or a wish to help another patient because one 'identifies' with aspects of their story or life history [31, pp. 131–132]. Further, when the patient is talking in concrete terms about wanting something bad taken out of them, it is important to consider what this means at a more symbolic or relational level, taking into consideration their history – for example, the presence of trauma or neglect. At St Marks, the presence of psychodynamic psychotherapists, 'in-house' with regular meetings and case discussions for staff groups, provides containment for some of the more intolerable anxieties, and this, as much as the direct work with patients, probably underpins the consistent support for the service from clinical staff" [31, pp. 131–132]. Psychodynamic approaches are thus helpful in managing the risk of iatrogenic investigation, medication and surgery.

In the absence of this containment, anxieties can become overwhelming or lead to problematic barriers to optimal care among staff and institutions. For example, Menzies Lyth [32] vividly described how many of the tasks of patient care were set up to create distance between patient and nurse, with the function of protecting staff members against the potentially overwhelming feelings evoked when working with death, disease and bodily distress. However, by precluding more intimate relationships with patients, much of the satisfaction derived from nursing is eliminated, leading to high rates of anxiety, burnout and staff turnover [32] – a problem exacerbated by increasing demands on services and the expectation for clinical staff to work harder and be more empathic without the provision of extra resources, support or training [33].

Current limitations/future directions

Despite promising findings, the pathways to improvements from psychodynamic therapies for FBDs, the 'active ingredients' of therapy and any long-term effects specific to psychodynamic interventions remain unclear [27]. Meta-analyses compiled of studies with small effects are being used to guide treatment for IBS, but they are being published more frequently than original studies [34]. This is particularly pertinent in psychological treatments where the mechanisms of therapy require further elucidation.

The body of high-level evidence for psychodynamic interventions for FBDs is notably small and the importance of such research, especially by Guthrie and colleagues, cannot be underestimated. The pioneering work by psychoanalysts, grounded in extensive clinical material, focusing on psychic struggles, enactments and the institutional defences surrounding patients, informs and enriches the field. A key current issue for psychological therapies broadly, but specifically psychodynamic therapies, which have been relatively 'slow off the mark' in establishing a strong evidence base, is the tension between demonstrating efficacy with large-scale RCTs and exploring the 'active ingredients' of therapy, a task which fits with the psychodynamic tradition of reflective practice, detailed verbatim notes and single case studies. This should be borne in mind when considering the recommendations ahead.

Practical recommendations

- Longer-term studies are needed to differentiate intervention effects from non-specific treatment effects.
- Treatment studies in this area have not distinguished IBS from other FBDs. This is a limitation. However, given the heterogeneity of IBS patients and comorbidity with other functional somatic disorders, future research and treatment might fruitfully delineate patients based on profiles, such as the presence of early adverse experiences, rather than on diagnoses.
- A consideration of emotional, relational and psychological contributors to FBD symptomatology along with an understanding of transference phenomena can facilitate a holistic approach to care and help to avoid iatrogenic harm.
- Clinicians should not feel alone in the treatment of this group of patients. Integrated multidisciplinary care – including psychiatric and psychological presence within teams – can improve patient care and bolster support for staff.

Acknowledgments, competing interests, and funding

The authors are unaware of any competing interests in relation to this chapter. No external funding was received for this chapter.

References

1 Drossman, D.A.: Presidential address: Gastrointestinal illness and the biopsychosocial model. *Psychosom Med* 1998, **60**(3): 258–267.

2 Mayer, E.A., Tillisch, K.: The brain-gut axis in abdominal pain syndromes. *Annu Rev Med* 2011, **62**: 381–396.

3 Rapps, N., van Oudenhove, L., Enck, P., Aziz, Q.: Brain imaging of visceral functions in healthy volunteers and IBS patients. *J Psychosom Res* 2008, **64**(6): 599–604.
4 Palsson, O.S., Drossman, D.A.: Psychiatric and psychological dysfunction in irritable bowel syndrome and the role of psychological treatments. *Gastroentero! Clin N Am* 2005, **34**(2): 281–303.
5 Fond, G., Loundou, A., Hamdani, N., Boukouaci, W., Dargel, A., Oliveira, J., Roger, M., Tamouza, R., Leboyer, M., Boyer, L.: Anxiety and depression comorbidities in irritable bowel syndrome (IBS): A systematic review and meta-analysis. *Eur Arch Psychiat Clin Neurosc* 2014, **264**(8): 651–660.
6 Drossman, D.A.: Review article: An integrated approach to the irritable bowel syndrome. *Aliment Pharm Ther* 1999, **13**(s2): 3–14.
7 Lackner, J.M., Gurtman, M.B.: Patterns of interpersonal problems in irritable bowel syndrome patients: A circumplex analysis. *J Psychosom Res* 2005, **58**(6): 523–532.
8 Freud, S., Breuer, J.: Studies on hysteria. In: *Standard edition of the complete psychological works of Sigmund Freud.* Volume 2, 1895: 1–309.
9 Stern, J.M.: 'No entry', an invitation to intrude, or both? Reflections on a group of anorexic patients. *Int J Psychoanal* 2013, **94**(4): 689–713.
10 Stern, J.: Home parenteral nutrition and the psyche: Psychological challenges for patient and family. *Proc Nut Soc* 2006, **65**(3): 222–226.
11 Stern, J., Jacyna, N., Lloyd, D.: Psychological aspects of HPN, abnormal illness behaviour, and risk of self-harm in patients with central venous catheters. *Aliment Pharmacol Therap* 2008, **17**: 175–184.
12 Stern, J.M.: Psycho-analytical psychotherapy in a medical setting. *Psychoanal Psychother* 1999, **13**(1): 51–68.
13 Stern, J.: Thirty years of abdominal pain. *Psychoanal Psychother* 2003, **17**(4): 300–311.
14 Bergner, S.: The analytic environment in times of bodily dysfunction: The effect of psychoanalytic psychosomatic theories. *Psychoanal Psychol* 2009, **26**(4): 362.
15 Wessely, S., White, P.D.: There is only one functional somatic syndrome. *Br J Psychiat* 2004, **185**(2): 95–96.
16 Luyten, P., Van Houdenhove, B., Lemma, A., Target, M., Fonagy, P.: Vulnerability for functional somatic disorders: A contemporary psychodynamic approach. *J Psychother Integrat* 2013, **23**(3): 250.
17 Henrich, J.F., Knittle, K., De Gucht, V., Warren, S., Dombrowski, S U., Maes, S.: Identifying effective techniques within psychological treatments for irritable bowel syndrome: A meta-analysis. *J Psychosom Res* 2015, **78**(3): 205–222.
18 Guthrie, E., Creed, F., Dawson, D., Tomenson, B.: A controlled trial of psychological treatment for the irritable bowel syndrome. *Gastroenterology* 1991, **100**(2): 450–457.
19 Svedlund, J., Ottosson, J-O, Sjödin, I., Dotevall, G.: Controlled study of psychotherapy in irritable bowel syndrome. *Lancet* 1983, **322**(8350): 589–592.
20 Guthrie, E., Creed, F., Dawson, D., Tomenson, B.: A randomised controlled trial of psychotherapy in patients with refractory irritable bowel syndrome. *Br J Psychiat* 1993, **163**(3): 315–321.
21 Creed, F., Fernandes, L., Guthrie, E., Palmer, S., Ratcliffe, J., Read, N., Rigby, C., Thompson, D., Tomenson, B., Group NoEIR: The cost-effectiveness of psychotherapy and paroxetine for severe irritable bowel syndrome. *Gastroenterology* 2003, **124**(2): 303–317.
22 Creed, F., Guthrie, E., Ratcliffe, J., Fernandes, L., Rigby, C., Tomenson, B., Read, N., Thompson, D.G.: Does psychological treatment help only those patients with severe irritable bowel syndrome who also have a concurrent psychiatric disorder? *Aus NZ J Psychiat* 2005, **39**(9): 807–815.
23 Hyphantis, T., Guthrie, E., Tomenson, B., Creed, F.: Psychodynamic interpersonal therapy and improvement in interpersonal difficulties in people with severe irritable bowel syndrome. *PAIN®* 2009, **145**(1): 196–203.
24 Creed, F., Ratcliffe, J., Fernandez, L., Tomenson, B., Palmer, S., Rigby, C., Guthrie, E., Read, N., Thompson, D.: Health-related quality of life and health care costs in severe, refractory irritable bowel syndrome. *Annal Inter Med* 2001, **134**(9_Part_2): 860–868.

25 Dalrymple, J., Bullock, I.: Guidelines: Diagnosis and management of irritable bowel syndrome in adults in primary care: Summary of NICE guidance. *BMJ* 2008, **336**(7643): 556–558.
26 Altayar, O., Sharma, V., Prokop, L.J., Sood, A., Murad, M.H.: Psychological therapies in patients with irritable bowel syndrome: A systematic review and meta-analysis of randomized controlled trials. *Gastroenterol Res Pract* 2015, 2015: 549308.
27 Zijdenbos, I.L., de Wit, N.J., van der Heijden, G.J., Rubin, G., Quartero, A.O.: Psychological treatments for the management of irritable bowel syndrome. *Cochrane Lib* 2009, Issue 1: Art. No.: CD006442.
28 Spiller, R., Aziz, Q., Creed, F.: Guidelines on the irritable bowel syndrome: Mechanisms and practical management (vol. 56, pg. 1770, 2007). *Gut* 2008, **57**(12): 1743–1743.
29 Bharucha, A.E., Pemberton, J.H., Locke III, G.R.: American gastroenterological association technical review on constipation. *Gastroenterology* 2013, **144**(1): 218.
30 Digestive health foundation. *Irritable bowel syndrome: Clinical update.* Gastroenterol Soc Aus. 2006.
31 Stern, J: The relevance of applied psychoanalytic practice and thinking to the treatment of medically symptomatic patients. Ch. 8 in: *Off the couch: Contemporary psychoanalytic application.* Edited by Lemma, A., Patrick, M. 2010: 130–142. Routledge, London.
32 Lyth, I.M.: Social systems as a defense against anxiety. *Hum Relat* 1960, **13**: 95–123.
33 Evans, M.: 'I'm beyond caring', a response to the Francis Report: The failure of social systems in health care to adequately support nurses and nursing in the clinical care of their patients. *Psychoanal Psychother* 2014, **28**(2): 193–210.
34 Camilleri, M., Mayer, E.A.: Developing irritable bowel syndrome guidelines through meta-analyses: Does the emperor really have new clothes? *Gastroenterology* 2009, **137**(3): 766–769.

Chapter 15

Functional bowel disorders (IBS and non-IBS)

Hypnosis

Perjohan Lindfors
Jenny Lövdahl
Magnus Simrén

The aim of this chapter is to review the current evidence supporting the use of gut-directed hypnotherapy for patients with functional bowel disorders. Practical recommendations are provided.

Learning points

- In clinical hypnosis, a hypnotic state is first induced, after which the therapist can use targeted verbal suggestions and therapeutic imagery to encourage symptom improvement.
- Results from randomised controlled trials (RCTs) and several meta-analyses support the efficacy of gut-directed hypnotherapy for patients with IBS, but the quality of studies conducted to date is not optimal.
- Long-term results of gut-directed hypnotherapy are excellent, with positive long-term effects on IBS symptoms, psychological symptoms and quality of life in the majority of responders.

Introduction

The function of the gastrointestinal (GI) tract is primarily controlled by the enteric nervous system (ENS) in a semi-autonomous fashion, and many of the routine actions in the GI tract occur without influence of the central nervous system (CNS). However, the CNS and the ENS communicate via nerves, hormones and the immune system. This pathway of communication plays an important role in adjusting the function in the GI tract and is referred to as the 'brain-gut axis' [1]. The CNS continuously monitors the actions of the ENS and can modify GI perception and activity in the ENS via descending pathways and filter ascending signals from the ENS, preventing unnecessary signals from reaching the cortex. The influence of CNS on ENS function is affected by the emotional state of the individual and by internal and external stressors [1, 2]. This interaction has been demonstrated in studies using hypnosis, where induction of different emotions clearly affects colonic sensorimotor function in patients with IBS [3, 4]. Moreover, chronic stress and psychological symptoms affect the severity of GI symptoms negatively in patients with functional bowel disorders (FBD) [5, 6], and stressful life events trigger exacerbations of symptoms in many patients [7]. Psychological factors also constitute important risk factors for developing chronic GI symptoms after an acute infectious gastroenteritis – namely, post-infectious IBS [8] – and comorbid psychiatric disorders are common in patients with FBD [9]. Taken together, these observations supporting the importance of gut-brain interactions in FBD provide the rationale for using psychological interventions to improve symptoms in these patients, and to use the brain-gut axis and the ability of the CNS to affect the function of the ENS as a therapeutic strategy in FBD.

One psychological treatment that has been most widely studied in patients with FBD is gut-directed hypnotherapy, which has been assessed in several RCTs in patients with IBS, as well as in some other functional GI disorders, with good overall results (see ahead) [10, 11]. However, so far no studies have been published on hypnosis and non-IBS FBDs.

Gut-directed hypnotherapy in functional bowel disorders

Hypnotherapy is a verbal intervention that uses a special mental state of enhanced receptivity to suggestions in order to facilitate psychological and physiological changes. First a hypnotic state is induced, after which the therapist can use targeted verbal suggestions and therapeutic imagery to encourage symptom improvement [10]. Most studies investigating the clinical effect of gut-directed hypnotherapy for GI disorders have studied adults with IBS; these studies are reviewed ahead (see Table 15.1). No clinical trials evaluating gut-directed hypnotherapy exist for the other functional bowel disorders – that is, functional constipation, functional diarrhoea, functional abdominal bloating/distension or opioid-induced constipation [12].

A small number of studies report a positive effect of hypnotherapy in children with IBS [13]. In adults, single studies suggesting a positive effect in inflammatory bowel disease (IBD) [14], non-cardiac chest pain [15] and functional dyspepsia [16] have been published, but more studies are needed before recommending gut-directed hypnotherapy for these patient groups in clinical practice.

Effects of gut-directed hypnotherapy on IBS symptoms

Results from randomized controlled trials (RCTs)

Gut-directed hypnotherapy as treatment in severe, refractory IBS was first described by the Manchester group in 1984 [17]. Thirty IBS patients, refractory to other therapies, were randomly allocated to treatment with gut-directed hypnotherapy or supportive psychotherapy and placebo. The hypnotherapy group reported less abdominal pain, less distension and more regular bowel habits compared to the control group. The reported general well-being was also greatly improved in the hypnotherapy group and the post-treatment difference compared to the control condition was highly significant. In the hypnotherapy group, symptoms were either mild or absent in all 15 patients. The authors concluded that hypnotherapy was highly effective in the treatment of refractory IBS, and a follow-up study to evaluate the long-term effects was presented by the same group in 1987 [18]. The original 15 hypnotherapy patients had by then been followed for an average of 18 months and had booster sessions every third month during this time.

At the end of the follow-up, all patients remained in remission with symptoms not significantly different from the end of the previous study. In this study, another 35 IBS patients with refractory IBS had also been treated and the combined results of the whole group of patients were presented in an uncontrolled fashion with an overall success rate of 84%. Patients reported significant improvements in all parameters (abdominal pain, distension, bowel habits and general well-being) when comparing pre- versus post-treatment measurements.

Subsequently Harvey *et al.* [19] studied 33 patients randomized to group or individual hypnotherapy. The treatment consisted of five 40-minute sessions of either group or individual hypnotherapy with decreasing intensity over a five-month period. No significant difference in effect was found between the patients who had been treated individually or in group. Sixty per cent of the patients were at least somewhat improved, but when comparing the result with earlier studies, considering the symptom-free group as responders, only 33% were responders compared to 84% in the previous (Manchester) studies.

In an attempt to replicate the original Manchester study, Galovski and Blanchard [20] included 12 patients in a randomized controlled study, comparing a 12-week course of hypnotherapy to a symptom monitoring control condition. The control patients were crossed over to hypnotherapy treatment after six weeks. In the hypnotherapy group 80% of the patients were clinically improved, compared to 0% in the control condition. When the controls were crossed over to hypnotherapy, 67% also reached clinically significant improvement. In an RCT using the North Carolina protocol (see ahead) [21, 42] patients were treated via hypnotherapy or served as waiting list controls. Significant improvements were seen within the hypnotherapy groups for abdominal pain, bloating, stool frequency and consistency. No effects were seen within the control group and the overall change in IBS symptoms differed between the groups after treatment. The patients provided a global rating of symptom status ten months after treatment, and the mean estimated degree of improvement in IBS symptoms compared with pre-treatment level was 68%.

In a primary care setting [22], patients were randomized to five 30-minute, weekly sessions of gut-directed hypnotherapy or to 'standard management'. At three months, the intervention group had significantly less pain, less diarrhoea and lower overall symptom scores compared to the control group, but the differences were not maintained over time. The results from these RCTs support the findings that gut-directed hypnotherapy is effective in treating refractory IBS, without reaching the impressive level of efficacy of the original Manchester study.

More recent studies from Sweden confirm hypnotherapy as an effective treatment when delivered outside specialized hypnotherapy centres; in these studies too, the efficacy was not quite as impressive as in the original trials (about 50% response rate) [23]. A Cochrane review (2007) concluded that the therapeutic effect of hypnotherapy was superior to that of a waiting list control or usual medical management, for abdominal pain and composite primary IBS symptoms, in the short term in patients who had failed standard medical therapy, but the authors also concluded that the results of these studies should be interpreted with caution due to poor methodological quality and small size [24]. Similar conclusions were also drawn from other systematic reviews [25–27], and one of these reported a favourable number needed to treat of four [25].

Clinical audits

The Manchester group has reported results from their clinical service in two publications (n=250 and n=1000, respectively), which confirm the effectiveness of the intervention in reducing both IBS symptoms and extraintestinal symptoms [28, 29]. In the larger trial, 76% met the primary endpoint (a 50-point reduction in the IBS Symptom Severity Score (IBS-SSS): total scale range 0–500) [29]. Moreover, the long-term effects on IBS symptoms have also been assessed [30], where patients, previously treated with hypnotherapy, were investigated 1–6 years after treatment. Of the 71% of patients initially responding to treatment, 81% maintained their improvement at follow-up. There was also a positive long-term effect on extraintestinal symptoms. These positive long-term effects of gut-directed hypnotherapy on IBS symptoms were confirmed in a Swedish cohort (mean follow-up four years) [31]. In children with functional abdominal pain and IBS, impressive long-term results have also been demonstrated, with two thirds of treated patients still in remission after almost five years [32].

Table 15.1 Summary of the current evidence regarding gut-directed hypnotherapy for FBDs.

Condition	*Level of evidence*	*Comments*
IBS	Level I	Several meta-analyses support the efficacy of gut-directed hypnotherapy for adult patients with IBS, but the quality of included trials has been judged to be poor [24–27]. A systematic review also suggests that the therapeutic effects of hypnotherapy seem superior to standard medical care in children with functional abdominal pain or IBS [13].
	Level II	Several RCTs have demonstrated that gut-directed hypnotherapy improves GI symptoms and quality of life more than the control condition in adult patients with IBS (supportive therapy +/- placebo pills, medical treatment, waiting list, (non-hypnotic) audiotapes) [18, 20]– [23, 33], and three positive RCTs with positive results have been published in children with functional abdominal pain or IBS [34–36].

Effects of gut-directed hypnotherapy on psychological comorbidity, quality of life and health economy

Hypnotherapy in general is reported to have a positive effect on psychological symptoms, such as anxiety, depression and somatization [37], and improvements in anxiety, depression and somatization have also been reported in trials in IBS patients using gut-directed hypnotherapy [20, 21, 23]. A group of 25 IBS patients previously treated with gut-directed hypnotherapy was compared to patients on the waiting list for the same intervention; the treated patients reported fewer severe IBS symptoms and extraintestinal symptoms, and quality of life was also favourably influenced by hypnotherapy. Patients treated with gut-directed hypnotherapy were also significantly less likely to take time off work and visit their general practitioner compared to the control group [38].

In another study from the Manchester group [39], specifically designed to investigate cognitive effects of hypnotherapy treatment in IBS patients, there was a significant improvement in quality of life, depression and anxiety post- versus pre-treatment, but also an improvement in IBS-related cognitions. Furthermore, the improvement of these IBS-related cognitions after treatment was correlated to the improvement in IBS symptoms. The authors concluded that the improvement of cognitions could be a mechanism behind the effect of hypnotherapy in treating IBS. In the clinical audits from Manchester, improvements pre- versus post-treatment were seen in quality of life, depression and anxiety [30], and positive long-term effects on these parameters have also been described as well as a decrease in health-care utilization and use of symptom-modifying medication among responders to hypnotherapy [30]. Gut-directed hypnotherapy is also associated with a high degree of patient satisfaction, which is surprisingly also seen in a substantial patients without a reduction in IBS symptom severity [40].

Availability of hypnotherapy – solutions for clinical practices

The availability of this treatment option is generally low and finding ways to increase availability is important. One approach is to educate and train health-care professionals other than psychologists to deliver the treatment. Our research group in Gothenburg recently evaluated nurse-administered hypnotherapy. In an uncontrolled study the verbatim protocol from the North Carolina group was used (see ahead) [41], and 85 patients with IBS were treated once a week for 12 weeks. With a responder definition of a reduction with at least 50 points on the IBS-SSS the responder rate was 59%. At follow-up 6 and 12 months after the intervention 86% and 79% of the initial responders maintained their responder status. Another interesting result was that early response (6 weeks) to treatment was a strong predictor to being a responder at the end of treatment (12 weeks) [42].

Another way to increase the availability is via group treatment. Moser *et al.* compared group hypnotherapy with "support and medical treatment". Hypnotherapy was superior to the control condition post-treatment and at follow-up after 12 months. The responder rate in this study was 61% post-treatment and 54% at follow-up after 15 months [33].

Another attractive approach to increase the number of subjects who can have access to hypnotherapy is home hypnotherapy, and the efficacy of home therapy is supported by a small pilot study [43]. Moreover, the use of the Internet to reach more subjects should also be tried for hypnotherapy [44].

Use of hypnotherapy for IBS in clinical practice

Hypnotherapy for IBS patients is most often administered with the help of a script, a standardized gut-focused protocol [41, 45]. This enables the therapy to be standardized across centres, which strengthens reliability. This approach makes it possible for health-care providers with basic training in hypnosis to deliver the treatment and increase availability of treatment. Hypnotherapy can be administered on an individual basis or in group settings, and both approaches have been shown to be efficient for patients with IBS [28, 33]. Most centres do not recommend gut-directed hypnotherapy for IBS patients with severe psychiatric disease or a significant history of trauma. In the clinical audit from Manchester female gender and higher anxiety scores at baseline were predictors for a better treatment response.

A widely used protocol, the North Carolina protocol, has been translated into different languages, can be used regardless of IBS bowel habit subtype or hypnotic ability, and is suited for effectively treating individuals with highly chronic or intractable symptoms. It has been thoroughly evaluated in different settings [21, 42, 46], including as home treatment in a pilot study [43]. Pain-specific suggestions are used in the protocol, with the aim to reduce somatic focus of attention and to lower the patient's beliefs about the importance of the symptoms and their impact in daily life. Patients receive a relaxation tape, which they are instructed to use daily. The protocol consists of seven written sessions delivered every other week for a period of three months. Although the different sessions differ from each other, the basic structure is always the same. The session starts with an induction of the hypnotic state through eye fixation. This is followed by a guided physical relaxation. The therapist then helps the patient to deepen the hypnotic state, and at the same time describes a gradual movement downwards, such as sinking downwards while sitting comfortably on a cloud. The session is continued by the therapist describing beautiful and pleasant scenery, often in nature. The patient is asked to imagine being in this particular place, feeling comfortable and relaxed. The scenery is used as a metaphor for inner tranquillity and feeling at ease. Therapeutic suggestions are used in order to improve gut function and to relieve symptoms. The therapist ends the session while counting backwards, suggesting the patient start waking up [41].

Practical recommendations

- Hypnotherapy for IBS patients should be administered with the help of a standardized gut-focused protocol, which enables the therapy to be standardized across centres.

- After hypnotic induction, pain-specific suggestions are used with the aim to reduce somatic focus of attention and to lower the patient's beliefs about the importance of the symptoms and their impact in daily life.
- Usually 7–12 hypnotherapy sessions over a three-month period are offered.
- To enhance treatment effects, patients are encouraged to use a relaxation tape at home on a daily basis throughout the treatment period.
- Different ways may increase the availability of this treatment: educate and train health-care professionals other than psychologists to deliver the treatment; treatment in a group format; home hypnotherapy.

Current limitations/future considerations

- Despite positive results from existing RCTs of gut-directed hypnotherapy in IBS, these results should be interpreted with caution due to poor methodological quality and small size.
- No RCTs have assessed the effect of gut-directed hypnotherapy for FBDs other than IBS.
- The availability of gut-directed hypnotherapy in clinical practice is limited.

Acknowledgments, competing interests, and funding

The authors are unaware of any competing interests in relation to this chapter. No external funding was received for this chapter.

References

1 Mayer, E.A., Tillisch, K.: The brain-gut axis in abdominal pain syndromes *Annu Rev Med* 2011, **62**: 381–396.
2 Van Oudenhove, L., Demyttenaere, K., Tack, J., Aziz, Q.: Central nervous system involvement in functional gastrointestinal disorders. *Best Pract Res Clin Gastroenterol* 2004, **18**(4): 663–680.
3 Houghton, L.A., Calvert, E.L., Jackson, N.A., Cooper, P., Whorwell, P.J. Visceral sensation and emotion: A study using hypnosis. *Gut* 2002, **51**(5): 701–704.
4 Whorwell, P.J., Houghton, L.A., Taylor, E.E., Maxton, D.G.: Physiological effects of emotion: Assessment via hypnosis. *Lancet* 1992, **340**(8811): 69–72.
5 Suarez, K., Mayer, C., Ehlert, U., Nater, U.M.: Psychological stress and self-reported functional gastrointestinal disorders. *J Nerv Ment Dis* 2010, **198**(3): 226–229.
6 Van Oudenhove, L., Crowell, M.D., Drossman, D.A., Halpert, A.D., Keefer, L., Lackner, J.M., Murphy, T.B., Naliboff, B.D., Levy, R.L.: Biopsychosocial aspects of functional gastrointestinal disorders. *Gastroenterology* 2016, **150**(6): 1355–1367.e1352.
7 Blanchard, E.B., Lackner, J.M., Jaccard, J., Rowell, D., Carosella, A.M., Powell, C., Sanders, K., Krasner, S., Kuhn, E.: The role of stress in symptom exacerbation among IBS patients. *J Psychosom Res* 2008, **64**(2): 119–128.
8 Thabane, M., Kottachchi, D.T., Marshall, J.K.: Systematic review and meta-analysis: The incidence and prognosis of post-infectious irritable bowel syndrome. *Aliment Pharmacol Ther* 2007, **26**(4): 535–544.
9 Whitehead, W.E., Palsson, O., Jones, K.R.: Systematic review of the comorbidity of irritable bowel syndrome with other disorders: What are the causes and implications? *Gastroenterology* 2002, **122**(4): 1140–1156.

10 Palsson, O.S., Whitehead, W.E.: Psychological treatments in functional gastrointestinal disorders: A primer for the gastroenterologist. *Clin Gastroenterol Hepatol* 2013, **11**(3): 208–216; quiz e222–203.

11 Palsson, O.S.: Hypnosis treatment of gastrointestinal disorders: A comprehensive review of the empirical evidence. *Am J Clin Hypn* 2015, **58**(2): 134–158.

12 Lacy, B.E., Mearin, F., Chang, L., Chey, W.D., Lembo, A.J., Simren, M., Spiller, R.: Bowel disorders. *Gastroenterology* 2016, **150**(6): 1393–1407.e1395.

13 Rutten, J.M., Reitsma, J.B., Vlieger, A.M., Benninga, M.A.: Gut-directed hypnotherapy for functional abdominal pain or irritable bowel syndrome in children: A systematic review. *Arch Dis Child* 2013, **98**(4): 252–257.

14 Keefer, L., Taft, T.H., Kiebles, J.L., Martinovich, Z., Barrett, T.A., Palsson, O.S.: Gut-directed hypnotherapy significantly augments clinical remission in quiescent ulcerative colitis. *Aliment Pharmacol Ther* 2013, **38**(7): 761–771.

15 Jones, H., Cooper, P., Miller, V., Brooks, N., Whorwell, P.J.: Treatment of non-cardiac chest pain: A controlled trial of hypnotherapy. *Gut* 2006, **55**(10): 1403–1408.

16 Calvert, E.L., Houghton, L.A., Cooper, P., Morris, J., Whorwell, P.J.: Long-term improvement in functional dyspepsia using hypnotherapy. *Gastroenterology* 2002, **123**(6): 1778–1785.

17 Whorwell, P.J., Prior, A., Faragher, E.B.: Controlled trial of hypnotherapy in the treatment of severe refractory irritable-bowel syndrome. *Lancet* 1984, **2**(8414): 1232–1234.

18 Whorwell, P.J., Prior, A., Colgan, S.M.: Hypnotherapy in severe irritable bowel syndrome: Further experience. *Gut* 1987, **28**(4): 423–425.

19 Harvey, R.F., Hinton, R.A., Gunary, R.M., Barry, R.E.: Individual and group hypnotherapy in treatment of refractory irritable bowel syndrome. *Lancet* 1989, **1**(8635): 424–425.

20 Galovski, T.E., Blanchard, E.B.: The treatment of irritable bowel syndrome with hypnotherapy. *Appl Psychophysiol Biofeedback* 1998, **23**(4): 219–232.

21 Palsson, O.S., Turner, M.J., Johnson, D.A., Burnett, C.K., Whitehead, W.E.: Hypnosis treatment for severe irritable bowel syndrome: Investigation of mechanism and effects on symptoms. *Dig Dis Sci* 2002, **47**(11): 2605–2614.

22 Roberts, L., Wilson, S., Singh, S., Roalfe, A., Greenfield, S.: Gut-directed hypnotherapy for irritable bowel syndrome: Piloting a primary care-based randomised controlled trial. *Br J Gen Pract* 2006, **56**(523): 115–121.

23 Lindfors, P., Unge, P., Arvidsson, P., Nyhlin, H., Bjornsson, E., Abrahamsson, H., Simren, M.: Effects of gut-directed hypnotherapy on IBS in different clinical settings-results from two randomized, controlled trials. *Am J Gastroenterol* 2012, **107**(2): 276–285.

24 Webb, A.N., Kukuruzovic, R.H., Catto-Smith, A.G., Sawyer, S.M.: Hypnotherapy for treatment of irritable bowel syndrome. *Cochrane Database Syst Rev* 2007, **4**: CD005110.

25 Ford, A.C., Talley, N.J., Schoenfeld, P.S., Quigley, E.M., Moayyedi, P.: Efficacy of antidepressants and psychological therapies in irritable bowel syndrome: Systematic review and meta-analysis. *Gut* 2009, **58**(3): 367–378.

26 Lee, H.H., Choi, Y.Y., Choi, M.G.: The efficacy of hypnotherapy in the treatment of irritable bowel syndrome: A systematic review and meta-analysis. *J Neurogastroenterol Motil* 2014, **20**(2): 152–162.

27 Wilson, S., Maddison, T., Roberts, L., Greenfield, S., Singh, S., Birmingham IBSRG: Systematic review: The effectiveness of hypnotherapy in the management of irritable bowel syndrome. *Aliment Pharmacol Ther* 2006, **24**(5): 769–780.

28 Gonsalkorale, W.M., Houghton, L.A., Whorwell, P.J.: Hypnotherapy in irritable bowel syndrome: A large-scale audit of a clinical service with examination of factors influencing responsiveness. *Am J Gastroenterol* 2002, **97**(4): 954–961.

29 Miller, V., Carruthers, H.R., Morris, J., Hasan, S.S., Archbold, S., Whorwell, P.J.: Hypnotherapy for irritable bowel syndrome: An audit of one thousand adult patients. *Aliment Pharmacol Ther* 2015, **41**(9): 844–855.

30 Gonsalkorale, W.M., Miller, V., Afzal, A., Whorwell, P.J.: Long term benefits of hypnotherapy for irritable bowel syndrome. *Gut* 2003, **52**(11): 1623–1629.

31 Lindfors, P., Unge, P., Nyhlin, H., Ljotsson, B., Bjornsson, E.S., Abrahamsson, H., Simren, M.: Long-term effects of hypnotherapy in patients with refractory irritable bowel syndrome. *Scand J Gastroenterol* 2012, **47**(4): 414–420.

32 Vlieger, A.M., Rutten, J.M., Govers, A.M., Frankenhuis, C., Benninga, M.A.: Long-term follow-up of gut-directed hypnotherapy vs. standard care in children with functional abdominal pain or irritable bowel syndrome. *Am J Gastroenterol* 2012, **107**(4): 627–631.

33 Moser, G., Tragner, S., Gajowniczek, E.E., Mikulits, A., Michalski, M., Kazemi-Shirazi, L., Kulnigg-Dabsch, S., Fuhrer, M., Ponocny-Seliger, E., Dejaco, C., *et al.*: Long-term success of GUT-directed group hypnosis for patients with refractory irritable bowel syndrome: A randomized controlled trial. *Am J Gastroenterol* 2013, **108**(4): 602–609.

34 van Tilburg, M.A., Chitkara, D.K., Palsson, O.S., Turner, M., Blois-Martin, N., Ulshen, M., Whitehead, W.E.: Audio-recorded guided imagery treatment reduces functional abdominal pain in children: A pilot study. *Pediatrics* 2009, **124**(5): e890–897.

35 Weydert, J.A., Shapiro, D.E., Acra, S.A., Monheim, C.J., Chambers, A.S., Ball, T.M.: Evaluation of guided imagery as treatment for recurrent abdominal pain in children: A randomized controlled trial. *BMC Pediatr* 2006, **6**: 29.

36 Vlieger, A.M., Menko-Frankenhuis, C., Wolfkamp, S.C., Tromp, E., Benninga, M.A.: Hypnotherapy for children with functional abdominal pain or irritable bowel syndrome: A randomized controlled trial. *Gastroenterology* 2007, **133**(5): 1430–1436.

37 Gould, R.C., Krynicki, V.E.: Comparative effectiveness of hypnotherapy on different psychological symptoms. *Am J Clin Hypn* 1989, **32**(2): 110–117.

38 Houghton, L.A., Heyman, D.J., Whorwell, P.J.: Symptomatology, quality of life and economic features of irritable bowel syndrome – the effect of hypnotherapy. *Aliment Pharmacol Ther* 1996, **10**(1): 91–95.

39 Gonsalkorale, W.M., Toner, B.B., Whorwell, P.J.: Cognitive change in patients undergoing hypnotherapy for irritable bowel syndrome. *J Psychosom Res* 2004, **56**(3): 271–278.

40 Lindfors, P., Ljotsson, B., Bjornsson, E., Abrahamsson, H., Simren, M.: Patient satisfaction after gut-directed hypnotherapy in irritable bowel syndrome. *Neurogastroenterol Motil* 2013, **25**(2): 169–e186.

41 Palsson, O.S.: Standardized hypnosis treatment for irritable bowel syndrome: The North Carolina protocol. *Int J Clin Exp Hypn* 2006, **54**(1): 51–64.

42 Lovdahl, J., Ringstrom, G., Agerforz, P., Tornblom, H., Simren, M.: Nurse-administered, gut-directed hypnotherapy in IBS: Efficacy and factors predicting a positive response. *Am J Clin Hypn* 2015, **58**(1): 100–114.

43 Palsson, O.S., Turner, M.J., Whitehead, W.E.: Hypnosis home treatment for irritable bowel syndrome: A pilot study. *Int J Clin Exp Hypn* 2006, **54**(1): 85–99.

44 Ljotsson, B., Hedman, E., Andersson, E., Hesser, H., Lindfors, P., Hursti, T., Rydh, S., Ruck, C., Lindefors, N., Andersson, G.: Internet-delivered exposure-based treatment vs. stress management for irritable bowel syndrome: A randomized trial. *Am J Gastroenterol* 2011, **106**(8): 1481–1491.

45 Gonsalkorale, W.M.: Gut-directed hypnotherapy: The Manchester approach for treatment of irritable bowel syndrome. *Int J Clin Exp Hypn* 2006, **54**(1): 27–50.

46 Palsson, O.S., van Tilburg, M.: Hypnosis and guided imagery treatment for gastrointestinal disorders: Experience with scripted protocols developed at the University of North Carolina. *Am J Clin Hypn* 2015, **58**(1): 5–21.

Chapter 16

Functional bowel disorders (IBS and non-IBS)

Cognitive behavioural therapy

Laurie Keefer

The aim of this chapter is to describe the structure, approach and efficacy for cognitive behavioural therapy (CBT) as it applies to irritable bowel syndrome and other functional bowel disorders. Practical recommendations regarding psychological approaches to manage these conditions will be provided.

Learning points

- CBT is applicable to functional gastrointestinal disorders because of its flexibility, compatibility with the biopsychosocial model of illness and its ability to specifically target the cognitive-affective skills necessary for symptom control.
- Providers should be familiar with the goals, structure and efficacy of CBT to generate an effective referral.

Introduction

Cognitive behavioural therapy (CBT) is a group of psychotherapies that operate under the assumption that problems arise from skills deficits that are either initiated or maintained by one's current environment [1]. CBT combines the goals of two types of therapy: *cognitive therapy*, which addresses maladaptive beliefs or attitudes believed to drive negative emotion, and *behaviour therapy*, a therapy focused on replacing maladaptive behaviours or habits with healthier ones. Both theories emphasize that factors that initiate a problem are not always those that perpetuate a problem. CBT focuses on interrupting and changing one or more overlapping components of the cycle: beliefs/thoughts, emotions and/or behaviours. There are several core components of CBT across disease groups: it is based on a collaborative relationship between patient and therapist, it is short-term and goal-oriented (usually 4–12 sessions) and it includes ongoing assessment and monitoring of progress. Furthermore, CBT – based on the best available evidence – is always being refined and adapted to different types of problem behaviours. CBT is well-researched and perhaps the most popular treatment for various mental health conditions, including major depressive disorder and several anxiety disorders. In many cases, it is superior to medications, such as antidepressants and anxiolytics [2].

Why is CBT applicable to functional gastrointestinal disorders (FGIDs)?

In FGIDs, the brain and the gut (connected via the 'brain-gut axis') are believed to become dysregulated through different pathways, and this results in gastrointestinal (GI) symptoms. First, dysregulation can occur when there is a downregulation of visceral sensation through the central nervous system (CNS) and the spinal cord. Here, thoughts and emotions impact on GI sensation and motility, and conversely, the same GI sensation and motility can affect pain perception, emotions (especially anxiety and fear) and behaviour. Another way in which dysregulation occurs is through *visceral hypersensitivity*, which can occur through either an increased activation of visceral afferent pathways (through injury or insult) or through central amplification of normal visceral sensations. A relevant (and patient-friendly) example of visceral hypersensitivity is the case of post-infectious IBS (PI-IBS), which reflects up to 30% of new IBS cases after acute gastroenteritis [3]. Here, patients with PI-IBS continued to experience abdominal discomfort, bloating and diarrhoea well after the acute infection has resolved [4]. Interestingly, premorbid anxiety, depression, somatization and neuroticism have been implicated as risk factors for the development of PI-IBS, as well as increased life stress within the past year and negative illness beliefs (Rhodes & Wallace, 2006). Similar findings are noted in functional dyspepsia [5]. The example of post-infectious-FGIDs is helpful for patients who feel validated that their symptoms are real, that something biological (vs psychological) sets off their symptoms but their reactions to symptoms in the absence of infection can be altered to improve symptoms.

What are the core components of CBT for FGIDs?

Older versions of CBT for FGIDs were based on manuals for the treatment of generalized anxiety disorder and delivered over 12–16 sessions [6–8]. They focused on stress management and worry control (about symptoms and life events) and operated under the assumption that FGIDs were a somatic manifestation of chronic worry (psychosomatic hypothesis of IBS). CBT worked very well for patients with IBS who had comorbid anxiety disorders, particularly generalized anxiety disorder [9]. Treatments included skills training in the areas of assertiveness training, perfectionism and neuroticism, worry control, problem solving and muscle tension. CBT was effectively delivered in groups and individual formats [10]. However, these earlier interventions were primarily conducted in psychological centres rather than gastroenterology practices, making selection bias towards psychological treatments high.

A large subset of patients did not benefit from this CBT that focused on stress management for IBS; it was hypothesized by emerging CBT scholars that this could be because: (1) psychopathology and stress were not the only drivers of FGID symptoms; and (2) focus on symptom-specific anxiety and associated avoidance behaviours may be more consistent with what is currently known about the pathophysiology of FGIDs, particularly IBS. Thus newer, more targeted CBT programs for FGIDs focus on targeting only a few skills deficits and emphasize skills generalization outside of the therapy setting through homework and self-directed readings [11, 12].

Psychoeducation remains a critical piece of CBTs for FGIDs because it enhances motivation, increases buy-in and collaboration between patient and therapist and reduces stigma around the FGID being psychologically or stress-related. During psychoeducation, often introduced at the first session, therapists review the brain-gut connection, describe the fight or flight response as it relates to gut responsivity and emphasize that how the brain interprets information related to the GI tract (e.g., cramps, bloating, urgency, diarrhoea, constipation, nausea) can be altered. Common examples that relate to patients include food aversion (feeling nauseous when eating a rotten fruit), classical conditioning (chemotherapy patients feeling nauseous driving past the hospital) or butterflies in one's stomach before an important event. Therapists focus on how initially such gut sensations were informative because they allowed the patient to do what was necessary to maintain their health or avoid harm, but that over time, their brain and gut became misaligned and now the brain is falsely interpreting normal signals (needing to have a bowel movement, fullness after eating) as threatening. The therapist spends much time with similar examples as buy-in to therapy, and increased locus of control over outcome increases the likelihood that the patient will respond rapidly to CBT with beneficial symptom relief over time [13].

Modification of arousal is part of most CBT interventions and is particularly relevant to FGIDs given that disruptions in the autonomic nervous system and stress response drive gastrointestinal motility and reduce pain thresholds. There are many ways to reduce arousal, and patient preference in collaboration with the therapist often dictates what type of arousal modification technique is recommended. Examples include progressive muscle relaxation [14], diaphragmatic breathing, which is more commonly employed in modern approaches and across a wider range of FGIDs, including rumination syndrome [15], and less often, guided imagery [16] or relaxation response meditation [17, 18]. Each technique has empirical support, giving wide flexibility to the CBT therapist. Mindfulness-based stress reduction may also be paired with CBT.

Cognitive restructuring makes up the majority of CBT for FGID programs, because of evidence that FGID patients have specific ways of thinking that amplify symptoms and impair coping. Specific cognitive skills deficits include pain catastrophizing, symptom-specific anxiety, somatic amplification and attentional bias/hypervigilance to perceived threats [19]. The therapist must introduce to the patient that (a) thoughts can be identified and characterized with self-awareness; (b) thoughts are open for debate/challenge; and (c) thoughts can affect emotions and behaviours. Common CBT techniques include the patient keeping a thought record in which they identify the situations in which they are experiencing symptoms, what they thought, how they felt physically and emotionally and what they did to cope. The therapist can help them recognize cognitive errors, such as overestimating the likelihood of an event occurring ('I just know I will have diarrhoea at the restaurant') or underestimating their likelihood of being able to cope ('I would die of embarrassment if I had to excuse myself during dinner'). The patient may need help with perspective taking if they are unable to identify certain unhelpful thoughts – this can be done by asking them to pretend they are talking to a friend and giving advice, asking them to come up with three alternative explanations to their worry or using 'Socratic questioning' to get at whether the worst-case scenario is really all that bad. CBT therapy for FGIDs thus focuses more than usual on thoughts and feelings as they relate to GI symptoms or fear of GI consequences.

Behavioural experimentation is another component of many CBT programs for FGIDs and focuses on the maladaptive responses patients develop as a result of their symptoms or cognitions. Avoidance of people, places and situations where symptoms are likely to occur or in which if symptoms were to occur if there is no escape is the most common maladaptive behaviour in FGID. Examples might include avoiding a child's baseball game because no bathroom is available, or cancelling movie plans because one hasn't had a bowel movement yet. The CBT therapist works to help the patients manage arousal and cognitions – for instance, by encouraging the patient to try certain behaviours they have been avoiding. This is a concrete way of demonstrating how the patient's avoidance or maladaptive cognitions may impact negatively on their quality of life or symptom severity. Behavioural experimentation is also possible among patients who engage in 'safety behaviour', such as wearing adult pull-ups for fear of incontinence, or who carry a safety backpack with a change of clothes or bathroom deodorizer lest they get caught having to use the bathroom outside of the home.

Coping flexibility is a newer feature of CBT for FGIDs and stems from earlier findings that FGID patients are biased towards solving problems, regardless of their 'solvability' [20]. Flexible coping training encourages patients to break down problems into smaller pieces, determine which aspects are solvable and apply appropriate coping – problem-focused coping in situations where a solution is apparent and emotion-focused when distress tolerance is more appropriate [21].

Other areas of CBT that may be featured in treatment include an emphasis on relapse prevention, a discussion of underlying core beliefs or underlying schemas (perfectionism, expecting approval) that may drive symptoms or drive maladaptive cognitions in a subset of patients [19]. Once these features are identified, they can be challenged through cognitive restructuring and behavioural experimentation.

What is the evidence for CBT for FGIDs?

Cognitive behavioural therapy is well supported by >30 RCTs in the areas of IBS [22] and paediatric functional abdominal pain [23, 24]. It has demonstrated efficacy against inert and active control conditions across many modes of delivery with a recent number needed to treat of 2.5 [25] and an associated durability [26]. While most commonly delivered individually, there is evidence of its efficacy in small groups [6, 27–30]. Newer CBT trials emphasize gastrointestinal symptom-based outcomes, self-management and minimal-contact techniques to improve accessibility to what are traditionally time-intensive and potentially expensive interventions. This approach is partially driven by data suggesting that a large subset of patients respond to CBT respond within the first four weeks of treatment [13]. No specific data exist regarding the efficacy of CBT in centrally mediated abdominal pain syndrome, functional constipation, diarrhoea or bloating/abdominal distension or unspecified functional bowel disorders (see Table 16.1).

While more research needs to be done in this area, Rome IV recommends the following as positive predictors for referral: patient has some insight into

Table 16.1 Summary of the current evidence base regarding medical and allied health approaches.

Treatment approach	*Level of evidence*	*Comments*
Cognitive behavioural therapy for IBS Level I Evidence	Strongest >32 RCTs, superior to placebo and attention controls, conducted in groups and individually, durability up to 4 years, number needed to treat (NNT) = 2.5	Not compared directly to psychotropic medication or to other forms of psychotherapy; minimal-contact or Internet-based approaches are recommended due to lack of accessibility of the treatment in general practice.
CBT for abdominal pain disorders Level I Evidence paediatrics Level V Evidence adults	Strongest Several RCTs for paediatric functional abdominal pain, seems to be equally effective as medical treatment 1 year after treatment in children ages 7–18 Low No RCTs in adults, CBT is recommended in Rome IV based on evidence in both IBS and other pain disorders more broadly.	Paediatric functional abdominal pain and adult functional abdominal pain (now called centrally mediated abdominal pain) are believed to be distinct entities and therefore the high evidence for paediatric FAP should not be extrapolated.
CBT for functional constipation Level V Evidence	Low No studies specific to this population	
CBT for functional diarrhoea Level V Evidence	Low No studies specific to this population	
CBT for functional bloating/distension Level V Evidence	Low No studies specific to this population	
CBT for unspecified functional bowel disorder Level V Evidence	Low No studies specific to this population	

the connection between psychological and physical factors, patient is willing to participate in self-management, patient has expectation that psychological treatment may be helpful, and patient has some perceived control over symptoms. Finally, patients with shorter duration of illness and with fewer pain sites tend to do best in CBT, further highlighting the need to refer early when possible. Patients who do the least well are those with more severe psychiatric comorbidities, low insight or motivation, scepticism around benefit of psychological therapies, and a longer duration of symptoms and multiple pain sites [19] – they may do better with other, less skills-based psychotherapies.

Practical recommendations

Medical providers can best serve FGID patients if they identify the potential for CBT early. Including CBT in an initial list of treatment options, along with whatever classes of drugs aimed at symptom management one might offer, makes it more easily adopted when these interventions fail or when the patient responds suboptimally. To facilitate a discussion around the role of CBT in FGID care, medical providers should create or refine a personalized 'elevator pitch' that they can use with patients. This may even include examples from other patients or colleagues as a way to reduce the perception or enactment of stigma around FGIDs as psychological disorders.

To further enhance belief in CBT for FGIDs, medical providers who are not already affiliated with a health psychologist should find 1–2 health psychologists in the community with whom they can develop a professional working relationship. This facilitates communication between the psychologist and medical provider, increases trust from the patient that the medical provider is not 'dumping them' to a psychologist and increases support for both the medical and psychological providers.

Practical recommendations

- Discuss CBT as a treatment early on; then it does not feel like it is a last resort when patients are referred.
- Create or refine a personalized 'elevator pitch' regarding the benefit of CBT for FGIDs so that you seem confident when recommending it.
- Find 1–2 health psychologists in the community with whom you can collaborate.
- Familiarize yourself with a good self-help book with CBT themes that you might recommend.

Current limitations/future considerations

- A limitation of CBT for FGIDs is the lack of specialized psychologists who provide the treatment.
- Attempts to increase access through health technology and minimal therapist contact are in place and will likely be widely adopted in the future.

- Despite >32 RCTs on CBT for FGIDs, none have been studied against other evidence-based psychotherapies, such as interpersonal psychotherapy, hypnotherapy or mindfulness-based stress reduction, or against an effective medication group.
- Interoceptive exposure-based CBT, which targets the subset of FGID patients who specifically demonstrate fear conditioning to benign internal sensations [31–33], is potentially beneficial.
- Mindfulness has also been paired with CBT techniques and may augment existing CBT therapies [34].
- Online delivery of CBT in various forms [34–37] and minimal-contact delivery [11] are also being tested to increase the availability of these therapies to FGID patients.

Acknowledgments, competing interests, and funding

The author is unaware of any competing interests in relation to this chapter. No external funding was received for this chapter.

References

1 Thoma, N., Pilecki, B., McKay, D.: Contemporary cognitive behavior therapy: A review of theory, history, and evidence. *Psychodyn Psychiatry* 2015, **43**(3): 423–461.
2 Hollon, S.D., Stewart, M.O., Strunk, D.: Enduring effects for cognitive behavior therapy in the treatment of depression and anxiety. *Annu Rev Psychol* 2006, **57**: 285–315.
3 Thabane, M., Marshall, J.K.: Post-infectious irritable bowel syndrome. *World J Gastroenterol* 2009, **15**(29): 3591–3596.
4 Gwee, K.A.: Post-infectious irritable bowel syndrome, an inflammation-immunological model with relevance for other IBS and functional dyspepsia. *J Neurogastroenterol Motil* 2010, **16**(1): 30–34.
5 Fock, K.M.: Functional dyspepsia, H. pylori and post infectious FD. *J Gastroenterol Hepatol* 2011, **26**(Suppl 3): 39–41.
6 Blanchard, E.B., Lackner, J.M., Sanders, K., Krasner, S., Keefer, L., Payne, A., Gudleski, G.D., Katz, L., Rowell, D., Sykes, M., *et al.*: A controlled evaluation of group cognitive therapy in the treatment of irritable bowel syndrome. *Behav Res Ther* 2007, **45**(4): 633–648.
7 Blanchard, E.B., Schwarz, S.P., Suls, J.M., Gerardi, M.A., Scharff, L., Greene, B., Taylor, A.E., Berreman, C., Malamood, H.S.: Two controlled evaluations of multicomponent psychological treatment of irritable bowel syndrome. *Behav Res Ther* 1992, **30**(2): 175–189.
8 Drossman, D.A., Toner, B.B., Whitehead, W.E., Diamant, N.E., Dalton, C.B., Duncan, S., Emmott, S., Proffitt, V., Akman, D., Frusciante, K., *et al.*: Cognitive-behavioral therapy versus education and desipramine versus placebo for moderate to severe functional bowel disorders. *Gastroenterology* 2003, **125**(1): 19–31.
9 Sykes, M.A., Blanchard, E.B., Lackner, J., Keefer, L., Krasner, S.: Psychopathology in irritable bowel syndrome: Support for a psychophysiological model. *J Behav Med* 2003, **26**(4): 361–372.
10 Lackner, J.M., Mesmer, C., Morley, S., Dowzer, C., Hamilton, S.: Psychological treatments for irritable bowel syndrome: A systematic review and meta-analysis. *J Consult Clin Psychol* 2004, **72**(6): 1100–1113.
11 Lackner, J.M., Keefer, L., Jaccard, J., Firth, R., Brenner, D., Bratten, J., Dunlap, L.J., Ma, C., Byroads, M., Group IR: The Irritable Bowel Syndrome Outcome Study (IBSOS): Rationale and design of a randomized, placebo-controlled trial with 12 month follow

up of self- versus clinician-administered CBT for moderate to severe irritable bowel syndrome. *Contemp Clin Trials* 2012, **33**(6): 1293–1310.

12 Lackner, J.M., Jaccard, J., Krasner, S.S., Katz, L.A., Gudleski, G.D., Holroyd, K.: Self-administered cognitive behavior therapy for moderate to severe irritable bowel syndrome: Clinical efficacy, tolerability, feasibility. *Clin Gastroenterol Hepatol* 2008, **6**(8): 899–906.

13 Lackner, J.M., Gudleski, G.D., Keefer, L., Krasner, S.S., Powell, C., Katz, L.A.: Rapid response to cognitive behavior therapy predicts treatment outcome in patients with irritable bowel syndrome. *Clin Gastroenterol Hepatol* 2010, **8**(5): 426–432.

14 Blanchard, E.B., Greene, B., Scharff, L., Schwarz-McMorris, S.P.: Relaxation training as a treatment for irritable bowel syndrome. *Biofeedback Self Regul* 1993, **18**(3): 125–132.

15 Halland, M., Parthasarathy, G., Bharucha, A.E., Katzka, D.A.: Diaphragmatic breathing for rumination syndrome: Efficacy and mechanisms of action. *Neurogastroenterol Motil* 2016, **28**(3): 384–391.

16 Boltin, D., Sahar, N., Gil, E., Aizic, S., Hod, K., Levi-Drummer, R., Niv, Y., Dickman, R.: Gut-directed guided affective imagery as an adjunct to dietary modification in irritable bowel syndrome. *J Health Psychol* 2015, **20**(6): 712–720.

17 Keefer, L., Blanchard, E.B.: A one year follow-up of relaxation response meditation as a treatment for irritable bowel syndrome. *Behav Res Ther* 2002, **40**(5): 541–546.

18 Keefer, L., Blanchard, E.B.: The effects of relaxation response meditation on the symptoms of irritable bowel syndrome: Results of a controlled treatment study. *Behav Res Ther* 2001, **39**(7): 801–811.

19 Van Oudenhove, L., Crowell, M.D., Drossman, D.A., Halpert, A.D., Keefer, L., Lackner, J.M., Murphy, T.B., Naliboff, B.D., Levy, R.L.: Biopsychosocial aspects of functional gastrointestinal disorders. *Gastroenterology* 2016, **150**(6): 1355–1367.

20 Cheng, C., Hui, W.M., Lam, S.K.: Coping style of individuals with functional dyspepsia. *Psychosom Med* 1999, **61**(6): 789–795.

21 Cheng, C., Chan, A.O., Hui, W.M., Lam, S.K.: Coping strategies, illness perception, anxiety and depression of patients with idiopathic constipation: A population-based study. *Aliment Pharmacol Ther* 2003, **18**(3): 319–326.

22 Palsson, O.S., Whitehead, W.E.: Psychological treatments in functional gastrointestinal disorders: A primer for the gastroenterologist. *Clin Gastroenterol Hepatol* 2013, **11**(3): 208–216.

23 Rutten, J.M., Korterink, J.J., Venmans, L.M., Benninga, M.A., Tabbers, M.M.: Nonpharmacologic treatment of functional abdominal pain disorders: A systematic review. *Pediatrics* 2015, **135**(3): 522–535.

24 Rutten, J.M., Vlieger, A.M.: Non-pharmacological treatment for abdominal pain. *J Pediatr Gastroenterol Nutr* 2011, **53**(Suppl 2): S41–S42.

25 Ford, A.C., Quigley, E.M., Lacy, B.E., Lembo, A.J., Saito, Y.A., Schiller, L.R., Soffer, E.E., Spiegel, B.M., Moayyedi, P.: Effect of antidepressants and psychological therapies, including hypnotherapy, in irritable bowel syndrome: systematic review and meta-analysis. *Am J Gastroenterol* 2014, **109**(9): 1350–1365, quiz 1366.

26 Laird, K.T., Tanner-Smith, E.E., Russell, A.C., Hollon, S.D., Walker, L.S.: Short-term and long-term efficacy of psychological therapies for irritable bowel syndrome: A systematic review and meta-analysis. *Clin Gastroenterol Hepatol* 2016, **14**(7): 937–947 e934.

27 Payne, A., Blanchard, E.B.: A controlled comparison of cognitive therapy and self-help support groups in the treatment of irritable bowel syndrome. *J Consult Clin Psychol* 1995, **63**(5): 779–786.

28 Lammert, M., Ratner, M.: Group treatment of patients with irritable bowel syndrome. *Soc Work Health Care* 1986, **12**(1): 67–92.

29 Toner, B.B., Segal, Z.V., Emmott, S., Myran, D., Ali, A., DiGasbarro, I., Stuckless, N.: Cognitive-behavioral group therapy for patients with irritable bowel syndrome. *Int J Group Psychother* 1998, **48**(2): 215–243.

30 van Dulmen, A.M., Fennis, J.F., Bleijenberg, G.: Cognitive-behavioral group therapy for irritable bowel syndrome: Effects and long-term follow-up. *Psychosom Med* 1996, **58**(5): 508–514.

31 Craske, M.G., Wolitzky-Taylor, K.B., Labus, J., Wu, S., Frese, M., Mayer, E.A., Naliboff, B.D.: A cognitive-behavioral treatment for irritable bowel syndrome using interoceptive exposure to visceral sensations. *Behav Res Ther* 2011, **49**(6–7): 413–421.
32 Keefer, L.: Extinguishing fear of gastrointestinal symptoms to treat functional gastrointestinal disorders. *Clin Gastroenterol Hepatol* 2016, **14**(11): 1559–1561.
33 Boersma, K., Ljotsson, B., Edebol-Carlman, H., Schrooten, M., Linton, S.J., Brummer, R.J.: Exposure-based cognitive behavioral therapy for irritable bowel syndrome: A single-case experimental design across 13 subjects. *Cogn Behav Ther* 2016, **45**(6): 415–430.
34 Ljotsson, B., Falk, L., Vesterlund, A.W., Hedman, E., Lindfors, P., Ruck, C., Hursti, T., Andreewitch, S., Jansson, L., Lindefors, N., *et al.*: Internet-delivered exposure and mindfulness based therapy for irritable bowel syndrome – a randomized controlled trial. *Behav Res Ther* 2010, **48**(6): 531–539.
35 Andersson, E., Ljotsson, B., Smit, F., Paxling, B., Hedman, E., Lindefors, N., Andersson, G., Ruck, C.: Cost-effectiveness of internet-based cognitive behavior therapy for irritable bowel syndrome: Results from a randomized controlled trial. *BMC Public Health* 2011, **11**: 215.
36 Ljotsson, B., Hedman, E., Lindfors, P., Hursti, T., Lindefors, N., Andersson, G., Ruck, C.: Long-term follow-up of internet-delivered exposure and mindfulness based treatment for irritable bowel syndrome. *Behav Res Ther* 2011, **49**(1): 58–61.
37 Ljotsson, B., Hedman, E., Andersson, E., Hesser, H., Lindfors, P., Hursti, T., Rydh, S., Ruck, C., Lindefors, N., Andersson, G.: Internet-delivered exposure-based treatment vs. stress management for irritable bowel syndrome: A randomized trial. *Am J Gastroenterol* 2011, **106**(8): 1481–1491.

Chapter 17

Functional bowel disorders (IBS and non-IBS)

Stress management and mindfulness-based approaches

Simon Knowles
Kaveh Monshat

Long-term or chronic stress can alter the function of the gastrointestinal tract, and stress often precedes or exacerbates symptoms of functional bowel disorders (FBD). The aim of this chapter is to briefly outline what stress management is, the role of arousal reduction approaches in stress management and the efficacy of stress management in relation to FBDs. The efficacy of mindfulness-based training for FBDs is reviewed. Practical recommendations and current limitations to the current use of stress management practices are outlined.

Learning points

- Long-term stress can alter the stress response and impact the functions of the gastrointestinal tract.
- Stress intensity has considerable impact on IBS symptoms.
- Stress management involves strategies to identify and mitigate stress at its sources and to reduce its impact on the body, and is beneficial for individuals with FBDs.

Introduction

What is stress management?

Stress is defined as an acute threat to homeostasis, with short- and long-term consequences to the immune system and gastrointestinal tract [1]. While acute stress increases sensitivity to gastrointestinal symptoms, long-term stress alters the stress response and the communication between the brain and the gut through the autonomic nervous system and the hypothalamic-pituitary-adrenal axis. This can affect the functions of the gastrointestinal tract and often precedes the onset of functional bowel disorders (FBD) [2].

Lasting changes in gastrointestinal motor activity, gastric secretion and emptying, electrolyte absorption and inflammation can be associated with abdominal pain, dyspepsia or diarrhoea, such as those observed in visceral hypersensitivity [1, 2]. In the context of prolonged stress, irritable bowel syndrome (IBS) sufferers (especially males) can experience intense gastrointestinal discomfort after even minor stimulation [3, 4]. In a distention experiment involving 33 women with

IBS, those with a lower rectal pressure tolerance (visceral hypersensitivity) had altered pain perception: pain remained intense irrespective of the intensity of anticipation or stimulation [5].

IBS sufferers frequently report a history of major stressful life events [2]. A study of 49 IBS patients showed that out of a number of factors, including stress, neuroticism, anxiety and depression, the only predictor of IBS symptom perpetuation was the intensity of stress ($r = .47, p < .01$) [6]. Stress explained 24% of the variance in IBS symptoms, with depression explaining 10% of stress intensity. However, some authors [7] suggest instead that IBS symptoms may be more strongly perpetuated by IBS symptoms themselves and only weakly influenced by concurrent stress.

Stress management is recommended in FBDs [8, 9]. This includes cognitive approaches that target ways of thinking, or arousal reduction strategies (the focus of the rest of this chapter) oriented towards behavioural change [10]. Training in problem solving has elements of both. It allows a better understanding of one's relationship with stressors and effecting appropriate strategies to manage these and may include effective planning, evaluation and organizing skills to allow better coping and self-care [11]. Coping refers to the efforts taken to overcome, tolerate or reduce the impact of the demand [12]. Self-care involves maintaining an awareness of one's own needs and seeking to fulfil these needs [13].

Arousal reduction approaches in stress management

Arousal reduction strategies include progressive muscle relaxation, biofeedback, time management, communication skills, assertiveness, problem solving, breathing techniques, diet, exercise and mindfulness training [10, 14, 15]. These are most extensively explored in IBS, though the results are likely relevant in non-IBS FBDs given the symptom overlap among all FBDs.

Relaxation training approaches include progressive muscle relaxation, which involves tensing and relaxing specific muscle groups [16], and slow breathing, which reduces physiological arousal in a number of ways, including through changes in the O_2/CO_2 ratio [17]. Exercise reduces tension through a number of channels, including improvements in cardiovascular function [14]. Biofeedback uses many techniques, including sensors providing visual feedback of physiological processes, such as heart rate, to aid in relaxation [18].

Techniques including relaxation training [19–27], biofeedback [28], autogenic therapy [29] and body awareness therapy [30] have been effective in reducing IBS symptoms. A Cochrane review found that stress management techniques, especially relaxation training, led to reductions in IBS symptoms, including pain, and improved quality of life compared to controls for up to two months [31], although the quality of evidence was low [32].

Stress management has been seldom compared with cognitive behavioural therapy (CBT) in reducing IBS symptoms. While preliminary findings suggest that they can be effective either individually or when used together [33], mindfulness-based approaches appear more effective overall [34].

Focus on mindfulness training

An intentional, non-judgemental and compassionate awareness of the present moment allows seeing beyond anxiety-provoking cognitive sets about the past or the future [35]. Mindfulness-based stress reduction (MBSR) is the most highly researched mindfulness training package, originally devised for hospital outpatients where allopathic interventions had been exhausted [35]. It involves 27 hours of contact time in groups of up to 25 persons, with home practice and exercises of up to an hour a day supported by audio recordings. Body awareness is cultivated through various forms of lying, sitting, walking, movement and eating meditation and framed within applied stress physiology and cognitive behavioural principles [36].

A meta-analysis showed lowered symptoms of anxiety (Hedges' $g = 0.63$) and depression (Hedges' $g = 0.59$; 39 studies, n = 1,140) [37]. A systematic review of 18 studies shows improvements in many physical symptoms of chronic illness, such as pain in various cancers, and rash [38]. Specifically relating to stress, a 21-study systematic review [39] found that MBSR decreased stress and distress and improved overall mental health compared with control conditions in all except one study. Similar results were found in studies involving college students (57 studies) [40].

A seven-study meta-analysis of mindfulness-based therapies involving FBDs (six IBS, one IBD with IBS) [41] reported promising initial findings: reductions in FBD symptoms post-intervention (Pooled $d = 0.60$; 95% CI = 0.33, 0.86) and at follow-up (Pooled $d = 0.35$; 95% CI = 0.11, 0.59), as well as improvements in quality of life (Pooled $d = 0.56$; 95% CI = 0.34, 0.79).

A large RCT examining mindfulness in IBS (n = 73 divided between an MBSR and a social support group) showed that IBS symptom severity and quality of life were significantly improved at post-treatment and at three months follow-up [42]. Symptom improvements were also clinically significant at both time points (symptom reduction of 26.4% versus 6.2% post-treatment, and 38.2% versus 11.8% at three months) [42]. In a randomly allocated sample of 24 individuals with IBS, MBSR led to greater IBS symptom reduction compared with an eight-week CBT group and 12 healthy control participants [34]. Another RCT (of Iranian IBS patients $n = 24$) found significantly greater improvements in IBS-related quality of life in the MBSR vis-à-vis the control group [43]. In contrast, an uncontrolled study involving US veterans with IBS ($n = 93$) found no significant differences in IBS-related symptom severity, quality of life or visceral sensitivity [44]. Although underlying biological effects are not well understood [45], and the evidence predominantly concerns IBS, MBSR is a promising approach for reducing symptoms and improving quality of life in FBDs.

Irritable bowel syndrome

Table 17.1 summarizes the current evidence regarding stress management in IBS. The largest volume of evidence is for relaxation training, especially in reducing overall symptom severity [19–27]. Mindfulness research – a newer

Table 17.1 Summary of the current evidence base regarding stress management approaches in IBS.

Approach	*Level of evidence*	*Comments*
Autogenic training	II [29]	Autogenic training involving muscular exercise and relaxation can improve symptoms and quality of life [29].
Biofeedback	III-1 [54], IV [22, 23, 25, 28]	Using gut-directed biofeedback with a computer game giving scores for muscle relaxation may help to improve muscle relaxation and IBS symptoms [28]. When combining biofeedback of vasodilation in hand with progressive muscle relaxation, IBS education and cognitive therapy, reductions in abdominal pain, diarrhoea, nausea and flatulence may be achieved [22, 23, 25, 54].
Body awareness therapy	III-2 [30]	Better awareness of bodily movements, breathing and posture can help reduce cortisol levels, IBS and other symptoms [30]
Comprehensive self-management	II [50–52]	Comprehensive self-management, including education, relaxation training, diet and CBT, may help reduce IBS symptoms and improve quality of life [50–52].
Mindfulness-based stress reduction (MBSR)	I [46], II [34, 42, 43, 47– 49, 55], IV [44]	Focusing on experience in the present moment is helpful with pain, symptom severity and quality of life [34, 42, 46–49] (this finding is not always consistent [44]).
Relaxation	I [20], II [26, 27, 29, 56– 61], III-1 [62, 63], III-2 [19], IV [21–25]	Relaxation has many benefits, including reducing symptom severity [19–27], pain [63] and impairment [57], as well as reductions in flatulence, belching, bloating and diarrhoea [56].
Self-regulatory therapy	II [33], III-1 [22, 23], IV [53]	Self-regulatory treatments that include relaxation, biofeedback and cognitive therapy can decrease levels of anxiety, depression and somatization in individuals with IBS [22, 23, 33, 53].

and consequently smaller field – suggests symptom improvement, especially pain, but also improved overall quality of life [34, 42, 46–49]. Although more head-to-head comparison studies are called for, it is difficult to compare the two approaches since mindfulness-based programs always include some degree of relaxation training. A combination of approaches can be effective in relieving the symptoms of IBS [50–52], as well as other comorbid symptoms of depression, anxiety and somatization [22, 23, 33, 53]. MBSR is indeed a combination approach, including elements of relaxation training, CBT and psychoeducation.

Practical recommendations

- Psychoeducation regarding the relationship between stress and gut dysfunction and training in stress management strategies are best provided as routine components of FBD management.
- Multiple stress management strategies are available, so techniques are best chosen in a collaborative and exploratory process.
- Stress management training, boasting the strongest evidence base (e.g., relaxed breathing techniques), should be offered routinely and concomitant with other cognitive and/or behavioural approaches.
- Where available, and acceptable to patients, a MBSR course, or variant thereof, may be an excellent starting point, as it includes a range of interventions, including psychoeducation, relaxation training and body awareness.

Current limitations/future directions

- Most research focuses on IBS. Similarity of symptoms (e.g., between functional diarrhoea and diarrhoea-predominant IBS) is used to extrapolate findings for other FBDs.
- Future studies are needed to investigate stress management in non-IBS FBDs, especially problem solving, slow breathing and exercise, where there is currently no non-IBS evidence base. Greater head-to-head comparison studies of different approaches are also desirable.

Acknowledgements, competing interests and funding

Thanks to Sarina Cook for assistance with the literature search and compilation. The authors are unaware of any competing interests in relation to this chapter. No external funding was received for this chapter.

References

1 Konturek, P.C., Brzozowski, T., Konturek, S.J.: Stress and the gut: Pathophysiology, clinical consequences, diagnostic approach and treatment options. *J Physiol Pharmacol* 2011, **62**(6): 591–599.

2 Bhatia, V., Tandon, R.K.: Stress and the gastrointestinal tract. *J Gastroenterol Hepatol* 2005, **20**(3): 332–339.
3 Moloney, R.D., Johnson, A.C., O'Mahony, S.M., Dinan, T.G., Meerveld, G.V., Cryan, J.F.: Stress and the microbiota – gut – brain axis in visceral pain: Relevance to irritable bowel syndrome. *CNS Neurosci Ther* 2016, **22**(2): 102–117.
4 Tillisch, K., Mayer, E.A., Labus, J.S., Stains, J., Chang, L., Naliboff, B.D.: Sex specific alterations in autonomic function among patients with irritable bowel syndrome. *Gut* 2005, **54**(10): 1396–1401.
5 Lowén, M.B.O., Mayer, E., Tillisch, K., Labus, J., Naliboff, B., Lundberg, P., Thorell, L.H., Ström, M., Engström, M., Walter, S.: Deficient habituation to repeated rectal distensions in irritable bowel syndrome patients with visceral hypersensitivity. *Neurogastroenterol Motil* 2015, **27**(5): 646–655.
6 Pletikosić, S., Tkalčić, M.: The role of stress in IBS symptom severity. *Psihologijske Teme* 2016, **25**(1): 29–43.
7 Blanchard, E.B., Lackner, J.M., Jaccard, J., Rowell, D., Carosella, A.M., Powell, C., Sanders, K., Krasner, S., Kuhn, E.: The role of stress in symptom exacerbation among IBS patients. *J Psychosom Res* 2008, **64**(2): 119–128.
8 Eriksson, E.M., Andrén, K.I., Kurlberg, G.K., Eriksson, H.T.: Aspects of the non-pharmacological treatment of irritable bowel syndrome. *WJG* 2015, **21**(40): 11439–11449.
9 Tanaka, Y., Kanazawa, M., Fukudo, S., Drossman, D.A.: Biopsychosocial model of irritable bowel syndrome. *J Neurogastroenterol Motil* 2011, **17**(2): 131–139.
10 Bunce, D.: What factors are associated with the outcome of individual-focused worksite stress management interventions? *J Occup Org Psychol* 1997, **70**(1): 1–17.
11 Largo-Wight, E., Peterson, P.M., Chen, W.W.: Perceived problem solving, stress, and health among college students. *Am J Health Behav* 2005, **29**(4): 360–370.
12 Folkman, S.: Personal control and stress and coping processes: A theoretical analysis. *J Pers Soc Psychol* 1984, **46**(4): 839–852.
13 Oberst, M.T., Hughes, S.H., Chang, A.S., McCubbin, M.A.: Self-care burden, stress appraisal, and mood among persons receiving radiotherapy. *Cancer Nurs* 1991, **14**(2): 71–78.
14 Daubenmier, J.J., Weidner, G., Sumner, M.D., Mendell, N., Merritt-Worden, T., Studley, J., Ornish, D.: The contribution of changes in diet, exercise, and stress management to changes in coronary risk in women and men in the Multisite Cardiac Lifestyle Intervention Program. *Annal Behav Med* 2007, **33**(1): 57–68.
15 Telch, C.F., Telch, M.J.: Group coping skills instruction and supportive group therapy for cancer patients: A comparison of strategies. *J Consult Clin Psychol* 1986, **54**(6): 802–808.
16 McCallie, M.S., Blum, C.M., Hood, C.J.: Progressive muscle relaxation. *J Hum Behav Soc Environ* 2006, **13**(3): 51–66.
17 Brown, R.P., Gerbarg, P.L.: Sudarshan Kriya yogic breathing in the treatment of stress, anxiety, and depression: Part I – Neurophysiologic model. *J Alter Complement Med* 2005, **11**(1): 189–201.
18 Nakao, M., Yano, E., Nomura, S., Kuboki, T.: Blood pressure-lowering effects of biofeedback treatment in hypertension: A meta-analysis of randomized controlled trials. *Hypertension Res* 2003, **26**(1): 37–46.
19 Kellow, J.E., Langeluddecke, P.M., Eckersley, G.M., Jones, M.P., Tennant, C.C.: Progressive muscular relaxation and motility of the small intestine: Studies in normal subjects and patients with irritable bowel syndrome. *J Gastrointest Motil* 1992, **4**(1): 47–52.
20 Park, S.H., Han, K.S., Kang, C.B.: Relaxation therapy for irritable bowel syndrome: A systematic review. *Asian Nurs Res* 2014, **8**(3): 182–192.
21 Blanchard, E.B., Greene, B., Scharff, L., Schwarz-McMorris, S.P.: Relaxation training as a treatment for irritable bowel syndrome. *Biofeedback Self-Regulation* 1993, **18**(3): 125–132.
22 Blanchard, E.B., Radnitz, C., Schwarz, S.P., Neff, D.F., Gerardi, M.A.: Psychological changes associated with self-regulatory treatments of irritable bowel syndrome. *Biofeedback Self-Regulation* 1987, **12**(1): 31–37.

23 Blanchard, E.B., Schwarz, S.P., Neff, D.F.: Two-year follow-up of behavioral treatment of irritable bowel syndrome. *Behav Ther* 1988, **19**(1): 67–73.

24 Lynch, P.M., Zamble, E.: Stress management training for irritable bowel syndrome: A preliminary investigation. *Clin Biofeedback Health* 1987, **10**(2): 123–134

25 Schwarz, S.P., Taylor, A.E., Scharff, L., Blanchard, E.B.: Behaviorally treated irritable bowel syndrome patients: A four-year follow-up. *Behav Res Ther* 1990, **28**(4): 331–335.

26 Shaw, G., Srivastava, E.D., Sadlier, M., Swann, P., James, J.Y., Rhodes, J.: Stress management for irritable bowel syndrome: A controlled trial. *Digestion* 1991, **50**(1): 36–42.

27 Van Der Veek, P.P.J., Van Rood, Y.R., Masclee, A.A.M.: Clinical trial: Short- and long-term benefit of relaxation training for irritable bowel syndrome. *Aliment Pharm Ther* 2007, **26**(6): 943–952.

28 Leahy, A., Clayman, C., Mason, I., Lloyd, G., Epstein, O.: Computerised biofeedback games: A new method for teaching stress management and its use in irritable bowel syndrome. *J R Coll Phys London* 1998, **32**(6): 552–556.

29 Shinozaki, M., Kanazawa, M., Kano, M., Endo, Y., Nakaya, N., Hongo, M., Fukudo, S.: Effect of autogenic training on general improvement in patients with irritable bowel syndrome: A randomized controlled trial. *Appl Psychophysiol Biofeedback* 2010, **35**(3): 189–198.

30 Eriksson, E.M., Möller, I.E., Söderberg, R.H., Eriksson, H.T., Kurlberg, G.K.: Body awareness therapy: A new strategy for relief of symptoms in irritable bowel syndrome patients. *WJG* 2007, **13**(23): 3206–3214.

31 Zijdenbos, I.L., De Wit, N.J., Van Der Heijden, G.J., Rubin, G., Quartero, A.O.: Psychological treatments for the management of irritable bowel syndrome. *Cochrane Database Sys Rev* 2009, **1**: CD006442.

32 Ford, A.C., Moayyedi, P., Lacy, B.E., Lembo, A.J., Saito, Y.A., Schiller, L.R., Soffer, E.E., Spiegel, B.M.R., Quigley, E.M.M.: American college of gastroenterology monograph on the management of irritable bowel syndrome and chronic idiopathic constipation. *Am J Gastroenterol* 2014, **109**(Suppl 1): S2–S26.

33 Neff, D.F., Blanchard, E.B.: A multi-component treatment for irritable bowel syndrome. *Behav Ther* 1987, **18**(1): 70–83.

34 Zomorodi, S., Tabatabaee, S.K.R., Arbabi, M., Falah, P.A., Daryani, N.E.: Comparative efficacy of cognitive-behavioral therapy and mindfulness therapy on reducing symptoms and improving quality of life in patients with the irritable bowel syndrome. *Biomed Pharm J* 2014, **7**(1): 63–74.

35 Kabat-Zinn, J.: Mindfulness-based interventions in context: Past, present, and future. *Clin Psychol Sci Pract* 2003, **10**(2): 144–156.

36 Reibel, D.K., Greeson, J.M., Brainard, G.C., Rosenzweig, S.: Mindfulness-based stress reduction and health-related quality of life in a heterogeneous patient population. *Gen Hosp Psychiat* 2001, **23**(4): 183–192.

37 Hofmann, S.G., Sawyer, A.T., Witt, A.A., Oh, D.: The effect of mindfulness-based therapy on anxiety and depression: A meta-analytic review. *J Consul Clin Psychol* 2010, **78**(2): 169–183.

38 Niazi, A.K., Niazi, S.K.: Mindfulness-based stress reduction: A non-pharmacological approach for chronic illnesses. *N Am J Med Sci* 2011, **3**(1): 20–23.

39 Fjorback, L.O., Arendt, M., Ørnbøl, E., Fink, P., Walach, H.: Mindfulness-based stress reduction and mindfulness-based cognitive therapy – a systematic review of randomized controlled trials. *Acta Psych Scand* 2011, **124**(2): 102–119.

40 Bamber, M.D., Kraenzle Schneider, J.: Mindfulness-based meditation to decrease stress and anxiety in college students: A narrative synthesis of the research. *Edu Res Rev* 2016, **18**: 1–32.

41 Aucoin, M., Lalonde-Parsi, M.J., Cooley, K.: Mindfulness-based therapies in the treatment of functional gastrointestinal disorders: A Meta-analysis. *Evid Complement Alter Med* 2014, 2014: 140724.

42 Gaylord, S.A., Palsson, O.S., Garland, E.L., Faurot, K.R., Coble, R.S., Mann, J.D., Frey, W., Leniek, K., Whitehead, W.E.: Mindfulness training reduces the severity of irritable bowel

syndrome in women: Results of a randomized controlled trial. *Am J Gastroenterol* 2011, **106**(9): 1678–1688.

43 Zomorrodi, S., Tabatabaie, S.K.R., Azadfallah, P., Ebrahimidaryani, N., Arbabi, M.: Long term effects of mindfulness on quality of life in irritable bowel syndrome. *Iran J Psychiat* 2015, **10**(2): 100–105.

44 Kearney, D.J., McDermott, K., Martinez, M., Simpson, T.L.: Association of participation in a mindfulness programme with bowel symptoms, gastrointestinal symptom-specific anxiety and quality of life. *Aliment Pharmacol Ther* 2011, **34**(3): 363–373.

45 Kim, S., Chang, L.: A mindful way through IBS: Reducing abdominal pain and improving quality of life. *Gastroenterology* 2012, **142**(5): 1247–1250.

46 Lakhan, S.E., Schofield, K.L.: Mindfulness-based therapies in the treatment of somatization disorders: A systematic review and meta-analysis. *PLoS ONE* 2013, **8**(8): e71834.

47 Berrill, J.W., Sadlier, M., Hood, K., Green, J.T.: Mindfulness-based therapy for inflammatory bowel disease patients with functional abdominal symptoms or high perceived stress levels. *J Crohn's Colitis* 2014, **8**(9): 945–955.

48 Kafi, M., Afshar, H., Moghtadaei, K., Ariaporan, S., Daghaghzadeh, H., Salamat, M.: Effectiveness of mindfulness-based cognitive-therapy on psychological signs women with irritable bowel syndrome. *Koomesh* 2014, **15**(2): 255–264.

49 Zernicke, K.A., Campbell, T.S., Blustein, P.K., Fung, T.S., Johnson, J.A., Bacon, S.L., Carlson, L.E.: Mindfulness-based stress reduction for the treatment of irritable bowel syndrome symptoms: A randomized wait-list controlled trial. *Int J Behav Med* 2013, **20**(3): 385–396.

50 Deechakawan, W., Cain, K.C., Jarrett, M.E., Burr, R.L., Heitkemper, M.M.: Effect of self-management intervention on cortisol and daily stress levels in irritable bowel syndrome. *Biol Res Nurs* 2013, **15**(1): 26–36.

51 Deechakawan, W., Heitkemper, M.M., Cain, K.C., Burr, R.L., Jarrett, M.E.: Anxiety, depression, and catecholamine levels after self-management intervention in irritable bowel syndrome. *Gastroenterol Nurs* 2014, **37**(1): 24–32.

52 Jarrett, M.E., Cain, K.C., Burr, R.L., Hertig, V.L., Rosen, S.N., Heitkemper, M.M.: Comprehensive self-management for irritable bowel syndrome: Randomized trial of in-person vs. combined in-person and telephone sessions. *Am J Gastroenterol* 2009, **104**(12): 3004–3014.

53 Blanchard, E.B., Schwarz, S.P., Neff, D.F., Gerardi, M.A.: Prediction of outcome from the self-regulatory treatment of irritable bowel syndrome. *Behav Res Ther* 1988, **26**(2): 187–190.

54 Blanchard, E.B., Schwarz, S.P., Suls, J.M., Gerardi, M.A., Scharff, L., Greene, B., Taylor, A.E., Berreman, C., Malamood, H.S.: Two controlled evaluations of multicomponent psychological treatment of irritable bowel syndrome. *Behav Res Ther* 1992, **30**(2): 175–189.

55 Zomorodi, S., Abdi, S., Tabatabaee, S.K.R.: Comparison of long-term effects of cognitive-behavioral therapy versus mindfulness-based therapy on reduction of symptoms among patients suffering from irritable bowel syndrome. *Gastroenterol Hepatol Bed Bench* 2014, **7**(2): 118–124.

56 Keefer, L., Blanchard, E.B.: The effects of relaxation response meditation on the symptoms of irritable bowel syndrome: Results of a controlled treatment study. *Behav Res Ther* 2001, **39**(7): 801–811.

57 Lahmann, C., Röhricht, F., Sauer, N., Noll-Hussong, M., Ronel, J., Henrich, G., Von Arnim, A., Loew, T.: Functional relaxation as complementary therapy in irritable bowel syndrome: A randomized, controlled clinical trial. *J Alter Complement Med* 2010, **16**(1): 47–52.

58 Lindfors, P., Unge, P., Arvidsson, P., Nyhlin, H., Björnsson, E., Abrahamsson, H., Simrén, M.: Effects of gut-directed hypnotherapy on IBS in different clinical settings – results from two randomized, controlled trials. *Am J Gastroenterol* 2012, **107**(2): 276–285.

59 Moser, G., Trägner, S., Gajowniczek, E.E., Mikulits, A., Michalski, M., Kazemi-Shirazi, L., Kulnigg-Dabsch, S., Führer, M., Ponocny-Seliger, E., Dejaco, C., *et al.*: Long-term

success of GUT-directed group hypnosis for patients with refractory irritable bowel syndrome: A randomized controlled trial. *Am J Gastroenterol* 2013, **108**(4): 602–609.

60 Roberts, L., Wilson, S., Singh, S., Roalfe, A., Greenfield, S.: Gut-directed hypnotherapy for irritable bowel syndrome: Piloting a primary care-based randomised controlled trial. *Br J Gen Pract* 2006, **56**(523): 115–121.

61 Whorwell, P.J., Prior, A., Faragher, E.B.: Controlled trial of hypnotherapy in the treatment of severe refractory irritable-bowel syndrome. *Lancet* 1984, **324**(8414): 1232–1234.

62 Arn, I., Theorell, T., Uvnäs-Moberg, K., Jonsson, C.O.: Psychodrama group therapy for patients with functional gastrointestinal disorders – a controlled long-term follow-up study. *Psychother Psychosom* 1989, **51**(3): 113–119.

63 Voirol, M.W., Hipolito, J.: Relaxation in the treatment of irritable gut: Results after 40 months. *Schweizerische Medizinische Wochenschrift* 1987, **117**(29): 1117–1119.

Chapter 18

Diagnostic and treatment approaches associated with centrally mediated abdominal pain syndrome (CAPS)

Ami D. Sperber

This chapter aims to review and raise awareness of centrally mediated abdominal pain syndrome (CAPS), a poorly recognized functional gastrointestinal disorder. It will focus on the major contribution of central pain processing in the disorder and in doing so address differences in the way doctors and patients may explain the symptoms.

Learning points

- CAPS is a relatively uncommon functional GI disorder.
- Its prevalence is unclear, but has been reported in the range of 0.5%–2.0%.
- The predominant symptom is persistent abdominal pain unrelated to physiological events.
- CAPS patients have high rates of functional and psychosocial comorbidity.
- The major pathophysiological feature is central sensitization rather than visceral hypersensitivity.
- CAPS patients are often considered to be particularly difficult to treat.
- A positive doctor-patient therapeutic partnership is the basis for successful treatment.
- Treatment programs should be tailored to the patient and include a combination of pharmacological and non-pharmacological therapies.

Introduction

One of the less-recognized and less prevalent functional gastrointestinal disorders (FGID), centrally mediated abdominal pain syndrome (CAPS) was previously known as the functional abdominal pain syndrome (FAPS). In the Rome IV diagnostic classification, it is listed as a centrally mediated disorder of gastrointestinal pain. CAPS, a challenging disorder for both clinicians and researchers, is often misdiagnosed as severe irritable bowel syndrome (IBS). While CAPS patients may also have irregular bowel movements, the latter are not associated with the abdominal pain as in IBS (see Figure 18.1). Because it is relatively uncommon and potentially underdiagnosed, it is often not included in epidemiological and pathophysiological studies of FGIDs, or in clinical treatment trials.

Although there are some reports of prevalence rates for CAPS, little is actually known about its prevalence or associated factors. It is clearly less common

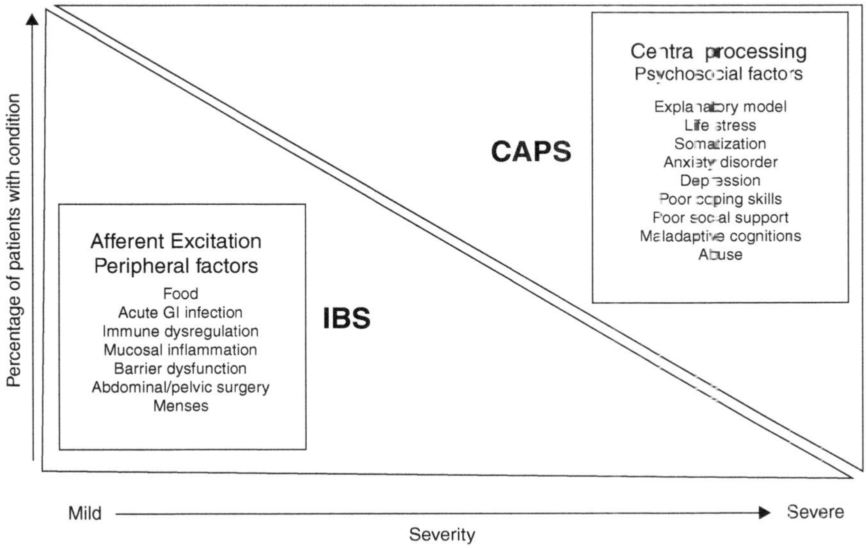

Figure 18.1 Modified from: Sperber A.D., Drossman D.A. 2011, 'Review Article: The Functional Abdominal Pain Syndrome', *Aliment Pharmacol Ther*, vol. 33, pp. 514–24 [5].

than IBS and other FGIDs, with a prevalence rate reported to range between 0.5% and 2.1% [1]. These rates are based on varying diagnostic criteria and research methods, so, as with IBS [2], the actual prevalence rate of CAPS is unclear. Some studies have shown it to be more prevalent in women than in men [1, 3]. As would be expected in a condition with high clinical severity, the consultation rate with gastroenterologists is high compared to other conditions, at least based on data from the UK [4]. The same UK study also reported a high rate of abdominal and pelvic surgery in CAPS patients.

While all FGIDs have a mix of peripheral and central pathophysiological components, one of the features of CAPS is its dominant central contribution. As can be seen in Figure 18.1, one reason that CAPS may be confused with severe IBS is that central mechanisms also become more prominent in IBS as its severity increases. In contrast to IBS, the relative prevalence of CAPS increases with the level of severity, whereas in IBS it decreases.

In contrast to IBS, a multifactorial disorder, CAPS appears to predominantly involve abnormal processing of normal visceral input through impaired central mechanisms, a process often referred to as central sensitization. As stated by Woolf:

> Central sensitization introduces another dimension, one where the CNS can change, distort or amplify pain, increasing its degree, duration and spatial extent in a manner that no longer directly reflects the specific qualities of peripheral noxious stimuli, but rather the particular functional states

> of circuits in the CNS. With the discovery of central sensitization, pain conceptually at least had become 'centralized' instead of being exclusively peripherally driven.
>
> (pp. S3–S4) [6]

Thus, although the initial stimulus may be peripheral, when central sensitization develops the symptoms become chronic even though the original stimulus is no longer operative.

Chronic pain and its subjective experience have a multidimensional nature involving the interaction of sensory-discriminative, affective-motivational and cognitive evaluative components [7]. This is one of the bases of the effectiveness of behavioural therapy in the treatment of chronic abdominal pain [8].

The results of a study conducted in Japan lend support to the presence of central pain sensitivity in CAPS [9]. In this small-scale study, the authors assessed 13 healthy controls, 7 patients with IBS and 6 with CAPS, by looking at sensitivity thresholds to rectal balloon distention. They found that while the patients with IBS had low thresholds and were thus hypersensitive to this peripheral stimulation, the patients with CAPS had normal thresholds to rectal distention, even though they suffered clinically from severe abdominal pain. Thus, their pain could not be attributed to peripheral mechanisms, such as visceral hypersensitivity.

Differential diagnosis

The Rome IV diagnostic criteria for CAPS are shown in Table 18.1.

Since many gastrointestinal diseases are characterized by abdominal pain, the differential diagnosis is broad. However, a careful history, focused physical

Table 18.1 Centrally mediated abdominal pain syndrome* (CAPS),

D1 Diagnostic criteria* for Centrally Mediated Abdominal Pain Syndrome**
Must include **all** of the following:

1. Continuous or nearly continuous abdominal pain
2. No or only occasional relationship of pain with physiological events (e.g., eating, defecation or menses)†
3. Pain limits some aspect of daily functioning.††
4. The pain is not feigned.
5. Pain is not explained by another structural or functional gastrointestinal disorder or other medical condition.

* CAPS is typically associated with psychosocial comorbidity, but there is no specific profile that can be used for diagnosis.

** Criteria fulfilled for the last three months with symptom onset at least six months prior to diagnosis

† Some degree of gastrointestinal dysfunction may be present.

†† Daily function could include impairments in work, intimacy, social/leisure, family life and caregiving for self or others.

Diagnostic criteria taken from P.J. Whorwell, L. Keefer, D.A. Drossman, E. Guthrie, M. Simrén, K. Tillisch and K. Olden [10], Centrally Mediated Disorders of Gastrointestinal Pain, Chapter 12, page 1066 of the *Rome IV Functional Gastrointestinal Disorders: Disorders of Gut-Brain Interaction*. Reproduction approved by Professor Douglas Drossman 23/10/2016.

examination and a minimal workup should be enough to reach the diagnosis. The most common difficulty is differentiating CAPS from severe IBS. Compared to IBS, in patients with CAPS it is clear that pain is their worst symptom and that it is not associated with physiological events. The pain is usually constant and daily, without periods or even days of relief. Other common disorders that can be confused with CAPS are chronic pelvic pain, including endometriosis, and possibly post-surgical adhesions, although the evidence for an association between adhesions and chronic abdominal pain is not clear. If the pain is in the upper right or mid-abdomen the origin of the pain could be gastroduodenal, gallbladder or sphincter of Oddi. If the pain has a clear temporal association with eating, especially in older patients, chronic mesenteric ischemia must be considered.

Common patient concerns and issues associated with CAPS

The concept of central sensitization may be difficult for doctors to grasp. It can lead to a 'paradoxical' situation in that while the pain experience is real, it is no longer caused by noxious peripheral stimulation. This may lend support to the statement that patients often hear from doctors that 'there's nothing wrong with you' or 'it's all in your head'. Basically, these patients are labelled as having a psychosomatic disorder (with a negative connotation) or somatization. If doctors lack the skill to legitimize what may be perceived as imagined pain it becomes very difficult for them to communicate with or treat patients with these conditions. The doctor-patient dialogue can become ineffective or even detrimental, leading to frustration and dissatisfaction on both sides, especially if psychosocial and cultural factors play a central role in symptom generation, severity, interpretation and reporting.

Eliciting the patient's understanding, concerns and outcome expectations is critical to the nurturing of a positive therapeutic doctor-patient relationship, the cornerstone of care for these patients. Patients have symptom- or disease-related beliefs that affect their concerns, anxieties and expectations from the health-care process. This set of beliefs has been called the explanatory model [11]. The patient's explanatory model is often manifested in illness beliefs [12], symptom expression and learned coping patterns.

Medical and allied health standard care treatment approaches for CAPS

Doctor-patient partnership

As in IBS, the development of a therapeutic relationship with an empathetic, non-judgemental listening style is the basis for treatment of CAPS patients [13]. It is essential to elucidate the patient's expectations from treatment (often complete cure) and to formulate realistic expectations for symptom reduction and improvement of quality of life. This can be explained on the basis of models of chronic disease, where the goal of treatment is to gain control of rather than cure the disease. To do this the treating doctor has to take into account not only the physiological basis of the disorder but also the psychosocial aspects.

Several simple questions that patients ask themselves in formulating an explanatory model can be explored by the doctor. These include: *What caused my sickness? Why did I become sick? How does the illness work inside my body? What will this illness do to me? How should it be treated*? If the doctor can explain symptoms in a way that is understood and accepted by the patient, this can be reassuring and disrupt the vicious cycle of increasing anxiety, hypervigilance and symptom severity.

The treatment strategy should be agreed upon by the doctor and the patient, with the patient playing an active role. The doctor presents various treatment options, including pharmacological and non-pharmacological, and then a mutual decision is reached as to the initial course to follow. Based on the strategy of augmentation therapy, as developed for the care of patients with depression, a combination of these options is usually more beneficial than monotherapy [14]. Finally, since IBS is a chronic disorder, continuity of care is essential and can increase the chance of achieving the agreed-upon treatment goals, with the patient learning to take control of symptoms and care [15].

Summary of the current evidence base regarding medical and allied health standard care treatment approaches for IBS

Symptomatic therapy – namely, for pain, diarrhoea, constipation and flatulence – is not effective in CAPS, so the treatment strategy should focus on centrally active treatments, both pharmacological and non-pharmacological. The discussion ahead is based on data on severe IBS because there are no good data on treatment in CAPS (Table 18.2). The assumption is that since severe IBS has a strong component of central sensitization, the treatment strategy should be effective in CAPS as well.

Non-pharmacological treatment

Three types of non-pharmacological therapy have been shown in clinical trials to be effective in severe IBS. These are hypnosis, cognitive behavioural therapy

Table 18.2 Summary of the current evidence base regarding medical and allied health approaches.

Treatment approach	*Level of evidence*
Medical/ pharmaceutical/ psychological/ behavioural	There is no good scientific evidence for the effectiveness of any treatment for CAPS. Treatment assumptions are based on treatment of severe IBS (see Chapter 12 of this book).

(CBT) and dynamic interpersonal psychotherapy [16]. These modalities are not available in all settings, but where available should be utilized if the patient is receptive. These behavioural treatments can be cost-effective in the treatment of chronic pain [17]. One problem in treating CAPS patients is that they often deny the psychosocial components of their illness and are focused on 'organic' causes and treatment. Part of the 'art' of clinical care is to help patients overcome this barrier and see their illness in a holistic context [15]. Moreover, patients with CAPS perceive their symptoms and condition in a catastrophic context and are usually not aware of these maladaptive thought patterns. CBT can help the patient to recognize these thoughts, understand their relevance to symptom generation and develop ways to increase control over them [18]. Hypnosis, which has been studied extensively in IBS, has been shown to have a long-term beneficial effect [19]. Other potentially beneficial modalities that have not been studied enough to make evidence-based recommendations are acceptance commitment therapy [20], mindfulness-based stress reduction [21] and biofeedback, although one study from Iran concluded that mindfulness therapy is better than CBT for IBS [22].

Recently a literature review of Chinese herbal medicine for CAPS was published. Although many studies were reviewed, their overall quality was low and the authors could not reach any solid conclusions or recommendations regarding this treatment modality [23].

Pharmacological treatment

Because CAPS patients have severe debilitating pain that has a negative effect on daily function they often demand pain-killing agents, in particular narcotics. This is especially the case in busy overloaded family and community practices and in emergency rooms. Add to this the lack of recognition of CAPS, as discussed earlier, and these drugs can be prescribed inappropriately. As a result some CAPS patients may develop the narcotic bowel syndrome, another centrally mediated abdominal pain syndrome, with its ensuing spiral of escalating pain with increasing pain-killer doses [24]. Thus, in chronic pain conditions these agents should be avoided. The main alternative is treatment with psychotropic agents that can have the double advantage of treating the chronic pain condition as well as psychological comorbidity.

The use of antidepressants and other psychotropic agents is well chronicled in severe IBS [25, 26] with an number needed to treat (NNT) of four. Tricyclic antidepressants have been shown to be beneficial in a meta-analysis [27]. They and serotonin-noradrenaline reuptake inhibitors (SNRIs) are used in chronic pain syndromes, including fibromyalgia [28] as well as cancer and noncancer neuropathic pain, although their true effectiveness is not clear in some of these conditions due to the low quality of the studies [29]. Knowledge of the receptor activity profile and potential adverse effects can facilitate the tailored selection of specific agents to individual patients.

Practical recommendations

- Differentiate from other sources of pain – gynaecological, urological and so forth.
- Verify perception of pain as the predominant symptom.
- Elicit associated psychosocial factors and cultural influences.
- Document psychological comorbidity – primarily anxiety, depression and somatization.
- Rule out alarm features, or conduct additional testing when indicated.
- Develop a therapeutic partnership based on the patient's explanatory model.
- Use combination therapy rather than monotherapy.

Current limitations/future considerations

- Our knowledge and understanding of CAPS are limited and relevant studies are negligible.
- Most of our assumptions, including modalities of treatment, are based on severe IBS.
- More focus should be centred on the training of doctors to understand and treat patients with centrally mediated pain disorders.
- Basic research and clinical trials should be conducted on CAPS. Because of the low prevalence rates, multicentre studies will be required to achieve this end.

Acknowledgments, competing interests, and funding

The author is unaware of any competing interests in relation to this chapter. No external funding was received for this chapter.

References

1 Drossman, D.A., Li, Z., Andruzzi, E., Temple, R.D., Talley, N.J., Thompson, W.G., Whitehead, W.E., Janssens, J., Funch-Jensen, P., Corrazziari, E.: U.S. householder survey of functional GI disorders: Prevalence, sociodemography and health impact. *Dig Dis Sci* 1993, **38**: 1569–1580.

2 Sperber, A.D., Dumitrascu, D., Fukudo, S., Gerson, C., Ghoshal, U.C., Gwee, K.A., Hungin, A.P., Kang, J.Y., Minhu, C., Schmulson, M., *et al.*: The global prevalence of IBS in adults remains elusive due to the heterogeneity of studies: A Rome Foundation working team literature review. *Gut* 2016.

3 Thompson, W.G., Irvine, E.J., Pare, P., Ferrazzi, S., Rance, L.: Functional gastrointestinal disorders in Canada: First population-based survey using Rome II criteria with suggestions for improving the questionnaire. *Dig Dis Sci* 2002, **47**: 225–235.

4 Maxton, D.G., Whorwell, P.J.: Use of medical resources and attitudes to health care of patients with "chronic abdominal pain". *Br J Med Econ* 1992, **2**: 75–79.

5 Sperber, A.D., Drossman, D.A.: Review article: The functional abdominal pain syndrome. *Aliment Pharmacol Ther* 2011, **33**(5): 514–524.

6 Woolf, C.J.: Central sensitization: Implications for the diagnosis and treatment of pain. *Pain* 2011, **152**(3 Suppl): S2–15.

7 Moayedi, M., Davis, K.D.: Theories of pain: From specificity to gate control. *J Neurophysiol* 2013, **109**: 5–12.

8 Keefer, L., Mandal, S.: The potential role of behavioral therapies in the management of centrally mediated abdominal pain. *Neurogastroenterol Motil* 2015, **27**: 313–323.

9 Nozu, T., Kudaira, M.: Altered rectal sensory response induced by balloon distention in patients with functional abdominal pain syndrome. *Biopsychosoc Med* 2009, **3**: 13.
10 Whorwell, P.J., Keefer, L., Drossman, D.A., Guthrie, E., Simrén, M., Tillisch, K., Olden, K.: Centrally mediated disorders of gastrointestinal pain. In: *Rome IV functional gastrointestinal disorders: Disorders of gut-brain interaction*. Edited by Chang, L., Chey, W.D., Kellow, J., Tack, J., Whitehead, W.E., The Rome IV Committees. Raleigh, NC: Rome Foundation, 2016: 1059–1116.
11 Eisenberg, L.: Disease and illness: Distinctions between professional and popular ideas of sickness. *Cult Med Psychiatry* 1977, **1**: 9–23.
12 Rothschild, S.K.: Cross-cultural issues in primary care medicine. *Dis Mon* 1998, **44**: 293–319.
13 Drossman, D.A.: Psychosocial sound bites: Exercises in the patient-doctor relationship. *Am J Gastroenterol* 1997, **92**: 1418–1423.
14 Trivedi, M.H., Fava, M., Wisniewski, S.R., Thase, M.E., Quitkin, F., Warden, D., Ritz, L., Nierenberg, A.A., Lebowitz, B.D., Biggs, M.M. *et al.*: Medication augmentation after the failure of SSRIs for depression. *N Engl J Med* 2006, **354**: 1243–1252.
15 Sperber, A.: Treating IBS patients: The science of the art of medicine. *US Gastroenterology Review* 2006: 73–75.
16 Creed, F., Fernandes, L., Guthrie, E., Palmer, S., Ratcliffe, J., Read, N., Rigby, C., Thompson, D., Tomenson, B.: The cost-effectiveness of psychotherapy and paroxetine for severe irritable bowel syndrome. *Gastroenterology* 2003, **124**: 303–317.
17 Lamb, S.E., Hansen, Z., Lall, R., Castelnuovo, E., Withers, E.J., Nichols, V., Potter, R., Underwood, M.R., Back Skills Training Trial i.: Group cognitive behavioural treatment for low-back pain in primary care: A randomised controlled trial and cost-effectiveness analysis. *Lancet* 2010, **375**: 916–923.
18 Drossman, D.A., Toner, B.B., Whitehead, W.E., Diamant, N.E., Dalton C.B., Duncan, S., Emmott, S., Proffitt, V., Akman, D., Frusciante, K *et al.*: Cognitive-behavioral therapy versus education and desipramine versus placebo for moderate to severe functional bowel disorders. *Gastroenterology* 2003, **125**: 19–31.
19 Gonsalkorale, W.M., Miller, V., Afzal, A., Whorwell, P.J.: Long term benefits of hypnotherapy for irritable bowel syndrome. *Gut* 2003, **52**: 1623–1629.
20 Dahl, J., Lundgren, T.: Acceptance and Commitment Therapy (ACT) in the treatment of chronic pain. In: *Mindfulness-based treatment approaches: Clinician's guide to evidence base and applications*. Edited by Baer, R.A. Burlington, VT: Academic Press, 2006: 285–306.
21 Kabat-Zinn, J., Lipworth, L., Burney, R.: The clinical use of mindfulness meditation for the self-regulation of chronic pain. *J Behav Med* 1985, **8**: 163–190
22 Zomorodi, S., Abdi, S., Tabatabaee, S.K.: Comparison of long-term effects of cognitive-behavioral therapy versus mindfulness-based therapy on reduction of symptoms among patients suffering from irritable bowel syndrome. *Gastroenterol Hepatol Bed Bench* 2014, **7**: 118–124.
23 Liu, T., Wang, N., Zhang, L., Zhong, L.: Chinese herbal medicine for functional abdominal pain syndrome: From clinical findings to basic understandings. *Evid Based Complement Alternat Med* 2016, **2016**, Epub 2016: 8652523.
24. Grunkemeier, D.M., Cassara, J.E., Dalton, C.B., Drossman, D.A.: The narcotic bowel syndrome: Clinical features, pathophysiology, and management. *Clin Gastroenterol Hepatol* 2007, **5**: 1126–1139.
25 Drossman, D.A.: Beyond tricyclics: New ideas for treating patients with painful and refractory functional gastrointestinal symptoms. *Am J Gastroenterol* 2009, **104**: 2897–2902.
26 Dekel, R., Drossman, D.A., Sperber, A.D.: The use of psychotropic drugs in irritable bowel syndrome. *Expert Opin Investig Drugs* 2013, **22**: 329–339.
27 Ford, A.C., Talley, N.J., Schoenfeld, P.S., Quigley, E.M.M., Moayyedi, P.: Efficacy of antidepressants and psychological therapies in irritable bowel syndrome: Systematic review and meta-analysis. *Gut* 2009, **58**: 367–378.
28 Moret, C., Briley, M.: Antidepressants in the treatment of fibromyalgia. *Neuropsychiatr Dis Treat* 2006, **2**: 537–548.
29 van den Beuken-van Everdingen, M.H., de Graeff, A., Jongen, J.L., Dijkstra, D., Mostovaya, I., Vissers, K.C.: Pharmacological Treatment of Pain in Cancer Patients: The Role of Adjuvant Analgesics, a Systematic Review. *Pain Pract* 2017, **17**(3): 409–419.

Chapter 19

Diagnostic and treatment approaches associated with functional gallbladder and sphincter of Oddi disorders

David O. Prichard

In the absence of overt organic pathology, biliary-type pain is attributed to dysfunction of the gallbladder or sphincter of Oddi: functional gallbladder disorder (FGBD) and functional biliary sphincter disorder (FBSD) respectively. The aim of this chapter is to provide an overview for the management of these conditions in a biopsychosocial context.

Learning points

- Correctly identifying biliary-type pain is the cornerstone for diagnosing functional biliary disorders.
- Education and reassurance regarding the benign nature of these diseases are crucial in managing individuals with these conditions.
- Functional gallbladder disorders can be managed surgically. Moderate-quality data suggest beneficial outcomes in selected individuals.
- Functional biliary sphincter disorder can be treated successfully by pharmacological means. In selected patients, endoscopic sphincterotomy may offer benefit.
- Functional pancreatic sphincter disorder requires stringent diagnosis prior to considering endoscopic sphincterotomy.

Introduction

Biliary-type pain (right upper quadrant or epigastric pain lasting greater than 30 minutes) in the absence of organic pathology is attributed to functional gallbladder disorder (FGBD) or functional biliary sphincter disorder (FBSD) [1]. The prevalence of biliary pain in patients with intact gallbladders and without sonographic evidence of gallstones ranges from 2% to 27% [2, 3]. The bidirectional relationship between gallstone pathophysiology (cholesterol saturation, crystals, microlithiasis and gallstones) and disordered biliary motility, in combination with the high rate of gallstone genesis in patients who report biliary-type pain, ensures that occult gallstone disease and FGBD are difficult to differentiate clinically [3, 4]. Where biliary-type pain presents in a post-cholecystectomy patient, FBSD is suggested. FBSD is estimated to affect 1.5%–5% of the general population, with a female preponderance [2, 3, 5].

The socioeconomic consequences of these disorders are substantial. Almost half of cholecystectomies performed in the US are performed for FGBD. Moreover, although difficult to compare directly with current diagnostic criteria, data suggest that a diagnosis of sphincter of Oddi dysfunction (SOD, which encompasses FBSD, papillary stenosis, pancreatic sphincter dysfunction and other conditions also) is associated with impaired quality of life and significant absenteeism from work [5, 6]. The pancreatic corollary of FBSD is functional pancreatic sphincter dysfunction (FPSD). This condition is suggested clinically by recurrent acute pancreatitis in the absence of other aetiologies.

Diagnostic criteria for functional gallbladder disorder and sphincter of Oddi disorders

Rome IV criteria define FGBD or FBSD based on the presence of biliary-type pain, the results of diagnostic testing and a patient's response to cholecystectomy (see Table 19.1) [7]. The current diagnosis of FBSD (requiring pain and *either* biliary dilation or abnormal liver function tests) differs from

Table 19.1 Diagnostic criteria for functional gallbladder and sphincter of Oddi (SO) disorders.

E1. Biliary pain[1] Diagnostic criteria Pain located in the epigastrium and/or right upper quadrant and all of the following: 1. Builds up to a steady level and lasts 30 minutes or longer 2. Occurring at different intervals (not daily) 3. Severe enough to interrupt daily activities or lead to an emergency department visit 4. Not significantly (<20%) related to bowel movements 5. Not significantly (<20%) relieved by postural change or acid suppression Supportive criteria The pain may be associated with: 1. Nausea and vomiting 2. Radiation to the back and/or right infra subscapular region 3. Waking from sleep
E1a. Functional gallbladder disorder[2] Diagnostic criteria Must include **both** of the following: 1. Criteria for biliary pain* 2. Absence of gallstones or other structural pathology Supportive criteria 1. Low ejection fraction on gallbladder scintigraphy 2. Normal liver enzymes, conjugated bilirubin and amylase/lipase * Criteria for biliary pain: Pain located in the epigastrium and/or right upper quadrant and all of the following: 1. Builds up to a steady level and lasts 30 minutes or longer. 2. Occurring at different intervals (not daily). 3. Severe enough to interrupt daily activities or lead to an emergency department visit. 4. Not significantly (<20%) related to bowel movements. 5. Not significantly (<20%) relieved by postural change or acid suppression.

(*Continued*)

Table 19.1 (Continued)

E1b. Functional biliary sphincter of Oddi disorder[3]
Diagnostic criteria Must include **all** of the following:
1. Criteria for biliary pain*
2. Elevated liver enzymes or dilated bile duct, but not both
3. Absence of bile duct stones or other structural abnormalities

Supportive criteria
1. Normal amylase/lipase
2. Abnormal sphincter of Oddi manometry
3. Hepatobiliary scintigraphy

* Criteria for biliary pain: Pain located in the epigastrium and/or right upper quadrant and all of the following: 1. Builds up to a steady level and lasts 30 minutes or longer. 2. Occurring at different intervals (not daily). 3. Severe enough to interrupt daily activities or lead to an emergency department visit. 4. Not significantly (<20%) related to bowel movements. 5. Not significantly (<20%) relieved by postural change or acid suppression.

E2. Functional pancreatic sphincter of Oddi disorder[4]
Diagnostic criteria Must include **all** of the following:
1. Documented recurrent episodes of pancreatitis (typical pain with amylase or lipase >3 times normal and/or imaging evidence of acute pancreatitis)
2. Other aetiologies of pancreatitis excluded
3. Negative endoscopic ultrasound
4. Abnormal sphincter manometry

* Diagnostic criteria taken from G.H. Elta, P.B. Cotton, C.R. Carter, E.S. Corazziari and P.J. Pasricha [1], Gallbladder and Sphincter of Oddi Disorders, Chapter 13, pages [1]1131, [2]1133, [3]1144, [4]1162 of the *Rome IV Functional Gastrointestinal Disorders: Disorders of Gut-Brain Interaction*. Reproduction approved by Professor Douglas Drossman 23/10/2016.

the previously utilized Milwaukee Classification, which categorized SOD into three subgroups [8]. FBSD equates to biliary SOD type II in that classification system. Biliary-type pain in association with both dilation and abnormal liver function tests was termed SOD type I; it is now regarded as a fixed organic papillary stenosis. Pain in the absence of either (previously SOD type III) is now regarded as non-biliary in origin. Diagnosing FPSD requires documented recurrent episodes of acute pancreatitis, the exclusion of alternate aetiologies of recurrent acute pancreatitis, a normal endoscopic ultrasound and documentation of abnormal sphincter manometry.

Differential diagnosis

Epigastric or right upper quadrant pain can arise from a variety of structures. A detailed history is required to establish that the pain is biliary in origin (see Table 19.1) [7]. Pain occurring daily or constantly is unlikely to be of biliary origin [9]. Pain lasting longer than six hours is more likely to represent non-biliary pain or a complication of biliary disease (e.g., ascending cholangitis or pancreatitis). Daily pain, especially when postprandial, suggests dyspepsia. Symptoms of nausea, bloating, belching, flatulence or heartburn are not symptoms of biliary disease [10]; however, the association between functional biliary disorders and other functional gastrointestinal disorders means that these symptoms are encountered frequently in this patient cohort [11–13].

When biliary pain is suspected, organic causes (e.g., stones or strictures) should be excluded with laboratory testing and imaging. If these are normal, further testing with endoscopic ultrasound and/or biliary scintigraphy may be indicated. Endoscopic ultrasound is more sensitive than transabdominal ultrasonography or computerized tomography for diagnosing microlithiasis or sludge [14]. During biliary scintigraphy, an abnormal gallbladder ejection fraction in response to cholecystokinin is considered suggestive of FGBD. However, this finding does not predict symptomatic response to cholecystectomy [15, 16].

In post-cholecystectomy patients, where FBSD is suspected, sphincter of Oddi manometry can be considered. Previously considered the reference standard for a diagnosis of SOD, manometry is currently considered a supportive criterion only. Although the reproducibility of manometry is questioned, studies have demonstrated a prognostic role for this investigation [8, 17–19]. However, even in experienced hands, there are definite risks associated with this procedure and a low prevalence of abnormal manometry (sphincter hypertension) in patients post-cholecystectomy [20]. Therefore, prior to considering FBSD as a diagnosis, reports of pain similar to that experienced prior to cholecystectomy should initially provoke re-evaluation of the pain characteristics and upper abdominal organs.

For patients with presumed FPSD, *all* alternate causes of recurrent acute pancreatitis should be excluded by clinical evaluation, laboratory testing, cross-sectional imaging and endoscopic ultrasonography. Genetic testing should be considered in the appropriate clinical context. If no other cause is found, sphincter manometry should be performed prior to considering treatment.

Common patient concerns and issues associated with functional gallbladder and sphincter of Oddi disorders

- Missed organic pathology
- Loss of social functioning due to unpredictable symptoms
- The absence of specific diagnostic tests
- An unclear prognosis

Medical and allied health-care treatment approaches for functional gallbladder and sphincter of Oddi disorders

See summary of the current evidence base regarding medical and allied health approaches to the treatment of functional biliary disorders in Table 19.2.

Functional gallbladder disorder

Medical and psychological therapy

Although not reported as FGBD triggers, it is prudent to discontinue medications which inhibit gallbladder function (e.g., anticholinergics, nifedipine, progesterone or loperamide) where possible [21]. Muscarinic agonists and serotonin receptor agonists promote gallbladder emptying but their effect on symptoms is unknown [22, 23].

A high prevalence of psychological comorbidity is reported among patients with FGBD and visceral hypersensitivity may play a role in symptom generation. As the long-term outcome of FBSD is benign, in willing patients it is reasonable to consider a trial of antidepressants or neuromodulators as in other functional gastrointestinal disorders [22]. However, in the absence of clinical trials, the efficacy of this strategy is unclear [23].

Surgical therapy

Few randomized trials support surgery for biliary dyskinesia [24]. However, cohort studies suggest that (i) the majority (52%–94%) of patients experience clinically relevant symptomatic relief after cholecystectomy [15] and (ii) biliary scintigraphy does not identify patients who will benefit from surgery [16]. Cholecystectomy has therefore gained acceptance as a therapeutic (and diagnostic) modality for managing acalculous biliary pain (i.e., FGBD or occult gallstone disease). However, patient factors influence outcome; high levels of anxiety pre-cholecystectomy and non-biliary symptoms (e.g., nausea, bloating, belching) predict poorer outcomes [10, 25]. If cholecystectomy is considered, patients should be counselled pre-operatively regarding the potential long-term complications (e.g., nausea, bloating and altered bowel habit) [2, 3].

Alternate strategies

Limited evidence suggests that acupuncture improves gallbladder function. Its effects on symptoms are unknown [26].

Functional biliary sphincter disorder

Medical and psychological therapy

One small prospective, double-blind, randomized, placebo-controlled, crossover trial demonstrated that nifedipine, administered at the highest tolerated dose, was effective for treating FBSD symptoms. Pain frequency and intensity, and the number of emergency room visits, were reduced in 75% of patients. However, symptomatic hypotension limited effective dosing in many patients [27]. A small cohort study demonstrated complete or partial response in 67% of type II SOD patients receiving trimebutine in combination with nitrates [28]. Other medications (e.g., nicardipine, ceruletide) which reduce biliary sphincter tone have not been evaluated clinically [29, 30]. Although unstudied, medications which increase sphincter pressure (e.g., morphine, codeine) should be discontinued where possible [31]. Studies have demonstrated associations between SOD, functional gastrointestinal disorders [11–13] and visceral hypersensitivity [32, 33]. Consistent with other functional gastrointestinal disorders, patients with SOD have a high prevalence of psychological symptoms (e.g., depression, anxiety, somatization, irritability – oversensitivity, somatization and hypochondriasis), distress and stressors (e.g., childhood sexual abuse) [34, 35]. These conditions should be treated appropriately. However, the impact of this intervention on FBSD symptoms is unknown.

Endoscopic therapy

The strongest data for endoscopic therapy of FBSD (type II SOD) come from a single randomized controlled trial involving 47 patients [8]. After one-year follow-up, fair to good improvement was reported in 65% of patients who underwent sphincterotomy and 30% of patients who had a sham procedure. Elevated sphincter pressure was the strongest predictor of clinical response; fair to good improvement in pain was reported by 91% of patients with elevated pressures after sphincterotomy compared to 25% after a sham procedure. After four years, almost all patients (17 of 18) who had demonstrated elevated sphincter pressures pre-sphincterotomy experienced sustained relief. Among patients with normal sphincter pressures the outcome was equivalent after sphincterotomy or sham procedure; only one third reported improvement. However, other studies (predominantly of pooled cohorts of type I, II and III SOD) have demonstrated variable utility of abnormal manometry for predicting response to endoscopic sphincterotomy [36].

Alternate strategies

Transcutaneous electrical nerve stimulation and hepatobiliary system–specific acupuncture have been shown to reduce sphincter of Oddi pressure [37, 38]. Their role in clinical management is unclear.

Functional pancreatic sphincter disorder

No evidence suggests that medical therapy is beneficial in treating FPSD. Endoscopic sphincterotomy cannot be reliably endorsed at the current time, especially in view of the recent revision in diagnostic criteria [39, 40]. Referral to an experienced tertiary referral centre may be advisable if this diagnosis is considered.

Practical recommendations

- Clinical history remains central to diagnosing functional biliary disorders.
- A strong therapeutic alliance needs to exist between practitioner and patient to facilitate explanation of the diagnosis and to provide treatment in the context of our limited pathophysiological understanding.
- The strongest evidence for management of functional gallbladder disorder relates to cholecystectomy. Clinical evaluation is the most sensitive tool for predicting outcome.

Table 19.2 Summary of the current evidence base regarding medical and allied health approaches to the treatment of functional biliary disorders.

Condition	*Treatment approach and levels of evidence*		
	Medical/pharmaceutical	*Allied health*	*Comments and general recommendations*
E1a. Functional gallbladder disorder	Level II: • Cholecystectomy [10, 15, 16, 24, 25]	No studies conducted to date	• Explanation remains the cornerstone of management • Therapeutic decisions should be made in conjunction with the patient • In willing, well-counselled patients a neuromodulator trial may be considered. • Surgery may offer benefit to a select cohort of well-counselled patients.
E1b. Functional biliary sphincter disorder	Level II: • Nifedipine [27] • Endoscopic sphincterotomy [8]. Level III: • trimebutine in combination with nitrates [28]	No studies conducted to date	• Nifedipine and endoscopic sphincterotomy are categorized as level 2 evidence because of limited sample size in the respective studies. • Side effects (hypotension) limited effective dosing of nifedipine. • Abnormal sphincter manometry may predict response to endoscopic sphincterotomy.

E2. Functional pancreatic sphincter disorder	Level III: • Sphincterotomy	No studies conducted to date	• Data for surgical sphincterotomy are stronger than for endoscopic sphincterotomy. • In the context of new stringent diagnostic criteria, and the absence of high-quality evidence, management should be offered on an individualized basis at expert institutions only.

- For functional biliary sphincter disorder, empiric pharmacological treatment is reasonable. Manometry and/or endoscopic sphincterotomy should be considered if medications are not beneficial or are not tolerated.
- A diagnosis of functional pancreatic sphincter disorder should be considered only where *all* other causes of recurrent acute pancreatitis have been excluded. Sphincterotomy should not be considered in the absence of abnormal manometry.

Current limitations/future considerations

- There is a need for further research regarding the pathophysiology of functional biliary disorders.
- The re-classification of functional biliary and pancreatic sphincter disorders refines the diagnoses into clearer entities. This allows for better clinical communication and more focused research regarding pathophysiology and management.
- Prospective data need to be gathered regarding the natural history, pharmacological, endoscopic and/or surgical management of functional biliary disorders.

Acknowledgments, competing interests, and funding

The author is unaware of any competing interests in relation to this chapter. No external funding was received for this chapter.

References

1 Elta, G.H., Cotton, P.B., Carter, C.R., Corazziari, E.S., Pasricha, P.J.: Gallbladder and Sphincter of Oddi disorders. In: *Rome IV functional gastrointestinal disorders: Disorders of gut-brain interaction*. Edited by Chang, L., Chey, W.D., Kellow, J., Tack, J., Whitehead, W.E., The Rome IV Committees. Raleigh, NC: Rome Foundation, 2016: 1117–1178.

2 Barbara, L., Sama, C., Morselli Labate, A.M., Taroni, F., Rusticali, A.G., Festi, D., Sapio, C., Roda, E., Banterle, C., Puci, A., *et al.*: A population study on the prevalence of gallstone disease: The Sirmione study. *Hepatology* 1987, **7**(5): 913–917.

3 Festi, D., Dormi, A., Capodicasa, S., Staniscia, T., Attili, A.F., Loria, P., Pazzi, P., Mazzella, G., Sama, C., Roda, E., *et al.*: Incidence of gallstone disease in Italy: Results from a multicenter, population-based Italian study (the MICOL project). *World J Gastroenterol* 2008, **14**(34): 5282–5289.

4 Velanovich, V.: Biliary dyskinesia and biliary crystals: A prospective study. *Am Surg* 1997, **63**(1): 69–74.

5 Drossman, D.A., Li, Z., Andruzzi, E., Temple, R.D., Talley, N.J., Thompson, W.G., Whitehead, W.E., Janssens, J., Funch-Jensen, P., Corazziari, E., *et al.*: U.S. householder survey of functional gastrointestinal disorders: Prevalence, sociodemography, and health impact. *Dig Dis Sci* 1993, **38**(9): 1569–1580.

6 Winstead, N.S., Wilcox, C.M.: Health-related quality of life, somatization, and abuse in Sphincter of Oddi dysfunction. *J Clin Gastroenterol* 2007, **41**(8): 773–776.

7 Cotton, P.B., Elta, G.H., Carter, C., Pasricha, P.J., Corazziari, E.S.: Gallbladder and Sphincter of Oddi disorders. *Gastroenterology* 2016, **150**(6): 1420–1429.e1422.

8 Geenen, J.E., Hogan, W.J., Dodds, W.J., Toouli, J., Venu, R.P.: The efficacy of endoscopic sphincterotomy after cholecystectomy in patients with sphincter-of-Oddi dysfunction. *N Engl J Med* 1989, **320**(2): 82–87.

9 Dibaise, J.K.: Evaluation and management of functional biliary pain in patients with an intact gallbladder. *Expert Rev Gastroenterol Hepatol* 2009, **3**(3): 305–313.
10 Mertens, M.C., Roukema, J.A., Scholtes, V.P., De Vries, J.: Risk assessment in cholelithiasis: Is cholecystectomy always to be preferred? *J Gastrointest Surg* 2010, **14**(8): 1271–1279.
11 Evans, P.R., Dowsett, J.F., Bak, Y.T., Chan, Y.K., Kellow, J.E.: Abnormal sphincter of Oddi response to cholecystokinin in postcholecystectomy syndrome patients with irritable bowel syndrome: The irritable sphincter. *Dig Dis Sci* 1995, **40**(5): 1149–1156.
12 Sood, G.K., Baijal, S.S., Lahoti, D., Broor, S.L.: Abnormal gallbladder function in patients with irritable bowel syndrome. *Am J Gastroenterol* 1993, **88**(9): 1387–1390.
13 Chun, A., Desautels, S., Slivka, A., Mitrani, C., Starz, T., Dilorenzo, C., Wald, A.: Visceral Algesia in irritable bowel syndrome, fibromyalgia, and Sphincter of Oddi dysfunction, type III. *Digest Dis Sci* 1999, **44**(3): 631–636.
14 Dahan, P., Andant, C., Levy, P., Amouyal, P., Amouyal, G., Dumont, M., Erlinger, S., Sauvanet, A., Belghiti, J., Zins, M *et al.*: Prospective evaluation of endoscopic ultrasonography and microscopic examination of duodenal bile in the diagnosis of cholecystolithiasis in 45 patients with normal conventional ultrasonography. *Gut* 1996, **38**(2): 277–281.
15 Ponsky, T.A., DeSagun, R., Brody, F.: Surgical therapy for biliary dyskinesia: A meta-analysis and review of the literature. *J Laparoendosc Adv Surg Tech A* 2005, **15**(5): 439–442.
16 Delgado-Aros, S., Cremonini, F., Bredenoord, A.J., Camilleri, M.: Systematic review and meta-analysis: Does gall-bladder ejection fraction on cholecystokinin cholescintigraphy predict outcome after cholecystectomy in suspected functional biliary pain? *Aliment Pharmacol Ther* 2003, **18**(2): 167–174.
17 Guelrud, M., Mendoza, S., Rossiter, G., Villegas, M.I.: Sphincter of Oddi manometry in healthy volunteers. *Dig Dis Sci* 1990, **35**(1): 38–46.
18 Cheon, Y.K.: How to interpret a functional or motility test – sphincter of Oddi manometry. *J Neurogastroenterol Motil* 2012, **18**(2): 211–217.
19 Suarez, A.L., Pauls, Q., Durkalski-Mauldin, V., Cotton, P.B.: Sphincter of Oddi Manometry: Reproducibility of measurements and Effect of sphincterotomy in the EPISOD study. *J Neurogastroenterol Motil* 2016, **22**(3): 477–482.
20 Bar-Meir, S., Halpern, Z., Bardan, E., Gilat, T.: Frequency of papillary dysfunction among cholecystectomized patients. *Hepatology* 1984, **4**(2): 328–330.
21 Marzio, L.: Factors affecting gallbladder motility: Drugs. *Dig Liver Dis* 2003, **35**(Suppl 3): S17–S19.
22 Bielefeldt, K., Saligram, S., Zickmund, S.L., Dudekula, A., Olyaee, M., Yadav, D.: Cholecystectomy for biliary dyskinesia: How did we get there? *Dig Dis Sci* 2014, **59**(12): 2850–2863.
23 Rastogi, A., Slivka, A., Moser, A.J., Wald, A.: Controversies concerning pathophysiology and management of acalculous biliary-type abdominal pain. *Dig Dis Sci* 2005, **50**(8): 1391–1401.
24 Gurusamy, K.S., Junnarkar, S., Farouk, M., Davidson, B.R.: Cholecystectomy for suspected gallbladder dyskinesia. *Cochrane Database Syst Rev* 2009, **1**: CD007086.
25 Thistle, J.L., Longstreth, G.F., Romero, Y., Arora, A.S., Simonson, J.A., Diehl, N.N., Harmsen, W.S., Zinsmeister, A.R.: Factors that predict relief from upper abdominal pain after cholecystectomy. *Clin Gastroenterol Hepatol* 2011, **9**(10): 891–896.
26 Min, B-I, Kim, J-H, Cho, Y-W, Lee, S-K, Kim, M-H: Effects and mechanisms of acupuncture on biliary system motility. *International Congress Series* 2002, **1238**: 157–162.
27 Khuroo, M.S., Zargar, S.A., Yattoo, G.N.: Efficacy of nifedipine therapy in patients with sphincter of Oddi dysfunction: A prospective, double-blind, randomized, placebo-controlled, cross over trial. *Br J Clin Pharmacol* 1992, **33**(5): 477–485.
28 Vitton, V., Delpy, R., Gasmi, M., Lesavre, N., Abou-Berdugo, E., Desjeux, A., Grimaud J-C, Barthet, M.: Is endoscopic sphincterotomy avoidable in patients with sphincter of Oddi dysfunction? *Eur J Gastroenterol Hepatol* 2008, **20**(1): 15–21.
29 Craig, A., Toouli, J.: Sphincter of Oddi dysfunction: Is there a role for medical therapy? *Curr Gastroenterol Rep* 2002, **4**(2): 172–176.
30 Fullarton, G.M., Falconer, S., Campbell, A., Murray, W.R.: Controlled study of the effect of nicardipine and ceruletide on the sphincter of Oddi. *Gut* 1992, **33**(4): 550–553.

31 Staritz, M.: Pharmacology of the Sphincter of Oddi. *Endoscopy* 1988, **20**(S 1): 171–174.
32 Desautels, S.G., Slivka, A., Hutson, W.R., Chun, A., Mitrani, C., DiLorenzo, C., Wald, A.: Postcholecystectomy pain syndrome: Pathophysiology of abdominal pain in sphincter of Oddi type III. *Gastroenterology* 1999, **116**(4): 900–905.
33 Kurucsai, G., Joo, I., Fejes, R., Szekely, A., Szekely, I., Tihanyi, Z., Altorjay, A., Funch-Jensen, P., Varkonyi, T., Madacsy, L.: Somatosensory hypersensitivity in the referred pain area in patients with chronic biliary pain and a Sphincter of Oddi dysfunction: New aspects of an almost forgotten pathogenetic mechanism. *Am J Gastroenterol* 2008, **103**(11): 2717–2725.
34 Kovács, Z., Kovács, F., Pap, Á.: Psychological disturbances in patients with Sphincter of Oddi dysfunction. *J Clin Psychol Med Settings* 2005, **12**(4): 377–381.
35 Bennett, E., Evans, P., Dowsett, J., Kellow, J.: Sphincter of Oddi dysfunction: Psychosocial distress correlates with manometric dyskinesia but not stenosis. *WJG* 2009, **15**(48): 6080–6085.
36 Rosenblatt, M.L., Catalano, M.F., Alcocer, E., Geenen, J.E.: Comparison of sphincter of Oddi manometry, fatty meal sonography, and hepatobiliary scintigraphy in the diagnosis of sphincter of Oddi dysfunction. *Gastrointest Endosc* 2001, **54**(6): 697–704.
37 Guelrud, M., Rossiter, A., Souney, P.F., Mendoza, S., Mujica, V.: The effect of transcutaneous nerve stimulation on sphincter of Oddi pressure in patients with biliary dyskinesia. *Am J Gastroenterol* 1991, **86**(5): 581–585.
38 Lee, S.K., Kim, M.H., Kim, H.J., Seo, D.S., Yoo, K.S., Joo, Y.H., Min, Y.I., Kim, J.H., Min, B.I.: Electroacupuncture may relax the sphincter of Oddi in humans. *Gastrointest Endosc* 2001, **53**(2): 211–216.
39 Wilcox, C.M.: Endoscopic therapy for Sphincter of Oddi dysfunction in idiopathic pancreatitis: From empiric to scientific. *Gastroenterology* 2012, **143**(6): 1423–1426.
40 Coté, G.A., Imperiale, T.F., Schmidt, S.E., Fogel, E., Lehman, G., McHenry, L., Watkins, J., Sherman, S.: Similar efficacies of biliary, with or without pancreatic, sphincterotomy in treatment of idiopathic recurrent acute pancreatitis. *Gastroenterology* 2012, **143**(6): 1502–1509.e1501.

Chapter 20

Diagnostic and treatment approaches for functional anorectal disorders

Henriette Heinrich
Mark Fox

The aim of this chapter is to review the diagnostic criteria, pathophysiology and differential diagnoses of functional anorectal disorders (faecal incontinence, functional anorectal pain and functional defecation disorders). Practical recommendations relating to management and treatment of functional anorectal disorders are provided.

Learning points

- Symptoms of FI, anal pain and evacuation difficulties significantly impact on quality of life and psychiatric health.
- Many patients reveal symptoms of anorectal dysfunction only if questioned directly.
- Diagnosis of functional anorectal disorders often requires both clinical and physiological assessment.
- Differential diagnosis of symptoms of faecal incontinence, anorectal pain and evacuation difficulties should be individualized to the symptom pattern.
- Management and treatment of functional anorectal disorders depend on the development of a trusting relationship.

Introduction

The definition of functional anorectal disorders has developed over the decades [1–4]. While specific symptoms continue to define our understanding of the pathophysiology of functional anorectal disorders, the evolution of diagnostic tests like high-resolution anorectal manometry (HR-ARM) and magnetic-resonance defecography (MR-D) has improved our understanding of anorectal structure and function.

The assessment of symptoms of anorectal dysfunction is complex as patients often have difficulties in recalling bowel symptoms; therefore, symptom and bowel diaries are recommended [5, 6]. The Rome IV criteria define three main groups of functional anorectal disorders: (1) faecal incontinence (FI), (2) functional anorectal pain and (3) functional defecation disorders (FDD) (Table 20.1).

Table 20.1 Diagnostic criteria for functional anorectal disorders.

F1. Faecal incontinence[1]
Diagnostic criterion*
Recurrent uncontrolled passage of faecal material in an individual with a developmental age of at least four years
* Criterion fulfilled for the last three months. For research studies, consider onset of symptoms of at least six months previously with 2–4 episodes of FI over four weeks.

F2. Functional ano rectal pain[2]
F2a. Levator ani syndrome
Diagnostic criteria* Must include *all* of the following:
1. Chronic or recurrent rectal pain or aching
2. Episodes last 30 minutes or longer
3. Tenderness during traction on the puborectalis
4. Exclusion of other causes of rectal pain, such as inflammatory bowel disease, intramuscular abscess, anal fissure, thrombosed haemorrhoids, prostatitis, coccygodynia and major structural alterations of the pelvic floor
* Criteria fulfilled for the last three months with symptom onset at least six months prior to diagnosis

F2b. Unspecified functional anorectal pain[3]
Diagnostic criteria*
Symptom criteria for chronic levator ani syndrome but no tenderness during posterior traction on the puborectalis muscle
* Criteria fulfilled for the last three months with symptom onset at least six months prior to diagnosis

F2c. Proctalgia fugax[4]
Diagnostic criteria* Must include *all* of the following:
1. Recurrent episodes of pain localized to the rectum and unrelated to defecation
2. Episodes last from seconds to minutes with a maximum duration of 30 minutes.
3. There is no anorectal pain between episodes.
4. Exclusion of other causes of rectal pain, such as inflammatory bowel disease, intramuscular abscess, anal fissure, thrombosed haemorrhoids, prostatitis, coccygodynia and major structural alterations of the pelvic floor
* For research purposes, criteria must be fulfilled for three months with symptom onset at least six months prior to diagnosis

F3. Functional defecation disorders[5]
Diagnostic criteria* Must include *all* of the following:
1. The patient must satisfy diagnostic criteria for functional constipation and/or irritable bowel syndrome with constipation.
2. During repeated attempts to defecate, there must be features of impaired evacuation, as demonstrated by *two of the following three* tests:
a. Abnormal balloon expulsion test
b. Abnormal anorectal evacuation pattern with manometry or anal surface EMG
c. Impaired rectal evacuation by imaging
* Criteria fulfilled for the last three months with symptom onset at least six months prior to diagnosis
Subcategories F3a and F3b apply to patients who satisfy criteria for FDD.

F3a. Inadequate defecatory propulsion[6]
Diagnostic criterion*
Inadequate propulsive forces as measured with manometry with or without inappropriate contraction of the anal sphincter and/or pelvic floor muscles**
* Criterion fulfilled for the last three months with symptom onset at least six months prior to diagnosis
** This criterion is defined by age- and gender-appropriate normal values for the technique.

F3b. Dyssynergic defecation[7]
Diagnostic criterion*
Inappropriate contraction of the pelvic floor as measured with anal surface EMG or manometry with adequate propulsive forces during attempted defecation**
* Criterion fulfilled for the last three months with symptom onset at least six months prior to diagnosis
** This criterion is defined by age- and gender-appropriate normal values for the technique.
Diagnostic criteria taken from A.E. Bharucha, S.S.C. Rao, R. Felt-Bersma, G. Chiaroni, C.H. Knowles, A. Malcolm and A. Wald [27], Anorectal Disorders, Chapter 14, pages [1] 1187, [2, 3, 4] 1203, [5, 6, 7] 1209 of the *Rome IV Functional Gastrointestinal Disorders: Disorders of Gut-Brain Interaction.* Reproduction approved by Professor Douglas Drossman 23/10/2016.

Faecal incontinence

Continence for stool is generally achieved after the age of four years when toilet training is complete [7]. FI afflicts all age groups and sexes; however, its prevalence is highest among middle-aged and elderly women and nursing home residents of both sexes [8, 9]. FI is often an 'unvoiced' symptom as it is associated with embarrassment and social stigma [10]. This not only delays diagnosis and treatment but also has profound effects on quality of life and healthcare costs [11]. FI is often multifactorial, with both structural and functional pathology present. Anal sphincter dysfunction, impaired rectal sensation and compliance are key pathophysiological factors in FI [12]. However, the single most important risk factor for FI is diarrhoea that 'overwhelms' the reservoir function of the anorectum [13].

Functional anorectal pain

The prevalence of functional anorectal pain has been estimated to be 8%–18%, with both sexes affected equally across almost all age groups in the community [17]. The pathophysiology of these conditions is not well defined; however, abnormal smooth muscle function with 'spasm' of the pelvic floor muscles, high anal resting tone and disturbed recto anal coordination have been proposed as pathophysiological mechanisms for the *levator ani syndrome, proctalgia fugax* and *unspecified anorectal pain*. Stressful life events, anxiety and perfectionist, hypochondriac and anxious personality traits have been associated with all these conditions [18].

Functional defecation disorders

Functional defecation disorders (FDDs) are part of the spectrum of chronic constipation with outlet obstruction, characterized by paradoxical contraction, insufficient relaxation of pelvic floor muscles or inadequate propulsive forces. Symptoms of FDDs include excessive straining, feeling of incomplete evacuation and digital facilitation of defecation. As diagnosis based on symptoms cannot distinguish other causes of chronic constipation from FDDs, physiologic testing is often necessary for diagnosis.

As specialist tests and clinical expertise are necessary for diagnosis, the prevalence of FDDs is difficult to assess and ranges between 20% and 80% in patients with chronic constipation in the literature [19–21]. Furthermore, the high rate of false positive results in the diagnosis of dyssynergic defecation with conventional manometry and HR-ARM could lead to a systematic overestimate of the prevalence of FDDs. Women seem to be affected more frequently than men. FDDs can be found in all age groups and are associated with IBS and psychiatric comorbidities [22–24].

Diagnostic criteria for functional anorectal disorders (table 20.1)

Faecal incontinence

FI can range from faecal seepage to complete loss of bowel control. While the staining of underwear is part of the current classification, flatus is not part of the Rome IV criteria. A detailed history must be taken and can provide information on the underlying pathophysiology. If present, causes of diarrhoea should be investigated. Although the diagnosis of FI can be based on symptoms, anal manometry, endoanal ultrasound and anorectal sensory testing are useful in patients who fail conservative treatment [12].

Functional anorectal pain

For the diagnosis of all forms of functional anorectal pain, other causes, including IBD and local causes, must be excluded. Important overlap exists between the *levator ani syndrome*, *unspecified functional anorectal pain* and *proctalgia fugax*. Generally, these entities are distinguished by the duration of pain and the presence or absence of anorectal tenderness.

Functional defecation disorders

The diagnosis of FDDs is based on symptoms and physiological testing. In the Rome IV criteria patients are required to fulfil diagnostic criteria of functional constipation and/or IBS with constipation. The criteria now include IBS with constipation, as there is emerging evidence for an association between IBS and pelvic floor dysfunction [25]. Two of three tests of anorectal physiology (balloon expulsion, manometry, surface EMG or imaging) must show impaired anorectal function. Functional defecation disorders are further subdivided into *inadequate defecatory propulsion* and *dyssynergic defecation*. Data regarding the performance of anal manometry in detecting dyssynergic defecation are conflicting: While high-resolution anorectal manometry has a high diagnostic accuracy in comparison to MRI defecography, patterns of dyssynergic defecation are frequently seen in health, thus limiting diagnostic ability until further quantitative metrics are developed and validated [26].

Differential diagnosis of functional anorectal disorders

Before the diagnosis of a functional anorectal disorder can be made important differential diagnoses have to be ruled out. The symptoms of functional anorectal disorders cover the spectrum of faecal incontinence, anal and rectal pain and constipation with evacuation difficulties; therefore history and diagnostic tests are required to rule out the presence of local pathology and metabolic conditions.

Common patient concerns and issues associated with functional anorectal disorders

For the investigation of symptoms of functional anorectal disorders, establishing a trusting relationship between the clinician and the patient is key. Symptoms of faecal incontinence, anal and rectal pain and evacuation difficulties are hard to voice for patients due to shame, embarrassment and fear [3, 6, 10]. In the case of FI only 10%–30% of patients report symptoms of stool loss to their treating physician [6]. In most cases, patients prefer to be actively asked about the quality, duration and severity of FI [29].

In FI symptoms often have significant impact on the social life of patients, restricting their range of movement and food intake [30], and are associated with a higher rate of anxiety, depression and stress [4].

Medical and allied health standard care treatment approaches for functional anorectal disorders

Faecal incontinence

Supportive management and dietary approaches for FI include identification and avoidance of food components which can cause diarrhoea. Psyllium is the only fibre supplement that has shown in trials to have a beneficial effect in FI patients in comparison to placebo [32]. Caffeinated beverages and brisk physical activity after a meal may lead to more rapid colonic transit, increasing the risk of urgency and stool loss [33–35]. Ritualizing food intake, bowel habit and cognitive training, especially in institutionalized patients, has been shown to decrease episodes of faecal incontinence in up 60% of patients [36]. It is vital to recognize soiling in institutionalized patients and immediately clean the skin to prevent excoriation [37].

Bowel habit modification with pharmacological interventions plays an important role in FI as liquid or loose stools are an important risk factor for FI. Stool consistency, intestinal transit time and resting anal sphincter tone can be improved by administration of a small dose of loperamide taken 30 minutes before a meal [38]. However, some patients suffer from side effects, making careful dosage titration necessary. Diphenoxylate and atropine can provide symptomatic relief in patients with FI; however, the patient's ability to retain rectal contents remains unaltered and anticholinergic side effects are common [39]. Although limited data exist in the literature, tricyclic antidepressants, such as amitriptyline, seem to have a beneficial effect in FI, especially in IBS patients, by slowing transit time and reducing visceral hypersensitivity and reactivity [40]. In patients with FI due to faecal impaction with overflow or with neurogenic bowel dysfunction, osmotive laxatives, suppositories, enemas and fibre supplementation are recommended [41]. Rectal irrigation and plug devices are available for patients who fail pharmacological intervention and biofeedback.

Biofeedback therapy is indicated in patients with FI with a weak, easily fatigued anal sphincter and impaired rectal sensation. This form of neuromuscular training based on operant conditioning and instrumental learning has been shown to be effective in improving objective measures of anorectal function, symptoms of FI and quality of life in randomized controlled trials [42, 43]. Many protocols for biofeedback therapy exist but none has been shown to be superior [44].

Surgery is reserved for patients who fail conservative measures and biofeedback therapy. Although overlapping sphincter repair is widely performed immediately after obstetric injury, long-term success rates in FI patients with evidence of past injury are disappointing, with less than 50% having long-term improvement of symptoms [45]. Bulking agents injected into the sphincter show modest improvement rates of approximately 50% for FI in contrast to sham injections, with the effect lasting up to three years [46, 47]. Dynamic graciloplasty and implantation of artificial bowel sphincters (ABS) require major surgery, and case series report up to 50% revision rate with insufficient long-term symptom improvement [48]. At this time no studies have compared the efficacy of surgical versus pharmacologic or biofeedback treatment for FI.

Sacral nerve stimulation has been shown to be effective in the reduction of FI episodes but, so far, only in uncontrolled trials [49]. Sacral neurostimulation has been shown to improve sphincter pressures and modulate rectal sensation, possibly influencing anorectal function via afferent pelvic and central pathways [50].

Functional anal pain

Treatment of *levator ani syndrome* comprises reassurance, sitzbaths and pharmacological therapy. Nonsteroidal anti-inflammatory drugs (NSAIDs), sublingual nifedipine and clonidine have all been reported to benefit patients with this condition in non-randomized controlled trials. In contrast, botulinum toxin injection was not shown to be of benefit in comparison to a placebo.

For *proctalgia fugax* no treatment is necessary due to its brief nature. Most patients benefit from reassurance and explanation. For those with frequent episodes, inhaled salbutamol has been shown to improve symptoms in one randomized controlled trial [52, 53].

Functional defecation disorders

Biofeedback is considered the first-line treatment for FDD, especially in patients with dyssynergic defecation, and has been shown to be superior to sham therapy, pelvic floor exercises, laxatives and pharmacologic therapy, with long-term success. [54–56]. Success for biofeedback has been shown to be associated with the absence of psychological comorbidity and diarrhoea, greater motivation, higher anal resting pressure and prolonged balloon expulsion time at baseline [57].

A summary of the current evidence base regarding medical and allied health standard care treatment approaches for functional anorectal disorders can be found in Tables 20.2 and 20.3.

Table 20.2 Summary of the current evidence base regarding medical and allied health approaches for faecal incontinence.

Treatment approach	*Level of evidence*	*Comments*
Basic supportive management	III-IV	Ritualizing bowel habit, recognition of soiling, skin cleaning, avoidance of triggering foods, physical activity after eating [33, 35–37]
Medical/pharmaceutical	II	Bowel habit modification by psyllium, loperamide, antidepressants [32, 38, 40, 41]
Behavioural	I	Biofeedback [43]
Neurostimulation	II	Sacral neurostimulation; recent evidence indicates that tibial nerve stimulation lacks efficacy [49, 51]
Surgery	III	Sphincter raphe or augmentation, artificial bowel sphincters [35, 45–47]

Table 20.3 Summary of the current evidence base regarding medical and allied health approaches for functional anorectal pain and FDD.

Treatment approach	*Level of evidence*	*Comments*
Basic supportive management	III	Massage, sitzbaths, electrical stimulation for levator ani syndrome [53]
Medical/ pharmaceutical	III-IV	NSAIDS, sublingual nifedipine or clonidine for levator ani syndrome [58] Salbutamol for proctalgia fugax [52]
Behavioural	I	Biofeedback for FDD and levator ani syndrome [54–57]

Practical recommendations

- Establish a trusting doctor-patient relationship
- Obtain a thorough history of bowel dysfunction. Use stool diaries and standardized questionnaires.
- Other causes of FI, anal pain and evacuation difficulties should be ruled out by appropriate investigations before diagnosis of a functional anorectal disorder is made.
- Patients failing first-line management with modification of bowel function and generic pelvic floor training should undergo physiologic testing.
- FI treatment with stool regulation and biofeedback improves symptoms and quality of life. Sacral neurostimulation is reserved for patients who fail conservative treatment.
- Biofeedback is the most effective treatment option for levator ani syndrome. Proctalgia fugax usually needs no treatment.
- Biofeedback is the most effective treatment approach for inadequate defecatory propulsion and dyssynergic defecation.

Current limitations/future considerations

- Agreement between diagnostic tests in FDD is suboptimal. Studies using new technologies and objective metrics that assess both anal sphincter and rectal function are needed to better phenotype patients and stratify treatment.
- Randomized controlled trials are needed to identify effective medical and surgical treatments of FI.
- More data on epidemiology, diagnostic features and treatment modalities are needed to better assess and treat functional anorectal pain syndromes.

Acknowledgements, competing interests and funding

Thank you to Drs Smith and Wells for their feedback regarding earlier drafts. The authors are unaware of any competing interests in relation to this chapter. No external funding was received for this chapter.

References

1 Wald, A.: Disorders of defecation and fecal continence. *Cleve Clin J Med* 1989, **56**(5): 491–501.

2 Diamant, N.E., Kamm, M.A., Wald, A., Whitehead, W.E.: AGA technical review on anorectal testing techniques. *Gastroenterology* 1999, **116**(3): 735–760.

3 Bharucha, A.E., Wald, A., Enck, P., Rao, S.: Functional anorectal disorders. *Gastroenterology* 2006, **130**(5): 1510–1518.

4 Rao, S.S., Bharucha, A.E., Chiarioni, G., Felt-Bersma, R., Knowles, C., Malcolm, A., Wald, A.: Functional anorectal disorders. *Gastroenterology* 2016, **150**(6): 1430–1442.

5 Ashraf, W., Park, F., Lof, J., Quigley, E.M.: An examination of the reliability of reported stool frequency in the diagnosis of idiopathic constipation. *Am J Gastroenterol* 1996, **91**(1): 26–32.

6 Bharucha, A.E., Seide, B.M., Zinsmeister, A.R., Melton, L.J.: Insights into normal and disordered bowel habits from bowel diaries. *Am J Gastroenterol* 2008, **103**(3): 692–698.
7 Bongers, M.E., Tabbers, M.M., Benninga, M.A.: Functional nonretentive fecal incontinence in children. *J Pediatr Gastroenterol Nut* 2007, **44**(1): 5–13.
8 Nelson, R., Furner, S., Jesudason, V.: Fecal incontinence in Wisconsin nursing homes: Prevalence and associations. *Dis Colon Rectum* 1998, **41**(10): 1226–1229.
9 Perry, S., Shaw, C., McGrother, C., Matthews, R.J., Assassa, R.P., Dallosso, H., Williams, K., Brittain, K.R., Azam, U., Clarke, M., *et al.*: Prevalence of faecal incontinence in adults aged 40 years or more living in the community. *Gut* 2002, **50**(4): 480–484.
10 Leigh, R.J., Turnberg, L.A.: Faecal incontinence: the unvoiced symptom. *Lancet (London, England)* 1982, **1**(8285): 1349–1351.
11 Cotterill, N., Norton, C., Avery, K.N.L, Abrams, P., Donovan, J.L.: A patient-centered approach to developing a comprehensive symptom and quality of life assessment of anal incontinence. *Dis Colon Rectum* 2008, **51**(1): 82–87.
12 Rao, S.S.: Pathophysiology of adult fecal incontinence. *Gastroenterology* 2004, **126**(1 Suppl 1): S14–S22.
13 Bharucha, A.E., Zinsmeister, A.R., Schleck, C.D., Melton III, L.J.: Bowel disturbances are the most important risk factors for late onset fecal incontinence A population-based case-control study in women. *Gastroenterology* 2010, **139**(5): 1559–1566.
14 Bharucha, A.E., Zinsmeister, A.R., Schleck, C.D., Melton III, L.J.: Bowel disturbances are the most important risk factors for late onset fecal incontinence A population-based case-control study in women. *Gastroenterology* 2010, **139**(5): 1559–1566.
15 Nelson, R., Norton, N., Cautley, E., Furner, S.: Community-based prevalence of anal incontinence. *JAMA* 1995, **274**(7): 559–561.
16 Bols, E.M.J., Hendriks, E.J.M., Berghmans, B.C.M., Baeten, C.G.M.I., Nijhuis, J.G., De Bie, R.A.: A systematic review of etiological factors for postpartum fecal incontinence. *Acta Obstetricia et Gynecologica Scandinavica* 2010, **89**(3): 302–314.
17 de Parades, V., Etienney, I., Bauer, P., Taouk, M., Atienza, P.: Proctalgia fugax: Demographic and clinical characteristics: What every doctor should know from a prospective study of 54 patients. *Dis Colon Rectum* 2007, **50**(6): 893–898.
18 Karras, J.D., Angelo, G.: Proctalgia fugax: Clinical observations and a new diagnostic aid. *Dis Colon Rectum* 1963, **6**(2): 130–134.
19 Nullens, S., Nelsen, T., Camilleri, M., Burton, D., Eckert, D., Iturrino, J., Vazquez-Roque, M., Zinsmeister, A.R.: Regional colon transit in patients with dys-synergic defaecation or slow transit in patients with constipation. *Gut* 2012, **61**(8): 1132–1139.
20 Duthie, G.S., Bartolo, D.C.C.: Anismus: The cause of constipation? Results of investigation and treatment. *WJS* 1992, **16**(5): 831–835.
21 Wald, A., Caruana, B.J., Freimanis, M.G., Bauman, D.H., Hinds, J.P.: Contributions of evacuation proctography and anorectal manometry to evaluation of adults with constipation and defecatory difficulty. *Dig Dis Sci* 1990, **35**(4): 481–487.
22 Grossi, U., Carrington, E.V., Bharucha, A.E., Horrocks, E.J., Scott, S.M., Knowles, C.H.: Diagnostic accuracy study of anorectal manometry for diagnosis of dyssynergic defecation. *Gut* 2016, **65**(3): 447–455.
23 Ratuapli, S.K., Bharucha, A.E., Noelting, J., Harvey, D.M., Zinsmeister, A.R.: Phenotypic identification and classification of functional defecatory disorders using high-resolution anorectal manometry. *Gastroenterology* 2013, **144**(2): 314–322.e312.
24 Rao, S.S.C., Tuteja, A.K., Vellema, T., Kempf, J., Stessman, M.: Dyssynergic defecation: Demographics, symptoms, stool patterns, and quality of life. *J Clin Gastroenterol* 2004, **38**(8): 680–685.
25 Prott, G., Shim, L., Hansen, R., Kellow, J., Malcolm, A.: Relationships between pelvic floor symptoms and function in irritable bowel syndrome. *Neurogastroenterol Motil* 2010, **22**(7): 764–769.
26 Heinrich, H., Sauter, M., Fox, M., Weishaupt, D., Halama, M., Misselwitz, B., Buetikofer, S., Reiner, C., Fried, M., Schwizer, W., *et al.*: Assessment of obstructive defecation by high-resolution anorectal manometry compared with magnetic resonance defecography. *Clin Gastroenterol Hepatol* 2015, **13**(7): 1310–1317 e1311.

27 Bharucha, A.E., Rao, S.S.C., Felt-Bersma, R., Chiaroni, G., Knowles, C.H., Malcolm, A., Wald, A.: Anorectal disorders. In: *Rome IV functional gastrointestinal disorders: Disorders of gut-brain interaction*. Edited by Chang, L., Chey, W.D., Kellow, J., Tack, J., Whitehead, W.E., The Rome IV Committees. Raleigh, NC: Rome Foundation, 2016: 1179–1236.
28 Tantiphlachiva, K., Rao, P., Attaluri, A., Rao, S.S.: Digital rectal examination is a useful tool for identifying patients with dyssynergia. *Clin Gastroenterol Hepatol* 2010, **8**(11): 955–960.
29 Kunduru, L., Kim, S.M., Heymen, S., Whitehead, W.E.: Factors that affect consultation and screening for fecal incontinence. *Clin Gastroenterol Hepatol* 2015, **13**(4): 709–716.
30 Hull, T.: Fecal incontinence. *Clin Colon Rectal Surg* 2007, **20**(2): 118–124.
31 Grover, M., Busby-Whitehead, J., Palmer, M.H., Heymen, S., Palsson, O.S., Goode, P.S., Turner, M., Whitehead, W.E.: Survey of geriatricians on the effect of fecal incontinence on nursing home referral. *J Am Geriatr Soc* 2010, **58**(6): 1058–1062.
32 Bliss, D.Z., Savik, K., Jung, H.J., Whitebird, R., Lowry, A., Sheng, X.: Dietary fiber supplementation for fecal incontinence: A randomized clinical trial. *Res Nurs Health* 2014, **37**(5): 367–378.
33 Rao, S.S., Welcher, K., Zimmerman, B., Stumbo, P.: Is coffee a colonic stimulant? *Eur J Gastroenterol Hepatol* 1998, **10**(2): 113–118.
34 Rao, S.S., Sadeghi, P., Beaty, J., Kavlock, R., Ackerson, K.: Ambulatory 24-h colonic manometry in healthy humans. *Am J Physiol Gastrointest Liver Physiol* 2001, **280**(4): G629–G639.
35 Rao, S.S., Beaty, J., Chamberlain, M., Lambert, P.G., Gisolfi, C.: Effects of acute graded exercise on human colonic motility. *Am J Physiol* 1999, **276**(5 Pt 1): G1221–G1226.
36 Chassagne, P., Jego, A., Gloc, P., Capet, C., Trivalle, C., Doucet, J., Denis, P., Bercoff, E.: Does treatment of constipation improve faecal incontinence in institutionalized elderly patients? *Age Ageing* 2000, **29**(2): 159–164.
37 Leung, F.W., Schnelle, J.F.: Urinary and fecal incontinence in nursing home residents. *Gastroenterol Clin North Am* 2008, **37**(3): 697–707, x.
38 Fox, M., Stutz, B., Menne, D., Fried, M., Schwizer, W., Thumshirn, M.: The effects of loperamide on continence problems and anorectal function in obese subjects taking orlistat. *Dig Dis Sci* 2005, **50**(9): 1576–1585.
39 Omar, M.I., Alexander, C.E.: Drug treatment for faecal incontinence in adults. *Cochrane Database Syst Rev* 2013, **6**: CD002116.
40 Santoro, G.A., Eitan, B.Z., Pryde, A., Bartolo, D.C.: Open study of low-dose amitriptyline in the treatment of patients with idiopathic fecal incontinence. *Dis Colon Rectum* 2000, **43**(12): 1676–1681, discussion 1681–1672.
41 Bharucha, A.E., Pemberton, J.H., Locke III, G.R.: American gastroenterological association technical review on constipation. *Gastroenterology* 2013, **144**(1): 218–238.
42 Rao, S.S., Benninga, M.A., Bharucha, A.E., Chiarioni, G., Di Lorenzo, C., Whitehead, W.E.: ANMS-ESNM position paper and consensus guidelines on biofeedback therapy for anorectal disorders. *Neurogastroenterol Motil* 2015, **27**(5): 594–609.
43 Norton, C., Cody, J.D.: Biofeedback and/or sphincter exercises for the treatment of faecal incontinence in adults. *Cochrane Database Syst Rev* 2012, **7**: CD002111.
44 Schouten, W.R., van Vroonhoven, T.J.: A simple method of anorectal manometry. *Dis Colon Rectum* 1983, **26**(11): 721–724.
45 Malouf, A.J., Norton, C.S., Engel, A.F., Nicholls, R.J., Kamm, M.A.: Long-term results of overlapping anterior anal-sphincter repair for obstetric trauma. *Lancet (London, England)* 2000, **355**(9200): 260–265.
46 Mellgren, A., Matzel, K.E., Pollack, J., Hull, T., Bernstein, M., Graf W, The Nasha Dx Study Group: Long-term efficacy of NASHA Dx injection therapy for treatment of fecal incontinence. *Neurogastroenterol Motil* 2014, **26**(8): 1087–1094.
47 Graf, W., Mellgren, A., Matzel, K.E., Hull, T., Johansson, C., Bernstein, M.: Efficacy of dextranomer in stabilised hyaluronic acid for treatment of faecal incontinence: A randomised, sham-controlled trial. *Lancet*, **377**(9770): 997–1003.

48 Gladman, M.A., Knowles, C.H.: Surgical treatment of patients with constipation and fecal incontinence. *Gastroenterol Clin North Am* 2008, **37**(3): 605–625, viii.
49 Thaha, M.A., Abukar, A.A., Thin, N.N., Ramsanahie, A., Knowles, C.H.: Sacral nerve stimulation for faecal incontinence and constipation in adults. *Cochrane Database Syst Rev* 2015, **8**: Cd004464.
50 Carrington, E.V., Evers, J., Grossi, U., Dinning, P.G., Scott, S.M., O'Connell, P.R., Jones, J.F.X., Knowles, C.H.: A systematic review of sacral nerve stimulation mechanisms in the treatment of fecal incontinence and constipation. *Neurogastroenterol Motil* 2014, **26**(9): 1222–1237.
51 Knowles, C.H., Horrocks, E.J., Bremner, S.A., Stevens, N., Norton, C., O'Connell, P.R., Eldridge, S., Group COs: Percutaneous tibial nerve stimulation versus sham electrical stimulation for the treatment of faecal incontinence in adults (CONFIDeNT): A double-blind, multicentre, pragmatic, parallel-group, randomised controlled trial. *Lancet (London, England)* 2015, **386**(10004): 1640–1648.
52 Eckardt, V.F., Dodt, O., Kanzler, G., Bernhard, G.: Treatment of proctalgia fugax with salbutamol inhalation. *Am J Gastroenterol* 1996, **91**(4): 686–689.
53 Chiarioni, G., Nardo, A., Vantini, I., Romito, A., Whitehead, W.E.: Biofeedback is superior to electrogalvanic stimulation and massage for treatment of levator ani syndrome. *Gastroenterology* 2010, **138**(4): 1321–1329.
54 Rao, S.S., Valestin, J., Brown, C.K., Zimmerman, B., Schulze, K.: Long-term efficacy of biofeedback therapy for dyssynergic defecation: Randomized controlled trial. *Am J Gastroenterol* 2010, **105**(4): 890–896.
55 Rao, S.S., Seaton, K., Miller, M., Brown, K., Nygaard, I., Stumbo, P., Zimmerman, B., Schulze, K.: Randomized controlled trial of biofeedback, sham feedback, and standard therapy for dyssynergic defecation. *Clin Gastroenterol Hepatol* 2007, **5**(3): 331–338.
56 Chiarioni, G., Whitehead, W.E., Pezza, V., Morelli, A., Bassotti, G.: Biofeedback is superior to laxatives for normal transit constipation due to pelvic floor dyssynergia. *Gastroenterology* 2006, **130**(3): 657–664.
57 Shim, L.S., Jones, M., Prott, G.M., Morris, L.I., Kellow, J.E., Malcolm, A.: Predictors of outcome of anorectal biofeedback therapy in patients with constipation. *Aliment Pharmacol Ther* 2011, **33**(11): 1245–1251.
58 Whitehead, W.E.: Functional anorectal disorders. *Sem Gastrointest Dis* 1996, **7**(4): 230–236.

Chapter 21

Functional gastrointestinal disorders and the elderly

Richard J. Saad

The aim of the chapter is to review the differences in the aetiology of gastrointestinal symptoms, adverse drug reactions and efficacy of treatment for functional gastrointestinal disorders (FGIDs) in elderly cohorts.

Learning points

- Differences in the aetiology of gastrointestinal symptoms suggestive of a functional gastrointestinal disorder (FGID) in the elderly compared to the general adult population.
- Special considerations when treating elderly adults for FGIDs given the higher risk of adverse drug reactions.
- Evidence for the safety and efficacy of treatment strategies in the elderly adult with an FGID.

Introduction

Given the high prevalence and chronicity of functional gastrointestinal disorders in the general population coupled with the rapid growth of the elderly (those aged 65 years of age and older), health-care providers will need to be cognizant of the many nuances associated with the evaluation, diagnosis and treatment of FGIDs in this population. The elderly represent the fastest-growing age cohort, anticipated to double from 8.5% of the global population in 2015 to 17% by 2050 [1]. Furthermore, given the chronicity of FGIDs, many younger adults are likely to carry their FGID into their elder years [2]. Symptoms may also fluctuate over time, moving from one FGID to another [2]. While the prevalence of most FGIDs is known to either decrease or remain stable with age, symptoms of dysphagia [3], constipation [4] and faecal incontinence [5] have been shown to increase with age.

The clinical challenge in this population is twofold. First is the separation of organic causes from functional causes of presenting symptoms. Once an FGID is established, the second challenge is the identification of a safe and effective treatment. This represents the greater challenge as most clinical trials of FGIDs have not been powered to adequately answer the question of safety and efficacy of treatment in the elderly [6]. Therefore, clinicians must extrapolate results from the general adult population and apply them to the elderly. In many cases, it is a gross oversimplification to consider the elderly simply as older adults. Age-related changes in physiology and structure, differences in the pharmacokinetics and pharmacodynamics of drugs, polypharmacy, comorbidity, frailty and a variety of social issues can have significant ramifications on the safety, tolerance and efficacy of treatment considerations.

Age-related change in gastrointestinal and other organ systems

Age-related motor changes of the oropharynx include a prolongation of the oral and pharyngeal phase of swallowing [7], and a reduction in tongue pulsion and pharyngeal wall contraction [8]. Age-related changes in oropharyngeal sensory function include a decline in taste discrimination [9], increase in the pharyngeal swallow threshold [10] and a reduction in sensation of the hypopharynx, other supraglottic structures and the laryngo-upper oesophageal sphincter reflex [11, 12]. Motor changes of the oesophagus include a reduction in resting upper oesophageal sphincter pressure as well as lower oesophageal sphincter relaxation; a diminished oesophageal contractile strength velocity and duration; reduced primary and secondary oesophageal peristalsis; and increased tertiary peristalsis [13–15]. The oesophagus also demonstrates an age-related reduction in visceral sensation [16]. Decreased visceral sensation of the small bowel and colon has been reported [17]. Anal sphincter rest and squeeze tone decreases with age [18]. The rectum also demonstrates decreased sensation with age [19]. The gut microbiota appears to change with age [20]. Other age-related changes potentially impacting FGID symptoms include demises in gait, balance, cognition, memory, renal function, immune function and sleep.

Pharmacologic considerations in the elderly

Medications can frequently be the source of gastrointestinal symptoms mistaken for an FGID. Common gastrointestinal side effects of medications include nausea, vomiting, anorexia, dyspepsia, abdominal pain, bloating, abdominal cramping, constipation and diarrhoea [21]. Furthermore, adverse drug reactions increase with advancing age [22].

Medications used to treat FGIDs can cause side effects or drug-drug interactions with other prescribed or over-the-counter agents. A recent publication illustrates the potential for interactions between medications used to treat acid peptic disease and medications used to treat five common diseases in the geriatric population, including hypertension, diabetes, hyperlipidaemia, arthritis and psychiatric illnesses [23]. In this scenario, a proton pump inhibitor could interact with a diuretic, resulting in hypomagnesemia, promote the premature breakdown of enteric-coated naproxen, leading to dyspeptic symptoms, or increase diazepam levels, resulting in over-sedation or psychomotor impairment.

The elderly are more susceptible to medication side effects. Age-related changes affecting drug pharmacokinetics and pharmacodynamics include reductions in lean muscle mass and water content, increased body fat, decreased albumin, reduced liver mass and perfusion, and decreased glomerular filtration rates [24]. Polypharmacy is also exceedingly common, with one study illustrating an average of more than 13 prescribed medications in a cohort of elderly patients upon hospitalization discharge [25]. Studies have also shown that adults 60 years of age and older receiving outpatient medical care take an average of 6–8 prescribed medications a day [26]. More alarming are studies indicating that one in six hospitalizations in adults 60 years of age and older is for adverse drug reactions, a number which increases to one in three for those 75 years of age and older [27]. Medications must always be carefully reviewed for potential drug-drug interactions as well other adverse effects, including an individual's presenting gastrointestinal symptoms.

Comorbidity in the elderly

Comorbid physical and mental illness can have a significant impact on the aetiology, presentation and treatment of gastrointestinal syndromes. Degenerative neurologic conditions, endocrinopathies and infiltrative conditions, such as amyloidosis, can negatively impact swallowing, gastric emptying, peristalsis and defecation. Cardiac disease resulting in congestive heart failure can impair liver function and intestinal absorptive function. Renal dysfunction, obstructive pulmonary disease and musculoskeletal disease can prompt symptoms of nausea, anorexia and constipation. Among the most common comorbidities in the elderly is that of neuropsychiatric illness, including depression, anxiety and dementia. These chronic and often time-progressive conditions can not only exacerbate physical illness but also arise as a result of such physical illnesses and impart poor treatment response, compliance and increased mortality [28].

Evaluation

The first step is the exclusion of organic disease. Most malignancies, particularly gastrointestinal cancers, increase in incidence with advancing age and frequently present with symptoms overlapping those of FGIDs. Appropriate structural evaluation should be the first step in the evaluation. Medications and other non-malignant diseases should also be considered and excluded as the source of symptoms before concluding that an FGID exists. Other caveats include the increased incidence of small intestinal bacterial overgrowth in the elderly, which may explain common symptoms, such as diarrhoea, bloating and excessive flatulence [29]. Depression and generalized anxiety disorders can also present with a variety of common gastrointestinal symptoms, including loss of appetite, weight loss and abdominal pain [30]. Major depression is reported to affect nearly 5% of the elderly population, with depressive symptoms affecting as many as 16% [31]. Furthermore, older adults with depression are more likely than their younger counterparts to report somatic gastrointestinal symptoms in association with their depression [32]. Therefore, an important component of an evaluation includes screening for the presence of depression or an anxiety disorder. Diarrhoea and faecal incontinence can frequently be the result of underlying constipation with faecal loading [33].

Treatment considerations

Virtually no pharmacologic or non-pharmacologic clinical trials have been adequately powered to assess safety and efficacy in the elderly. Care must be taken to use medications with the lowest side effects profile. Furthermore, other medications and medical conditions need to be carefully considered when choosing therapy. An elderly patient with advanced dementia or memory impairment may not be a good candidate for behavioural therapy. Likewise, a patient with limited mobility or a poor social support structure is not a good candidate for neuromuscular reeducation of a pelvic floor problem, which will require frequent visits over a short period of time.

When choosing pharmacologic therapy, consider using one of several clinical tools to assist with the selection of safe medications, such as the Beers criteria, the STOPP (Screening Tool of Older Person's Potentially inappropriate prescriptions) criteria and the START (Screening Tool to Alert doctors to Right Treatment) criteria. The Beers criteria consist of three lists of medications deemed by an expert panel within the American Geriatrics Society to be potentially unsafe in the elderly [34]. These three lists, last updated in 2015, include medications to be avoided independent of diagnosis, medications to be avoided when considering the diagnosis, and those medications to be used with caution (see Table 21.1). STOPP is a validated clinical tool consisting of 65 clinically significant criteria for potentially inappropriate prescribing in older persons [35]. This can be used in tandem with the START criteria which consists of 22 evidence-based prescribing indicators for commonly encountered medical conditions in the elderly [35].

Regarding the treatment of constipation, a recent systematic review was performed on controlled trials assessing the use of laxatives in the elderly [36]. Nine small studies were identified. A senna-fibre laxative was found to be effective and well tolerated in two studies totalling 107 patients. Although the osmotic laxatives were associated with bloating, flatulence, diarrhoea and nausea, polyethylene glycol was as safe and effective in the geriatric cohort as the general population. A sub-analysis and pooled analysis of open-labelled trials found lubiprostone to be more effective than placebo and associated with fewer side effects than a younger adult cohort. Nausea was the most commonly reported adverse effect in this study. Analysis of a subpopulation of 30 geriatric

Table 21.1 Commonly used drugs for FGIDs on the Beers list to avoid in the elderly (adapted from American Geriatrics Society [34]).

Anticholinergics	*Promethazine*
Antispasmodics	Atropine, Belladonna Alkaloids, Clidinium-Chlordiazepoxide, Dicyclomine, Hyoscyamine, Propanthelline, Scopolamine
Antidepressants	Amitriptyline, Desipramine, Nortriptyline, Paroxeitine
Gastrointestinal	Metoclopramide, mineral oil, proton pump inhibitor (avoid scheduled use > 8 weeks unless there is high-risk reason for chronic use)

patients found linaclotide to be as effective as in overall group, with no difference in reported side effects compared to those receiving placebo. Two dose-ranging studies of prucalopride demonstrated superiority to placebo, although there was an increased likelihood of diarrhoea. More importantly, there were no dose-related effects on laboratory studies, vital signs, EKG or Holter monitor findings compared to placebo. Realizing that these studies share the same methodological flaws as studies on the general population, there were several small studies suggestive of efficacy of and tolerance to yoghurt containing probiotic, abdominal and manual massage, and biofeedback therapy [37]. Although studies assessing the efficacy and safety of antidepressants and behavioural therapy in the elderly are lacking, the increased presence of anxiety and depression and its negative impact on coexistent gastrointestinal symptoms would suggest that such therapy would be effective. However, efficacy must be weighed against the risk of medication side effects, limits related to dementia and memory loss, and the social support system an elderly patient may have. Speaking anecdotally, this author has found Remeron effective and well tolerated for symptoms of nausea, abdominal pain and weight loss. The author has also found the use of a behavioural therapist and dietician effective in elderly patients with FGIDs.

Practical recommendations

- Exclude organic disease and medications before concluding an elderly patient has an FGID.
- Awareness of age-related changes in motor and sensory function of the oropharynx and oesophagus and impact on dysphagia, altered oral intake and weight loss.
- Awareness of age-related changes in motor and sensory function of the anorectum and impact on altered bowel habits and faecal incontinence.
- Consider constipation as a cause of faecal incontinence.
- Awareness of depression promoting somatic gastrointestinal symptoms.
- Careful consideration of side effects and drug-drug interactions when selecting pharmacologic therapy to treat an FGID in the elderly.
- Over-the-counter laxatives senna and polyethylene glycol are safe and effective first-line treatment options for constipation.
- Probiotics and behavioural therapy provide reasonable treatment options in the elderly.
- Biofeedback is effective for constipation and faecal incontinence; however, dementia, memory loss and a poor social support system are important considerations.

Current limitations/future considerations

- Virtually no existing FGID treatment trials are adequately powered to evaluate the elderly.
- Future FGID treatment trials need larger elderly cohorts.

Acknowledgements, competing interests and funding

The authors are unaware of any competing interests in relation to this chapter. No external funding was received for this chapter.

References

1 He, W., Goodkind, D., Kowal, P.: U.S. Census Bureau, International Population Reports, P95/16-1, An aging world: 2015, 2016: Washington, DC: U.S. Government Publishing Office.
2 Agreus, L., Svardsudd, K., Talley, N.J., Jones, M.P., Tibblin, G.: Natural history of gastroesophageal reflux disease and functional abdominal disorders: A population-based study. *Am J Gastroenterol* 2001, **96**(10): 2905–2914.
3 Smithard, D.G.: Dysphagia: Prevalence, management and the community nurse. *Community Pract* 2015, **88**(10): 32–35.
4 Choung, R.S., Locke, G.R., 3rd, Schleck, C.D., Zinsmeister, A.R., Talley, N.J.: Cumulative incidence of chronic constipation: A population-based study 1988–2003. *Aliment Pharmacol Ther* 2007, **26**(11–12): 1521–1528.
5 Ng, K.S., Sivakumaran, Y., Nassar, N., Gladman, M.A.: Fecal incontinence: Community prevalence and associated factors – a systematic review. *Dis Colon Rectum* 2015, **58**(12): 1194–1209.
6 Shenoy, P., Harugeri, A.: Elderly patients' participation in clinical trials. *Perspect Clin Res* 2015, **6**(4): 184–189.
7 Cook, I.J., Weltman, M.D., Wallace, K., Shaw, D.W., McKay, E., Smart, R.C., Butler, S.P.: Influence of aging on oral-pharyngeal bolus transit and clearance during swallowing: Scintigraphic study. *Am J Physiol* 1994, **266**(6 Pt 1): G972–G977.
8 Dejaeger, E., Pelemans, W., Ponette, E., Joosten, E.: Mechanisms involved in postdeglutition retention in the elderly. *Dysphagia* 1997, **12**(2): 63–67.
9 Fukunaga, A., Uematsu, H., Sugimoto, K.: Influences of aging on taste perception and oral somatic sensation. *J Gerontol A Biol Sci Med Sci* 2005, **60**(1): 109–113.
10 Shaker, R., Ren, J., Zamir, Z., Sarna, A., Liu, J., Sui, Z.: Effect of aging, position, and temperature on the threshold volume triggering pharyngeal swallows. *Gastroenterology* 1994, **107**(2): 396–402.
11 Aviv, J.E., Martin, J.H., Jones, M.E., Wee, T.A., Diamond, B., Keen, M.S., Blitzer, A.: Age-related changes in pharyngeal and supraglottic sensation. *Ann Otol Rhinol Laryngol* 1994, **103**(10): 749–752.
12 Ren, J., Xie, P., Lang, I.M., Bardan, E., Sui, Z., Shaker, R.: Deterioration of the pharyngo-UES contractile reflex in the elderly. *Laryngoscope* 2000, **110**(9): 1563–1566.
13 Ren, J., Shaker, R., Kusano, M., Podvrsan, B., Metwally, N., Dua, K.S., Sui, Z.: Effect of aging on the secondary esophageal peristalsis: Presbyesophagus revisited. *Am J Physiol* 1995, **268**(5 Pt 1): G772–G779.
14 Dejaeger, E., Pelemans, W., Bibau, G., Ponette, E.: Manofluorographic analysis of swallowing in the elderly. *Dysphagia* 1994, **9**(3): 156–161.
15 Grande, L., Lacima, G., Ros, E., Pera, M., Ascaso, C., Visa, J., Pera, C.: Deterioration of esophageal motility with age: A manometric study of 79 healthy subjects. *Am J Gastroenterol* 1999, **94**(7): 1795–1801.
16 Lasch, H., Castell, D.O., Castell, J.A.: Evidence for diminished visceral pain with aging: Studies using graded intraesophageal balloon distension. *Am J Physiol* 1997, **272**(1 Pt 1): G1–G3.
17 Hall, K.E.: Aging and neural control of the GI tract. II. Neural control of the aging gut: Can an old dog learn new tricks? *Am J Physiol Gastrointest Liver Physiol* 2002, **283**(4): G827–G832.

18 Bannister, J.J., Abouzekry, L., Read, N.W.: Effect of aging on anorectal function. *Gut* 1987, **28**(3): 353–357.
19 Lagier, E., Delvaux, M., Vellas, B., Fioramonti, J., Bueno, L., Albarede, J.L., Frexinos, J.: Influence of age on rectal tone and sensitivity to distension in healthy subjects. *Neurogastroenterol Motil* 1999, **11**(2): 101–107.
20 O'Toole, P.W., Jeffery, I.B.: Gut microbiota and aging. *Science* 2015, **350**(6265): 1214–1215.
21 Jain, V., Pitchumoni, C.S.: Gastrointestinal side effects of prescription medications in the older adult. *J Clin Gastroenterol* 2009, **43**(2): 103–110.
22 Nolan, L., O'Malley, K.: Prescribing for the elderly. Part I.: Sensitivity of the elderly to adverse drug reactions. *J Am Geriatr Soc* 1988, **36**(2): 142–149.
23 Singh, M., Chaudhary, S., Azizi, S., Green, J.: Gastrointestinal drug interactions affecting the elderly. *Clin Geriatr Med* 2014, **30**(1): 1–15.
24 Lavan, A.H., Gallagher, P.: Predicting risk of adverse drug reactions in older adults. *Ther Adv Drug Saf* 2016, **7**(1): 11–22.
25 Rohrer, J.E., Garrison, G., Oberhelman, S.A., Meunier, M.R.: Epidemiology of polypharmacy among family medicine patients at hospital discharge. *J Prim Care Community Health* 2013, **4**(2): 101–105.
26 Pretorius, R.W., Gataric, G., Swedlund, S.K., Miller, J.R.: Reducing the risk of adverse drug events in older adults. *Am Fam Physician* 2013, **87**(5): 331–336.
27 Chan, M., Nicklason, F., Vial, J.H.: Adverse drug events as a cause of hospital admission in the elderly. *Intern Med J* 2001, **31**(4): 199–205.
28 Kennedy, G.J., Castro, J., Chang, M., Chauhan-James, J., Fishman, M.: Psychiatric and medical comorbidity in the primary care geriatric patient-an update. *Curr Psychiatry Rep* 2016, **18**(7): 62.
29 Parlesak, A., Klein, B., Schecher, K., Bode, J.C., Bode, C.: Prevalence of small bowel bacterial overgrowth and its association with nutrition intake in nonhospitalized older adults. *J Am Geriatr Soc* 2003, **51**(6): 768–773.
30 Wetherell, J.L., Ayers, C.R., Nuevo, R, Stein M.B., Ramsdell, J, Patterson T.L.: Medical conditions and depressive, anxiety, and somatic symptoms in older adults with and without generalized anxiety disorder. *Aging Ment Health* 2010, **14**(6): 764–768.
31 Taylor, W.D.: Clinical practice: Depression in the elderly. *N Engl J Med* 2014, **371**(13): 1228–1236.
32 Hegeman, J.M., Kok, R.M., van der Mast, R.C., Giltay, E.J.: Phenomenology of depression in older compared with younger adults: meta-analysis. *Br J Psychiatry* 2012, **200**(4): 275–281.
33 Roach, M., Christie, J.A.: Fecal incontinence in the elderly. *Geriatrics* 2008, **63**(2): 13–22.
34 American Geriatrics Society: 2015 Updated Beers criteria for potentially inappropriate medication use in older adults. *J Am Geriatr Soc* 2015, **63**(11): 2227–2246.
35 Gallagher, P., Ryan, C., Byrne, S., Kennedy, J., O'Mahony, D.: STOPP (Screening Tool of Older Person's Prescriptions) and START (Screening Tool to Alert doctors to Right Treatment). Consensus validation. *Int J Clin Pharmacol Ther* 2008, **46**(2): 72–83.
36 Izzy, M., Malieckal, A., Little, E., Anand, S.: Review of efficacy and safety of laxatives use in geriatrics. *World J Gastrointest Pharmacol Ther* 2016, **7**(2): 334–342.
37 Cherniack, E.P.: Use of complementary and alternative medicine to treat constipation in the elderly. *Geriatr Gerontol Int* 2013, **13**(3): 533–538.

Chapter 22

Diagnostic and treatment approaches associated with functional gastrointestinal disorders in children and adolescents

Sara E. Williams
Brenda Bursch

The aim of this chapter is to provide information on the diagnosis and treatment of functional gastrointestinal disorders (FGIDs) in children and adolescents, with a particular focus on efficacious psychological approaches. There are effective psychological approaches to manage these conditions in children and adolescents, particularly for pain-related FGIDs, including cognitive behavioural therapy and hypnotherapy.

Learning points

- FGIDs are common among children and adolescents.
- Children with FGIDs go on to experience those and other health problems as adults.
- There are effective psychological interventions for children with FGIDs.
- Psychological treatment improves function, coping and symptom management.
- Practical recommendations include discussing treatment in a biopsychosocial context and referring for/providing psychological intervention.

Introduction

Symptoms related to functional gastrointestinal disorders (FGIDs), such as chronic or intermittent nausea, vomiting, abdominal pain and constipation, are common complaints among children and adolescents. For instance, population studies show that many children experience abdominal pain at some point during development, with up to 43% of school children reporting transient abdominal pain [1] and 13.5% of children reporting chronic abdominal pain problems, more common in girls [2]. Studies of FGID prevalence among paediatric patients in the medical setting have shown that 2%–4% of all paediatric primary care patients are seen for abdominal pain complaints and up to 50% of paediatric gastroenterology patients have a pain-related FGID [3].

As with adults, FGIDs are understood to be a physiological disorder generated by a combination of disruptions in enteric and central nervous system activity [4]. Alterations at the enteric level can lead to changes in intestinal motility, which in turn can result in abdominal pain, diarrhoea, constipation and nausea. Visceral hypersensitivity, a result of nerves in the gastrointestinal (GI) tract becoming over-sensitized, contributes to the production of pain or discomfort from normal stimuli. Communication between the brain and gut also becomes dysregulated, resulting in increased signals and perception of symptoms. Psychosocially, disturbances in mood and functioning amplify the symptom experience and adversely affect children with FGIDs. FGIDs are disruptive to normal childhood development. Anxiety, depression and somatic symptoms are associated with FGIDs in children and adolescents, as well as poor quality of life, school absence and health-care utilization [2, 5].

Research has identified several factors that may predispose children to develop FGIDs. Genetics play a role in making it more likely for a child to develop physiological disruptions in the GI tract [6]. Early life events have been identified as precursors to the development of visceral hypersensitivity (e.g., physical or psychological stress) [7]. Parent and family factors also play an important role (e.g., family interaction around illness, parent coping and mental health); there is a clustering of chronic pain in families that may occur through parental modelling of illness behaviour and/or through shared genetics [8].

Because of the complex relationship between these factors that contribute to the presentation of FGIDs, it is widely agreed that these disorders are best understood through a biopsychosocial model [4, 9]. The biopsychosocial model "integrates biological science with the unique features of the individual and determines the degree to which biological and psychosocial factors interact to explain the disease, illness, and outcome" (p. 262) [9]. In other words, in addition to the biological process, psychological, social, environmental and behavioural factors are recognized as contributing and interacting factors in patients' experience of FGIDs. Using this model to explain the problem can enable children and parents to understand the need for a comprehensive approach to treatment.

Diagnostic criteria

The Rome IV includes specific FGID diagnoses for children and adolescents [10]; infant and toddler diagnoses are also available [11], which are not reviewed in detail in this chapter but are summarized in Table 22.1. Rome IV focuses on symptom-based diagnosis for these paediatric conditions. This represents a shift from a prior focus on ruling out organic disease to a positive diagnosis format, which is based on symptom presentation when medical evaluation has determined that symptoms are not associated with another condition or are found to co-exist with another condition. There are 11 child and adolescent FGIDs in Rome IV presented in three categories: *Functional Nausea and Vomiting Disorders* (Cyclic Vomiting Syndrome, Functional Nausea and Functional Vomiting, Rumination Syndrome, Aerophagia), *Functional Abdominal Pain Disorders* (Functional Dyspepsia, Irritable Bowel Syndrome, Abdominal Migraine, Functional Abdominal Pain Not Otherwise Specified), *Functional Defecation Disorders* (Functional Constipation, Nonretentive Faecal Incontinence). The diagnostic criteria are also presented in Table 22.1.

Table 22.1 Diagnostic criteria for childhood functional gastrointestinal disorders: neonate/toddler and child/adolescent.

G1. Infant regurgitation[1]
Diagnostic criteria Must include *both* of the following in otherwise healthy infants 3 weeks to 12 months of age:
1. Regurgitation two or more times per day for three or more weeks
2. No retching, hematemesis, aspiration, apnoea, failure to thrive, feeding or swallowing difficulties, or abnormal posturing

G2. Rumination syndrome[2]
Diagnostic criteria Must include *all* of the following for at least two months:
1. Repetitive contractions of the abdominal muscles, diaphragm and tongue
2. Effortless regurgitation of gastric contents, which are either expelled from the mouth or rechewed and reswallowed
3. Three or more of the following:
    a. Onset between 3 and 8 months
    b. Does not respond to management for GERD and regurgitation
    c. Unaccompanied by signs of distress
    d. Does not occur during sleep and when the infant is interacting with individuals in the environment

G3. Cyclic vomiting syndrome (CVS)[3]
Diagnostic criteria Must include *all* of the following:
1. Two or more periods of unremitting paroxysmal vomiting with or without retching, lasting hours to days within a six-month period
2. Episodes are stereotypical in each patient.
3. Episodes are separated by weeks to months with return to baseline health between episodes of vomiting.

G4. Infant colic[4]
Diagnostic criteria For clinical purposes, must include *all* of the following:
1. An infant who is less than 5 months of age when the symptoms start and stop
2. Recurrent and prolonged periods of infant crying, fussing or irritability reported by caregivers that occur without obvious cause and cannot be prevented or resolved by caregivers
3. No evidence of infant failure to thrive, fever or illness

'Fussing' refers to intermittent distressed vocalization and has been defined as "behaviour that is not quite crying but not awake and content either." Infants often fluctuate between crying and fussing, so that the two symptoms are difficult to distinguish in practice.

For clinical research, a diagnosis of infant colic must meet the preceding diagnostic criteria *and also include both* of the following:
1. Caregiver reports infant has cried or fussed for three or more hours/day during three or more days in seven days in a telephone or face-to-face screening interview with a researcher or clinician.
2. Total 24-hour crying plus fussing in the selected group of infants is confirmed to be three hours or more when measured by at least one prospectively kept 24-hour behaviour diary.

G5. Functional diarrhoea[5]
Diagnostic criteria Must include *all* of the following:
1. Daily painless, recurrent passage of four or more large, unformed stools
2. Symptoms last more than four weeks
3. Onset between 6 and 60 months of age
4. No failure to thrive if caloric intake is adequate

(Continued)

Table 22.1 (Continued)

G6. Infant dyschezia[6]
Diagnostic criteria Must include in an infant less than 9 months of age:
1. At least ten minutes of straining and crying before successful or unsuccessful passage of soft stools
2. No other health problems

G7. Functional constipation (FC)[7]
Diagnostic criteria Must include *one month of at least two* of the following in infants up to 4 years of age:
1. Two or fewer defecations per week
2. History of excessive stool retention
3. History of painful or hard bowel movements
4. History of large-diameter stools
5. Presence of a large faecal mass in the rectum
In toilet-trained children, the following additional criteria may be used:
6. At least one episode/week of incontinence after the acquisition of toileting skills
7. History of large-diameter stools which may obstruct the toilet

H1. Functional nausea and vomiting disorders
H1a. Cyclic vomiting syndrome (CVS)[8]
Diagnostic criteria Must include *all* of the following:
1. Two or more periods of intense, unremitting nausea and paroxysmal vomiting, lasting hours to days within a six-month period
2. Episodes are stereotypical in each patient.
3. Episodes are separated by weeks to months with return to baseline health between episodes.
4. After appropriate evaluation, the symptoms cannot be attributed to another medical condition.

H1b. Functional nausea and functional vomiting[9]
H1b1. Functional nausea[10]
Diagnostic criteria* Must include *all* of the following:
1. Bothersome nausea as the predominant symptom, occurring at least twice per week, and generally not related to meals
2. Not consistently associated with vomiting
3. After appropriate evaluation, the nausea cannot be fully explained by another medical condition.
* Criteria fulfilled for at least two months prior to diagnosis

H1b2. Functional vomiting[11]
Diagnostic criteria* Must include *all* of the following:
1. On average, one or more episodes of vomiting per week
2. Absence of self-induced vomiting or criteria for an eating disorder or rumination
3. After appropriate evaluation, the vomiting cannot be fully explained by another medical condition.
* Criteria fulfilled for at least two months prior to diagnosis

H1c. Rumination syndrome[12]
Diagnostic criteria* Must include *all* of the following:
1. Repeated regurgitation and rechewing or expulsion of food that:
a. Begins soon after ingestion of a meal
b. Does not occur during sleep

2. Not preceded by retching
3. After appropriate evaluation, the symptoms cannot be fully explained by another medical condition. An eating disorder must be ruled out.

* Criteria fulfilled for at least two months prior to diagnosis

H1d. Aerophagia[13]

Diagnostic criteria* Must include *all* of the following:

1. Excessive air swallowing
2. Abdominal distension due to intraluminal air which increases during the day
3. Repetitive belching and/or increased flatus
4. After appropriate evaluation, the symptoms cannot be fully explained by another medical condition.

* Criteria fulfilled for at least two months prior to diagnosis

H2. Functional abdominal pain disorders

H2a. Functional dyspepsia (FD)[14]

Diagnostic criteria Must include *one or more* of the following bothersome symptoms at least four times a month for at least two months prior to diagnosis:

1. Postprandial fullness
2. Early satiation
3. Epigastric pain or burning not associated with defecation
4. After appropriate evaluation, the symptoms cannot be fully explained by another medical condition.

Within FD the following subtypes are now adopted:

H2a1. *Postprandial distress syndrome (PDS)*[15] includes bothersome postprandial fullness or early satiation which prevents finishing a regular meal. Supportive features include upper abdominal bloating, postprandial nausea or excessive belching.

H2a2. *Epigastric pain syndrome (EPS)*[16], which includes all of the following: bothersome (severe enough to interfere with normal activities) pain or burning localized to the epigastrium. The pain is not generalized or localized to other abdominal or chest regions and is not relieved by defecation or passage of flatus. Supportive criteria can include (a) burning quality of the pain but without a retrosternal component, (b) commonly induced or relieved by ingestion of a meal but may occur while fasting.

H2b. Irritable bowel syndrome (IBS)[17]

Diagnostic criteria* Must include *all* of the following:

1. Abdominal pain at least four days per month over at least two months associated with *one or more* of the following:
   a. Related to defecation
   b. A change in frequency of stool
   c. A change in form (appearance) of stool
2. In children with abdominal pain and constipation, the pain does not resolve with resolution of the constipation (children in whom the pain resolves have functional constipation, not IBS).
3. After appropriate evaluation, the symptoms cannot be fully explained by another medical condition.

* Criteria fulfilled for at least two months prior to diagnosis

H2c. Abdominal migraine[18]

Diagnostic criteria* Must include *all* of the following occurring at least twice:

(Continued)

Table 22.1 (Continued)

1. Paroxysmal episodes of intense, acute periumbilical, midline or diffuse abdominal pain lasting one hour or more (should be the most severe and distressing symptom)
2. Episodes are separated by weeks to months.
3. The pain is incapacitating and interferes with normal activities.
4. Stereotypical pattern and symptoms in the individual patient
5. The pain is associated with *two or more* of the following:

a. Anorexia
b. Nausea
c. Vomiting
d. Headache
e. Photophobia
f. Pallor

6. After appropriate evaluation, the symptoms cannot be fully explained by another medical condition.

* Criteria fulfilled for at least six months prior to diagnosis

H2d. Functional abdominal pain – not otherwise specified[19]
Diagnostic criteria* Must be fulfilled at least four times per month and include *all* of the following:

1. Episodic or continuous abdominal pain that does not occur solely during physiologic events (e.g., eating, menses)
2. Insufficient criteria for irritable bowel syndrome, functional dyspepsia or abdominal migraine
3. After appropriate evaluation, the abdominal pain cannot be fully explained by another medical condition.

* Criteria fulfilled for at least two months prior to diagnosis

H3. Functional defecation disorders
H3a. Functional constipation (FC)[20]
Diagnostic criteria Must include *two or more* of the following occurring at least once per week for a minimum of one month with insufficient criteria for a diagnosis of IBS:

1. Two or fewer defecations in the toilet per week in a child of a developmental age of at least 4 years
2. At least one episode of faecal incontinence per week
3. History of retentive posturing or excessive volitional stool retention
4. History of painful or hard bowel movements
5. Presence of a large faecal mass in the rectum
6. History of large-diameter stools which can obstruct the toilet
7. After appropriate evaluation, the symptoms cannot be fully explained by another medical condition.

H3b. Nonretentive faecal incontinence[21]
Diagnostic criteria Must include at least a one-month history in a child with a developmental age older than 4 years of *all* of the following:

1. Defecation in places inappropriate to the sociocultural context
2. No evidence of faecal retention
3. After appropriate evaluation, the faecal incontinence cannot be explained by another medical condition.

Diagnostic criteria taken from S Nurko, MA Benninga, C Faure, PE Hyman, NL Schechter, I St. James-Roberts [12], Childhood functional gastrointestinal disorders: Neonate/Toddler, chapter 15, pages [1]1243, [2]1247, [3]1250, [4]1256, [5]1263, [6]1266, [7]1268 and CD Lorenzo, JS Hyams, M Saps, RJ Shulman, A Staiano and MAL van Tilburg [13], Childhood functional gastrointestinal disorders: Child/Adolescent, chapter 16, pages [8]1300, [9,10,11]1307, [12]1310, [13]1315, [14,15,16]1319, [17]1324, [18]1333, [19]1337, [20]1342, [21]1348 of the *Rome IV functional gastrointestinal disorders: Disorders of gut-brain interaction*. Reproduction approved by Professor Douglas Drossman 23/10/2016.

In this chapter, we will primarily review the literature and focus discussion on diagnoses in the Functional Abdominal Pain Disorders category, both because this category encompasses the most common FGID diagnosis in children and adolescents and because it is the most well-researched in terms of efficacy of psychological interventions. While there are some studies in the literature examining behavioural treatment of constipation, there are no trials examining treatment in functional nausea or vomiting conditions [14].

Differential diagnosis

Although the range of diagnoses differs [10], the general approach to differential diagnosis for paediatric FGIDs is broad and does not substantially differ from adults. It includes assessment for malabsorptive conditions, inflammatory bowel disease, dietary factors, psychiatric conditions, infections, malignancies and other conditions.

Clinicians evaluating children and adolescents with symptoms of a pain-related FGID may be challenged by specific subsets of these patients. For example, there is a greater prevalence of GI symptoms among children with autism spectrum disorders (ASD) compared to typically developing children [15]. Evaluation may be complicated because some individuals with ASDs have great difficulty identifying and/or communicating about symptoms. For others, behavioural problems may cloud the picture, such as adolescents who trigger gastroparesis due to intentional or unintentional restricted intake of food [16]. These issues underscore the value of evaluations that are conducted by paediatric specialists who are aware of such nuances in children and adolescents.

Common patient concerns and issues

Children and adolescents with FGIDs have more anxious, depressive and somatic symptoms, experience poorer quality of life and have more school absences than healthy children [2, 5]. Specifically, in one study, 79% and 43% of children with FAP were found to have anxiety and depression, respectively, compared to only 11% of healthy children with anxiety and 8% with depression (effect size, .68 for anxiety and .40 for depression) [5]. In addition, children with FAP have been shown to have increased depression, more somatic symptoms and greater functional impairment compared to children with gastrointestinal disease [17]. A long-term study of 31 children with FAP found that they continued to have more abdominal pain episodes, functional impairment and health service utilization five years after initial evaluation compared to 31 healthy children; in that sample, only 1 child with FAP received a later diagnosis of another medical condition to explain symptoms [18]. One third of children with FAP continue to have abdominal pain as adults and go on to develop other chronic pain conditions [19]. Finally, adults with a childhood history of FAP have a significantly higher lifetime prevalence rate of anxiety and depressive disorders (51% and 40%, respectively) compared to adults who were healthy as children (20% and 16%, respectively) [20].

Parents of children with FGIDs have a high level of anxiety [21] as well as their own history of FGIDs [9] compared to parents of healthy children. Parents of children with FAP also have high levels of distress about their children's symptoms [22]. These factors may lead to parents to reassure their children and protect them from harm by encouraging children to withdraw from activities. Although well-intended, protective parenting behaviour is associated with high levels of school absence and pain-related disability in paediatric FAP patients [23]. In contrast, distracting or coping-promoting parenting behaviour that draws children's attention away from symptoms and encourages function is associated with fewer symptom complaints among children with FAP [24].

Treatment approaches

Due to the lack of high-quality, placebo-controlled trials of pharmacologic treatment, there is insufficient evidence to support routine use of any pharmacologic therapy for paediatric pain-related FGIDs. Preliminary studies suggest that supplements and medications, such as peppermint oil, cyproheptadine and famotidine, are promising in terms of managing symptoms effectively; however, randomized controlled trials need to be conducted in paediatric populations [25]. Probiotics (LGG and VSL#3, which are beneficial bacteria that are thought to prevent overgrowth of potentially pathogenic bacteria, maintain the integrity of gut mucosa and/or alter intestinal inflammatory responses) have demonstrated benefit over placebo for children with FAP, IBS and functional dyspepsia. Those with IBS appear to benefit most from probiotics [26–29]. Consistent with a biopsychosocial treatment approach, pharmacologic treatment of medical and psychiatric comorbidities may reduce symptoms or improve functioning by reducing nociceptive input and/or allostatic load.

The best research support for the effective treatment of paediatric pain-related FGIDs comes from non-pharmacologic approaches. Due to concerns about side effects and impact on development, many parents are interested in or can be educated to accept a non-medication-based treatment approach for FGIDs. Psychological interventions, including psychotherapy/cognitive behavioural therapy (CBT), hypnotherapy/guided imagery and biofeedback with relaxation training, have direct effects on symptoms and promote self-efficacy by increasing the child's ability to manage symptoms. However, in order to help them understand the rationale for this recommendation, both children and families benefit from initial careful explanation of how psychosocially based techniques can alter physiological function for symptom relief.

Psychotherapy is used to reduce somatic and psychological symptoms, improve coping and functioning, increase communication and problem solving and reduce stress load. CBT refers to psychotherapy focused on achieving these goals by modifying unhelpful cognitions, assumptions, beliefs and behaviours, and it is the most common form of psychotherapy delivered to children and adolescents with the largest evidence base. Techniques may include developing a biopsychosocial view of symptoms; briefly keeping a diary of symptoms and associated events, feelings, thoughts and/or behaviours (to identify triggers and outcomes that could be targeted for intervention); learning relaxation and distraction techniques to aid in symptom management; questioning cognitions, assumptions and beliefs that may be unhelpful or unrealistic and trying new ones; and gradually facing activities that have been avoided. Anxiety and depression are also effectively treated with CBT in children and adolescents, and this treatment can be incorporated into FGID treatment as well when there are comorbid concerns. Parent training is included as part of CBT to facilitate acceptance of a rehabilitation approach to treatment, alter family patterns that maintain disability or exacerbate symptoms, help parents better tolerate children's distress, and develop behavioural plans that support the child's self-management of symptoms and independent functioning.

Hypnotherapy and guided imagery interventions are like deep relaxation or meditative experiences in which the child imagines a pleasant scene either independently or as directed by a therapist. The experience takes attention away from symptoms, alters sensory experiences, reduces distress, induces relaxation, reframes symptom experiences, facilitates dissociation from pain and enhances feelings of mastery. 'Gut-directed' hypnotherapy includes abdomen-specific suggestions that can facilitate a more pleasant physical sensation (e.g., imagining a pleasant sensation in the gut).

Biofeedback uses a computer to generate a visual or auditory indicator of muscle tension, peripheral skin temperature, heart rate or muscle control (e.g., anal rectal manometry), allowing the child to have external validation of physiological symptoms that he or she can then observe changing when using relaxation and symptom management techniques. Relaxation includes techniques such as progressive muscle relaxation and diaphragmatic breathing, which directly alter pain perception by facilitating a relaxation response.

Psychological therapies have a solid evidence base for paediatric pain-related FGIDs, especially. Study results are summarized in Table 22.2.

Table 22.2 Summary of the current evidence for allied health approaches.

Treatment approach	*Level of evidence*	*Comments*
Biofeedback	Level II	One RCT [30] and a review [31] show good effects for children pain-related FGIDs, rumination and constipation. Heart-rate variability biofeedback changes vagal tone, which may be a mediator for symptom improvement [32].
CBT	Level I	Multiple randomized controlled trials (RCTs) and systematic reviews show efficacy among paediatric patients with FAP and IBS in particular [33–35]. Decreasing maladaptive parent and child cognitions may mediate symptom improvement [36].
Hypnotherapy	Level I	Multiple RCTs and review show superior therapeutic effects compared to standard medical care [35].
Yoga	Level III-1	Two small trials show symptom improvement compared to standard care [37, 38].

Practical recommendations

- Based on the evidence, it is recommended to refer and provide psychological intervention for children with pain-related FGIDs.
- It is helpful to describe these approaches to children and families in practical terms to improve understanding of the efficacy of the intervention and the likelihood of following through with the recommendation, which can be described in the following ways.
- Psychological intervention typically involves CBT performed individually with the child, or with the child and family. The goal of CBT is for children to learn to reduce their symptoms by reducing central nervous system arousal and by improving their resilience to stressors. This is done by teaching the child body-based and cognitive coping skills (e.g., relaxation techniques, positive thinking strategies), and how to effectively communicate and problem-solve related to their chronic stressors and to adopt a functional coping approach (e.g., adopting active and distracting coping skills to continue with regular activities).
- It is also essential for the treating provider to work with the child's school and family to ensure that the functional pain coping approach is supported in the child's school and family settings.
- Biofeedback and self-hypnosis/guided imagery are additional evidence-based skills that can be taught to assist the child or adolescent with symptom self-management, either within a CBT framework or as an added treatment.

Current limitations/future considerations

- While there is good evidence for the efficacy of psychological intervention for children and adolescents with pain-related FGIDs, efficacy for other FGIDs needs to be evaluated.
- Limitation to delivery of psychological intervention includes availability of resources, insurance access, stigma of mental health–based approaches, rarity of providers with expertise in this area, and need for multiple treatment sessions.
- Studies of psychological interventions are limited by definitions of pain and sample sizes.
- Optimal health care is based on the combination of medical and allied health practices; more studies of integrated interdisciplinary care are needed.
- Recommendations for future research are inclusion of comorbid psychopathology, well-defined inclusion and exclusion criteria, and standardized outcome measures of symptoms, function and mental health.

Acknowledgements, competing interests and funding

Dr Williams is an author for Guilford Press and receives royalty payments. Dr Bursch is an author for Oxford Press and receives royalty payments. No external funding was received for this chapter.

References

1 Roth-Isigkeit, A., Thyen, U., Stöven, H., Schwarzenberger, J., Schmucker, P.: Pain among children and adolescents: Restrictions in daily living and triggering factors. *Pediatrics* 2005, **115**(2): e152–e162.

2 Korterink, J.J., Diederen, K., Benninga, M.A., Tabbers, M.M.: Epidemiology of pediatric functional abdominal pain disorders: A meta-analysis. *PloS one* 2015, **10**(5): e0126982.

3 Rouster, A.S., Karpinski, A.C., Silver, D., Monagas, J., Hyman, P.E.: Functional gastrointestinal disorders dominate pediatric gastroenterology outpatient practice. *J Pediat Gastroenterol Nut* 2016, **62**(6): 847–851.

4 Chiou, E., Nurko, S.: Management of functional abdominal pain and irritable bowel syndrome in children and adolescents. *Exp Rev Gastroenterol Hepatol* 2010, **4**(3): 293–304.

5 Campo, J.V., Bridge, J., Ehmann, M., Altman, S., Lucas, A., Birmaher, B., Di Lorenzo, C., Iyengar, S., Brent, D.A.: Recurrent abdominal pain, anxiety, and depression in primary care. *Pediatrics* 2004, **113**(4): 817–824.

6 Talley, N.J.: Genetics and functional bowel disease. *J Pediat Gastroenterol Nut* 2008, **47**(5): 680–682.

7 Miranda, A.: Early life events and the development of visceral hyperalgesia. *J Pediatr Gastroenterol Nut* 2008, **47**(5): 682–684.

8 Levy, R.L., Whitehead, W.E., Von Korff, M.R., Feld, A.D.: Intergenerational transmission of gastrointestinal illness behavior. *Am J Gastroenterol* 2000, **95**(2): 451–456.

9 Drossman, D.A.: Gastrointestinal illness and the biopsychosocial model. *Psychosom Med* 1998, **60**(3): 258–267.

10 Hyams, J.S., Di Lorenzo, C., Saps, M., Shulman, R.J., Staiano, A., van Tilburg, M.: Childhood functional gastrointestinal disorders: Child/adolescent. *Gastroenterology* 2016, **150**(6): 1456–1468. e1452.

11 Benninga, M.A., Nurko, S., Faure, C., Hyman, P.E., Roberts, I.S.J., Schechter, N.L.: Childhood functional gastrointestinal disorders: Neonate/toddler. *Gastroenterology* 2016, **150**(6): 1443–1455. e1442.

12 Nurko, S., Benninga, M.A., Faure, C., Hyman, P.E., Schechter, N.L., St. James-Roberts, I: Childhood functional gastrointestinal disorders: Neonate/Toddler. In: *Rome IV functional gastrointestinal disorders: Disorders of gut-brain interaction*. Edited by Chang, L., Chey, W.D., Kellow, J., Tack, J., Whitehead, W.E., The Rome IV Committees. Raleigh, NC: Rome Foundation, 2016: 1237–1296.

13 Lorenzo, C.D., Hyams, J.S., Saps, M., Shulman, R.J., Staiano, A., van Tilburg, M.A.L.: Childhood functional gastrointestinal disorders: Child/adolescent. In: *Rome IV functional gastrointestinal disorders: Disorders of gut-brain interaction*. Edited by Chang, L., Chey, W.D., Kellow, J., Tack, J., Whitehead, W.E., The Rome IV Committees. Raleigh, NC: Rome Foundation, 2016: 1297–1372.

14 Russell, A.C., Stone, A.L., Walker, L.S.: Functional nausea in children: A review of the literature and need for diagnostic criteria. *Children* 2016, **3**(1): 5.

15 McElhanon, B.O., McCracken, C., Karpen, S., Sharp, W.G.: Gastrointestinal symptoms in autism spectrum disorder: A meta-analysis. *Pediatrics* 2014, **133**(5): 872–883.

16 De Caprio, C., Pasanisi, F., Contaldo, F.: Gastrointestinal complications in a patient with eating disorders. *Eat Weight Disord* 2000, **5**(4): 228–230.

17 Walker, L.S., Garber, J., Greene, J.W.: Psychosocial correlates of recurrent childhood pain: A comparison of pediatric patients with recurrent abdominal pain, organic illness, and psychiatric disorders. *J Abnorm Psychol* 1993, **102**(2): 248.

18 Walker, L.S., Garber, J., Van Slyke, D.A., Greene, J.W.: Long-term health outcomes in patients with recurrent abdominal pain. *J Pediatr Psychol* 1995, **20**(2): 233–245.

19 Walker, L.S., Dengler-Crish, C.M., Rippel, S., Bruehl, S.: Functional abdominal pain in childhood and adolescence increases risk for chronic pain in adulthood. *Pain* 2010, **150**(3): 568–572.

20 Shelby, G.D., Shirkey, K.C., Sherman, A.L., Beck, J.E., Haman, K., Shears, A.R., Horst, S.N., Smith, C.A., Garber, J., Walker, L.S.: Functional abdominal pain in childhood and long-term vulnerability to anxiety disorders. *Pediatrics* 2013, **132**(3): 475–482.

21 Garber, J., Zeman, J., Walker, L.S.: Recurrent abdominal pain in children: Psychiatric diagnoses and parental psychopathology. *J Am Acad Child Adolescent Psychiat* 1990, **29**(4): 648–656.

22 van Tilburg, M.A., Venepalli, N., Ulshen, M., Freeman, K.L., Levy, R., Whitehead, W.E.: Parents' worries about recurrent abdominal pain in children. *Gastroenterol Nurs* 2006, **29**(1): 50–55.

23 Walker, L.S., Zeman, J.L.: Parental response to child illness behavior. *J Pediatr Psychol* 1992, **17**(1): 49–71.

24 Walker, L.S., Williams, S.E., Smith, C.A., Garber, J., Van Slyke, D.A., Lipani, T.A.: Parent attention versus distraction: Impact on symptom complaints by children with and without chronic functional abdominal pain. *Pain* 2006, **122**(1): 43–52.

25 Korterink, J.J., Rutten, J.M., Venmans, L., Benninga, M.A., Tabbers, M.M.: Pharmacologic treatment in pediatric functional abdominal pain disorders: A systematic review. *J Pediatr* 2015, **166**(2): 424–431. e426.

26 Bausserman, M., Michail, S.: The use of Lactobacillus GG in irritable bowel syndrome in children: A double-blind randomized control trial. *J Pediatr* 2005, **147**(2): 197–201.

27 Francavilla, R., Miniello, V., Magistà, A.M., De Canio, A., Bucci, N., Gagliardi F, Lionetti, E., Castellaneta, S., Polimeno, L., Peccarisi, L.: A randomized controlled trial of Lactobacillus GG in children with functional abdominal pain. *Pediatrics* 2010, **126**(6): e1445–e1452.

28 Gawrońska, A., Dziechciarz, P., Horvath, A., Szajewska, H.: A randomized double-blind placebo-controlled trial of Lactobacillus GG for abdominal pain disorders in children. *Aliment Pharmacol Ther* 2007, **25**(2): 177–184.

29 Guandalini, S., Magazzu, G., Chiaro, A., La Balestra, V., Di Nardo, G., Gopalan, S., Sibal, A., Romano, C., Canani, R.B., Lionetti, P.: VSL# 3 improves symptoms in children with irritable bowel syndrome: A multicenter, randomized, placebo-controlled, double-blind, crossover study. *J Pediatric Gastroenterol Nut* 2010, **51**(1): 24–30.

30 Schurman, J.V., Wu, Y.P., Grayson, P., Friesen, C.A.: A pilot study to assess the efficacy of biofeedback-assisted relaxation training as an adjunct treatment for pediatric functional dyspepsia associated with duodenal eosinophilia. *J Pediatr Psychol* 2010, **35**(8): 837–847.

31 Desantis, D.J., Leonard, M.P., Preston, M.A., Barrowman, N.J., Guerra, L.A.: Effectiveness of biofeedback for dysfunctional elimination syndrome in pediatrics: A systematic review. *J Pediatr Urol* 2011, **7**(3): 342–348.

32 Sowder, E., Gevirtz, R., Shapiro, W., Ebert, C.: Restoration of vagal tone: A possible mechanism for functional abdominal pain. *Appl Psychophysiol Biofeedback* 2010, **35**(3): 199–206.

33 Eccleston, C., Palermo, T.M., Williams, A.C.d.C., Lewandowski, A., Morley, S.: Psychological therapies for the management of chronic and recurrent pain in children and adolescents. *Cochrane Lib* 2009: CD003968.

34 Fisher, E., Heathcote, L., Palermo, T.M., de C Williams, A.C., Lau J, Eccleston, C.: Systematic review and meta-analysis of psychological therapies for children with chronic pain. *J Pediatr Psychol* 2014, **39**(8): 763–782.

35 Rutten, J.M., Korterink, J.J., Venmans, L.M., Benninga, M.A., Tabbers, M.M.: Nonpharmacologic treatment of functional abdominal pain disorders: A systematic review. *Pediatrics* 2015, **135**(3): 522–535.

36 Levy, R.L., Langer, S.L., Romano, J.M., Labus, J., Walker, L.S., Murphy, T.B., Van Tilburg, M., Feld, L.D., Christie, D.L., Whitehead, W.E.: Cognitive mediators of treatment outcomes in pediatric functional abdominal pain. *Clin J Pain* 2014, **30**(12): 1033.

37 Evans, S., Lung, K.C., Seidman, L.C., Sternlieb, B., Zeltzer, L.K., Tsao, J.C.: Iyengar yoga for adolescents and young adults with irritable bowel syndrome. *J Pediatr Gastroenterol Nut* 2014, **59**(2): 244.

38 Korterink, J.J., Ockeloen, L.E., Hilbink, M., Benninga, M.A., Deckers-Kocken, J.M.: Yoga therapy for abdominal pain related-functional gastrointestinal disorders in children: A randomized controlled trial. *J Pediatr Gastroenterol Nut* 2016, **3**(5): 481–487.

Part IV

Working with complex psychological issues in functional gastrointestinal disorders

Chapter 23

Functional gastrointestinal disorders and eating disorders

Catherine Boyd

The aim of this chapter is to summarize the evidence in relation to the comorbidity of eating disorders (EDs) in FGIDs cohorts and provide recommendation relating to treatment.

Learning points

- Gastrointestinal symptoms in patients with eating disorders are common, and may be due to functional gastrointestinal disorders.
- Standardized criteria for the assessment of functional gastrointestinal disorders can be used in patients with eating disorders.
- There is individual variation, though the functional gastrointestinal disorders in patients with eating disorders may be related to eating-disordered behaviour and characteristics, and psychological dysfunction.
- Functional gastrointestinal complaints and disorders should be monitored during recovery from the eating disorder, and may persist.

Introduction

The EDs, anorexia nervosa, bulimia nervosa, binge eating disorder and the unspecified EDs (ED not otherwise specified (EDNOS), as per *Diagnostic and Statistical Manual 5* [DSM-5; 1], or other specified feeding or ED (OSFED), or unspecified feeding or ED (UFED), are serious, chronic psychiatric disorders, affecting young women and men in Western and Western-influenced cultures. The cardinal feature of the EDs is attempted or actual weight loss. There is usually a fear of gaining weight or becoming fat, and a preoccupation with body shape and food intake, which results in either restrictive eating, or binge eating, and increased energy output (excessive exercise or purging). Feelings of loss of control over one's eating behaviour and body weight and associated guilt are common. EDs have a chronic course, and without treatment, are characterized by periods of remission and relapse. The mortality rate at ten years for anorexia nervosa is among the highest of the psychiatric disorders, at approximately 5% [2].

The pathogenesis of EDs is complex. As summarized by Abraham [3], risk factors for the eating disorders may include genetic propensity, childhood experiences (e.g., abuse, illness, loss or separation), family attributes (e.g., inadequate modelling of eating behaviour, medical or psychiatric illness in family member, parent-child interactions) and sociocultural attitudes (emphasis on success, beauty, thinness). These risk factors, and the physical and psychological changes associated with puberty (particularly in women), in the presence of actual or attempted weight loss (e.g., due to viral illness, excessive exercising for performance, or depression) are among the predisposing, precipitating and/or maintaining factors of an eating disorder.

The variability of the behavioural (e.g., food restriction, purging, excessive exercise), psychological (e.g., concerns about shape and weight, depression, anxiety) and physical (e.g., weight loss, somatic complaints) symptoms between people with eating disorders, and even temporally within an individual, necessitates long-term, multidisciplinary management. Dietary, medical, psychological and psychiatric realms must be addressed, with the addition of family therapy for younger patients.

There are some common features between EDs and FGIDs. These include the preponderance of females who seek medical attention for both eating disorders and FGIDs (despite there being similar numbers of women and men with FGIDs in community samples). Patients with eating disorders focus on dietary intake and output, and many develop food preferences. Similarly, patients with FGIDs may relate some gastrointestinal symptoms to particular food types, and this may result in a restrictive diet. As with EDs, the expression of functional gastrointestinal disorders is complex and multifactorial, and may be understood in the biopsychosocial model proposed by Drossman [4].

Gastrointestinal symptoms in patients with EDs

The occurrence of gastrointestinal symptoms in patients with EDs is well documented. Symptoms attributable to the entire gastrointestinal tract have been described in patients with anorexia nervosa [5–11] and bulimia nervosa [5, 10, 12–15].

Functional gastrointestinal disorders in patients with EDs

FGIDs or 'functional gastrointestinal disorder-like' symptoms are a common feature of ED patients, with a prevalence of over 90% among anorexia nervosa, bulimia nervosa or eating disorder not otherwise specified patients [16–18], though there are variations depending on the standardized instrument administered [19]. Moreover, in FGID patients, a higher than expected proportion (16%) report a past history of EDs [17]. The most prevalent FGIDs in eating disorder inpatient populations include irritable bowel syndrome (52%–57% patients), functional constipation (24%–27% patients) and functional heartburn (26%–51%), though other FGIDs involving the entire gastrointestinal tract are also common [16, 19]. Interestingly, between 34% and 52% of patients fulfil the criteria for at least three coexistent FGIDs in these studies. Functional dyspepsia was reported to be common in patients with a range of eating-disordered behaviour in one study, though the presence of other FGIDs wasn't examined.

FGIDs have also been recognized in other psychiatric conditions, with irritable bowel syndrome also being the most common diagnosis [20, 21].

Organic gastrointestinal disease in patients with EDs

In most people with EDs, there are no structural or biochemical abnormalities to account for gastrointestinal symptoms or weight loss. A careful clinical assessment, including detailed history of food intake, purging behaviours (including vomiting, laxative abuse and excessive exercise) and psychological assessment, will reveal behaviour which is contributing to a negative energy balance. However, a degree of caution should be reserved, as 'anorexia' or appetite suppression may be due to chronic illness. Baseline laboratory assessments for patients with EDs will include complete blood count, electrolytes, urea and creatinine, liver function tests, calcium, magnesium, phosphate, thyroid function and serology for coeliac disease. Further tests to assess for the presence of organic gastrointestinal disease should be reserved when gastrointestinal symptoms are severe, or when 'alarm symptoms', persisting weight loss or poor weight gain despite adequate caloric intake, persisting abnormal laboratory results, or significant comorbid illness are present. Second-line investigations may include urine and stool microscopy and culture, serum and stool inflammatory markers, tests of pancreatic function, imaging of the abdomen and possible endoscopy. There are few reports of duodenal ulcers and erosive oesophagitis in patients with bulimia nervosa [12, 22–24, and rare instances of acute gastric dilatation or rupture associated with binge eating [25–28].

In patients with EDs, are functional gastrointestinal symptoms due to the eating-disordered characteristics?

One may presume that the high prevalence of gastrointestinal symptoms in patients with eating disorders is simply due to eating-disordered characteristics (e.g., low or fluctuating weight, long duration of illness) or behaviours (e.g., binge eating, vomiting, severe food restriction, excessive exercise), but few studies have demonstrated any such connection. One study [5] reported no significant differences in symptoms between people with anorexia nervosa and bulimia nervosa, though others have reported a relationship between the number of bulimic behaviours and higher measures of gastrointestinal symptom severity in a group of patients with bulimia nervosa [13]. Binge-eating behaviour was a significant predictor of functional heartburn in a group of inpatients with eating disorders [16], though other disordered eating characteristics, including weight, were not predictors. In a study of obese and normal-weight binge eaters, the obese individuals had a higher prevalence of gastrointestinal symptoms [29].

Gastrointestinal motility and emptying in patients with eating disorders

Altered gastrointestinal motility has been postulated as one of the mechanisms contributing to the expression of function gastrointestinal disorders in an individual, and has been examined in patients with eating disorders in multiple studies. The overall average half emptying time is delayed in patients with anorexia nervosa compared to controls[6–9, 30–37], yet as reported by some researchers, normal emptying is present in at least 50% of adults and children with anorexia nervosa [10, 33, 38]. Gastric emptying characteristics are less well defined in patients with bulimia nervosa; delayed [22, 37–39], rapid [39] and normal gastric emptying [10, 14] have been reported. Despite the changes in gastrointestinal motility in some patients, most studies have not observed a correlation between alterations in gastrointestinal motility and gastrointestinal symptoms[6, 8, 10, 36]. Moreover, whether gastrointestinal motility in patients with eating disorders relates to physiological parameters, such as body weight or nutritional state [6, 7, 10, 22], eating disorder behaviour [22, 34, 38] or psychological factors [36, 37] remains unclear.

Do gastrointestinal symptoms reflect altered psychological states?

There are few studies examining the relationship between psychological features and gastrointestinal symptoms in patients with eating disorders. Depression has been found to be the most important determinant of gastrointestinal symptoms in a group of patients before and after inpatient treatment of bulimia nervosa [13]. Psychological features (somatization, neuroticism, state and trait anxiety) were among the significant predictors of specific and >=3 coexistent FGIDs in a group of female inpatients with eating disorders [16]. Another study found no correlation between gastric symptoms and psychopathological measures [36].

Persistence of gastrointestinal symptoms in patients with eating disorders

A few prospectively designed studies have addressed whether gastrointestinal symptoms in patients with eating disorders persist after treatment. Chami and colleagues [13] reported that the gastrointestinal symptoms in patients with bulimia nervosa improved after an average of six weeks of inpatient treatment, yet remained worse than control subjects. Further, when these data were controlled for the concurrent improvement in depression, the effects of treatment on gastrointestinal symptoms were no longer significant – highlighting the effect of psychological dysfunction on gastrointestinal symptoms. A follow-up study on patients with anorexia nervosa also demonstrated an improvement in gastrointestinal symptoms after an average of 12 weeks of treatment, but these symptoms remained higher than in control subjects [11].

A follow-up study examining functional gastrointestinal disorders in women during treatment and at 12 months' follow-up showed that the prevalence of

FGIDs remains high (77% at follow-up compared with 97% at admission), and there was a significant decrease in only two FGIDs – functional heartburn and functional dyspepsia [40]. Similar to the presence of FGIDs in non-ED patients, however, was a considerable turnover of FGIDs, and the appearance of new FGIDs was not restricted to the original (admission) FGID regional category. Most patients in this study were recovering from the eating disorder at the follow-up point, and there was no apparent relationship between the turnover of the FGIDs and the ED behaviours of self-induced vomiting, laxative use or binge eating, body weight change or psychological variables. This suggest that the FGIDs in this group of patients with eating disorders at follow-up behave more like those in non-ED patients and seem unlikely to be related to the physiologic aspects of active weight-losing behaviours characteristic of EDs. Thus, it is feasible that mechanisms similar to the FGIDs in non-ED patients may be in operation in ED patients.

Porcelli and colleagues [18] found that patients with FGIDs were five times more likely to have had a past eating disorder than those presenting with gallstone disease. Interestingly, most of these patients developed gastrointestinal symptoms during the eating disorder period, which persisted after recovery from the eating disorder. The finding that those with a past history of an eating disorder had higher depression scores than their counterparts with FGID with no history of an eating disorder highlights the impact of psychological features on the persistence of gastrointestinal symptoms. Another group described greater eating disorder symptomatology in female IBS patients compared to female patients with organic gastrointestinal disease [41].

Recommendations for a holistic approach and conclusions

Management of functional gastrointestinal disorders in patients with eating disorders is not dissimilar to patients with FGIDs who do not suffer from an eating disorder. This involves correct identification of the disorder, using symptom-based criteria in the absence of alarm symptoms [42]. This approach will result in rationalizing and potentially avoiding invasive tests. Patients with both ED and FGIDs will benefit from acknowledgement of their symptoms, reassurance and explanation of their symptoms in a functional context. Medical and adjunctive therapy of functional gastrointestinal disorders is evolving and will be discussed in separate chapters. Cognitive behavioural therapy has also proved efficacious in selected patients [42].

Patients with eating disorders and FGIDs should be counselled that with recovery of the eating disorder, an overall improvement in the FGIDs symptoms is expected, though there may be different types of functional gastrointestinal symptoms experienced by an individual over time. The effect of specific therapies used for the treatment of eating disorders (e.g., cognitive behavioural therapy, family therapy, medications) on gastrointestinal symptoms in this group of patients is not known. Psychological factors may have an impact on the persistence of functional gastrointestinal disorders over time in patients with eating disorders, and should be monitored and treated, especially if there are ongoing gastrointestinal complaints. Similarly, persistence of a functional gastrointestinal disorder in patients with a history of an eating disorder should prompt the clinician to enquire about the presence of eating-disordered behaviours and psychological symptoms.

Patients with eating disorders have a high morbidity and mortality, and best practice of the management of patients with eating disorders is to involve a multidisciplinary team as early as possible in the treatment of the illness. Treatment of the eating disorder must not be delayed while investigation of gastrointestinal complaints is undertaken.

The risk of iatrogenesis in this group of patients should not be underestimated. A paper comparing ED patients presenting to an eating disorder unit with those presenting to a GI hospital [43] and an in-depth psychoanalytic paper looking at unnecessary, catastrophic surgery in such a patient make interesting reading [44].

Summary of practical recommendations

- In patients with eating disorders and gastrointestinal complaints, a careful history and assessment for the presence of alarm symptoms are important.
- Most patients with eating disorders and gastrointestinal symptoms do not require extensive investigations.
- Symptom-based criteria to assess functional gastrointestinal symptoms (e.g., the Rome III criteria) should be employed.
- Treatment of patients with both an eating disorder and functional gastrointestinal disorder should involve a multidisciplinary team, employing a biopsychosocial model of care.
- With recovery of the eating disorder, it is expected that the functional gastrointestinal symptoms will improve, though there may be crossover of symptoms over time.
- If there is persistence or worsening of gastrointestinal complaints, this should prompt further evaluation for the presence of eating-disordered behaviour and psychological distress, and careful assessment for the uncommon occurrence of organic gastrointestinal disease.

Current limitations

- There are no studies which look at the specific treatments for eating disorders and the effect these treatments have on gastrointestinal symptoms in these patients.
- Future studies which look at specific therapies for functional gastrointestinal symptoms may include patients with eating disorders.

Acknowledgements

Thank you to my dear friend and mentor, the late Associate Professor Suzanne Abraham, who continues to influence my writing and clinical practice. The author is unaware of any competing interests in relation to this chapter. No external funding was received for this chapter.

References

1 American Psychiatric Association: *Diagnostic and statistical manual of mental disorders*, 5th edn. Washington, DC: Author, 2013.

2 Arcelus, J., Mitchell, A.J., Wales, J., Nielsen, S.: Mortality rates in patients with anorexia nervosa and other eating disorders: A meta-analysis of 36 studies. *Arch Gen Psychiat* 2011, **68**(7): 724–731.

3 Abraham, S.: Dieting, body weight, body image and self-esteem in young women: Doctors' dilemmas. *Med J Aust* 2003, **178**: 607–611.

4 Drossman, D.A.: *Rome II: The functional gastrointestinal disorders*, 2nd edn. McLean, VA: Degnon Associates, 2000.

5 Kamal, N., Chami, T., Andersen, A., Rosell, F.A., Schuster, M.M., Whitehead, W.E.: Delayed gastrointestinal transit times in anorexia nervosa and bulimia nervosa. *Gastroenterology* 1991, **101**(5): 1320–1324.

6 Abell, T.L., Malagelada, J.R., Lucas, A.R., Brown, M.L., Camilleri, M., Go, V.L., Azpiroz, F., Callaway, C.W., Kao, P.C., Zinsmeister, A.R.: Gastric electromechanical and neurohormonal function in anorexia nervosa. *Gastroenterology* 1987, **93**(5): 958–965.

7 McCallum, R.W., Grill, B.B., Lange, R., Planky, M., Glass, E.E., Greenfeld, D.G.: Definition of a gastric emptying abnormality in patients with anorexia nervosa. *Dig Dis Sci* 1985, **30**: 713–722.

8 Rigaud, D., Bedig, G., Merrouche, M., Vulpillat, M., Bonfils, S., Apfelbaum, M.: Delayed gastric emptying in anorexia nervosa is improved by completion of a renutrition program. *Dig Dis Sci* 1988, **33**(919–925).

9 Stacher, G., Kiss, A., Wiesnagrotzki, S., Bergmann, H., Hobart, J., Schneider, C.: Oesophageal and gastric motility disorders in patients categorized as having primary anorexia nervosa. *Gut* 1986, **27**: 1120–1126.

10 Hutson, W.R., Wald, A.: Gastric emptying in patients with bulimia nervosa and anorexia nervosa. *Am J Gastroenterol* 1990, **85**(1): 41–46.

11 Waldholtz, B.D., Andersen, A.E.: Gastrointestinal symptoms in anorexia nervosa: A prospective study. *Gastroenterology* 1990, **98**: 1415–1419.

12 Nickl, N.J., Brazer, S.R., Rockwell, K., Smith, J.W.: Patterns of oesophageal motility in patients with stable bulimia. *Am J Gastroenterol* 1996, **91**(12): 2544–2547

13 Chami, T.N., Andersen, A.E., Crowell, M.D., Schuster, M.M., Whitehead, W.E.: Gastrointestinal symptoms in bulimia nervosa: Effects of treatment. *Am J Gastroenterol* 1995, **90**: 88–92.

14 Koch, K.L., Bingaman, S., Tan, L., Stern, R.M.: Visceral perceptions and gastric myoelectrical activity in healthy women and in patients with bulimia nervosa. *Neurogastroenterol Motil* 1998, **10**(1): 3–10.

15 Abraham, S.F., Beumont, P.J.V.: How patients describe bulimia or binge eating. *Psychol Med* 1982, **12**: 625–635.

16 Boyd, C., Abraham, S., Luscombe, G.: Exercise behaviours and feeling in eating disorder and non-eating disorder groups. *Eur Eating Dis Rev* 2007, **15**(2): 112–118.

17 Perkins, S.J., Keville, S., Schmidt, U., Chalder, T.: Eating disorders and irritable bowel syndrome: Is there a link? *J Psychosom Res* 2005, **59**(2): 57–64.

18 Porcelli, P., Leandro, G., Carne, M.D.: Functional gastrointestinal disorders and eating disorders – Relevance of the association in clinical management. *Scand J Gastroenterol* 1998, **33**(6): 577–582.

19 Wang, X., Luscombe, G.M., Boyd, C., Kellow, J., Abraham, S.: Functional gastrointestinal disorders in eating disorder patients: Altered distribution and predictors using ROME III compared to ROME II criteria. *WJG* 2014, **20**(43): 16293–16299

20 Garakani, A., Win, T., Virk, S., Gupta, S., Kaplan, D., Masand, P.S.: Comorbidity of irritable bowel syndrome in psychiatric patients: A review. *Am J Ther* 2003, **10**(1): 61–67.

21 Whitehead, W.E., Palsson, O., Jones, K.R.: Systematic review of the comorbidity of irritable bowel syndrome with other disorders: What are the causes and implications? *Gastroenterology* 2002, **122**(4): 1140–1156.

22 Kiss, A., Bergmann, H., Abatzi, T-A, Schneider, C., Wiesnagrotzki, S., Hobart, J., Steiner-Mittelbach, G., Gaupmann, G., Kugi, A., Stacher-Janotta, G.: Oesophageal and gastric motor activity in patients with bulimia nervosa. *Gut* 1990, **31**(3): 259–265.
23 Kiss, A., Wiesnagrotzki, S., Abatzi, T-A, Meryn, S., Haubenstock, A., Base, W.: Upper gastrointestinal endoscopy findings in patients with long-standing bulimia nervosa. *Gastrointest Endosc* 1989, **35**(6): 516–518.
24 Cuellar, R.E., Kaye, W.H., al LKGHe: Upper gastrointestinal tract dysfunction in bulimia. *Dig Dis Sci* 1988, **33**: 1549–1553.
25 Russell, G.F.: Acute dilatation of the stomach in a patient with anorexia nervosa. *Br J Psychiatry* 1966, **112**(483): 203–207.
26 Scobie, B.A.: Acute gastric dilatation and duodenal ileus in anorexia nervosa. *Med J Aus* 1973, **2**: 923–924.
27 Jennings, K.P., Klidjian, A.M.: Acute gastric dilatation in anorexia nervosa. *Br Med J* 1974, **2**: 477–478.
28 Saul, S.H., Dekker, A., Watson, C.G.: Acute gastric dilatation with infarction and perforation. *Gut* 1981, **22**: 978–983.
29 Crowell, M.D., Cheskin, L.J., Musial, F.: Prevalence of gastrointestinal symptoms in obese and normal weight binge eaters. *Am J Gastroenterol* 1994, **89**: 387–391.
30 Holt, S., Ford, M.J., Grant, S., Heading, R.C.: Abnormal gastric emptying in primary anorexia nervosa. *Br J Psychiatry* 1981, **139**: 550–552.
31 Stacher, G., Bergmann, H., Wiesnagrotzki, S., Kiss, A., Schneider, C., Mittelbach, G., Gaupmann, G., Hobart, J.: Intravenous cisapride accelerates delayed gastric emptying and increases antral contraction amplitudes in patients with primary anorexia nervosa. *Gastroenterology* 1987, **92**(4): 1000–1006.
32 Dubois, A., Gross, H.A., Ebert, M.H., Castell, D.O.: Altered gastric emptying and secretion on primary anorexia nervosa. *Gastroenterology* 1979, **77**: 319–323.
33 Domstad, P.A., Shih, W.J., Humphries, L., Deland, F.H., Digenis, G.A.: Radionuclide gastric emptying studies in patients with anorexia nervosa. *J Nucl Med* 1987, **28**: 816–819.
34 Robinson, P.H., Clark, M., Barrett, J.: Determinants of delayed gastric emptying in anorexia nervosa and bulimia nervosa. *Gut* 1988, **29**: 458–464.
35 Saleh, J.W., Lebwohl, P.: Metoclopramide induced gastric emptying in patients with anorexia nervosa. *Am J Gastroenterol* 1980, **74**: 127–132.
36 Luigi, B., Todesco, T., Dalle Grave, R., Deiorio, F., Salandini, L., Vantini, I.: Gastric emptying in patients with restricting and binge/purging subtypes of anorexia nervosa. *Am J Gastroenterol* 2004, **99**: 1448–1454.
37 Inui, A., Okano, H., Miyamoto, M., Aoyama, N., Uemoto, M., Baba, S., Kasuga, M.: Delayed gastric emptying in bulimic patients. *Lancet* 1995, **346**: 1240.
38 Diamante, A., Bracci, F., Gambarara, M., Ciofetta, G.C., Sabbi, T., Ponticelli, A., Montecchi, F., Marinucci, S., Bianco, G., Castro, M.: Gastric electric activity assessed by electrogastrography and gastric emptying scintigraphy in adolescents with eating disorders. *J Pediatr Gastroenterol Nut* 2003, **37**: 35–41.
39 Shih, W.J., Humphries, L., Digenis, G.A., Castellanos, F.X., Domstad, P.A., DeLand, F.H.: Tc-99m labeled tetraamine polysyrene resin gastric emptying studies in bulimia patients. *Eur J Nucl Med Mol Imaging* 1987, **13**(4): 192–196.
40. Boyd, C., Abraham, S., Kellow, J.: Appearance and disappearance of functional gastrointestinal disorders in patients with eating disorders. *Neurogastroenterol Motil* 2010, **22**(12): 1279–1283.
41 Guthrie, E.A., Creed, F.H., Whorwell, P.J.: Eating disorders in patients with the irritable bowel syndrome: A comparison with inflammatory bowel disease and peptic ulceration. *J Gastroenterol Hepatol* 1990, **2**: 471–473.
42 Brandt, LJ, Bjorkman, D., Fennerty, M., Locke, G.R., Olden, K., Peterson, W., Quigley, E., Schoenfeld, P., Schuster, M., Talley, N.: Systematic review on the management of irritable bowel syndrome in North America. *Am J Gastroenterol* 2002, **97**(11): S7–S26.
43 Emmanuel, A.V., Stern, J., Treasure, J., Forbes, A., Kamm, M.A.: Anorexia nervosa in gastrointestinal practice. *Eur J Gastroenterol Hepatol* 2004, **16**(11): 1135–1142.
44 Stern, J.M.: 'No entry', an invitation to intrude, or both? Reflections on a group of anorexic patients. *Int J Psychoanal* 2013, **94**(4): 689–713.

Chapter 24

Functional gastrointestinal disorders and psychotropic medication

Elspeth Carruthers
Julian Stern

The aim of this chapter is to review the mechanism of psychotropic medication action, specifically for selective serotonin reuptake inhibitors (SSRIs) and tricyclic antidepressants (TCAs), as well as other psychotropic agents, and explore current theories relating to pharmacological action both on the GI tract and centrally. Other areas discussed in this chapter include clinical indications, adherence challenges and the interaction with psychological therapies.

Learning points

- Prevalence and rationale for prescribing of antidepressants in FGIDs
- Mechanisms of action of SSRI medication
- Mechanisms of action of TCA medication
- Side effects, challenges with adherence, and communicating with the patient
- Interaction with psychological therapies

Introduction

At least one in eight patients with irritable bowel syndrome (IBS) is offered a psychotropic agent, almost invariably an antidepressant. Dekel, Drossman and Sperber [1] cite research showing prescribing rates of up to 50%. Psychotropic medications are often incorporated into the management of functional gastrointestinal disorders. Although nearly 70% of patients seeking secondary or tertiary care for functional gastrointestinal disorders (FGIDs) meet diagnostic criteria for a psychiatric disorder, this leaves 30% who do not, yet response to psychopharmacological agents in FGIDs is not predicated on psychiatric comorbidity.

Mechanisms

IBS and other FGIDs are increasingly seen as disorders of the gut-brain axis – a dysregulation of signalling between the gastrointestinal tract and the brain. Research focuses on the role of serotonergic mechanisms in IBS. Camilleri [2] summarizes the evidence for the role of serotonin in IBS, including elevated serotonin blood plasma levels in IBS patients, increased concentration of serotonin-containing cells in rectal biopsies, and the empirical evidence that serotonergic agents, such as 5-HT3 antagonists (e.g., ondansetron), are effective in treating many symptoms of IBS. Garsed *et al.* [3] concluded from a randomized controlled trial of ondansetron in 120 IBS patients that ondansetron improved IBS symptom severity scores compared to placebo. This suggests that a key mechanism involved in the use of psychopharmacological agents to treat IBS and other FGIDs is the inhibition of serotonin and/or norepinephrine reuptake by serotonergic agents, such as tricyclic antidepressants (TCAs) and selective serotonin reuptake inhibitors (SSRIs). These work at the presynaptic level of the brain, affecting the central nervous system processes involved in the gut-brain axis, but may also work in the gastrointestinal system: the greatest concentration of serotonin is found in the enteric nervous system [4].

Grover and Camilleri [5] reviewed evidence for the effects of psychopharmacological agents on gastrointestinal functions, highlighting studies showing that the SSRI paroxetine and the serotonin-norepinephrine reuptake inhibitor (SNRI) venlafaxine, along with the anxiolytic buspirone, promoted gut transit and gastric accommodation in patients with functional dyspepsia. Nevertheless, they concluded only that the effects of antidepressants on the GI tract 'may' contribute to their potential efficacy in functional dyspepsia and IBS.

Clouse and Lustman [6, page 1335] concluded that "antidepressants may address mechanisms more specifically related to global distress than to correction of gut physiological abnormalities or individual gastrointestinal complaints", while also citing research showing that the level of global distress was a better predictor of health-related quality of life in IBS patients, rather than gastrointestinal symptoms. Other mechanisms involved in the effects of psychopharmacological agents on FGIDs are their broad analgesic and antiemetic effects. TCAs have an analgesic effect in functional pain syndromes, thought to relate to their inhibition of norepinephrine and serotonin reuptake, and these analgesic effects exist independently of their effect on mood [1]. Certain psychopharmacological agents are also known to have an antiemetic effect, which may prove generally therapeutic.

There are high rates of psychiatric comorbidity in FGIDs (including depression and anxiety): the prevalence of psychiatric disorders ranges from 40% to 60% in FGID patients presenting to tertiary care [1]. In such cases, psychotropic medications play a well-attested role in improving global well-being and reducing the symptoms of comorbid psychiatric disorders.

Main psychotropic agents used in treating FGIDs

Tricyclic antidepressants (TCAs)

TCAs (e.g., amitriptyline, nortriptyline, dosulepin, clomipramine) are the most widely used psychotropic agents for pain syndromes. Although their analgesic function is not fully understood, it is thought to relate to the inhibition of norepinephrine and serotonin uptake. Dekel, Drossman and Sperber [1] propose three explanations for why their effect may be unrelated to their antidepressant effect:

firstly, TCAs have been shown to have an effect in numerous pain syndromes in which there is no associated psychopathological comorbidity. Secondly, when used for pain (and for IBS) they are usually administered in much lower doses than when used for psychiatric indications, specifically depression. Thirdly, studies specifically addressing this issue have found that TCAs have an analgesic effect independent of their effect on mood. Clouse and Lustman [6] suggest that their effects on neurotransmitter physiology could explain their benefit in functional gastrointestinal disorders unrelated to their antidepressant effect.

Rahimi, Nikfar, Rezale and Abdollahi [7] conducted a systematic review of TCAs for the treatment of IBS, with a total number of 257 IBS patients, and found that TCAs reduce abdominal pain scores in IBS patients, with an effect size of TCA versus placebo of -44.15 (95% CI: -53.27 to -35.04, $P < 0.0001$). Given that antidepressant therapy in IBS aims to treat the dysregulation in the brain-gut axis, rather than concomitant depression, they suggested that the dosage required would be lower than for depression. They highlighted several problems with randomized controlled trials (RCTs) of antidepressants for IBS, including the high placebo response rate in IBS, and the difficulty of randomization given the prevalence of side effects with TCAs. There is also a lack of comparative studies between TCAs and SSRIs. Ruepert *et al.* [8], in their Cochrane review of antidepressants for IBS, found that their subgroup analysis of TCAs showed a statistically significant improvement in abdominal pain (320 patients) and symptom score (87 patients). The subgroup analysis also showed a statistically significant benefit for TCAs in improvement of global assessment (523 patients).

Grover and Camilleri [5] reviewed studies of TCAs for FGIDs, including IBS and functional dyspepsia. They found that studies have focused on amitriptyline, which reduced nausea symptoms in 28 healthy volunteers (after a drink test) and in 38 functional dyspepsia patients (over the entire course of treatment but not after a drink test). Another study has also shown significant benefits of amitriptyline over no treatment in 31 patients with functional dyspepsia. In patients with IBS and comorbid depression, one study found a significant improvement in depressive symptoms with desipramine. However, a trial of 90 paediatric FGID patients showed no benefit of the TCA over placebo. The authors caution that trials of antidepressants for IBS are generally small and the recommendations from meta-analyses are unreliable.

Ford *et al.* [9] reviewed 11 RCTs of TCAs for IBS with a total of 744 patients and concluded that TCAs were an effective treatment for IBS, pointing out that the broad estimates of the efficacy of TCAs had remained virtually unchanged since the previous review conducted by the authors five years ago. However, they also caution that further research is necessary, citing the small number of studies and risk of bias.

Selective serotonin reuptake inhibitors (SSRIs)

SSRIs inhibit the reuptake of serotonin only, rather than serotonin and norepinephrine: they therefore have a less powerful analgesic effect than TCAs. However, evidence suggests that they have an effect on global well-being in FGIDs.

In particular, they are recommended to alleviate anxiety-specific symptoms in IBS, and may be used in combination with other psychotropic agents, such as TCAs [1]. Ruepert *et al.* [8] found a statistically significant improvement in global assessment for SSRIs in the subgroup analysis of their Cochrane review (227 patients). However, subgroup analysis showed no benefit for SSRIs in improvement of abdominal pain (197 patients).

Grover and Camilleri [5] reviewed the use of SSRIs for FGIDs. One study showed that paroxetine accelerated orocecal transit in 18 IBS patients and healthy controls; another that paroxetine and psychotherapy improved health-related quality of life in IBS patients (257 participants); and another that paroxetine improved overall well-being in IBS patients, who nevertheless did not experience any improvement in pain, bloating or social functioning (98 participants). For fluoxetine, one 40-participant study showed that it improved pain scores, and another (44 participants) showed a decrease in abdominal pain and bloating and improvement in stool frequency and consistency. Their discussion of citalopram cites a small study showing increased colonic compliance after acute citalopram infusion in ten subjects, and another showing improved pain, bloating and overall symptom scores with citalopram in IBS (23 participants). However, another study of 51 IBS patients showed no benefit of citalopram over placebo for global IBS endpoints.

As with TCAs, the authors call for caution in interpreting the results of meta-analyses, given their sometimes unrepresentative results; for example, one trial of fluoxetine in 44 constipation-predominant IBS patients showed an unrepresentative 10% placebo response for discomfort and bloating. Meta-analyses of SSRIs and other antidepressants often use secondary endpoints when primary endpoints are not significant. Moreover, many studies, including several of those discussed earlier, include relatively small patient numbers.

Ford *et al.* [9] reviewed seven trials comparing SSRIs with placebo in a total of 356 IBS patients. A total of 45.5% of patients allocated to SSRIs had no improvement in symptoms, versus 67.2% of placebo patients. The number needed to treat with SSRIs was four, but with a wider confidence interval compared to TCAs. The authors highlighted statistically significant heterogeneity between studies of SSRIs for IBS. They also highlight one trial of citalopram which excluded depressed individuals and found no benefit of therapy over placebo in the remaining 54 participants: this suggests there is only weak evidence for citalopram in non-depressed IBS patients. Ford *et al.* thus recommend further studies which either exclude depressed and/or anxious individuals or stratify for psychological comorbidities.

Other agents (SNRIs, mirtazapine, buspirone, anti-psychotic agents)

There is some evidence for other classes of psychotropic medications in FGIDs. Certain SNRIs have some effect in functional pain disorders, such as fibromyalgia: Marks *et al.* [10], in a review of SNRIs for pain relief, conclude that the available data suggest greater effects from dual-acting antidepressants, such as

SNRIs, than for SSRIs. There is also some evidence for atypical antidepressants, such as mirtazapine (an atypical antidepressant with noradrenergic and specific serotonergic activity), and other drugs, such as the anxiolytic buspirone, a 5-HT1A receptor agonist.

Grover and Camilleri [5] reviewed studies of buspirone: in one study, buspirone enhanced gastric relaxation in 10 healthy participants, and in another it decreased symptom scores in 51 healthy participants after a liquid meal. A study of the effect of buspirone in 17 functional dyspepsia patients showed a reduction in symptom scores and overall dyspepsia severity scores, but no effect on gastric emptying or gastric sensation. In another study of lower GI functions in 60 healthy participants, buspirone had almost no effect. Looking at SNRIs, a study of 51 healthy volunteers showed that venlafaxine enhanced gastric accommodation, suggesting efficacy in treating functional dyspepsia. Another study compared venlafaxine to placebo in 160 functional dyspepsia patients, but showed no overall efficacy, with many drop-outs due to side effects. In a study of lower GI function in 60 healthy participants, venlafaxine increased colonic compliance and reduced pain sensation.

Dekel, Drossman and Sperber [1] conclude that there are little data on the effectiveness of SNRIs in IBS. They highlight adherence issues in conducting such trials: in a study of duloxetine in 15 non-depressed IBS patients, 7 dropped out due to side effects. Despite extensive research on venlafaxine in pain syndromes, the authors state there are no data concerning venlafaxine specifically in IBS.

Dekel, Drossman and Sperber [1] reviewed atypical antipsychotics, such as quetiapine and olanzapine, both of which have been trialled in functional pain disorders, such as fibromyalgia. A retrospective study found that in 21 patients with severe FGIDs, 6 reported improvement after low doses of quetiapine (although 10 subjects dropped out due to side effects). Olanzapine has been shown to decrease pain and improve quality of life in fibromyalgia, but has not been trialled in FGIDs. Dekel, Drossman and Sperber [1] also briefly reviewed mirtazapine, concluding that data regarding its use in FGIDs are limited.

Table 24.1 summarizes common psychotropic medications, side effects and relevance to treating primary FGID symptoms.

Clinical indications and contraindications

The Cochrane reviewers, Ruepert *et al.* [8], concluded that the positive effects of antidepressant medications were sufficient to warrant a discussion of their indication for FGIDs. Clouse and Lustman [6] advise that antidepressants are indicated for FGIDs patients who do not respond to the usual low-risk interventions, such as reassurance and diet. However, antidepressants are currently not used optimally, largely because their mechanisms are so poorly understood. Choosing the correct medication and dosage can therefore be a 'crude process' [6, 1334].

The choice of the right psychotropic agent depends on several factors. The patient's symptom profile is important: for example, given the potentially constipating effect of TCAs, TCAs are recommended for non-constipated patients but SNRIs for constipated patients. Other side effects should also be taken into

Table 24.1 Common psychotropic medications, side effects and relevance to treating primary FGID symptoms.

Type of medication	*Impact on predominant FGID symptom*					*Impact on psychological/psychiatric symptom*			
	Pain	*Diarrhoea*	*Constipation*	*Dyspepsia*	*Appetite*	*Depression*	*Anxiety*	*Insomnia*	*Suicidality*
Tricyclic antidepressants (TCAs). Examples: Amitriptyline, Nortriptylline, Clomipramine, Doxepin Dothiepin/ Dosulein, Trimipramine, Imipramine	✓ (sometimes used for FGID pain) A recent meta-analysis [8] showed a superiority of TCAs over placebo for abdominal pain.	✓ A placebo-controlled trial of amitriptyline for diarrhoea-predominant IBS [11] showed that patients receiving amitriptyline experienced fewer incidents of loose stool than the control group.	× Some TCAs are indeed constipating. See, for example, a recent evaluation of the net benefit of TCAs for IBS [12] which found that TCAs caused constipation in 13% of IBS patients.	✓ A meta-analysis of 1241 patients showed that TCAs had beneficial effects for functional dyspepsia patients [13].	× A placebo-controlled study of healthy volunteers showed that TCAs had no effect on satiation [14]. There is little research on the effect of TCAs on upper GI function.	✓ See, for example, [15]: Cochrane review of antidepressants in primary care.	× See, for example, [16] for a comparison of TCAs and benzodiazepines for anxiety disorders.	✓ Some are more sedating than others. See, for example, [17].	(beware in overdose)
Serotonin reuptake inhibition (SSRI). Examples: Citalopram, Escitalopram, Fluvoxamine, Fluoxetine, Sertraline, Paroxetine	× Ruepert, Quartero, de Wit, van der Heijden, Rubin and Muris [8] found no evidence for improvement of abdominal pain with	× See, for example, Van Nieuwenhoven and Kilkens [20].	✓ It is often reported that SSRIs decrease gut transit time (in comparison to TCAs, which increase	× See Lu, Chen, Huang and Tang [22].	Anecdotal evidence suggests that SSRIs suppress appetite.	✓ See NICE guidelines on treatment of depression for a summary of the literature on SSRIs and depression [23].	✓ See NICE guidelines on treatment of anxiety for a summary of the literature on SSRIs and anxiety [24].	× SSRI treatment has been linked with insomnia. See Asnis *et al.* [25].	SSRIs have been linked to a decreased risk of suicide in adults and an increased risk of suicide in young people. See Barbui, Esposito and Cipriani [26].

	SSRIs. Some smaller studies have shown benefit – e.g., Tack *et al.* [18], Vahedi *et al.* [19].		it). See, for example, Gorard, Libby and Farthing [21].						
Serotonin Noradrenaline reuptake inhibition (SNRI). Examples: Venlafaxine, Desvenlafaxine, Duloxetine.	✓ See, for example, Kaplan *et al.* [27].	✓	×	× See, for example, van Kerkhoven *et al.* [28].	??	✓ See Bradley and Lenox-Smith [29].	✓ See Silverstone [30].	✓ See Ensrud *et al.* [31].	A higher risk for suicide has been reported for venlafaxine compared to other antidepressants. See Rubino *et al.* [32].
Noradrenergic and specific serotonin antidepressant (NaSSA). Example: Mirtazapine.	?	?	× Often reported as a side effect of mirtazapine.	✓ A number of studies have reported benefits from mirtazapine in dyspepsia. See, for example, Tacket *al.* [33].	✓ See Tacket *al.* [33] for discussion of mirtazapine and early satiation.	✓ See Watanabe *et al.* [34].	✓ See Croom, Perry and Plosker [35].	✓ Mirtazapine can be helpful in patients who are struggling to sleep as it has a sedative effect. See Wichniak, Wierzbicka and Jernajczyk [36].	A higher rate of suicide associated with mirtazapine use has been reported in a cohort study [37].
Monoamine oxidase inhibitor (MAOI). Examples: Phenelzine, Tranylcypromine	?	MAOIs have been reported to have a constipating effect.	MAOIs have been reported to have a constipating effect.	?	?	✓ See Krishnan [38].	✓ MAOIs may benefit patients suffering from anxiety. See Culpepper [39].	× MAOIs have been associated with sleep disorders. See Robinson and Amsterdam [40].	

consideration, such as the nausea and weight loss often caused by antidepressants: clinicians should consider which psychotropic medications are more easily tolerated. Although it is important to take into account psychological comorbidity when prescribing psychotropic medication for IBS and other FGIDs, the presence or absence of this comorbidity should not determine whether these agents are prescribed: rather, there is consensus that psychotropic medications should be prescribed for moderate to severe FGIDs which have not responded to other treatments.

Issues with adherence and side effects

Adherence to psychotropic medication can be challenging. FGID patients may feel that when a clinician prescribes psychotropic medication for their physically experienced symptoms, this suggests that he or she thinks it is 'all in their head' or does not believe them. Even in trials of psychotropic medication for FGIDs, discontinuation rates reach 50%, partly because of the common side effects experienced as a result of psychotropic drugs.

There are a number of ways for clinicians to improve adherence to psychotropic medication among patients with FGIDs. Firstly, psychotropic medication should not generally be prescribed for patients with mild or intermittent IBS, and should be reserved for patients with moderate or severe symptoms, or whose symptoms cannot be managed with first-line treatments, such as diet, laxatives and bulking agents.

Where psychotropic medications are prescribed, this should be accompanied by a detailed conversation about the reasons for prescribing, the relationship between the gut and the brain, and how psychotropic medication can be effective in FGIDs. The clinician should also discuss side effects, risks and benefits, and alternatives. As the side effects of many psychotropic drugs are most acute in the first days of treatment, patients should be especially supported during this time.

All psychotropic medications have side effects, whether prescribed for IBS or for depression and/or anxiety, and these frequently pertain to the GI tract. IBS and other GI symptoms might be exacerbated by such medications. The National Institute of Mental Health [41] highlights the range and prevalence of the side effects of psychotropic agents: with antidepressants, the most common include nausea and vomiting, weight gain, diarrhoea, sleepiness and sexual problems. For antipsychotics, side effects include drowsiness, dizziness, restlessness, weight gain (the risk is higher with some atypical antipsychotics), dry mouth, constipation and nausea. For anxiolytics, the NIMH states that the most common side effects for benzodiazepines are drowsiness and dizziness [41]. Other possible side effects include dependence/addiction, nausea, depression, cognitive problems and delirium.

While psychotropic agents can be helpful in some FGIDs, they can also exacerbate GI symptoms or introduce new symptoms, which may affect adherence. Most importantly, when pharmacotherapy is considered in a patient with a FGID, the physician needs to ensure the patient feels listened to and understood, and not just 'fobbed off' with a prescription.

Psychotropic medications and talking therapies

Within the field of psychotherapy and psychiatry, there has been much debate about the sequential or combined use of psychotherapy and psychopharmacology. Gabbard [42] has written how in the last half of the twentieth century, many psychoanalytically oriented clinicians maintained that medications somehow submerged important conflicts and feelings, making psychotherapy and psychoanalysis less effective.

However, within contemporary mental health practice there is increasing recognition of the value of combined psychological and psychopharmacological approaches, sequentially or concurrently. For example, for some patients, only once their mood has begun to lift via initiation of an antidepressant are they able to make full use of a talking therapy. For others, despite being committed to a psychological approach, the severity of depression might mean that they and their therapist agree that the addition of a pharmacological agent could be helpful.

Different models of practice exist, each with its own benefits and risks. In some cases, when treatment is via a psychiatrist, the prescriber and the therapist are the same individual. In others the prescriber and therapist are different individuals, and there is a need for close co-working to avoid unhealthy splits and conflict both within the professional network and within the patient him- or herself. Clinicians need to be aware of a temptation to interfere in the privacy of the relationship between therapist and patient, and to be cautious about not intruding too forcefully, or impatiently, when psychotherapeutic progress is seen to be slow. A description of an integrated service in a specialist hospital for gastrointestinal disorders is provided by Stern [43].

Busch and Sandberg [44] (writing from the perspective of psychoanalytically oriented clinicians) pose questions which are relevant to psychotherapists of all persuasions: How should patients be introduced to medication? What are the clinical advantages of combined treatment? What is the impact of medication discussions and prescribing on the therapist's role and how is this best handled? The way in which this is discussed with, and conveyed to, the patient is crucial.

Practical recommendations

- Psychotropic agents may be prescribed for individuals with severe and refractory FGIDs who have not responded to first-line treatments.
- The choice of psychotropic agent depends on multiple factors, including the patient's symptom profile, psychological comorbidity and the side effects of the psychotropic drug.
- TCAs and SSRIs can improve global well-being and overall symptom score in individuals with FGIDs, although there is less evidence for an effect on specific gastrointestinal symptoms.

- There is less evidence for SNRIs, buspirone, mirtazapine and other antipsychotics.
- Physicians prescribing psychotropic agents for FGIDs must take into account any concerns the patient may have around 'psychiatric' medication for a physically experienced complaint. They must explain clearly their rationale for prescribing.
- To ensure adherence, patients must be supported adequately if they experience side effects during treatment, particularly at the beginning when the side effects of antidepressants may be most pronounced.
- There should be special attention paid to the possibility of gastrointestinal side effects and how these can be managed.
- Psychotropic medication can be usefully combined with psychological therapies, but careful thought must be given to how this combination will be managed and explained to the patient.

Current limitations/future considerations

- Limited understanding of the mechanisms behind the effect of psychotropic agents on FGIDs, leading to difficulties with prescribing and dosage.
- Lack of research on psychotropic agents and FGIDs: conclusions of meta-analyses may not always be valid.
- Small numbers of studies and small numbers of participants.
- Risk of bias with RCTs of psychotropic agents for FGIDs, such as the high placebo response rate in IBS.
- Inclusion of subjects suffering from depression/anxiety may distort results of RCTs.

Acknowledgements, competing interests and funding

The authors are unaware of any competing interests in relation to this chapter. No external funding was received for this chapter.

References

1 Dekel, R., Drossman, D.A., Sperber, A.D.: The use of psychotropic drugs in irritable bowel syndrome. *Exp Opin Investig Drugs* 2013, **22**(3): 329–339.
2 Camilleri, M.: Mechanisms in IBS: Something old, something new, something borrowed. *Neurogastroenterol Motil* 2005, **17**(3): 311–316.
3 Garsed, K., Chernova, J., Hastings, M., Lam, C., Marciani, L., Singh, G., Henry, A., Hall, I., Whorwell, P., Spiller, R.: A randomised trial of ondansetron for the treatment of irritable bowel syndrome with diarrhoea. *Gut* 2014, **63**(10): 1617–1625.
4 North, C.S., Hong, B.A., Alpers, D.H.: Relationship of functional gastrointestinal disorders and psychiatric disorders: Implications for treatment. *WJG* 2007, **13**(14): 2020–2027.
5 Grover, M., Camilleri, M.: Effects on gastrointestinal functions and symptoms of serotonergic psychoactive agents used in functional gastrointestinal diseases. *J Gastroenterol* 2013, **48**(2): 177–181.

6 Clouse, R.E., Lustman, P.J.: Use of psychopharmacological agents for functional gastrointestinal disorders. *Gut* 2005, **54**(9): 1332–1341.

7 Rahimi, R., Nikfar, S., Rezale, A., Abdollahi, M.: Efficacy of tricyclic antidepressants in irritable bowel syndrome: A meta-analysis. *WJG* 2009, **15**(13): 1548–1553.

8 Ruepert, L., Quartero, A.O., de Wit, N.J., van der Heijden, G.J., Rubin, G., Muris, J.W.: Bulking agents, antispasmodics and antidepressants for the treatment of irritable bowel syndrome. *Cochrane Database Syst Rev (Online)* 2011, **8**: CD003460.

9 Ford, A.C., Quigley, E.M., Lacy, B.E., Lembo, A.J., Saito, Y.A., Schiller, L.R., Soffer, E.E., Spiegel, B.M., Moayyedi, P.: Effect of antidepressants and psychological therapies, including hypnotherapy, in irritable bowel syndrome: Systematic review and meta-analysis. *Am J Gastroenterol* 2014, **109**(9): 1350–1365, quiz 1366.

10 Marks, D.M., Shah, M.J., Patkar, A.A., Masand, P.S., Park, G.Y., Pae, C.U.: Serotonin-norepinephrine reuptake inhibitors for pain control: Premise and promise. *Curr Neuropharmacol* 2009, **7**(4): 331–336.

11 Vahedi, H., Merat, S., Momtahen, S., Kazzazi, A.S., Ghaffari, N., Olfati, G., Malekzadeh, R.: Clinical trial: The effect of amitriptyline in patients with diarrhoea-predominant irritable bowel syndrome. *Aliment Pharm Ther* 2008, **27**(8): 678–684.

12 Shah, E., Pimentel, M.: Evaluating the functional net value of pharmacologic agents in treating irritable bowel syndrome. *Aliment Pharm Ther* 2014, **39**(9): 973–983.

13 Ford, A.C., Luthra, P., Tack, J., Boeckxstaens, G.E., Moayyedi, P., Talley, N.J.: Efficacy of psychotropic drugs in functional dyspepsia: Systematic review and meta-analysis. *Gut* 2015: gutjnl-2015-310721.

14 Bouras, E.P., Talley, N.J., Camilleri, M., Burton, D.D., Heckman, M.G., Crook, J.E., Richelson, E.: Effects of amitriptyline on gastric sensorimotor function and postprandial symptoms in healthy individuals: A randomized, double-blind, placebo-controlled trial. *Am J Gastroenterol* 2008, **103**(8): 2043–2050.

15 Arroll, B., Elley, C.R., Fishman, T., Goodyear-Smith, F.A., Kenealy, T., Blashki, G., Kerse, N., MacGillivray, S.: Antidepressants versus placebo for depression in primary care. *Cochrane Database Syst Rev* 2009, 3: CD007954.

16 Offidani, E., Guidi, J., Tomba, E., Fava, G.A.: Efficacy and tolerability of benzodiazepines versus antidepressants in anxiety disorders: A systematic review and meta-analysis. *Psychother Psychosom* 2013, **82**(6): 355–362.

17 Krystal, A.D., Durrence, H.H., Scharf, M., Jochelson, P., Rogowski, R., Ludington, E., Roth, T.: Efficacy and safety of doxepin 1 mg and 3 mg in a 12-week sleep laboratory and outpatient trial of elderly subjects with chronic primary insomnia. *Sleep* 2010, **33**(11): 1553–1561.

18 Tack, J., Broekaert, D., Fischler, B., Van Oudenhove, L., Gevers, A.M., Janssens, J.: A controlled crossover study of the selective serotonin reuptake inhibitor citalopram in irritable bowel syndrome. *Gut* 2006, **55**(8): 1095–1103.

19 Vahedi, H., Merat, S., Rashidioon, A., Ghoddoosi, A., Malekzadeh, R.: The effect of fluoxetine in patients with pain and constipation-predominant irritable bowel syndrome: A double-blind randomized-controlled study. *Aliment Pharm Ther* 2005, **22**(5): 381–385.

20 Van Nieuwenhoven, M.A., Kilkens, T.O.C.: The effect of acute serotonergic modulation on rectal motor function in diarrhea-predominant irritable bowel syndrome and healthy controls. *Eur J Gastroenterol Hepatol* 2012, **24**(11): 1259–1265.

21 Gorard, D.A., Libby, G.W., Farthing, M.J.G.: Influence of antidepressants on whole gut and orocaecal transit times in health and irritable bowel syndrome. *Aliment Pharmacol Ther* 1994, **8**(2): 159–166.

22 Lu, Y., Chen, M., Huang, Z., Tang, C.: Antidepressants in the treatment of functional dyspepsia: A systematic review and meta-analysis. *PLoS ONE* 2016, **11**(6): e0157798.

23 National Collaborating Centre for Mental Health: *Depression: The treatment and management of depression in adults*, updated edn. Leicester: British Psychological Society, 2010.

24 National Collaborating Centre for Mental Health: *Generalised anxiety disorder in adults: Management in primary, secondary and community care*. Leicester: British Psychological Society, 2011.
25 Asnis, G.M., Chakraburtty, A., DuBoff, E.A., Krystal, A., Londborg, P.D., Rosenberg, R., Roth-Schechter, B., Scharf, M.B., Walsh, J.K.: Zolpidem for persistent insomnia in SSRI-treated depressed patients. *J Clin Psychiat* 1999, **60**(10): 668–676.
26 Barbui, C., Esposito, E., Cipriani, A.: Selective serotonin reuptake inhibitors and risk of suicide: A systematic review of observational studies. *CMAJ* 2009, **180**(3): 291–297.
27 Kaplan, A., Franzen, M.D., Nickell, P.V., Ransom, D., Lebovitz, P.J.: An open-label trial of duloxetine in patients with irritable bowel syndrome and comorbid generalized anxiety disorder. *Int J Psychiat Clin Pract* 2014, **18**(1): 11–15.
28 van Kerkhoven, L.A.S., Laheij, R.J.F., Aparicio, N., De Boer, W.A., Van Den Hazel, S., Tan, A.C.I.T.L., Witteman, B.J.M., Jansen, J.B.M.J.: Effect of the antidepressant venlafaxine in functional dyspepsia: A randomized, double-blind, placebo-controlled trial. *Clinical Gastroenterology and Hepatology* 2008, **6**(7): 746–752.
29 Bradley, A.J., Lenox-Smith, A.J.: Does adding noradrenaline reuptake inhibition to selective serotonin reuptake inhibition improve efficacy in patients with depression? A systematic review of meta-analyses and large randomised pragmatic trials. *J Psychopharmacol* 2013, **27**(8): 740–758.
30 Silverstone, P.H.: Qualitative review of SNRIs in anxiety. *J Clin Psychiat* 2004, **65**(suppl 17): 19–28.
31 Ensrud, K.E., Guthrie, K.A., Hohensee, C., Caan, B., Carpenter, J.S., Freeman, E.W., LaCroix, A.Z., Landis, C.A., Manson, J.A., Newton, K.M., *et al.*: Effects of estradiol and venlafaxine on insomnia symptoms and sleep quality in women with hot flashes. *Sleep* 2015, **38**(1): 97–108.
32 Rubino, A., Roskell, N., Tennis, P., Mines, D., Weich, S., Andrews, E.: Risk of suicide during treatment with venlafaxine, citalopram, fluoxetine, and dothiepin: Retrospective cohort study. *Br Med J* 2007, **334**(7587): 242–245.
33 Tack, J., Ly, H.G., Carbone, F., Vanheel, H., Vanuytsel, T., Holvoet, L., Boeckxstaens, G., Caenepeel, P., Arts, J., Van Oudenhove, L.: Efficacy of mirtazapine in patients with functional dyspepsia and weight loss. *Clin Gastroenterol Hepatol* 2016, **14**(3): 385–392.e384.
34 Watanabe, N., Omori, I.M., Nakagawa, A., Cipriani, A., Barbui, C., Churchill, R., Furukawa, T.A.: Mirtazapine versus other antidepressive agents for depression. *Cochrane Database Syst Rev (Online)* 2011, 12: CD006528.
35 Croom, K.F., Perry, C.M., Plosker, G.L.: Mirtazapine: A review of its use in major depression and other psychiatric disorders. *CNS Drugs* 2009, **23**(5): 427–452.
36 Wichniak, A., Wierzbicka, A., Jernajczyk, W.: Sleep and antidepressant treatment. *Curr Pharm Des* 2012, **18**(32): 5802–5817.
37 Coupland, C., Hill, T., Morriss, R., Arthur, A., Moore, M., Hippisley-Cox, J.: Antidepressant use and risk of suicide and attempted suicide or self harm in people aged 20 to 64: Cohort study using a primary care database. *BMJ (Online)* 2015, 350: h517.
38 Krishnan, K.R.: Revisiting monoamine oxidase inhibitors. *J Clin Psychiat* 2007, **68**(Suppl 8): 35–41.
39 Culpepper, L.: The use of monoamine oxidase inhibitors in primary care. *J Clin Psychiat* 2012, **73**(Suppl 1): 37–41.
40 Robinson, D.S., Amsterdam, J.D.: The selegiline transdermal system in major depressive disorder: A systematic review of safety and tolerability. *J Affect Dis* 2008, **105**(1–3): 15–23.
41 Mental Health Medications [www.nimh.nih.gov/health/topics/mental-health-medications/index.shtml]
42 Gabbard, G.: *Textbook of psychotherapeutic treatments in psychiatry*. Washington, DC, London: American Psychiatric Publishing, 2008.
43 Stern, J.M.: Review article: Psychiatry, psychotherapy and gastroenterology – Bringing it all together. *Aliment Pharmacol Ther* 2003, **17**(2): 175–184.
44 Busch, F., Sandberg, L.: *Psychotherapy and medication: The challenge of integration*. London, New York: Routledge, 2007.

Chapter 25

Patient empowerment and working with complex patients with functional gastrointestinal disorders

Livia Guadagnoli
Simon Knowles
Laurie Keefer

The aim of this chapter is to review the factors that are associated with complex functional gastrointestinal disorders (FGIDs), the evidence for the role of patient empowerment in relation to FGIDs, and psychosocial barriers to patient empowerment. Recommendations for how to facilitate an effective physician-patient relationship are provided.

Learning points

- Discuss the complex features of FGIDs.
- Understand patient empowerment in FGIDs.
- Identify ways of implementing empowerment into practice

Introduction

FGIDs are accompanied by a variety of biological, psychological and social factors that contribute to their complexity and underscore the importance of multidisciplinary, comprehensive and patient-centred care. Factors driving complexity in both assessment and treatment of FGIDs are reviewed ahead.

The complex features of FGIDs: FGID pathology and related stigma

Unknown disease pathology and varying treatment efficacy can lead to patients feeling confused, frustrated, misunderstood and/or misdiagnosed, therefore straining the physician-patient relationship. Stigma is high in this group and significantly affects quality of life as well as clinical outcomes [1, 2].

The complex features of FGIDs: the impact of early life events

Consideration of abuse history

There is a high prevalence of abuse history in patients with FGIDs [3–5], which includes physical, sexual and emotional abuse. Further, the occurrence of general trauma in childhood, such as witnessing violence or being exposed to a natural disaster, is higher in patients with IBS than compared to healthy controls [3]. Current experiences of abuse are also relevant. For example, Perona *et al.* found that 71% of women reporting an episode of domestic violence met criteria for a FGID [6]. Thus, both past and current trauma and abuse are important to consider.

Oftentimes it is the case that patients are not asked about abuse or trauma by their health-care provider. Douglas A. Drossman, an expert in FGIDs, outlined a process of addressing potential abuse with a patient [7]. In brief, Drossman states that rapport should be established and communication should be respectful, thoughtful and empathetic. Further, the clinician should take both the patient's verbal and nonverbal responses as cues to lead the discussion. For example, if a patient endorses abuse but does not want to discuss further, the clinician should respect the patient's request but indicate that he or she is available to talk in the future or make an appropriate referral. Finally, educating the patient on the potential influence of psychosocial effects on FGID outcomes is important, especially when making referrals to mental health professionals.

Learned illness behaviours

Social learning theory proposes that behaviours are learned through the observation of others [8]. Levy (2011) provides evidence for intergenerational transmission in that gastrointestinal illness behaviour can be learned through mechanisms of social learning [9]. For example, if a child is rewarded for expressing GI symptoms, the parent is reinforcing the child and encouraging the behaviour to continue. Similarly, when the parent expects special consideration for his or her illness, the child models that behaviour and expects it as well. Changing these behaviours is hard, especially when they are learned and reinforced throughout the person's life. Therefore, it is important to understand how learned illness behaviours contribute to the presence and maintenance of a patient's illness.

The complex features of FGIDs: illness identity

There is a growing body of evidence that health outcomes are driven in part by an individual's identity and sense of self [10]. As part of adapting to a health-related condition, individuals have to successfully come to terms with changes to their lifestyle and potentially future life goals. Further, individuals have to adapt their lifestyle, often already involving multiple family and work responsibilities, to new demands, such as medical appointments, physical and psychological symptoms, and potentially increased financial pressures.

A key role of health providers is not only to support individuals living with FGIDs but also to promote insight, hope, self-esteem and adaptation/recovery. However, for some individuals with FGIDs, sense of identity changes from one about values and life goals to being overridden centrally by their symptoms and its impact upon them (e.g., I have IBS and can no longer care for my children, be a good wife, work as a teacher, study). As individuals become more focused upon their illness and its impact, a sense of learned helplessness may also develop.

The complex features of FGIDs: somatization and central sensitization disorders

Somatization (i.e., medically explained or unexplained symptoms that are associated with excessive thoughts, feelings and behaviours) is relatively common among people with FGIDs and has been directly associated with symptom severity in IBS [11]. Further, it is believed to be a contributing factor to the comorbidity between FGIDs and other functional somatic syndromes [5, 12]. As such, clinicians should be aware of the consequences and seek additional resources to help the patient manage these maladaptive thoughts, feeling and behaviours.

The complex features of FGIDs: psychiatric comorbidity

Anxiety and mood disorders

There is considerable psychiatric comorbidity in patients with FGIDs, and given the bidirectional nature of the brain-gut connection, both psychiatric and gut-based problems drive symptoms. Anxiety disorders are the most common psychiatric illnesses in FGID patients, affecting up to 50% of IBS patients [12–14]. This includes generalized anxiety disorder (GAD), panic disorder and post-traumatic stress disorder (PTSD). Of particular importance is GAD, as patients with GAD and an FGID tend to focus their worry on GI symptoms, which ultimately increases hypervigilance and symptom exacerbation. Panic disorder is also associated with catastrophizing sensations. As previously identified, trauma leading to PTSD is also an important potential comorbidity. Thus, PTSD, which is associated with hyperarousal of the autonomic nervous system, can facilitate FGID symptoms. While not as prevalent as anxiety disorders, mood disorders, affecting around 12%–30% [13, 14] of patients with IBS, can influence symptoms and treatment adherence and outcomes consequently adding to the complexity of working with FGID patients.

Personality disorders

Maladaptive personality traits or characteristics are frequently observed in patients with FGIDs. Most notably, neuroticism has been shown to be higher in patients with IBS compared to healthy adults [11, 15]. Although not as thoroughly researched, there is some evidence to illustrate the prevalence of personality disorders in the FGID patient population. Blanchard *et al.* [13] found that 30% of the patients with IBS met DSM-IV criteria for one or more Axis II disorders. Of these, cluster C disorders were the most common disorders (12% with obsessive-compulsive personality disorder, 5% meeting avoidant personality disorder). This is probably an overestimate as the study was conducted in a psychiatric sample. Although more research is needed to fully understand personality disorders in FGID patients, it is important to be aware of their existence and impact on a patient.

The complex features of FGIDs: summary

The chronic but fluctuating nature of FGIDs coupled with the aforementioned factors makes treatment management and patient engagement particularly challenging. Given this, there is even more reason to promote patient empowerment in this clinical cohort.

What is empowerment?

Empowerment is a patient-driven process focused on facilitating personal behaviour change as necessary to meet disease demands. Assumptions of empowerment are: (1) patients provide the majority of their own disease care in the context of day-to-day life; (2) because patients are in control of daily self-management, they are responsible for both their choices and their consequences; (3) the health-care provider cannot be responsible for the patient's self-management. These three components shift the physician-patient relationship away from the traditional compliance-oriented approach [16, 17] to one where patients are central to directing and managing their own care. To facilitate empowerment, health-care providers instead focus on helping patients acquire the knowledge, skills and autonomy they need to take full responsibility for various aspects of their illness management and decision-making [16, 18].

What is the evidence for patient empowerment in terms of outcomes in chronic illness and FGID cohorts?

Literature in several chronic illnesses supports the use of empowerment for management and care. Engaging in a diabetes self-management program has been shown to improve healthy lifestyle behaviours (e.g., healthy eating and reading food labels), promote physician-patient communication [19] and improve A1c levels [20]. Empowerment has even been shown to decrease health-care utilization through lower initial hospitalizations and emergency department visits [21]. Health-related benefits through the use of patient empowerment strategies have also been found in other chronic illness groups, such as cancer [22, 23] and asthma [24]. Enhancing patient empowerment through facilitating illness knowledge in FGID cohorts has demonstrated benefits; these include: increased quality of life in patients with functional dyspepsia [25], and increased confidence and ability to make better-informed decisions in IBS [26].

How do you help empower patients?

Health-care providers can integrate patient empowerment into their everyday practice, primarily through facilitating and encouraging health literacy. It is important for the patient to understand their illness and the behaviours they can engage in to help manage the illness. However, oftentimes patients hold misconceptions about their illness, especially FGIDs, where much uncertainty exists. One study examining the current knowledge and educational needs of IBS patients found that up to 50% of patients hold misconceptions about the illness, such as beliefs that it can develop into cancer or colitis [27]. Therefore, it is important for health-care professionals to educate patients about their illness to avoid these misconceptions. In addition, health literacy gives the patient the tools to make knowledge-based decisions and understand the behaviours they need to engage in to manage the illness [28].

Encouraging self-efficacy is another way health-care providers can help to empower patients. Improving a patient's self-efficacy arranges the foundation for successful self-management. Action plans are specific, short-term (1–2 week) behaviour changes that are voluntarily chosen by the patient and discussed with the clinician [29, 30]. Setting, monitoring and completing these action plans can increase patients' morale and confidence in themselves [30], which in turn can lead to more long-term behaviour change. Aside from action plans, another important approach includes highlighting skills the patient can (or does) utilize in everyday encounters, such as problem-solving or coping strategies to promote self-managing. By understanding places where he or she can impact the disorder the patient can learn how different decisions will influence health outcomes.

Fostering a healthy physician-patient relationship is an integral part of patient empowerment. Patients who trust, respect and value their physician are going to feel more comfortable becoming actively involved in care and adhere to medication protocols [31]. Encouraging communication by keeping an open dialogue and addressing the patient's questions and concerns are practical ways of enhancing this relationship. A strong physician-patient relationship is also necessary for shared decision-making. This gives the patient a stake in his or her health outcomes [32, 33], hence encouraging responsibility and autonomy over their own health management.

Promoting positive change and effective management in complex cases may be addressed through motivational interviewing techniques [34]. In motivational interviewing, the patient explores potential barriers and strengths to behaviour change, increasing the patient's awareness of his or her situation and resolving ambivalence. The five principles of motivational interviewing are as follows: (1) develop discrepancy between the patient's current behaviours and goals, (2) express empathy (3) amplify ambivalence by discussing the patient's hesitation to change, (4) roll with resistance as opposed to confrontation and (5) support self-efficacy [35]. These techniques encourage discussion about both the patient's willingness and ambivalence around change, in a manner that is non-confrontational and empathetic, thus facilitating patient empowerment.

Practical recommendations

- Explore potential complex features associated with patient FGIDs, such as trauma, psychopathology and personality.

- Promote health literacy through communication, illness education and addressing misconceptions with the patient.
- Cultivate a strong physician-patient communication and foster shared decision-making.
- Facilitate patient engagement with motivational interviewing and self-efficacy promoting strategies (e.g., setting action plans and goals).
- Identify personal strengths, skills and coping strategies the patient can utilize.

Current limitations/future considerations

- Further research is needed to explore the effect of perceived stigma, history of abuse and/or trauma, learned illness behaviours, illness identity, somatization and psychiatric comorbidity across all FGIDs.
- Complex FGID cases will continue to be part of medical practice; research is needed to assess the factors relating to the role of patient empowerment in FGIDs, and how it can be facilitated.
- There is currently no consensus of guidelines to aid medical professionals and patients with empowerment.

Acknowledgements, competing interests and funding

Livia Guadagnoli is supported by a training grant through the National Institute of Diabetes and Digestive and Kidney Diseases (1T32DK101363).

References

1 Taft, T.H., Riehl, M.E., Dowjotas, K.L., Keefer, L.: Moving beyond perceptions: Internalized stigma in the irritable bowel syndrome. *Neurogastroenterol Motil* 2014, **26**(7): 1026–1035.
2 Taft, T., Keefer, L., Artz, C., Bratten, J., Jones, M.: Perceptions of illness stigma in patients with inflammatory bowel disease and irritable bowel syndrome. *Qual Life Res* 2011, **20**(9): 1391–1399.
3 Bradford, K., Shih, W., Videlock, E.J., Presson, A.P., Naliboff, B.D., Mayer, E.A., Chang, L.: Association between early adverse life events and irritable bowel syndrome. *Clin Gastroenterol Hepatol* 2012, **10**(4): 385–390.e383.
4 Drossman, D.A., Li, Z., Leserman, J., Toomey, T.C., Hu, Y.J.: Health status by gastrointestinal diagnosis and abuse history. *Gastroenterology* 1996, **110**(4): 999–1007.
5 Van Oudenhove, L., Levy, R.L., Crowell, M.D., Drossman, D.A., Halpert, A.D., Keefer, L., Lackner, J.M., Murphy, T.B., Naliboff, B.D.: Biopsychosocial aspects of functional gastrointestinal disorders: How central and environmental processes contribute to the development and expression of functional gastrointestinal disorders. *Gastroenterology* 2016, **150**(6): 1355–1367.e1352.
6 Perona, M., Benasayag, R., Perello, A., Santos, J., Zarate, N., Zarate, P., Mearin, F.: Prevalence of functional gastrointestinal disorders in women who report domestic violence to the police. *Clin Gastroenterol Hepatol* 2005, **3**(5): 436–441.
7 Drossman, D.A.: Abuse, trauma, and GI illness: Is there a link? *Am J Gastroenterol* 2011, **106**(1): 14–25.
8 Bandura, A.: *Social learning theory*. Englewood Cliffs, NJ: Prentice Hall, 1977.

9 Levy, R.L.: Exploring the intergenerational transmission of illness behavior: From observations to experimental intervention. *Annal Behav Med* 2011, **41**(2): 174–182.

10 Yanos, P.T., Roe, D., Lysaker, P.H.: The impact of illness identity on recovery from severe mental illness. *Am J Psychiatr Rehabil* 2010, **13**(2): 73–93.

11 van Tilburg, M.A.L., Palsson, O.S., Whitehead, W.E.: Which psychological factors exacerbate Irritable Bowel Syndrome? Development of a comprehensive model. *J Psychosom Res* 2013, **74**(6): 486–492.

12 Hausteiner-Wiehle, C., Henningsen, P.: Irritable bowel syndrome: Relations with functional, mental, and somatoform disorders. *WJG* 2014, **20**(20): 6024–6030.

13 Blanchard, E.B., Keefer, L., Lackner, J.M., Galovski, T.E., Krasner, S., Sykes, M.A.: The role of childhood abuse in Axis I and Axis II psychiatric disorders and medical disorders of unknown origin among irritable bowel syndrome patients. *J Psychosom Res* 2004, **56**(4): 431–436.

14 Mikocka-Walus, A., Turnbull, D., Moulding, N., Wilson, I., Andrews, J M., Holtmann, G.: Psychological comorbidity and complexity of gastrointestinal symptoms in clinically diagnosed irritable bowel syndrome patients. *J Gastroenterol Hepatol* 2008, **23**(7 Pt 1): 1137–1143.

15 Farnam, A., Somi, M.H., Sarami, F., Farhang, S., Yasrebinia, S.: Personality factors and profiles in variants of irritable bowel syndrome. *WJG* 2007, **13**(47): 6414–6418.

16 Anderson, R.M., Funnell, M.M.: Patient empowerment: Myths and misconceptions. *Patient Educ Counsel* 2010, **79**(3): 277–282.

17 Aujoulat, I., d'Hoore, W., Deccache, A.: Patient empowerment in theory and practice: Polysemy or cacophony? *Patient Educ Couns* 2007, **66**(1): 13–20.

18 Fumagalli, L.P., Radaelli, G., Lettieri, E., Bertele, P., Masella, C.: Patient Empowerment and its neighbours: Clarifying the boundaries and their mutual relationships. *Health Policy* 2015, **119**(3): 384–394.

19 Lorig, K., Ritter, P.L., Villa, F.J., Armas, J.: Community-based peer-led diabetes self-management: A randomized trial. *Diabetes Educ* 2009, **35**(4): 641–651.

20 Bolen, S.D., Chandar, A., Falck-Ytter, C., Tyler, C., Perzynski, A.T., Gertz, A.M., Sage, P., Lewis, S., Cobabe, M., Ye, Y., *et al.*: Effectiveness and safety of patient activation interventions for adults with type 2 diabetes: Systematic review, meta-analysis, and meta-regression. *J Gen Inter Med* 2014, **29**(8): 1166–1176.

21 Wong, C.K., Wong, W.C., Wan, Y.F., Chan, A.K., Chan, F.W., Lam, C.L.: Effect of a structured diabetes education programme in primary care on hospitalizations and emergency department visits among people with Type 2 diabetes mellitus: Results from the Patient Empowerment Programme. *Diabet Med* 2015, **33**(10): 1427–1436.

22 Lovell, M.R., Luckett, T., Boyle, F.M., Phillips, J., Agar, M., Davidson, P.M.: Patient education, coaching, and self-management for cancer pain. *J Clin Oncol* 2014, **32**(16): 1712–1720.

23 Miaskowski, C., Dodd, M., West, C., Schumacher, K., Paul, S.M., Tripathy, D., Koo, P.: Randomized clinical trial of the effectiveness of a self-care intervention to improve cancer pain management. *J Clin Oncol* 2004, **22**(9): 1713–1720.

24 Londono, A.M., Schulz, P.J.: Influences of health literacy, judgment skills, and empowerment on asthma self-management practices. *Patient Educ Couns* 2015, **98**(7): 908–917.

25 Paré, P., Math, J.L.M., Hawes, I.A.: Counselling by primary care physicians may help patients with heartburn-predominant uninvestigated dyspepsia. *Can J Gastroenterol Hepatol* 2010, **24**(3): 189–195.

26 Hakanson, C., Sahlberg-Blom, E., Ternestedt, B.M., Nyhlin, H.: Learning about oneself through others: Experiences of a group-based patient education programme about irritable bowel syndrome. *Scand J Caring Sci* 2012, **26**(4): 738–746.

27 Halpert, A., Dalton, C.B., Palsson, O., Morris, C., Hu, Y., Bangdiwala S., Hankins, J., Norton, N., Drossman, D.: What patients know about irritable bowel syndrome (IBS) and what they would like to know. National Survey on Patient Educational Needs in IBS and development and validation of the Patient Educational Needs Questionnaire (PEQ). *Am J Gastroenterol* 2007, **102**(9): 1972–1982.

28 Schulz, P.J., Nakamoto, K.: Health literacy and patient empowerment in health communication: The importance of separating conjoined twins. *Patient Educ Couns* 2013, **90**(1): 4–11.
29 Lorig, K., Laurent, D.D., Plant, K., Krishnan, E., Ritter, P.L.: The components of action planning and their associations with behavior and health outcomes. *Chronic Illn* 2014, **10**(1): 50–59.
30 Bodenheimer, T., Lorig, K., Holman, H., Grumbach, K.: Patient self-management of chronic disease in primary care. *JAMA* 2002, **288**(19): 2469–2475.
31 Schneider, J., Kaplan, S.H., Greenfield, S., Li, W., Wilson, I.B.: Better physician-patient relationships are associated with higher reported adherence to antiretroviral therapy in patients with HIV infection. *J Gen Intern Med* 2004, **19**(11): 1096–1103.
32 Kambhampati, S., Ashvetiya, T., Stone, N.J., Blumenthal, R.S., Martin, S.S.: Shared decision-making and patient empowerment in preventive cardiology. *Curr Cardiol Rep* 2016, **18**(5): 49.
33 Hoffmann, T.C., Montori, V.M., Del Mar, C.: The connection between evidence-based medicine and shared decision making. *JAMA* 2014, **312**(13): 1295–1296.
34 Miller, W.R.: Motivational interviewing with problem drinkers. *Behav Cogn Psychother* 1983, **11**(02): 147–172.
35 Rollnick, S., Miller, W.R.: What is motivational interviewing? *Behav Cogn Psychother* 1995, **23**(04): 325–334.

Part V

Future directions in functional gastrointestinal disorders

Chapter 26

Future directions in functional gastrointestinal disorders – eHealth

Simon Knowles
Brjánn Ljótsson

The aim of this chapter is to provide an overview of the services that have been evaluated and are available to individuals with functional gastrointestinal disorders (FGIDs), and give recommendations on how eHealth can enrich the work in the biopsychosocial functional gastrointestinal disorder (FGID) clinics.

Learning points

- While eHealth can empower patients with FGIDs to seek the information and support they need, providers can help to further support patients to avoid some of the potential pitfalls.
- Although apps are an emerging avenue to support patients and have been demonstrated effective in some cases, cautious use is still required.
- While several eHealth FGID-specific psychological treatments have been shown to improve FGID symptoms and psychological well-being, they are not freely available to the wider FGID community.
- eHealth technology should be considered as an important component of optimal care and integrated into models of health care for patients with FGIDs.

Introduction

eHealth can be defined as "health services and information delivered or enhanced through the Internet and related technologies", and is not just a development in technology but also a new and connected approach to health care [1, p. 1]. Forms of eHealth technology include direct and interactive communication, such as email, video conferencing (e.g., Skype) or discussion boards (e.g., posting questions), or more passive information consumption through websites (e.g., medical organization information page), blogs (e.g., patient's sharing of experiences) or a database (e.g., scientific journals).

Research on individuals with functional gastrointestinal disorders (FGIDs) indicates that the majority of patients have used the Internet as a source of medical information and more than half would turn to it for information about their condition [2]. On the Internet, social support can also be found in other individuals who share the same FGID for not only information but also emotional support [3]. As such, the Internet offers not only a quick and convenient way to access information but also a means to find and connect with other individuals in a similar situation. Given these findings, providers are likely to find more and more FGID patients who are informed by resources on the Internet. This provides a unique opportunity to support patients in a new way.

For providers, eHealth contains many advantages in easily accessible, up-to-date monitoring and information that can be utilized without stretching the limitations of existing health-care services. eHealth also provides a new tool to communicate and work together with patients to address potentially embarrassing health-related concerns. Providers are in a unique and valuable place to help guide and refine desired medical information to a patient's specific circumstances and overcome these limitations, while providing essential one-on-one care.

The Internet as a primary source of information in FGID cohorts

The Internet is a popular source of medical information for individuals with FGIDs. For instance, in a sample of 1,242 individuals with irritable bowel syndrome (IBS), Halpert and colleagues [2] found that 92.6% have used the Internet to seek medical information. When asked about desiring to learn more about IBS, the Internet (55%) was the second most endorsed method, behind their doctor (67%). Younger patients (<30 compared to 30–45-year-old and >45 years) were more likely to report the use of Internet to find information about IBS, perceive it as helpful and use it in the future to attain information. With such frequent use of the Internet for medical information, similar to that of health-care providers, this places health-care providers under pressure to meet the informational needs of their patients.

In regard to the accuracy of patient IBS knowledge, Halpert *et al.* [4] assessed the accuracy of IBS-related medical knowledge in 1,216 individuals who were informed by health-care professionals, the Internet or both. Those who were informed by both health-care professionals and the Internet combined were significantly more knowledgeable about lifestyle factors (e.g., avoiding milk, caffeine, diets) and medications (e.g., fibre, antispasmodics) that may help them to manage their IBS than using one source alone. However, it should be noted that Halpert and colleagues [2] found in 1,242 individuals with IBS that it is just as likely that when using the Internet, medical information will be sought from a general Internet search (62%) as from websites supported by a medical organization. Although being informed by the Internet is helpful in adjunct to seeing a health-care professional, the information may be indiscriminately sought and the quality is often not verified. As such, health-care providers should support individuals with FGIDs becoming more skilled consumers of Internet-based medical information.

A structured general guide has been developed by Fortinsky *et al.* [5], see Table [4] for health-care providers to facilitate provider-patient discussion about using the Internet to seek medical information for non-functional gastrointestinal disorders; however, its premise is relevant to FGIDs. The Four D's approach is as follows: (1) *Determine* the information desired (e.g., side effects of medication, information about disease) and whether this could also be discussed directly, (2) *Direct* patients to reputable and accurate websites, (3) *Discuss* and review the information discovered online and (4) *Don't dismiss* the Internet as a source of information but rather encourage cautious use with comfortable discussion about what was found. It is important that the use of the Internet is careful and the discussion of information obtained from the Internet is not detrimental to the provider-patient relationship.

Although Fortinsky *et al.* [5] provided a list of recommended Internet resources for patients with inflammatory bowel disease (IBD), less research has been done on Internet resources for FGIDs. It can be helpful for providers to offer advice on safely using information online, combined with suggestions of recommended sites, such as the International Foundation for Functional Gastrointestinal Disorders (www.iffgd.org), the Mayo Clinic (www.mayoclinic.org/diseases-conditions/irritable-bowel-syndrome/basics/symptoms/con-20024578) or Health Direct (www.healthdirect.gov.au/irritable-bowel-syndrome-ibs).

In addition to direct information resources, message boards can offer social support in relation to emotions, information and symptoms [3]. However, only 20% of patients use health message boards [2]. Over all, the Internet is frequently used as a source of health information by patients. Health-care providers can help their patients to more safely approach this resource and offer comfortable discussion of medical information.

The role of mobile applications for FGID patients

Many mobile phones, known as smart phones, are now capable of running software applications ('apps') that can be downloaded to enable a phone to be used by users for a specific task or activity. For example, mental health apps have been developed to facilitate illness recovery and improve mental health in ways that are easily accessible [8, 9].

While there have been many apps developed for GI-oriented conditions, the validity and controlled comparative trials are lacking. In a review of apps for colorectal diseases, O'Neill and Brady [10] assessed 68 apps and found that only 29% had customer satisfaction reviews (only 5% had over 100 reviews), and only 33% had professional medical involvement in the development of the app. As such, O'Neill and Brady concluded that there is a risk that the content of the apps may not be referenced academically and may make misleading claims, for which more regulation, review and quality assurance are needed where medical conditions are involved.

In relation to FGIDs, very few studies evaluating apps are available. Zia and colleagues [11] explored using an app to self-monitor IBS symptoms and food intake in a sample of 11 IBS patients. The participants frequently used the app, as 24-hour compliance rates were high, with 90% of meals and 94% of symptoms tracked. Although there was not a significant difference in symptoms using the app, 73% of participants identified a significant association between a meal nutrient and symptom that helped them to identify trigger foods. However, it should be noted that although this information can be useful to enhance patient-provider communication and develop personalized treatment plans, there are potentially barriers, such as time limitations to review large amounts of data and difficulties associated with data standardization [12].

Based on the limited research to date, clinicians should be aware that although apps are an emerging avenue to support patients and have been demonstrated effective in some cases, cautious use is still required. Suggestions for apps that may be useful for patients with FGIDs include the Monash Uni low FODMAP diet app, in which a research-supported comprehensive database of trigger foods can help to manage symptoms [13], or other alternatives recommended by reputable sourcese.g., [14].

Evidence for the efficacy of eHealth interventions in FGID cohorts

By 2012, more than 100 randomized controlled trials investigating eHealth interventions for a wide range of both physical and psychiatric conditions were published [15]. Most studies show efficacy comparable to studies of regular face-to-face treatments – however, at lower cost for the treatment provider and more accessible for the patient. In the FGID field, there are currently only a small number of eHealth interventions for IBS. The interventions that have been studied can broadly be divided into interventions that are based on comprehensive self-management approaches to IBS and interventions that specifically address fear and avoidance behaviours in IBS.

Three studies by Oerlemans *et al.* [16], Everitt *et al.* [17] and Dorn *et al.* [18] included self-management interventions that involved education about IBS, self-observation of symptom triggers (e.g., dietary habits and stress), cognitive restructuring to address unhelpful beliefs about IBS, dietary advice, physical exercise advice, stress management and relaxation. As shown in Table 26.1, the interventions had generally low or non-significant effects on symptoms and quality of life.

As shown in Table 26.1, six studies have investigated eHealth interventions that address symptom-related fear and avoidance behaviour in IBS. This behavioural pattern has been associated with increased hypervigilance towards symptoms in IBS and also reduced quality of life and has been proposed to be a key factor in maintaining symptom severity and disability in IBS [19, 20]. The studies have been conducted by two research groups, with exposure therapy being the common element. In exposure therapy, patients gradually approach situations that they usually avoid (e.g., eating certain foods, physical and social activities), to learn that they can tolerate the symptoms and emotions that these situations provoke. Two of the studies based on exposure exercises have been conducted by Hunt *et al.* [21, 22], and Ljótsson *et al.* have published four studies [23–26]. eHealth interventions have generally large effect sizes compared to no-treatment control groups and also outperform active control groups.

Table 26.1 eHealth approaches for IBS based on self-management and targeting symptom-related fear and avoidance behaviour.

Authors	*Study design*	*Intervention description*	*Main findings at post-treatment*
Self-management interventions: All self-management interventions included education about IBS, self-observation of symptom triggers (e.g., dietary habits and stress), cognitive restructuring to address unhelpful beliefs about IBS, dietary advice, physical exercise advice, stress management and relaxation.			
Oerlemans *et al.* (2010) [16], the Netherlands	Randomized trial, N=76. PDA intervention vs standard care.	4-week intervention. PDAs that were for daily registrations of symptoms, activities, thoughts and emotions. Therapists provided feedback on registrations over SMS.	The intervention was superior to standard care control group in terms of symptom and quality of life improvement. However, effect sizes were quite small (Cohen's $d < 0.35$).
Everitt *et al.* (2013) [17], United Kingdom	Randomized trial, N= 135. Pure website vs website + 1 telephone call vs no intervention.	6-week website intervention with interactive content. One condition included 1 supportive telephone call with study nurse.	No differences in IBS symptom or quality-of-life outcomes between the study conditions.
Dorn *et al.* (2015) [18], USA	Pilot trial, no control group. N=40.	12-week website with educational information, self-management tools and a chat forum for communication between patients and an expert answering questions about IBS.	28% of the patients reported moderate or significant relief, while 50% reported slight relief of IBS symptoms. A significant improvement in quality of life was observed; however, the within-group effect size was small (Cohen's $d = 0.25$).
eHealth approaches for IBS targeting symptom-related fear and avoidance behaviour:			
Hunt *et al.* 2009 [22], USA	Randomized trial, N=54. Internet-CBT vs waiting list.	6-week intervention based on exposure exercises, relaxation exercises, cognitive restructuring and behavioural experiments. Therapist provided treatment material and continuous support over email. No website was used.	Internet-CBT was superior on IBS symptoms and quality-of-life outcomes with large effect sizes (Cohen's $d = 1.08–1.21$).
Hunt *et al.* 2015 [21], USA	Randomized trial, N=60. Internet-CBT vs waiting list.	Same interventions as earlier. No therapist contact except only one check-in email sent after 3 weeks' treatment. Treatment material available on a website or in hard copy.	Internet-CBT was superior on IBS symptoms and quality-of-life outcomes with moderate to large effect sizes (Cohen's $d = 0.76–0.96$). A large proportion of missing data (40%) make the effect sizes estimates uncertain.

(Continued)

Table 26.1 (Continued)

Authors	*Study design*	*Intervention description*	*Main findings at post-treatment*
Sweden	Randomized trial, N=85. Internet-CBT vs waiting list.	10-week intervention based on exposure exercises and brief mindfulness training. Treatment material was accessed through a website and written online therapist contact was provided 1–2 times/week.	Internet-CBT was superior on IBS symptoms and quality-of-life outcomes with large effect sizes (Cohen's d = 0.93–1.21).
Ljótsson *et al.* 2010 [23, 25], Sweden	Randomized trial, N=61. Internet-CBT vs waiting list. Patients consecutively recruited from one clinic.	Same as previous.	Internet-CBT was superior on IBS symptoms and quality-of-life outcomes with moderate to near large effect sizes (Cohen's d = 0.76–0.79).
Ljótsson *et al.* 2011 [24], Sweden	Randomized trial, N=195. Internet-CBT vs Internet-based stress management.	Internet-CBT was same as previous. Internet-based stress-management control group received education about IBS, dietary advice, physical exercise advice, stress management and relaxation. Mode of delivery and therapist support was identical to Internet-CBT.	Internet-CBT was superior to stress management on IBS symptoms and quality-of-life outcomes with small to moderate effect sizes (Cohen's d = 0.38–0.51).
Ljótsson *et al.* 2014 [26], Sweden	Randomized trial, N=309. Internet-CBT vs reduced Internet-CBT protocol	Internet-CBT was same as previous. The reduced protocol included all active ingredients of the Internet-CBT protocol with the exception of exposure – that is, a dismantling design.	Exposure was found to account for a significant proportion of the treatment effect on IBS symptoms and quality of life with small to near moderate effect sizes (Cohen's d = 0.26–0.48).

Abbreviations: PDA = personal digital assistant, SMS = short message service, Internet-CBT= Internet-based cognitive behavioural therapy.

In summary, recent research suggests that psychological treatments for IBS can be delivered over the Internet. Self-management approaches seem to produce lower effect sizes than interventions based on reducing IBS-related fear and avoidance behaviours through exposure exercises. However, the studies of self-management interventions have also included no or considerably less therapist support compared to the studies based on exposure exercises. Research on other disorders than IBS suggests that regular therapist contact may be an important component in eHealth interventions [27]. Moreover, less intensive self-management interventions may be more suitable for patients with mild symptoms and limited disability while exposure-based interventions are more helpful for patients with more severe symptoms and pronounced disability, although this has not been empirically investigated.

Conclusions

eHealth technology is frequently utilized by individuals as a source of information and support in relation to FGIDs. A challenge facing users of eHealth technology is identifying reliable and valid FGID information and services. Currently there is an abundance of information and treatment recommendations in relation to FGIDs on the Internet; however, very few are supported by medical organizations. Consequently, it is important that health-care providers help individuals with FGIDs identify reliable eHealth sources of information and support and to integrate this with traditional medical services. Several eHealth interventions, predominantly IBS-focused, have shown strong evidence for reducing symptom activity and improving psychological-well-being; however, these interventions are not freely available. Future eHealth interventions must include conducting studies on non-IBS FGIDs to determine the wider applicability of eHealth interventions for FGIDs.

Practical recommendations

- Expert-guided eHealth technology should be integrated into a holistic treatment approach to promote optimal patient care.
- Health professionals should help individuals with FGIDs by directing them to sites that they see as reliable and authoritative in the area.

Current limitations/future considerations

- The development and integration of eHealth technology for FGID management is likely to be facilitated by increasing health-care demands and limited resources.
- Most Internet information is not peer-reviewed and may contribute to misinformation and patient concerns/distress.
- While mobile applications are available to provide information and monitor symptoms, few have been evaluated for their effectiveness and usability.

- Optimal health care is likely to be based on the combination of traditional health-care practices (e.g., one-on-one assessments) and eHealth technology.
- eHealth interventions specifically developed for patients with IBS seem to be effective, but it is unclear which interventions are most effective for specific patients and if the results are applicable to all the FGIDs.
- Evaluation of how eHealth interventions can be embedded in traditional services is also needed.

Acknowledgements, competing interests and funding

Thank you to Sarina Cook for her assistance with the literature search and compilation. The authors are unaware of any competing interests in relation to this chapter. No external funding was received for this chapter.

References

1 Eysenbach, G.: What is e-health? *J Med Inter Res* 2001, **3**(2): e20.
2 Halpert, A., Dalton, C.B., Palsson, O., Morris, C., Hu, Y., Bangdiwala, S., Hankins, J., Norton, N., Drossman, D.A.: Patient educational media preferences for information about irritable bowel syndrome (IBS). *Dig Dis Sci* 2008, **53**(12): 3184–3190.
3 Coulson, N.S.: Receiving social support online: An analysis of a computer-mediated support group for individuals living with irritable bowel syndrome. *Cyberpsychol Behav* 2005, **8**(6): 580–584.
4 Halpert, A., Dalton, C.B., Palsson, O., Morris, C., Hu, Y., Bangdiwala, S., Hankins, J., Norton, N., Drossman, D.: What patients know about Irritable Bowel Syndrome (IBS) and what they would like to know. National survey on patient educational needs in IBS and development and validation of the Patient Educational Needs Questionnaire (PEQ). *Am J Gastroenterol* 2007, **102**(9): 1972–1982.
5 Fortinsky, K.J., Fournier, M.R., Benchimol, E.I.: Internet and electronic resources for inflammatory bowel disease: A primer for providers and patients. *Inflamm Bowel Dis* 2012, **18**(6): 1156–1163.
6 Advice to patients on the safe use of the Internet [www.hon.ch/HONcode/Pro/visitor_safeUse.html]
7 Health website evaluation tool [www.hon.ch/HONcode/Pro/HealthEvaluationTool.html]
8 Bakker, D., Kazantzis, N., Rickwood, D., Rickard, N.: Mental health smartphone apps: Review and evidence-based recommendations for future developments. *JMIR Mental Health* 2016, **3**(1): e7.
9 Donker, T., Petrie, K., Proudfoot, J., Clarke, J., Birch, M-R, Christensen, H.: Smartphones for smarter delivery of mental health programs: A systematic review. *J Med Inter Res* 2013, **15**(11): e247.
10 O'Neill, S., Brady, R.R.W.: Colorectal smartphone apps: Opportunities and risks. *Colorectal Dis* 2012, **14**(9): e530–e534.
11 Zia, J., Schroeder, J., Munson, S., Fogarty, J., Nguyen, L., Barney, P., Heitkemper, M., Ladabaum, U.: Feasibility and usability pilot study of a novel irritable bowel syndrome food and gastrointestinal symptom journal smartphone app. *Clin Trans Gastroenterol* 2016, **7**(3): e147.
12 Chung, C.F., Cook, J., Bales, E., Zia, J., Munson, S.A.: More than telemonitoring: Health provider use and nonuse of life-log data in irritable bowel syndrome and weight management. *J Med Inter Res* 2015, **17**(8): e203.

13 The Monash Uni low FODMAP Diet app [www.med.monash.edu.au/cecs/gastro/fodmap/iphone-app.html]
14 Top 5 iPhone and iPad apps for patients with irritable bowel syndrome [www.hcplive.com/medical-news/top-5-iphone-and-ipad-apps-for-patients-with-irritable-bowel-syndrome-]
15 Hedman E, Ljótsson B, Lindefors, N.: Cognitive behavior therapy via the Internet: A systematic review of applications, clinical efficacy and cost-effectiveness. *Exp Rev Pharmacoecon Outcomes Res* 2012, **12**(6): 745–764.
16 Oerlemans, S., van Cranenburgh, O., Herremans, P.J., Spreeuwenberg, P., van Dulmen, S.: Intervening on cognitions and behavior in irritable bowel syndrome: A feasibility trial using PDAs. *J Psychosom Res* 2011, **70**(3): 267–277.
17 Everitt, H., Moss-Morris, R., Sibelli, A., Tapp, L., Coleman, N., Yardley, L., Smith, P., Little, P.: Management of irritable bowel syndrome in primary care: The results of an exploratory randomised controlled trial of mebeverine, methylcellulose, placebo and a self-management website. *BMC Gastroenterol* 2013, **13**(1): 68.
18 Dorn, S.D., Palsson, O.S., Woldeghebriel, M., Fowler, B., McCoy, R., Weinberger, M., Drossman, D.A.: Development and pilot testing of an integrated, web-based self-management program for irritable bowel syndrome (IBS). *Neurogastroenterol Motil* 2015, **27**(1): 128–134.
19 Labus, J.S., Mayer, E.A., Chang, L., Bolus, R., Naliboff, B.D.: The central role of gastrointestinal-specific anxiety in irritable bowel syndrome: Further validation of the visceral sensitivity index. *Psychosom Med* 2007, **69**(1): 89–98.
20 Jerndal, P., Ringström, G., Agerforz, P., Karpefors, M., Akkermans, L.M., Bayati, A., Simrén, M.: Gastrointestinal-specific anxiety: An important factor for severity of GI symptoms and quality of life in IBS. *Neurogastroenterol Motil* 2010, **22**(6): 646–653+e179.
21 Hunt, M.G., Ertel, E., Coello, J.A., Rodriguez, L.: Empirical support for a self-help treatment for IBS. *Cogn Ther Res* 2015, **39**(2): 215–227.
22 Hunt, M.G., Moshier, S., Milonova, M.: Brief cognitive-behavioral internet therapy for irritable bowel syndrome. *Behav Res Ther* 2009, **47**(9): 797–802.
23 Ljótsson, B., Falk, L., Vesterlund, A.W., Hedman, E., Lindfors, P., Rück, C., Hursti, T., Andréewitch, S., Jansson, L., Lindefors, N., *et al.*: Internet-delivered exposure and mindfulness based therapy for irritable bowel syndrome – a randomized controlled trial. *Behav Res Ther* 2010, **48**(6): 531–539.
24 Ljótsson, B., Hedman, E., Andersson, E., Hesser, H., Lindfors, P., Hursti, T., Rydh, S., Rück, C., Lindefors, N., Andersson, G.: Internet-delivered exposure-based treatment vs. Stress management for irritable bowel syndrome: A randomized trial. *Am J Gastroenterol* 2011, **106**(8): 1481–1491.
25 Ljótsson, B., Andersson, G., Andersson, E., Hedman, E., Lindfors, P., Andréewitch, S., Rück, C., Lindefors, N.: Acceptability, effectiveness, and cost-effectiveness of internet-based exposure treatment for irritable bowel syndrome in a clinical sample: A randomized controlled trial. *BMC Gastroenterol* 2011, **11**(1): 110.
26 Ljótsson, B., Hesser, H., Andersson, E., Lackner, J.M., El Alaoui, S., Falk, L., Aspvall, K., Fransson, J., Hammarlund, K., Löfström, A., *et al.*: Provoking symptoms to relieve symptoms: A randomized controlled dismantling study of exposure therapy in irritable bowel syndrome. *Behav Res Ther* 2014, **55**(1): 27–39.
27 Baumeister, H., Reichler, L., Munzinger, M., Lin, J.: The impact of guidance on Internet-based mental health interventions – A systematic review. *Inter Intervent* 2014, **1**(4): 205–215.

Chapter 27

Future challenges and directions in functional gastrointestinal disorders – complementary medicine

Arine Marianne Vlieger
Marc Alexander Benninga

Many patients with functional gastrointestinal disorders (FGIDs) use complementary or alternative medicine (CAM). This chapter presents an overview of CAM treatment options for the most common FGIDs as well as discussing the safety of CAM therapies, and focuses on those treatments that have been studied best or are used most, including herbs, acupuncture, homeopathy and manual-based therapies, like chiropractics and osteopathy. Suggestions regarding directions for future research in this field are provided.

Learning points

- CAM use is prevalent in adult and paediatric patients with organic and functional gastrointestinal disorders.
- Some CAM therapies can have severe, sometimes fatal adverse reactions.
- Acupuncture is the best-studied CAM modality and may be a good alternative for patients with infantile colic, IBS, GER and functional constipation.
- Herbal medicine can be useful in FGIDs, but concerns exist about the lack of standard dosage, and adverse events.
- Given the high use of and lack of evidence for most CAM therapies, it is important to establish a more rigorous evidence base for CAM in FGIDs.

Introduction

Complementary and alternative medicine (CAM) is a group of medical products and practices generally not considered to be part of conventional medicine. The term 'CAM' incorporates many different approaches and methodologies, ranging from ancient techniques like acupuncture and Ayurvedic medicine to chiropractics, osteopathy, homeopathy, spiritual healing, massage and body-mind techniques, like yoga and meditation. CAM has huge popularity with gastroenterology patients, with a one-year prevalence of CAM use of 35%–51% in adults [1–4] and 36%–41% in paediatric patients [5, 6]. Its usage is common in patients both with organic disorders and with FGIDs [1–6]. Because of this prevalence and the fact that complementary therapies are not without adverse effects (and may interfere with allopathic medications), paediatricians and gastroenterologists should discuss these therapies with their patients. Many CAM therapies are considered 'natural' by the general public and thus safer and gentler in some way than the armamentarium of modern medicine. This may explain the high use of CAM in young infants – for example, in infants with regurgitation and reflux [6]. Another further reason for turning towards CAM by patients with FGIDs is the low perceived effect of conventional treatment [2, 6].

This chapter summarizes CAM treatment options for the most common FGIDs: infantile colic, IBS and functional dyspepsia, gastro-oesophageal reflux and constipation. Moreover, the safety of CAM therapies is discussed. Since research on the safety and efficacy of CAM treatments is limited, the chapter will focus on those treatments that have been studied best or are most popular, including herbs, acupuncture, homeopathy and manual-based therapies, like chiropractics and osteopathy.

Safety of CAM therapies

Many users consider CAM therapies as 'natural', equating this with safety. They are often unaware that many of these therapies have the potential for direct or indirect harm. No safety-based trials of CAM treatments have been carried out in FGID cohorts; however, several non-FGIDs studies show that acupuncture and homeopathy can be regarded as relatively safe treatments. A large observational study in over 200,000 acupuncture patients showed only mild adverse events, like hematoma, pain or pallor, in 8.6% of the patients [7]. A review of the safety of acupuncture in children found a risk of adverse events of only 1.5 in 100 treatments [8]. A systematic review on 6,000 patients receiving homeopathic treatments demonstrated that the proportion of patients experiencing adverse effects was similar for patients randomized to homeopathic treatment compared to patients randomized to placebo, and that adverse effects were not severe [9].

In contradistinction, herbal treatments can have severe, sometimes fatal adverse reactions. This is mostly due to contamination with metals, drug interactions or direct toxic effects. Serious concerns also exist about the safety of manipulative therapies, like chiropractic and osteopathy, especially when spinal manipulation is part of the treatment. Most adverse events involve transient neurological symptoms and increased neck pain, but more serious adverse events, including stroke and death, have been reported reviewed in [10].

CAM therapies can also have indirect harmful effects due to missed diagnoses, delay of more effective treatments, and discontinuation of prescribed drugs. However, these indirect effects are probably not of major concern in functional gastrointestinal disorders, in which spontaneous improvement often occurs and delay of more effective treatment seldom results in life-threatening situations.

Efficacy of CAM in FGIDs

Major flaws in study design and low numbers hamper most studies in the field of CAM. Therefore, definite conclusions on the efficacy of most individual CAM therapies for FGIDs cannot be drawn. Table 27.1 summarizes the current evidence regarding complementary therapies in FGIDs, with recommendations for use and further information in the section ahead.

Table 27.1 Summary of the current evidence base regarding complementary therapies in FGIDs.

FGID	*Recommendation for use (Class 1 to 3) and level of evidence (LoE I–V)*	*Comments*
Infantile colic	Acupuncture: Class 2a; LoE II [11, 12] Herbal medicine: Class 3; LoE II [13, 14] Homeopathy: Class 3, LoE III [15, 16] Osteopathy and chiropractics: class 3, LoE I [17, 18]	Concerns about the lack of standard dosages of herbs Serious adverse events after homeopathic remedy Fatal adverse events after spinal manipulation
IBS and functional dyspepsia	Acupuncture: Class 2a; LoE I [19] Herbal medicine: Class 1, LoE I [20–22] Homeopathy: Cass 2b, LoE II [23] Osteopathy: Class 2b, LoE I [24] Yoga: Class 2a, LoE I [25]	For patients with preferences for acupuncture Recommendation only for peppermint and STW5
Gastro-esophageal reflux	Acupuncture: Class 2b; LoE II [26] Herbs: Class 2b; LoE IV [27, 28] Osteopathy: Class 2b; LoE II [29, 30]	Recommendation only for Rikkunshito
Constipation and/ or faecal incontinence	Acupuncture: Class I; LoE I [31, 32] Senna: Class 1, LoE I [33] Chinese herbs: Class 2b; LoE, I [34] Massage: Class 2b; LoE I [35] Reflexology: Class 2b; LoE IV [36, 37] Osteopathy: Class 2b, LoE IV [38]	Effect is proven in adults, RCTs in children are lacking Serious adverse events with Chinese herbs have been reported

Recommendation: Class 1: treatment is useful/effective and is recommended; Class 2a: treatment may or can be useful; Class 2b: treatment might be considered or effect is unclear; Class 3: treatment is not recommended, because it is not effective or may be harmful.

Infantile colic

Acupuncture has long been used for infantile colic, especially in China, and three randomized control trials (RCTs) have been published, evaluating slight needling acupuncture in one single point in 121 children with excessive crying [12]. Two trials used the acupuncture points Large Intestine 4 and report a small but significant reduction in crying in the acupuncture groups compared to the control groups. A third RCT evaluating the effect of the acupuncture point Stomach 36 found no significant difference between groups. It is plausible that acupuncture can have effect in the treatment of colic, as acupuncture releases different neurotransmitters and hormones [11], but more studies are needed before acupuncture can be definitely recommended as an alternative to conventional care.

Two RCTs examined the effect of herbs in 210 infants with colicky symptoms and showed some effect on crying time for a phytotherapeutic agent with chamomile, fennel and lemon balm as well as a calming effect of fennel seed oil emulsion [13, 14]. However, the administration of herbal products in infants with colic raises concerns about the lack of standard dosages, the possible content of alcohol and possible contamination with hormones or metals. Data on the efficacy of homeopathic treatments in infants with colic are only observational.

A frequently used treatment for infantile colic is spinal manipulation, given by chiropractors, manual therapists, osteopaths or craniosacral therapists. Such therapists claim that spinal manipulation is a very effective treatment for colic, but good evidence is lacking [17]. Moreover, the recent reported severe ARs (adverse reactions) in infants, including three deaths, demonstrate that spinal manipulation has risks and therefore should not be recommended for infantile colic [18].

Irritable bowel syndrome and functional dyspepsia

The best-studied CAM therapy in IBS is acupuncture. A 2012 Cochrane systematic review evaluated 17 randomized controlled trials using acupuncture in IBS [19]. Four trials were of high quality, with adequate randomization, blinding and a low number of drop-outs. No benefits of acupuncture relative to a credible sham acupuncture control were found on IBS symptom severity or IBS-related quality of life. However, in comparative effectiveness trials, patients reported greater benefits from acupuncture than from pharmacological therapies. Thus acupuncture may be a reasonable alternative to drug therapy in patients with preferences for acupuncture.

Herbals and botanicals have been used for generations for abdominal complaints in both adults and children, but good scientific evidence of their effectiveness is sparse. A comprehensive review reviewed 23 studies on nine single and seven compound preparations for IBS [22]. Among the single preparations, the most evidence for efficacy was found for peppermint oil. The mechanism of action is thought to be from the menthol component that relaxes gastrointestinal smooth muscle by blocking calcium channels [21]. Some single preparations, including Aloe vera, Curcuma xanthorriza, Fumaria officinalis, show no benefit in IBS and results for the efficacy of Hypericum perforatum were conflicting. Among compound preparations, STW 5 (Iberogast), a formula containing nine herbs, shows positive results in IBS with different mechanisms of action, such as anti-inflammatory, prosecretory activity and affecting gastrointestinal motility [22]. STW 5 has also modest effect in patients with functional dyspepsia [20]. Another herb for functional dyspepsia with promising results is ginger. Evidence for homeopathic remedies in IBS or FD is lacking, with three low-quality trials totalling 213 participants suggesting minimal benefit [23].

A systematic review assessed the effect of osteopathic manipulation in IBS patients. Five studies, totalling 204 patients, showed more pronounced short-term improvements with osteopathy compared with sham therapy or standard care only. Osteopathic therapy might therefore be beneficial for patients with IBS [24]. However, larger studies are needed before osteopathy can be advocated as a treatment option for IBS.

Yoga might be also a feasible and safe adjunctive treatment for people with IBS. Six RCTs show a beneficial effect of yoga therapy over conventional treatment, with significantly decreased bowel symptoms, IBS severity and anxiety [25]. Because of major flaws in study methods, however, a recommendation regarding yoga as a routine intervention for patients with IBS cannot be made yet.

Gastro-esophageal reflux

Transient relaxations of the lower esophageal sphincter (LES) underlie most gastroesophageal reflux (GER) episodes in healthy volunteers and patients with Gastroesophageal reflux disease (GERD) [39]. Interestingly, it has been shown that acupuncture can influence the basal LOS pressure as well as the rate of transient LES relaxations [40, 41], suggesting that it is an interesting alternative for GERD patients. However, apart from a small RCT in 30 adult patients with persisting symptoms of heartburn that showed that adding acupuncture was more effective than doubling the proton pump inhibitor dose in controlling GER-related symptoms [26], evidence of the efficacy of acupuncture in the treatment of GERD is still lacking. Not much evidence supports the use of herbal or homeopathic products in patients with GERD. Two case studies with 17 patients suggest that Rikkunshito, a traditional Japanese medicine consisting of eight herbs, can improve gastric emptying and reduce acid reflux [27, 28]. Finally, also for manual-based therapies evidence in the treatment of GERD patients is scarce. A small RCT in 38 patients demonstrated that osteopathic manipulative techniques may produce a positive increment in the LES region, but data on clinical effects are lacking [29]. Another small RCT in 36 infants with GERD showed that massage therapy administered by a professional therapist did not affect symptoms of GERD differently than a sham treatment but did decrease infant stress levels [30].

Constipation

Acupuncture has been studied widely in patients with constipation. A meta-analysis of 15 Chinese RCTs containing 1,256 participants indicated that acupuncture for chronic functional constipation is probably as effective as conventional medical therapy in the change of bowel movements [32]. However, the quality of most studies was limited. Recently a large randomized, multicentre, sham-controlled trial from China and including 1075 patients showed that electro-acupuncture alleviated symptoms and improved quality of life in patients with chronic constipation during the eight-week treatment; these effects persisted throughout the 12-week follow-up [31]. Acupuncture-related adverse events during treatment were infrequent in both groups, and all were mild or transient. Thus, acupuncture can be recommended as a valuable option for adult patients with constipation [31, 32]. In children, only a small study has been performed, suggesting an increase in bowel movements after treatment [42].

Herbals and botanicals, especially traditional Chinese medicine, have been used in many cultures over thousands of years for defecation disorders in both children and adults. Although there are many Chinese herbal medicine (CHM) interventions available, and some have been verified by clinical trials, their efficacy and safety are still questioned by both patients and health-care providers worldwide. A systematic review identified a total of 62 papers, of which 35 were reviewed, including a total of 3,571 patients (ranging in age from 1 month to 93 years). Although the authors conclude that the results of the different studies included favoured the tested CHM interventions in comparison with controls, the results of these trials should be interpreted with caution due to the low methodological quality of most included studies [34]. The botanical agent senna has been used as a stimulant laxative already for decades and is approved by the Food and Drug Administration for the treatment of constipation in children over 2 years of age and adults; however, studies evaluating the safety and efficacy of these stimulants are still lacking [33].

In the field of manual-based treatments, abdominal massage is the only CAM modality that has been investigated thoroughly in patients with constipation. A systematic review evaluating 17 studies showed that massage increased defecation frequency and relieved abdominal pain, but could not decrease laxative use [35]. Unfortunately, most studies were of low quality. One pilot study in 13 patients suggests that osteopathic methods may be helpful as an alternative treatment in constipation [38].

The effect of reflexology – a form of foot massage – has been studied in 50 children, ages 3–14 years, with constipation and faecal incontinence. After six sessions, defecation frequencies increased and faecal incontinence decreased [36]. A small pilot study in 19 adult females with constipation also showed an improvement in colonic transit time after reflexology treatment [37].

Practical recommendations

- Acupuncture is the best-studied CAM modality and may be a good alternative for patients with infantile colic, IBS, GER and functional constipation.
- Herbal medicine may be useful in FGIDs, but concerns exist about the lack of standard dosages of herbs and adverse events.
- Spinal manipulation cannot be recommended in general and should be avoided in infants.

Current limitations/future considerations

- Since many patients use CAM and because some of these modalities are not devoid of risks, it is important for physicians to be familiar with these therapies.
- Education on CAM therapies is recommended in the training of (paediatric) gastroenterologists so they can discuss both possibilities and limitations of CAM options with their patients.
- Major flaws in study design and low subject numbers hamper most studies in the field of CAM. Therefore, definite conclusions on the efficacy and safety of most individual CAM therapies for FGIDs cannot be drawn.
- Given its popularity, it is important to establish better evidence on efficacy and safety of these therapies. This will promote integration of

evidence-based CAM modalities into the treatment of functional gastrointestinal disorders, where relevant, and the abandonment of ineffective and/or unsafe CAM modalities.

Acknowledgements, competing interests and funding

The authors are unaware of any competing interests in relation to this chapter. No external funding was received for this chapter.

References

1 Dossett, M.L., Davis, R.B., Lembo, A.J., Yeh, G.Y.: Complementary and alternative medicine use by US adults with gastrointestinal conditions: Results from the 2012 National Health Interview Survey. *Am J Gastroenterol* 2014, **109**(11): 1705–1711.
2 Hung, A., Kang, N., Bollom, A., Wolf, J.L., Lembo, A.: Complementary and alternative medicine use is prevalent among patients with gastrointestinal diseases. *Dig Dis Sci* 2015, **60**(7): 1883–1888.
3 Kong, S.C., Hurlstone, D.P., Pocock, C.Y., Walkington, L.A., Farquharson, N.R., Bramble, M.G., McAlindon, M.E., Sanders, D.S.: The incidence of self-prescribed oral complementary and alternative medicine use by patients with gastrointestinal diseases. *J Clin Gastroenterol* 2005, **39**(2): 138–141.
4 Van Tilburg, M.A.L., Palsson, O.S., Levy, R.L., Feld, A.D., Turner, M.J., Drossman, D.A., Whitehead, W.E.: Complementary and alternative medicine use and cost in functional bowel disorders: A six month prospective study in a large HMO. *BMC* 2008, 8: 46.
5 Day, A.S.: Use of complementary and alternative therapies and probiotic agents by children attending gastroenterology outpatient clinics. *J Paediatr Child Health* 2002, **38**(4): 343–346.
6 Vlieger, A.M., Blink, M., Tromp, E., Benninga, M.A.: Use of complementary and alternative medicine by pediatric patients with functional and organic gastrointestinal diseases: Results from a multicenter survey. *Pediatrics* 2008, **122**(2): e446–e451.
7 Witt, C.M., Pach, D., Brinkhaus, B., Wruck, K., Tag, B., Mank, S., Willich, S.N.: Safety of acupuncture: Results of a prospective observational study with 229,230 patients and introduction of a medical information and consent form. *Forschende Komplementarmedizin* 2009, **16**(2): 91–97.
8 Jindal, V., Ge, A., Mansky, P.J.: Safety and efficacy of acupuncture in children: A review of the evidence. *J Pediatr Hematol Oncol* 2008, **30**(6): 431–442.
9 Stub, T., Musial, F., Kristoffersen, A.A., Alræk, T., Liu, J.: Adverse effects of homeopathy, what do we know? A systematic review and meta-analysis of randomized controlled trials. *Complement Ther Med* 2016, **26**: 146–163.
10 Rozmovits, L., Mior, S., Boon, H.: Exploring approaches to patient safety: The case of spinal manipulation therapy. *BMC* 2016, **16**(1): 164.
11 Carlsson, C.: Acupuncture mechanisms for clinically relevant long-term effects – Reconsideration and a hypothesis. *Acupunct Med* 2002, **20**(2–3): 82–99.
12 Raith, W., Urlesberger, B., Schmölzer, G.M.: Efficacy and safety of acupuncture in preterm and term infants. *Evid Complement Alter Med* 2013, 2013: 739414.
13 Alexandrovich, I., Rakovitskaya, O., Kolmo, E., Sidorova, T., Shushunov, S.: The effect of fennel (Foeniculum vulgare) seed oil emulsion in infantile colic: A randomized, placebo-controlled study. *Alter Ther Health Med* 2003, **9**(4): 58–61.
14 Savino, F., Cresi, F., Castagno, E., Silvestro, L., Oggero, R.: A randomized double-blind placebo-controlled trial of a standardized extract of Matricariae recutita, Foeniculum

vulgare and Melissa officinalis (ColiMil®) in the treatment of breastfed colicky infants. *Phytother Res* 2005, **19**(4): 335–340.

15 Aviner, S., Berkovitch, M., Dalkian, H., Braunstein, R., Lomnicky, Y, Schlesinger, M.: Use of a homeopathic preparation for "infantile colic" and an apparent life-threatening event. *Pediatrics* 2010, **125**(2): e318–e323.

16 Glatstein, M., Danino, D., Wolyniez, I., Scolnik, D.: Seizures caused by ingestion of Atropa belladonna in a homeopathic medicine in a previously well infant: Case report and review of the literature. *Am J Ther* 2014, **21**(6): e196–e198.

17 Dobson, D., Lucassen, P.L., Miller, J.J., Vlieger, A.M., Prescott, P., Lewith, G.: Manipulative therapies for infantile colic. *Cochrane Database Sys Rev (Online)* 2012, 12: CD004796.

18 Todd, A.J., Carroll, M.T., Robinson, A., Mitchell, E.K.L.: Adverse events due to chiropractic and other manual therapies for infants and children: A review of the literature. *J Manipulat Physiol Ther* 2015, **38**(9): 699–712.

19 Manheimer, E., Cheng, K., Wieland, L.S., Min, L.S., Shen, X., Berman, B.M., Lao, L.: Acupuncture for treatment of irritable bowel syndrome. *Cochrane Database Syst Rev (Online)* 2012, 5: CD005111.

20 Cremonini, F.: Standardized herbal treatments on functional bowel disorders: Moving from putative mechanisms of action to controlled clinical trials. *Neurogastroenterol Motil* 2014, **26**(7): 893–900.

21 Hills, J.M., Aaronson, P.I.: The mechanism of action of peppermint oil on gastrointestinal smooth muscle: An analysis using patch clamp electrophysiology and isolated tissue pharmacology in rabbit and guinea pig. *Gastroenterology* 1991, **101**(1): 55–65.

22 Rahimi, R., Abdollahi, M.: Herbal medicines for the management of irritable bowel syndrome: A comprehensive review. *WJGastroenterol* 2012, **18**(7): 589–600.

23 Peckham, E.J., Nelson, E.A., Greenhalgh, J., Cooper, K., Roberts, E.R., Agrawal, A.: Homeopathy for treatment of irritable bowel syndrome. *Cochrane Database Syst Rev* 2013, 11: CD009710.

24 Müller, A., Franke, H., Resch, K.L., Fryer, G.: Effectiveness of osteopathic manipulative therapy for managing symptoms of irritable bowel syndrome: A systematic review. *J Am Osteopathic Assoc* 2014, **114**(6): 470–479.

25 Schumann, D., Anheyer, D., Lauche, R., Dobos, G., Langhorst, J., Cramer, H.: Effect of yoga in the therapy of irritable bowel syndrome: A systematic review. *Clin Gastroenterol Hepatol* 2016, **14**(12): 1720–1731.

26 Dickman, R., Schiff, E., Holland, A., Wright, C., Sarela, S.R., Han, B., Fass, R.: Clinical trial: Acupuncture vs. doubling the proton pump inhibitor dose in refractory heartburn. *Aliment Pharm Ther* 2007, **26**(10): 1333–1344.

27 Kawahara, H., Tazuke, Y., Soh, H., Yoneda, A., Fukuzawa, M.: Physiological analysis of the effects of rikkunshito on acid and non-acid gastroesophageal reflux using pH-multichannel intraluminal impedance monitoring. *Pediatr Surg Inter* 2014, **30**(9): 927–931.

28 Morita, T., Furuta, K., Adachi, K., Ohara, S., Tanimura, T., Koshino, K., Uemura, T., Naora, K., Kinoshita, T.: Effects of rikkunshito (TJ-43) on esophageal motor function and gastroesophageal reflux. *J Neurogastroenterol Motil* 2012, **18**(2) 181–186.

29 Da Silva, R.C.V., De Sá, C.C., Pascual-Vaca, A.O., De Souza Fontes, L.H., Herbella Fernandes, F.A.M., Dib, R.A., Blanco, C.R., Queiroz, R.A., Navarro-Rodriguez, T.: Increase of lower esophageal sphincter pressure after osteopathic intervention on the diaphragm in patients with gastroesophageal reflux. *Diseases of the Esophagus* 2013, **26**(5): 451–456.

30 Neu, M., Pan, Z., Workman, R., Marcheggiani-Howard, C., Furuta, G., Laudenslager, M.L.: Benefits of massage therapy for infants with symptoms of gastroesophageal reflux disease. *Biol Res Nurs* 2014, **16**(4): 387–397.

31 Liu, Z., Yan, S., Wu, J., He, L., Li, N., Dong, G., Fang, J., Fu, W., Fu, L., Sun, J.: Acupuncture for chronic severe functional constipation a randomized trial acupuncture for chronic constipation. *Annal Inter Med* 2016, **165**(11): 761–769.

32 Zhang, T., Chon, T.Y., Liu, B., Do, A., Li, G., Bauer, B., Wang, L., Lin, Z.: Efficacy of acupuncture for chronic constipation: A systematic review. *Am J Chin Med* 2013, **41**(4): 717–742.

33 Gordon, M., Naidoo, K., Akobeng, A.K., Thomas, A.G.: Osmotic and stimulant laxatives for the management of childhood constipation. *Cochrane Database Syst Rev (Online)* 2012, 7: CD009118.
34 Cheng, C.W., Bian, Z.X., Wu, T.X.: Systematic review of Chinese herbal medicine for functional constipation. *WJG* 2009, **15**(39): 4886–4895.
35 Wang, X., Yin, J.: Complementary and alternative therapies for chronic constipation. *Evid Complement Alter Med* 2015, 2015: 396396.
36 Bishop, E., McKinnon, E., Weir, E., Brown, D.W.: Reflexology in the management of encopresis and chronic constipation. *Paediatr Nurs* 2003, **15**(3): 20–21.
37 Woodward, S., Norton, C., Barriball, K.L.: A pilot study of the effectiveness of reflexology in treating idiopathic constipation in women. *Complement Ther Clin Pract* 2010, **16**(1): 41–46.
38 Tarsuslu, T., Bol, H., Şimşek, I.E., Toylan, I.E., Çam, S.: The effects of osteopathic treatment on constipation in children with cerebral palsy: A pilot study. *J Manipulat Physiol Ther* 2009, **32**(8): 648–653.
39 Boeckxstaens, G., El-Serag, H.B., Smout, A.J.P.M., Kahrilas, P.J.: Symptomatic reflux disease: The present, the past and the future. *Gut* 2014, **63**(7): 1185–1193.
40 Chang, F.Y., Chey, W.Y., Ouyang, A.: Effect of transcutaneous nerve stimulation on esophageal function in normal subjects – evidence for a somatovisceral reflex. *Am J Chin Med* 1996, **24**(02): 185–192.
41 Zou, D., Chen, W.H., Iwakiri, K., Rigda, R., Tippett, M., Holloway, R.H.: Inhibition of transient lower esophageal sphincter relaxations by electrical acupoint stimulation. *Am J Physiol Gastrointest Liver Physiol* 2005, **289**(2 52–2): G197–G201.
42 Broide, E., Pintov, S., Portnoy, S., Barg, J., Klinowski, E., Scapa, E.: Effectiveness of acupuncture for treatment of childhood constipation. *Dig Dis Sci* 2001, **46**(6): 1270–1275.

Chapter 28

Future directions in functional gastrointestinal disorders – microbiota, faecal transplants and pharmaceutical approaches

Michael Camilleri
Purna Kashyap
Madhusudan Grover

The aim of this chapter is to summarize the research relating to microbiota, faecal transplants and pharmaceutical approaches in FGIDs and provide practical recommendations in relation to these new approaches in managing functional gastrointestinal disorders.

Learning points

- Gut microbiota may play a role in the pathogenesis of IBS and functional gastrointestinal disorders.
- The gut microbiome represents a potential target for development of precise mechanism-based therapies.
- Several mechanisms based on neurotransmitter receptors and immune mechanisms are potential targets for current pharmacological interventions and novel pharmaceutical approaches in functional gastrointestinal disorders.

Introduction

Functional gastrointestinal disorders (FGIDs) are complex and heterogeneous disorders associated with peripheral and central pathophysiological mechanisms responsible for symptoms in subsets of patients [1]. Although traditional approaches emphasized the biopsychosocial context targeting these mechanisms and associated psychosocial comorbidities [2], considerable potential exists for treatment directed at the microbiome, faecal transplants and pathophysiological mechanisms.

Gut microbiota in irritable bowel syndrome

The gut microbiome is emerging as a key player in driving several peripheral and central mechanisms implicated in irritable bowel syndrome (IBS), including microbiota-gut-brain signalling, gastrointestinal motility, visceral hypersensitivity and epithelial barrier dysfunction. Studies using 16S rRNA-based composition analyses of microbial community have shown reduced microbial diversity and alterations in the composition of microbial community in patients with IBS compared to healthy individuals [3–7].

However, these findings lack consistency, which may be attributed to heterogeneous study populations, differing methodologies for sample preparation and analysis, limited patient numbers and lack of longitudinal data. More recent studies have therefore attempted to complement studies based on 16S rRNA-based microbial analyses of stool with clinical or physiological phenotypes. Thus, Jeffery *et al.* [8] recently identified correlations between specific symptoms and bacterial groups, allowing for exploration of further mechanistic links.

To date, most studies addressing mechanistic effects of colonic or faecal microbiome are limited to animal models, due to the inherent difficulty of conducting such studies in humans. Gut microbiota accelerate gastrointestinal motility (in part due to effects on the serotonergic system), transfer an increase in visceral sensation [9], alter intestinal barrier function [10] and modulate the gut-brain axis [11, 12], and some beneficial bacterial species (e.g., *Lactobacilli and Bifidobacteria*) inhibit the release of pro-inflammatory cytokines from dendritic cells. Conversely, there was an increase in cytokine-mediated inflammation in the absence of these 'friendly' bacteria [13]. Gut microbiota also increase colonic mucosal expression of receptors, such as Toll-like receptor-4 [14], increase circulating antibodies against components of indigenous microbiota, activate the mucosal immune response and increase activated mast cells [15]. These studies all support a role of gut microbiota in immune activation in IBS.

Opportunities for therapy directed at microbiome

Therapeutic approaches directed at the gut microbiota include broad dietary interventions, specific dietary substances, prebiotics, live biotherapeutic products, antibiotics and microbial community interventions, such as faecal microbiota transplant.

Dietary interventions: A low FODMAP (Fermentable Oligo- Di- Monosaccharides and Polyols) diet reduces symptoms in IBS patients; however, long-term benefit has not been demonstrated and there is concern regarding the potential loss of beneficial bacteria [16] or the development of nutritional or mineral deficiencies with excessively strict diets. Recent data show similar efficacy between a low FODMAP and traditional dietary intervention [17]. Prebiotics, such as trans-galacto-oligosaccharide mixtures, reduce symptoms in IBS patients [18], but larger scale studies with longer follow-up are needed.

Live biotherapeutic products have been extensively studied in IBS; the effect appears strain-specific with variable magnitude of clinical effect. Overall, they improve symptoms of abdominal distention and altered bowel pattern [19], with use of multispecies probiotics, such as probiotic combination VSL#3, which reduced flatulence scores and retarded colonic transit in patients with IBS-D [20] and IBS with bloating [21]. Another multispecies probiotic supplement

(*Lactobacillus* rhamnosus GG, L. rhamnosus Lc705, *Propionibacterium* freudenreichii ssp. shermanii JS and *Bifidobacterium* animalis ssp. lactis Bb12) also ameliorated symptoms [22]. Single species, such as *Bifidobacterium infantis* [23] and *Bifidobacterium lactis* [24], resulted in improvement in overall symptoms, including bloating, reduction in abdominal distention and decrease in transit time in patients with constipation-predominant IBS [24]. Anecdotal reports of benefit of *faecal microbiota transplant* in managing IBS symptoms [25–27] have been reported. Moreover a single-centre, retrospective study reported improvement in abdominal pain, dyspepsia, bloating and flatus in about 9/13 patients undergoing faecal microbiota transplant, using a non-validated questionnaire [28]. Conversely, 5/27 patients developed post-infectious IBS post-faecal microbiota transplant for recurrent *C. difficile* infection [29]. As recommended [6, 25, 28–31], robust clinical trials are needed to determine the utility of faecal microbiota transplant in IBS.

Antibiotics represent a double edged sword: antibiotic use is associated with the development of IBS (e.g., marolides and tetracycline) [32]; conversely, other poorly absorbed antimicrobials, such as rifaximin taken for two weeks, provide significant relief of bloating, abdominal pain and global IBS symptoms in patients with IBS without constipation [33]. The proposed mechanism of action is through treatment of small intestinal bacterial overgrowth (SIBO), but the prevalence and significance of SIBO in the pathophysiology of IBS are unclear [34]. The mechanism of rifaximin's action is largely unclear, with no significant effects on bowel symptoms, small bowel or colonic permeability, colonic transit and faecal bile acids, and only modest effects on microbial community richness [35]. Other studies have shown antibiotic use to possibly increase the risk of development of FGIDs [36]. Hence, one needs to exercise caution given the theoretical risk of developing resistant organisms.

Novel pharmaceutical approaches unrelated to microbiome

Bile acid diarrhoea, due to either increased bile acid synthesis or impaired reabsorption, occurs in up to one third of patients with chronic functional diarrhoea or diarrhoea-predominant IBS (IBS-D) [37]. Traditional bile acid sequestrants, such as cholestyramine, colestipol and colesevelam, help improve abdominal distention, pain severity, stool frequency and interference with daily life [38, 39]. An experimental alternative is obeticholic acid (or 6-ethyl chenodeoxycholic acid), a farnesoid X receptor agonist, that results in increased enterocyte synthesis of the hormone fibroblast growth factor (FGF)-19 that inhibits hepatic bile acid synthesis. It improves stool form and frequency [40].

A minority of patients with constipation have low levels of primary or secretory bile acids in the colon and in stool. Elobixibat, an ileal bile acid transport inhibitor, accelerates colonic transit and loosens stool consistency in functional constipation patients [41].

Hence, changing colonic availability of bioactive bile acids either pharmacologically or by modulation of gut microbiota may be an important treatment strategy for managing the spectrum of bowel dysfunction seen in IBS.

Opioid receptor modulation has been of long-standing interest in management of FGIDs, and loperamide is a mainstay of treatment of functional diarrhoea. Recently, eluxadoline, a μ and κ-receptor agonist and δ-receptor antagonist, received Food and Drug Administration (FDA) approval for the management of IBS-D. The μ receptor activity decreases abdominal pain and gastrointestinal (GI) propulsion. The δ-receptor activity prevents excessive inhibition of GI motility by the μ agonist activity of the drug, and provides analgesia without inducing tolerance. It improved diarrhoea and pain over 12 weeks [42].

Mast cell stabilization

Ebastine, a histamine receptor H1antagonist, reduced visceral hypersensitivity and abdominal pain scores and provided overall symptom relief [43]. Previously, ketotifen increased the rectal discomfort threshold in IBS patients with visceral hypersensitivity, reduced overall symptoms and improved health-related quality of life. Although stabilization of mast cells and effects on histamine and other mediators has been proposed to be the targeted mechanism, this was tested in these trials and was not confirmed [44]. Further studies are needed to understand the role of mast cells and to develop related pharmacotherapy.

Serotonergic agents alosetron and ondansetron effectively treat IBS-D. Ramosetron is a potent and selective 5-HT_3 receptor antagonist effective in improving stool consistency and other outcome measures (e.g., global symptoms) in IBS-D patients [45–47]. Ramosetron induced constipation in 11% of the participants, with no increased risk of severe constipation or ischemic colitis in contrast to prior experience with alosetron. YKP10811, a selective agonist of the 5-HT_4 receptor, accelerated colonic transit and improved stool consistency in patients with functional constipation [48]. Overall, serotonergic pathway modulation continues to remain attractive in treatment of FGIDs and is of interest for future drug development.

Antidepressant trials for IBS are reported to be associated with a number needed to treat of four [49]; however, this interpretation is limited due to significant heterogeneity in mechanism of action and doses of the diverse therapies, methods used to appraise outcomes, definition of endpoints, trial design and high heterogeneity scores [50]. The tricyclic antidepressant amitriptyline was beneficial in patients with ulcer-like (painful) dyspepsia, especially with normal gastric emptying [51], whereas escitalopram, a selective serotonin reuptake inhibitor, was not found to be effective.

Mirtazapine (antidepressant and antagonist at histamine receptor H1, α2 adrenergic receptor and serotonin receptors 5-HT_{2C} and 5-HT_3) was effective in improving early satiation, quality of life, gastrointestinal-specific anxiety, weight and nutrient tolerance in functional dyspepsia patients with >10% loss of body weight [52].

Considering the associated burden of psychosocial comorbidities, antidepressants will likely continue to be of interest for treated FGIDs, especially for those with moderate to severe disease who often have a significant central component in the pathophysiology of IBS. Alternatively, it is conceivable that the peripheral effects of the different classes of antidepressants may affect colonic motility or sensitivity. For example, tricyclic antidepressants are associated with reduced rectal motility [53] and reduced visceral sensitivity [54], which was associated with reduced severity of the gastrointestinal symptoms. Similarly, the serotonin-norepinephrine reuptake inhibitor venlafaxine reduces colonic sensation of pain [55], in contrast to the selective serotonin studied to date in humans [56].

Tachykinins induce smooth muscle contraction in the human colon in vitro via a direct excitatory action and by an inhibitory effect on nitrergic neurons. Ibodutant, a selective antagonist of neurokinin 2 receptors, has been shown to be effective only in females with IBS-D in a phase 2 trial [57]. Lack of efficacy in males is not fully understood and may reflect differences in pathophysiology of IBS-D or in expression and sensitivity of neurokinin 2 receptors among males and females; alternatively, the lower number of males included in the trials to date may have led to inadequate power to assess efficacy in males.

Acetylcholinesterase inhibitor acotiamide enhances gastric contractions ex vivo and is effective for postprandial symptoms of functional dyspepsia [58]. Studies indicate its effectiveness in both postprandial distress and epigastric pain predominant subsets of functional dyspepsia [59].

Guanylate cyclase C receptor agonist linaclotide is an effective agent for both IBS-C and chronic constipation with an number needed to treat (NNT) of 7 for achieving complete spontaneous bowel movements. A newer agent, plecanatide, improves the number of spontaneous bowel movements [60]; further trials are awaited.

Anti-inflammatory agent mesalazine did not result in satisfactory relief of abdominal pain/discomfort for patients with Rome III IBS, although a subset of patients showed sustained relief [61]. Beneficial effects on abdominal pain or bowel dysfunction were not replicated [62]. Further trials in subset of patients with post-infectious IBS with low-grade inflammation or immune dysregulation are required.

Modulation of intestinal permeability: There is evidence of reduced glutamine synthetase (possibly in association with epigenetic changes, such as increased micro RNA 29 expression) in the mucosa of a subset of patients with IBS [63]. In a preliminary report of 61 IBS-D patients, glutamine (10 g three times a day) improved abdominal pain, bloating and diarrhoea as well as restored small intestinal permeability when compared to placebo [64].

Practical recommendations

- Currently, limited evidence exists for microbiota-based therapies for treatment of global symptoms of IBS and other FGIDs.
- Next-generation microbiota-targeted therapies will include engineered probiotics and defined microbial communities.
- Pharmacological approaches focused on peripheral mechanisms, such as modulation of bile acids, opioidergic and serotonergic pathways, are the key for treatment of FGIDs.
- Clinical trials and practice tailored to target the key pathophysiological mechanism of FGIDs will likely provide better outcomes.

Current limitations/future considerations

- The current generation of microbiota-targeted therapies is largely empirical given the lack of specificity of therapeutic approaches possible. However, the efficacy of probiotic mixtures in improving symptoms of IBS is promising, highlighting the need for further investigation.
- Future studies delineating longitudinal changes in gut microbiota and their relationship to diet and symptoms will help identify more specific therapeutic targets.
- In future, defined microbial communities and engineered microbial strains producing specific metabolites, aiming to restore host function, will likely replace traditional probiotic approaches.
- The risk-benefit ratio of eluxadoline in the treatment of IBS-D needs further study, given the propensity to be associated with sphincter of Oddi dysfunction, especially in people with prior cholecystectomy and history of pancreatitis and in patients using excessive alcohol consumption.
- Additional studies are needed to understand the putative role of SIBO in the pathophysiology of IBS and effects of antibiotic treatment, including rifaximin, on pathophysiological mechanisms and symptoms in FGIDs.
- Future clinical practice in IBS will involve identifying and treating subsets with either unique or combinations of specific physiological alterations, such as bile acid diarrhoea, peripheral chemosensitivity and central sensitization.

Acknowledgements, competing interests and funding

Dr Grover is supported by NIDDK K23-DK103911. Dr Kashyap is supported by NIH K08-DK100638. Dr Camilleri is supported by NIH RO1-DK92179.

References

1 Camilleri, M.: Mechanisms of disease: Peripheral mechanisms in irritable bowel syndrome. *N Engl J Med* 2012, **367**(17): 1626–1635.
2 Grover, M., Drossman, D.A.: Psychopharmacologic and behavioral treatments for functional gastrointestinal disorders. *Gastrointest Endosc Clin N Am* 2009, **19**(1): 151–170.
3 Balsari, A., Ceccarelli, A., Dubini, F., Fesce, E., Poli, G.: The fecal microbial population in the irritable bowel syndrome. *Microbiologica* 1982, **5**(3): 185–194.
4 Malinen, E., Rinttilä, T., Kajander, K., Mättö, J., Kassinen, A., Krogius, L., Saarela, M., Korpela, R., Palva, A.: Analysis of the fecal microbiota of irritable bowel syndrome patients and healthy controls with real-time PCR. *Am J Gastroenterol* 2005, **100**(2): 373–382.
5 Mättö, J., Maunuksela, L., Kajander, K., Palva, A., Riitta, K., Anna, K., Saarela, M.: Composition and temporal stability of gastrointestinal microbiota in irritable bowel syndrome – A longitudinal study in IBS and control subjects. *FEMS Immunol Med Microbiol* 2005, **43**(2): 213–222.
6 Simrén, M., Barbara, G., Flint, H.J., Spiegel, B.M.R., Spiller, R.C., Vanner, S., Verdu, E.F., Whorwell, P.J., Zoetendal, E.G.: Intestinal microbiota in functional bowel disorders: A Rome foundation report. *Gut* 2013, **62**(1): 159–176.

7 Wang, Z.K., Yang, Y.S.: Upper gastrointestinal microbiota and digestive diseases. *WJG* 2013, **19**(10): 1541–1550.

8 Jeffery, I.B., O'Toole, P.W., Öhman, L., Claesson, M.J., Deane, J., Quigley E.M.M., Simrén, M.: An irritable bowel syndrome subtype defined by species-specific alterations in faecal microbiota. *Gut* 2012, **61**(7): 997–1006.

9 Crouzet, L., Gaultier, E., Del'Homme, C., Cartier, C., Delmas, E., Dapoigny, M., Fioramonti, J., Bernalier-Donadille, A.: The hypersensitivity to colonic distension of IBS patients can be transferred to rats through their fecal microbiota. *Neurogastroenterol Motil* 2013, **25**(4): e272–e282.

10 Patel, R.M., Myers, L.S., Kurundkar, A.R., Maheshwari, A., Nusrat, A., Lin, P.W.: Probiotic bacteria induce maturation of intestinal claudin 3 expression and barrier function. *Am J Pathol* 2012, **180**(2): 626–635.

11 Collins, S.M., Surette, M., Bercik, P.: The interplay between the intestinal microbiota and the brain. *Nat Rev Microbiol* 2012, **10**(11): 735–742.

12 Tillisch, K., Labus, J., Kilpatrick, L., Jiang, Z., Stains, J., Ebrat, B., Guyonnet, D., Legrain-Raspaud, S., Trotin, B., Naliboff, B., *et al.*: Consumption of fermented milk product with probiotic modulates brain activity. *Gastroenterology* 2013, **144**(7): 1394–1401.e1394.

13 Bailey, M.T., Coe, C.L.: Maternal separation disrupts the integrity of the intestinal microflora in infant rhesus monkeys. *Dev Psychobiol* 1999, **35**(2): 146–155.

14 Brint, E.K., MacSharry, J., Fanning, A., Shanahan, F., Quigley, E.M.M.: Differential expression of toll-like receptors in patients with irritable bowel syndrome. *Am J Gastroenterol* 2011, **106**(2): 329–336.

15 Hughes, P.A., Zola, H., Penttila, I.A., Blackshaw, L.A., Andrews, J.M., Krumbiegel, D.: Immune activation in irritable bowel syndrome: Can neuroimmune interactions explain symptoms. *Am J Gastroenterol* 2013, **108**(7): 1066–1074.

16 Halmos, E.P., Power, V.A., Shepherd, S.J., Gibson, P.R., Muir, J.G.: A diet low in FODMAPs reduces symptoms of irritable bowel syndrome. *Gastroenterology* 2014, **146**(1): 67–75.e65.

17 Böhn, L., Störsrud, S., Liljebo, T., Collin, L., Lindfors, P., Törnblom, H., Simrén, M.: Diet low in FODMAPs reduces symptoms of irritable bowel syndrome as well as traditional dietary advice: A randomized controlled trial. *Gastroenterology* 2015, **149**(6): 1399–1407.e1392.

18 Silk, D.B.A., Davis, A., Vulevic, J., Tzortzis, G., Gibson, G.R.: Clinical trial: The effects of a trans-galactooligosaccharide prebiotic on faecal microbiota and symptoms in irritable bowel syndrome. *Aliment Pharmacol Ther* 2009, **29**(5): 508–518.

19 Ford, A.C., Quigley, E.M., Lacy, B.E., Lembo, A.J., Saito, Y.A., Schiller, L.R., Soffer, E.E., Spiegel, B.M., Moayyedi, P.: Efficacy of prebiotics, probiotics, and synbiotics in irritable bowel syndrome and chronic idiopathic constipation: Systematic review and meta-analysis. *Am J Gastroenterol* 2014, **109**(10): 1547–1562.

20 Kim, H.J., Camilleri, M., McKinzie, S., Lempke, M.B., Burton, D.D., Thomforde, G.M., Zinsmeister, A.R.: A randomized controlled trial of a probiotic, VSL#3, on gut transit and symptoms in diarrhoea-predominant irritable bowel syndrome. *Aliment Pharmacol Ther* 2003, **17**(7): 895–904.

21 Kim, H.J., Vazquez Roque, M.I., Camilleri, M., Stephens, D., Burton D.D., Baxter, K., Thomforde, G., Zinsmeister, A.R.: A randomized controlled trial of a probiotic combination VSL# 3 and placebo in irritable bowel syndrome with bloating *Neurogastroenterol Motil* 2005, **17**(5): 687–696.

22 Kajander, K., Myllyluoma, E., Rajilić-Stojanović, M., Kyrönpalo, S., Rasmussen, M., Järvenpää, S., Zoetendal, E.G., De Vos, W.M., Vapaatalo, H., Korpela, R.: Clinical trial: Multispecies probiotic supplementation alleviates the symptoms of irritable bowel syndrome and stabilizes intestinal microbiota. *Aliment Pharmacol Ther* 2008, **27**(1): 48–57.

23 Whorwell, P.J., Altringer, L., Morel, J., Bond, Y., Charbonneau, D., O'Mahony, L., Kiely, B., Shanahan, F., Quigley, E.M.M.: Efficacy of an encapsulated probiotic Bifidobacterium infantis 35624 in women with irritable bowel syndrome. *Am J Gastroenterol* 2006, **101**(7): 1581–1590.

24 Agrawal, A., Houghton, L.A., Morris, J., Reilly, B., Guyonnet, D., Goupil, Feuillerat N, Schlumberger, A., Jakob, S., Whorwell, P.J.: Clinical trial: The effects of a fermented milk product containing Bifidobacterium lactis DN-173 010 on abdominal distension and gastrointestinal transit in irritable bowel syndrome with constipation. *Aliment Pharmacol Ther* 2009, **29**(1): 104–114.

25 Andrews, P., Borody, T.J., Shortis, N.P., Thompson, S.: Bacteriotherapy for chronic constipation: A long term follow-up. *Gastroenterology* 1995, **108**(Suppl 2): A563.

26 Borody, T.J., Khoruts, A.: Fecal microbiota transplantation and emerging applications. *Nat Rev Gastroenterol Hepatol* 2012, **9**(2): 88–96.

27 Zoller, V., Laguna, A.L., Prazeres Da Costa, O., Buch, T., Göke, B., Storr, M.: Fecal microbiota transfer (FMT) in a patient with refractory irritable bowel syndrome. *Deutsche Medizinische Wochenschrift* 2015, **140**(16): 1232–1236.

28 Pinn, D.M., Aroniadis, O.C., Brandt, L.J.: Is fecal microbiota transplantation the answer for irritable bowel syndrome? A single-center experience. *Am J Gastroenterol* 2014, **109**(11): 1831–1832.

29 Garg, S., Song, Y., Han, M.A.T., Girotra, M., Fricke, W.F., Dutta, S.: Post-infectious irritable bowel syndrome in patients undergoing fecal microbiota transplantation for recurrent Clostridium difficile colitis. *Gastroenterology* 2014, **146**(Suppl 1): S83–S84.

30 Pinn, D.M., Aroniadis, O.C., Brandt, L.J.: Is fecal microbiota transplantation (FMT) an effective treatment for patients with functional gastrointestinal disorders (FGID)? *Neurogastroenterol Motil* 2015, **27**(1): 19–29.

31 Shanahan, F., Quigley, E.M.M.: Manipulation of the microbiota for treatment of IBS and IBD – challenges and controversies. *Gastroenterology* 2014, **146**(6): 1554–1563.

32 Villarreal, A.A., Aberger, F.J., Benrud, R., Gundrum, J.D.: Use of broad-spectrum antibiotics and the development of irritable bowel syndrome. *Wis Med J* 2012, **111**(1): 17–20.

33 Pimentel, M., Lembo, A., Chey, W.D., Zakko, S., Ringel, Y., Yu, J., Mareya, S.M., Shaw, A.L., Bortey, E., Forbes, W.P.: Rifaximin therapy for patients with irritable bowel syndrome without constipation. *N Engl J Med* 2011, **364**(1): 22–32.

34 Spiegel, B.M.R.: Questioning the bacterial overgrowth hypothesis of irritable bowel syndrome: An epidemiologic and evolutionary perspective. *Clin Gastroenterol Hepatol* 2011, **9**(6): 461–469.

35 Acosta, A., Camilleri, M., Shin, A., Nord, S.L., O'Neill, J., Gray, A.V., Lueke, A.J., Donato, L.J., Burton, D.D., Szarka, L.A.: Effects of rifaximin on transit, permeability, fecal microbiome, and organic acid excretion in irritable bowel syndrome. *Clin Trans Gastroenterol* 2016, **7**(5): e173.

36 Paula, H., Grover, M., Halder, S.L., Locke, G.R., Schleck, C.D., Zinsmeister, A.R., Talley, N.J.: Non-enteric infections, antibiotic use, and risk of development of functional gastrointestinal disorders. *Neurogastroenterol Motil* 2015, **27**(11): 1580–1586.

37 Valentin, N., Camilleri, M., Altayar, O., Vijayvargiya, P., Acosta, A., Nelson, A.D., Murad, M.H.: Biomarkers for bile acid diarrhoea in functional bowel disorder with diarrhoea: A systematic review and meta-analysis. *Gut* 2016, **65**(12): 1951–1959.

38 Bajor, A., Törnblom, H., Rudling, M., Ung, K.A., Simrén, M.: Increased colonic bile acid exposure: A relevant factor for symptoms and treatment in IBS. *Gut* 2014, **64**(1): 84–92.

39 Camilleri, M., Acosta, A., Busciglio, I., Boldingh, A., Dyer, R.B., Zinsmeister, A.R., Lueke, A., Gray, A., Donato, L.J.: Effect of colesevelam on faecal bile acids and bowel functions in diarrhoea-predominant irritable bowel syndrome. *Aliment Pharmacol Ther* 2015, **41**(5): 438–448.

40 Walters, J.R.F., Johnston, I.M., Nolan, J.D., Vassie, C., Pruzanski, M.E., Shapiro, D.A.: The response of patients with bile acid diarrhoea to the farnesoid x receptor agonist obeticholic acid. *Aliment Pharmacol Ther* 2015, **41**(1): 54–64.

41 Chey, W.D., Camilleri, M., Chang, L., Rikner, L., Graffner, H.: A randomized placebo-controlled phase IIb trial of A3309, a bile acid transporter inhibitor, for chronic idiopathic constipation. *Am J Gastroenterol* 2011, **106**(10): 1803–1812.

42 Dove, L.S., Lembo, A., Randall, C.W., Fogel, R., Andrae, D., Davenport, J.M., McIntyre, G., Almenoff, J.S., Covington, P.S.: Eluxadoline benefits patients with irritable bowel syndrome with diarrhea in a phase 2 study. *Gastroenterology* 2013, **145**(2): 329–338.e321.

43 Wouters, M.M., Balemans, D., Van Wanrooy, S., Dooley, J., Cibert-Goton, V., Alpizar, Y.A., Valdez-Morales, E.E., Nasser, Y., Van Veldhoven, P.P., Vanbrabant, W., *et al.*: Histamine receptor H1-mediated sensitization of TRPV1 mediates visceral hypersensitivity and symptoms in patients with irritable bowel syndrome. *Gastroenterology* 2016, **150**(4): 875–887.e879.

44 Klooker, T.K., Braak, B., Koopman, K.E., Welting, O., Wouters, M.M., Van Der Heide, S., Schemann, M., Bischoff, S.C., Van Den Wijngaard, R.M., Boeckxstaens, G.E.: The mast cell stabiliser ketotifen decreases visceral hypersensitivity and improves intestinal symptoms in patients with irritable bowel syndrome. *Gut* 2010, **59**(9): 1213–1221.

45 Fukudo, S., Ida, M., Akiho, H., Nakashima, Y., Matsueda, K.: Effect of ramosetron on stool consistency in male patients with irritable bowel syndrome with diarrhea. *Clin Gastroenterol Hepatol* 2014, **12**(6): 953–959.e954.

46 Fukudo, S., Kinoshita, Y., Okumura, T., Ida, M., Akiho, H., Nakashima, Y., Nishida, A., Haruma, K.: Ramosetron reduces symptoms of irritable bowel syndrome with diarrhea and improves quality of life in Women. *Gastroenterology* 2016, **150**(2): 358–366e358.

47 Lee, K.J., Kim, N.Y., Kwon, J.K., Huh, K.C., Lee, O.Y., Lee, J.S., Choi, S.C., Sohn, C.I., Myung, S.J., Park, H.J., *et al.*: Efficacy of ramosetron in the treatment of male patients with irritable bowel syndrome with diarrhea: A multicenter, randomized clinical trial, compared with mebeverine. *Neurogastroenterol Motil* 2011, **23**(12): 1098–1104.

48 Shin, A., Acosta, A., Camilleri, M., Boldingh, A., Burton, D., Ryks, M., Rhoten, D., Zinsmeister, A.R.: A randomized trial of 5-Hydroxytryptamine4-receptor agonist, YKP10811, on colonic transit and bowel function in functional constipation. *Clin Gastroenterol Hepatol* 2015, **13**(4): 701–708.

49 Ford, A.C., Quigley, E.M., Lacy, B.E., Lembo, A.J., Saito, Y.A., Schiller, L.R., Soffer, E.E., Spiegel, B.M., Moayyedi, P.: Effect of antidepressants and psychological therapies, including hypnotherapy, in irritable bowel syndrome: Systematic review and meta-analysis. *Am J Gastroenterol* 2014, **109**(9): 1350–1365, quiz 1366.

50 Camilleri, M.: American college of gastroenterology monograph on the management of irritable bowel syndrome. *Exp Opin Pharmacother* 2015, **16**(5): 629–632.

51 Talley, N.J., Richard Locke, G., Saito, Y.A., Almazar, A.E., Bouras, E.P., Howden, C.W., Lacy, B.E., Dibaise, J.K., Prather, C.M., Abraham, B.P., *et al.*: Effect of amitriptyline and escitalopram on functional dyspepsia: A multicenter, randomized controlled study. *Gastroenterology* 2015, **149**(2): 340–349.e342.

52 Tack, J., Ly, H.G., Carbone, F., Vanheel, H., Vanuytsel, T., Holvoet, L., Boeckxstaens, G., Caenepeel, P., Arts, J., Van Oudenhove, L.: Efficacy of mirtazapine in patients with functional dyspepsia and weight loss. *Clin Gastroenterol Hepatol* 2016, **14**(3): 385–392.e384.

53 Santoro, G.A., Eitan, B.Z., Pryde, A., Bartolo, D.C., Orkin, B.A.: Open study of low-dose amitriptyline in the treatment of patients with idiopathic fecal incontinence. *Dis Colon Rectum* 2000, **43**(12): 1676–1682.

54 Poitras, P., Poitras, M.R., Plourde, V., Boivin, M., Verrier, P.: Evolution of visceral sensitivity in patients with irritable bowel syndrome. *Dig Dis Sci* 2002, **47**(4): 914–920.

55 Chial, H.J., Camilleri, M., Ferber, I., Delgado-Aros, S., Burton, D., McKinzie, S., Zinsmeister, A.R.: Effects of venlafaxine, buspirone, and placebo on colonic sensorimotor functions in healthy humans. *Clin Gastroenterol Hepatol* 2003, **1**(3): 211–218.

56 Kuiken, S.D., Tytgat, G.N.J., Boeckxstaens, G.E.E.: The selective serotonin reuptake inhibitor fluoxetine does not change rectal sensitivity and symptoms in patients with irritable bowel syndrome: A double blind, randomized, placebo-controlled study. *Clin Gastroenterol Hepatol* 2003, **1**(3): 219–228.

57 Tack, J., Schumacher, K., Tonini, G., Scartoni, S., Capriati, A., Maggi, C.A., Atanasov, I., Bochenek, A., Dochev, Y., Filip, R., *et al.*: The neurokinin-2 receptor antagonist ibodutant improves overall symptoms, abdominal pain and stool pattern in female patients in a phase II study of diarrhoea-predominant IBS. *Gut* In Press.

58 Matsushita, M., Masaoka, T., Suzuki, H.: Emerging treatments in neurogastroenterology: Acotiamade, a novel treatment option for functional dyspepsia. *Neurogastroenterol Motil* 2016, **28**(5): 631–638.

59 Yamawaki, H., Futagami, S., Kawagoe, T., Maruki, Y., Hashimoto, S., Nagoya, H., Sato, H., Kodaka, Y., Gudis, K., Akamizu, T., *et al.*: Improvement of meal-related symptoms

and epigastric pain in patients with functional dyspepsia treated with acotiamide was associated with acylated ghrelin levels in Japan. *Neurogastroenterol Motil* 2016, **28**(7): 1037–1047.

60 Miner, P.B., Surowitz, R., Fogel, R., Koltun, W., Drossman, D.A., Camilleri, M., Mangel, A., Barrow, L., Jacob, G.S., Shailubhai, K.: Plecanatide, a novel Guanylate Cyclase-C (GC-C) receptor agonist, is efficacious and safe in patients with Chronic Idiopathic Constipation (CIC): Results from a 951 patient, 12 week, multi-center trial. *Gastroenterology* 2013, **144**(Suppl 1) (5): S163–S164.

61 Barbara, G., Cremon, C., Annese, V., Basilisco, G., Bazzoli, F., Bellini, M., Benedetti, A., Benini, L., Bossa, F., Buldrini, P., *et al.*: Randomised controlled trial of mesalazine in IBS. *Gut* 2016, **65**(1): 82–90.

62 Lam, C., Tan, W., Leighton, M., Hastings, M., Lingaya, M., Falcone, Y., Zhou, X., Xu, L., Whorwell, P., Walls, A.F., *et al.*: A mechanistic multicentre, parallel group, randomised placebo-controlled trial of mesalazine for the treatment of IBS with diarrhoea (IBS-D). *Gut* 2016, **65**(1): 91–99.

63 Zhou, Q., Souba, W.W., Croce, C.M., Verne, G.N.: MicroRNA-29a regulates intestinal membrane permeability in patients with irritable bowel syndrome. *Gut* 2010, **59**(6): 775–784.

64 Basra, S., Verne, G.N., Zhou, Q.: Randomized placebo-controlled trial of glutamine for the treatment of diarrhea-predominant IBS. *Gastroenterology* 2013, **5**(144(Suppl 1)): S160.

Chapter 29

Future challenges and directions in functional gastrointestinal disorders – psychological approaches

Michael Jones
Alissa Beath

The aim of this chapter is to review current research on involvement of psychological processes in functional gastrointestinal disorders (FGIDs), with specific focus on how future research can address limitations of current understanding.

Learning points

- FGIDs are defined by their symptoms – an understanding of the involvement of psychological traits in potentially heterogeneous disorders, in the absence of a diagnostic gold standard, is particularly challenging
- While there are robust data implicating psychological traits (particularly maladaptive) in FGIDs, whether the association is causal, and if it is, what the causal direction is, has not been established; any causal pathways are likely bidirectional and multifaceted.
- Psychological therapies are effective in reducing gastrointestinal symptom burden for many patients. However, the mechanism through which they work is not understood, and furthermore, it is unclear whether the same mechanism applies across different types of therapy.

Introduction

FGIDs have strong connections with mental state in general and aspects of mental health in particular. The term 'brain-gut axis' has been coined to cover the study of the array of possible mechanisms by which this association might exist [1]. Despite promising research, many questions about the direct and indirect, causal mechanisms of the association between mind and gut remain unresolved. This chapter builds upon earlier chapters by outlining what is still unknown in the involvement of psychological factors in the FGIDs, with recommendations for future work. The chapter begins by outlining current understanding of the role of some key psychological traits in the aetiology of FGIDs, followed by limitations and future work on the role of psychological therapies as treatment for FGIDs.

Aetiology of FGIDs

A comprehensive understanding of the role of psychological processes in the aetiology of FGIDs is fundamentally important, and will aid in aspects of their diagnosis and treatment. However, understanding the aetiology of FGIDs is hampered by two particular challenges. Being *functional* disorders, any explicit cause, such as organic pathology, must be ruled out before a diagnosis can be made [2]. Second, heterogeneity exists both across specific FGIDs and within, again making it unlikely that simple causal pathways to disease exist.

Psychosocial aetiology: what is known

FGIDs, particularly irritable bowel syndrome (IBS) have strong associations with a range of psychological traits, including diagnosable psychological pathology (summarized in Table 29.1). Evidence demonstrates that a number of maladaptive psychological traits are consistently associated with FGIDs. These traits can be organized into a developmental framework of the biopsychosocial model [3] which posits that childhood predisposes individuals to more or less healthy adulthood, and a negative feedback loop affecting a bidirectional maintenance of psychological and gastrointestinal symptoms (see Figure 29.1).

Table 29.1 Overview of known psychological correlates of IBS.

Potential psychosocial aetiology	*Synopsis of findings*
Genetics	Some genetic involvement in IBS [4], serotonin transporter gene polymorphisms that predispose IBS individuals to depression but not other forms of psychological morbidity [5], >60 candidate genes identified for IBS but none well validated [6]. Similar comments apply to functional dyspepsia (FD) [7].
Early childhood	Physical/sexual abuse [8], trauma [9] and exposure to stress [10] elevated in IBS.
Personality	IBS [11] and FD [12] individuals score higher on neuroticism scales than healthy individuals [11].
Mood disorders	Anxiety levels [13] and diagnoses of anxiety and depressive disorders [14] higher in IBS [14] and FD [12].
Dysfunctional cognitions	IBS individuals over-attend to gastrointestinal symptoms [15], have a tendency to appraise sensations negatively [16] and tend to catastrophize painful sensations [17], which may exacerbate their suffering. Similar findings have been reported for FD [18].
Coping strategies	IBS individuals preferably utilize strategies for coping with problems that can be considered maladaptive [19]. Similarly, FD individuals do not use targeted coping strategies in times of stress [18].
Order of psychological and FGID morbidity	While inconclusive, psychological morbidity appears to precede gastrointestinal symptoms more often than the reverse [20, 21].

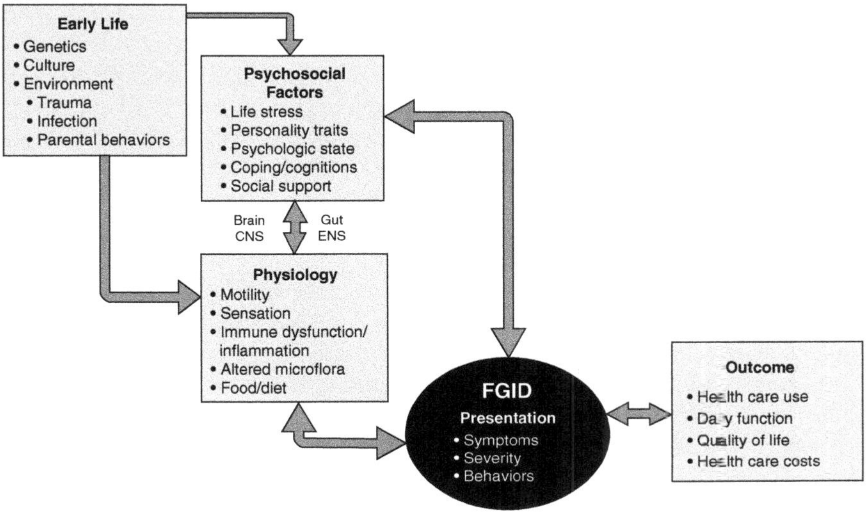

Figure 29.1 The biopsychosocial model adapted for FGIDs. It shows the interaction between brain and gut driving both symptoms and clinical outcome. Adapted from Drossman [4].

Psychosocial aetiology: what remains unknown

While Table 29.1 presents a summary of the knowledge base, there remain considerable uncertainties, particularly around causality.

Despite evidence that genetic inheritance might play a role in some FGIDs (Table 29.1) the search for the specific genes remains unfulfilled. Findings relating to promising candidate genes replicate poorly in subsequent studies. From a psychological perspective, the connection between inheritance accounting for some part of IBS prevalence and IBS individuals more often having a particular polymorphism related to depression (Table 29.1) provides a tantalizing but unproven connection. Similarly, personality is thought to be partly inherited and IBS and FD individuals score higher on neuroticism than normal controls on average. However, given that both FGIDs and neuroticism appear to have some genetic contribution, they are presumably both mostly driven by environmental factors.

A number of maladaptive psychological traits are present in higher levels in IBS than healthy individuals, including neuroticism, anxiety and depression (Table 29.1). However, whether there is a causal association between higher levels of these traits and IBS or other FGIDs remains unproven, and the possibility of a common cause cannot be ruled out. Nonetheless, psychological therapies targeting some traits have met with success in an appreciable percentage of IBS patients [22]. The problem with making causal interpretations from much of the available data is the proliferation of cross-sectional design studies from which causation cannot be inferred and the relative paucity of long-term longitudinal studies. Given the chronicity of FGIDs and their association with early life factors it is possible that causal understanding may require longitudinal studies with tracking commencing in early childhood. The causal direction of the association between maladaptive psychological traits and FGIDs remains unanswered. From the perspective of understanding the onset, with the long-term aim of identifying early interventions to limit the development of FGIDs into adulthood, it is central.

Some psychotherapies target dysfunctional cognitive processes found at higher levels in FGIDs (Table 29.1) but the significance of this is called into question by not all patients experiencing gastrointestinal symptom relief. The number needed to treat is between two to four for IBS [23]. Hence much greater understanding is needed of individual differences in whether dysfunctional cognitions have a role in FGIDs and among those where it does, whether there are individual differences in the importance of their role. Such understanding might offer the possibility of a more efficacious individualized therapy than a one-form-suits-all approach.

Some data suggest that FGID individuals engage in more maladaptive coping strategies in response to life challenges than healthy individuals [19]. If using poor coping strategies is one of the environmental factors discussed earlier and leads to higher levels of anxiety, for example, might training in coping skills at a young age prevent FGID onset in some cases, removing the need for a cure and the suffering that precedes cure?

Numerous psychological traits are involved in FGIDs, but how they are involved? Understanding the psychological causal pathways is complicated by their complexity and potential individual differences in the importance and which specific traits are involved. The relationship between psychological traits and gastrointestinal symptoms is bidirectional [1] and for some, the psychological disturbance predates gastrointestinal symptoms [20]; however, variation in the order of onset between individuals and the absence of psychopathology in some individuals with FGIDs remains unexplained. Long-term longitudinal studies are needed that collect data prospectively, commencing in early life, on all known FGID/psychological correlates.

In summary, there is substantial knowledge about how psychological traits and social environment are associated with functional gastrointestinal disorders but little understanding of the causal pathway.

Psychological therapy: future directions

Psychological therapies have reproducible, medium-sized effects on GI symptoms, and associated health-related quality-of-life outcomes [22]. The benefit of psychological therapies can be maintained up to a year after the end of treatment [23]. However, the specific mechanisms of action remain largely unknown. This section will discuss some of the future issues that should be addressed in this area.

Understanding the underlying mechanisms

There are multiple dysfunctional psychological processes in FGID patients, and each of these therapies acts upon multiple specific processes in order to decrease gastrointestinal symptom burden and increase health-related quality of life.

Improvements in FGID symptoms following psychological therapy have been correlated with a decrease in GI-specific catastrophizing [24], dysfunctional cognitions (a combination of GI-specific anxiety, catastrophizing and negative appraisal) [25], external locus of control (indicating a greater sense of personal control over their symptoms) [26] and an increase in interpersonal relationships [27]. However, while these studies have correlated changes in psychological constructs and changes in symptoms, both occurring following psychological therapy, this demonstrates only that both change as a result of therapy, not that a change in one results causally in a change in the other. It is possible that dysfunctional cognitions, negative emotions and interpersonal quality would benefit from an improvement in GI symptoms (and increased well-being), which, evidence has shown, result from therapeutic interventions. More sophisticated research methods are needed to investigate mediating effects and causal relationships between therapy and symptom burden.

Currently there is no gold standard study to identify causal mediating mechanisms, but a number of studies have investigated the *indirect* effects of psychological therapy on symptom change. Dysfunctional cognitions are targeted through psychological therapies: mindfulness therapy decreases visceral sensitivity and catastrophizing, and increases non-reactivity and reinterpreting pain sensations, which subsequently predicted decreased IBS symptoms and quality of life [28]. Brain imaging techniques show that hypnotherapy patients have decreased brain activity related to pain attention and processing, and are more similar to healthy controls after (compared with before) the intervention [29]. This is consistent with other, more correlational, hypnotherapy research [30].

Decreasing psychological distress is also likely to improve symptom burden. The biopsychosocial model demonstrates the bidirectional relationship between psychological distress (stress, anxiety, depression) and FGID symptoms. Since psychological therapies are known to act upon psychological distress, this decrease in distress may act to decrease FGID symptoms. One study found evidence that CBT predicted a decrease in bowel symptom scores via a decrease in anxiety [31] (contrasting with an earlier study [32]). Thus there is evidence for the role of psychological processes in the therapeutic effect: while data support the involvement of these processes in the therapeutic effect, research has not been conducted yet which would support causal interpretations.

Types of psychological therapies

Various psychological therapies have treated FGIDs, including cognitive behavioural therapy (CBT), relaxation, hypnotherapy and psychodynamic therapy (each independently reviewed earlier). Two meta-analyses demonstrate no difference between types of psychological therapies in their effects on FGID symptoms [23, 33]. Two possible explanations for this finding are: first, differences between therapies are surface-level, and there are similar mechanisms through which these therapies reduce symptoms. Alternatively, there are different underlying mechanisms, but these mechanisms are equally efficacious. Data also demonstrate similar efficacy between types of psychotherapy generally, supporting the 'common underlying mechanism' hypothesis, although this continues to be debated [34]. Clearly, more work is needed to understand the mechanisms through which each type of therapy works, and additionally, whether certain patient characteristics make some individuals more suited for a particular type of therapy.

Traditionally, psychological therapies have not been among the primary treatments recommended by primary care physicians, being recommended once, for example, other traditional treatments fail or in the context of psychological or psychiatric comorbidities [35, 36]. Limitations to psychological therapies include perceived high cost and lower feasibility; the number of sessions in a typical course of therapy is 10–12. However, novel therapeutic methods have emerged, such as self-managed therapy (the patient experiences limited face-to-face clinician sessions, taking responsibility for the ongoing monitoring of the therapy themselves) and online-delivered therapy (clinical intervention is delivered via computer, rather than in face-to-face sessions). Both types of implementations have promising data to suggest equivalent efficacy to traditional forms of therapy [24, 37]. While there are unique barriers, like low adoption, retention rates and stigma [38, 39], the benefits (lower cost, increased feasibility and often greater availability) may vastly outweigh the barriers. Future research should focus on how to increase patient engagement with therapy and retention, and identify the characteristics of patients for whom online and minimal-contact therapy is most suitable, compared with those who benefit more from face-to-face therapy.

Conclusions

Multiple mostly maladaptive psychological traits are strongly associated with FGIDs, with regard to symptom onset and the mechanism through which psychological therapy appears to reduce symptoms. However, there are substantial individual differences in the effect of psychological processes on FGID symptoms, and the mechanism of association remains incompletely understood. This lack of understanding of disease aetiology has practical consequences; it is unclear whether therapies are targeting underlying causes. Given the chronicity of both psychological and functional gastrointestinal disorders, long-term, ideally birth cohort studies are needed to understand how psychological traits and gastrointestinal symptoms are related, which would lead to improved therapeutic options and the possibility of early intervention, which in turn could potentially prevent FGID symptoms from developing. Finally, since the role of psychological processes is fundamental to the experience of these diseases, we believe that referral to a psychologist for psychotherapy should become part of clinicians' primary treatment of FGIDs, rather than left as a fall-back strategy when other treatments fail [35].

Practical recommendations

- Psychological treatments should be considered as first-line treatments.
- Develop further community understanding of the long-term negative impact that traumatic early life events and negative environmental effects have on subsequent development of FGIDs.
- Raise awareness of early intervention for children who experience negative early life events.
- A multidisciplinary approach is needed in managing FGID patients, and research into all elements of FGIDs.

Current limitations/future considerations

- Much research is cross-sectional; prospective longitudinal birth cohort studies are needed to properly understand cause and effect.
- Search for a marker as to whether a person has gut-driven or brain-driven disorder.
- Mediation studies for treatment effects, specifically the investigation of multiple concurrent mediators in any single study.
- Research to understand the differences among types of psychological therapies, and what therapy has the best chance of success for the individual.

Acknowledgements, competing interests and funding

The authors are unaware of any competing interests in relation to this chapter. No external funding was received for this chapter.

References

1 Carabotti, M., Scirocco, A., Maselli, M.A., Severi, C.: The gut-brain axis: Interactions between enteric microbiota, central and enteric nervous systems. *Annal Gastroenterol* 2015, **28**(2): 203–209.

2 Lacy, B.E., Mearin, F., Chang, L., Chey, W.D., Lembo, A.J., Simren, M., Spiller, R.: Bowel disorders. *Gastroenterology*, **150**(6): 1393–1407.e1395.

3 Drossman, D.A.: Gastrointestinal illness and the biopsychosocial model. *Psychosom Med* 1998, **60**(3): 258–267.

4 Lembo, A., Zaman, M., Jones, M., Talley, N.J.: Influence of genetics on irritable bowel syndrome, gastro-oesophageal reflux and dyspepsia: A twin study. *Aliment Pharmacol Ther* 2007, **25**(11): 1343–1350.

5 Jarrett, M.E., Kohen, R., Cain, K.C., Burr, R.L., Poppe, A., Navaja, G.P., Heitkemper, M.M.: Relationship of SERT polymorphisms to depressive and anxiety symptoms in irritable bowel syndrome. *Biol Res Nurs* 2007, **9**(2): 161–169.

6 Henström, M., D'Amato, M.: Genetics of irritable bowel syndrome. *Molecul Cell Pediatr* 2016, **3**: 7.

7 Oshima, T., Toyoshima, F., Nakajima, S., Fukui, H., Watari, J., Miwa, H.: Genetic factors for functional dyspepsia. *J Gastroenterol Hepatol* 2011, **26**(Suppl 3): 83–87.
8 Drossman, D.A.: Abuse, trauma, and GI illness: Is there a link? *Am J Gastroenterol* 2011, **106**(1): 14–25.
9 Halland, M., Almazar, A., Lee, R., Atkinson, E., Larson, J., Talley, N.J., Saito, Y.A.: A case-control study of childhood trauma in the development of irritable bowel syndrome. *Neurogastroenterol Motil* 2014, **26**(7): 990–998.
10 Klooker, T.K., Braak, B., Painter, R.C., de Rooij, S.R., van Elburg, R.M., van den Wijngaard, R.M., Roseboom, T.J., Boeckxstaens, G.E.: Exposure to severe wartime conditions in early life is associated with an increased risk of irritable bowel syndrome: A population-based cohort study. *Am J Gastroenterol* 2009, **104**(9): 2250–2256.
11 Koloski, N.A., Talley, N.J., Boyce, P.M.: Epidemiology and health care seeking in the functional GI disorders: A population-based study. *Am J Gastroenterol* 2002, **97**(9): 2290–2299.
12 Filipović, B.F., Randjelovic, T., Ille, T., Markovic, O., Milovanović, B., Kovacevic, N., Filipović, B.R.: Anxiety, personality traits and quality of life in functional dyspepsia-suffering patients. *Eur J Inter Med* 2013, **24**(1): 83–86.
13 Fond, G., Loundou, A., Hamdani, N., Boukouaci, W., Dargel, A., Oliveira, J., Roger, M., Tamouza, R., Leboyer, M., Boyer, L.: Anxiety and depression comorbidities in irritable bowel syndrome (IBS): A systematic review and meta-analysis. *Eur Arch Psychia Clin Neurosci* 2014, **264**(8): 651–660.
14 Mykletun, A., Jacka, F., Williams, L., Pasco, J., Henry, M., Nicholson, G.C., Kotowicz, M.A., Berk, M.: Prevalence of mood and anxiety disorder in self reported irritable bowel syndrome (IBS). An epidemiological population based study of women. *BMC Gastroenterol* 2010, **10**(1): 1–9.
15 Posserud, I., Svedlund, J., Wallin, J., Simren, M.: Hypervigilance in irritable bowel syndrome compared with organic gastrointestinal disease. *J Psychosom Res* 2009, **66**(5): 399–405.
16 McKinnon, A.C., Van Oudenhove, L., Tack, J., Jones, M.: The association of personality, appraisal, catastrophising and vigilance with gastrointestinal symptom-specific anxiety. *J Health Psychol* 2013: 1359105313503027.
17 Heymen, S., Maixner, W., Whitehead, W.E., Klatzkin, R.R., Mechlin, B., Light, K.C.: Central processing of noxious somatic stimuli in patients with irritable bowel syndrome compared with healthy controls. *Clin J Pain* 2010, **26**(2): 104–109.
18 Cheng, C., Chan, A.O.O., Hui, W.M., Lam, S.K.: Coping strategies, illness perception, anxiety and depression of patients with idiopathic constipation: A population-based study. *Aliment Pharmacol Ther* 2003, **18**(3): 319–326.
19 Knowles, S.R., Austin, D.W., Sivanesan, S., Tye-Din, J., Leung, C., Wilson, J., Castle, D., Kamm, M.A., Macrae, F., Hebbard, G.: Relations between symptom severity, illness perceptions, visceral sensitivity, coping strategies and well-being in irritable bowel syndrome guided by the common sense model of illness. *Psychol Health Med* 2016: 1–11.
20 Jones, M.P., Van Oudenhove, L., Talley, N.J.: Mo1007 Functional Gastrointestinal Disorders (FGIDs) and psychological disorders: Strong evidence that the link is bidirectional, but psychological distress is more likely to precede a new diagnosis of an FGID. *Gastroenterology* 2012, **142**(5): S–570.
21 Sykes, M., Blanchard, E., Lackner, J., Keefer, L., Krasner, S.: Psychopathology in irritable bowel syndrome: Support for a psychophysiological model. *J Behav Med* 2003, **26**(4): 361–372.
22 Ford, A.C.: Efficacy of antidepressants and psychological therapies in irritable bowel syndrome: Systematic review and meta-analysis. *Gut* 2009, **58**(3): 367–378.
23 Laird, K.T., Tanner-Smith, E.E., Russell, A.C., Hollon, S.D., Walker, L.S.: Short-term and long-term efficacy of psychological therapies for irritable bowel syndrome: A systematic review and meta-analysis. *Clin Gastroenterol Hepatol* 2016, **14**(7): 937–947.e934.
24 Oerlemans, S., van Cranenburgh, O., Herremans, P.J., Spreeuwenberg, P., van Dulmen, S.: Intervening on cognitions and behavior in irritable bowel syndrome: A feasibility trial using PDAs. *J Psychosom Res* 2011, **70**(3): 267–277.

25 Gonsalkorale, W.M., Toner, B.B., Whorwell, P.J.: Cognitive change in patients undergoing hypnotherapy for irritable bowel syndrome. *J Psychosom Res* 2004, **56**(3): 271–278.
26 Boyce, P.M., Talley, N.J., Balaam, B., Koloski, N.A., Truman, G.: A randomized controlled trial of cognitive behavior therapy, relaxation training, and routine clinical care for the irritable bowel syndrome. *Am J Gastroenterol* 2003, 98(10): 2209–2218.
27 Hyphantis, T., Guthrie, E., Tomenson, B., Creed, F.: Psychodynamic interpersonal therapy and improvement in interpersonal difficulties in people with severe irritable bowel syndrome. *Pain* 2009, **145**(1–2): 196–203.
28 Garland, E.L., Gaylord, S.A., Palsson, O., Faurot, K., Douglas Mann, J., Whitehead, W.E.: Therapeutic mechanisms of a mindfulness-based treatment for IBS: Effects on visceral sensitivity, catastrophizing, and affective processing of pain sensations. *J Behav Med* 2012, **35**(6): 591–602.
29 Lowen, M.B., Mayer, E.A., Sjoberg, M., Tillisch, K., Naliboff, B., Labus, J., Lundberg, P., Strom, M., Engstrom, M., Walter, S.A.: Effect of hypnotherapy and educational intervention on brain response to visceral stimulus in the irritable bowel syndrome. *Aliment Pharmacol Ther* 2013, **37**(12): 1184–1197.
30 Lea, R., Houghton, L.A., Calvert, E.L., Larder, S., Gonsalkorale, W.M., Whelan, V., Randles, J., Cooper, P., Cruickshanks, P., Miller, V., *et al.*: Gut-focused hypnotherapy normalizes disordered rectal sensitivity in patients with irritable bowel syndrome. *Aliment Pharmacol Ther* 2003, **17**(5): 635–642.
31 Jones, M., Koloski, N., Boyce, P., Talley, N.J.: Pathways connecting cognitive behavioral therapy and change in bowel symptoms of IBS. *J Psychosom Res* 2011, **70**(3): 278–285.
32. Lackner, J.M., Jaccard, J., Krasner, S.S., Katz, L.A., Gudleski, G.D., Blanchard, E.B.: How does cognitive behavior therapy for irritable bowel syndrome work? A mediational analysis of a randomized clinical trial. *Gastroenterology* 2007, **133**(2): 433–444.
33 Ford, A.C., Quigley, E.M.M., Lacy, B.E., Lembo, A.J., Saito, Y.A., Schiller, L.R., Soffer, E.E., Spiegel, B.M.R., Moayyedi, P.: Effect of antidepressants and psychological therapies, including hypnotherapy, in irritable bowel syndrome: Systematic review and meta-analysis. *Am J Gastroenterol* 2014, **109**(9): 1350–1365.
34 Baardseth, T.P., Goldberg, S.B., Pace, B.T., Wislocki, A.P., Frost, N.D., Siddiqui, J.R., Lindemann, A.M., Kivlighan, D.M., 3rd, Laska, K.M., Del Re, A.C., *et al.*: Cognitive-behavioral therapy versus other therapies: Redux. *Clin Psychol Rev* 2013, **33**(3): 395–405.
35 Tack, J., Vanuytsel, T., Corsetti, M.: Modern management of irritable bowel syndrome: More than motility. *Dig Dis* 2016, **34**(5): 566–573.
36 Van Oudenhove, L., Levy, R.L., Crowell, M.D., Drossman, D.A., Halpert, A.D., Keefer, L., Lackner, J.M., Murphy, T.B., Naliboff, B.D.: Biopsychosocial aspects of functional gastrointestinal disorders: How central and environmental processes contribute to the development and expression of functional gastrointestinal disorders. *Gastroenterology* 2016, **150**(6): 1355–1367.e1352.
37 Moss-Morris, R., McAlpine, L., Didsbury, L.P., Spence, M.J.: A randomized controlled trial of a cognitive behavioural therapy-based self-management intervention for irritable bowel syndrome in primary care. *Psycholog Med* 2010, **40**(1): 85–94.
38 Knowles, S.R., Mikocka-Walus, A.: Utilization and efficacy of internet-based eHealth technology in gastroenterology: A systematic review. *Scand J Gastroenterol* 2014, **49**(4): 387–408.
39 Wallin, E.E., Mattsson, S., Olsson, E.M.: The preference for internet-based psychological interventions by individuals without past or current use of mental health treatment delivered online: A survey study with mixed-methods analysis. *JMIR Mental Health* 2016, **3**(2): e25.

Chapter 30

Future challenges and directions in functional gastrointestinal disorders – integrated and biopsychosocial care approaches

Ecushla Linedale
Antonina Mikocka-Walus
Jane M. Andrews

The aim of this chapter is to review the current evidence for holistic care for functional gastrointestinal disorders (FGIDs) and suggest avenues for future gains. Specific areas reviewed in this chapter include the need for an integrated health-care approach, current recommendations for integrated care, benefits of integrated approaches, gaps between recommendations and practice and the evidence for models of integrated care.

Learning points

- Integrated care for individuals with a FGID should be patient-centred and holistic to facilitate accurate and timely diagnosis, effectively communicate both the cause of the symptoms and evidence-based information about treatment approaches, and co-ordinate relevant multidisciplinary caregivers, all with the specific purpose of enabling the individual to self-manage.
- Integrated care for FGIDs has been shown to be effective in nurse-navigated models in secondary and tertiary care and via remote care in the tertiary setting.
- Evaluation of integrated care in primary care settings is lacking.
- Practical and accessible guidelines to support FGID diagnosis and management, and clinical pathways for evidence-based treatment approaches are needed.

Introduction

It is well established that individuals with FGIDs are likely to experience multiple comorbidities and somatization and require an ongoing high level of health care [1]. Integrated care approaches are therefore necessary to address the multiple comorbid challenges associated with FGIDs. A holistic, integrated health-care approach that begins with the first medical consultation is required to address the biopsychosocial experience, comorbidities, somatization and suboptimal acceptance of functional disorders as a valid diagnosis. This type of integrated care requires a number of professionals, including general practitioners, gastroenterologists and allied health professionals (e.g., psychologists, dieticians), to optimally address these chronic complex conditions.

Defining integrated care

Integrated care has been a popular concept in health care since the 1960s, recommended by the World Health Organisation as current best practice in the management of people with complex, long-term conditions, offering a number of benefits (Figure 30.1) [2, 3].

Integrated care is an umbrella term which is used to describe multicomponent care [4]. Although there is no universally accepted definition of integrated care, it incorporates both the delivery and management of health-care services, in order to provide efficient, effective, high-quality, person-centred care [5]. Although the meaning of 'integrated care' and the individual elements of an integrated health-care program vary between countries and health-care systems, the founding principles include a holistic patient-centred approach (i.e., partnering with patients and carers) and facilitating access to and communication between health-care providers and services [4, 6]. While integrated care systems are not quick or easy to establish, integrated approaches have been shown to be successful in a number of global and financial settings and can be practically applied in any health system [5, 7].

The need for integrated FGID care

FGIDs are indeed both chronic and complex, with biopsychosocial triggers, shifting symptomology over time [8] and often involving multiple unexplained somatic complaints [9]. Many patients have symptoms which impair daily life and need to access a number of health-care services to maintain both physical and mental functioning [6]. This results in high levels of health-care utilization and costs [10–13], and often an overuse of unnecessary investigations

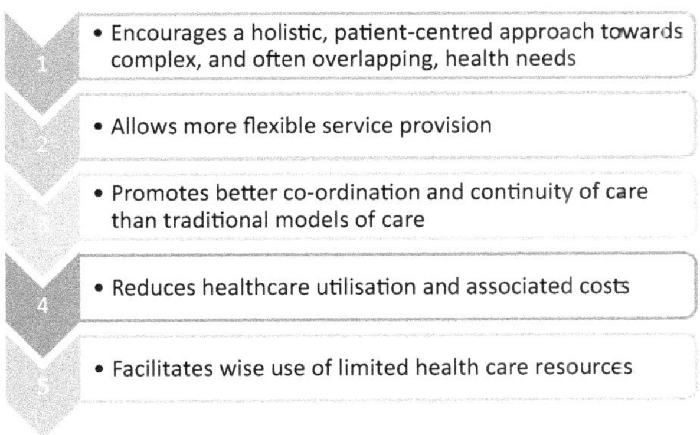

Figure 30.1 Benefits of an integrated approach to health care.

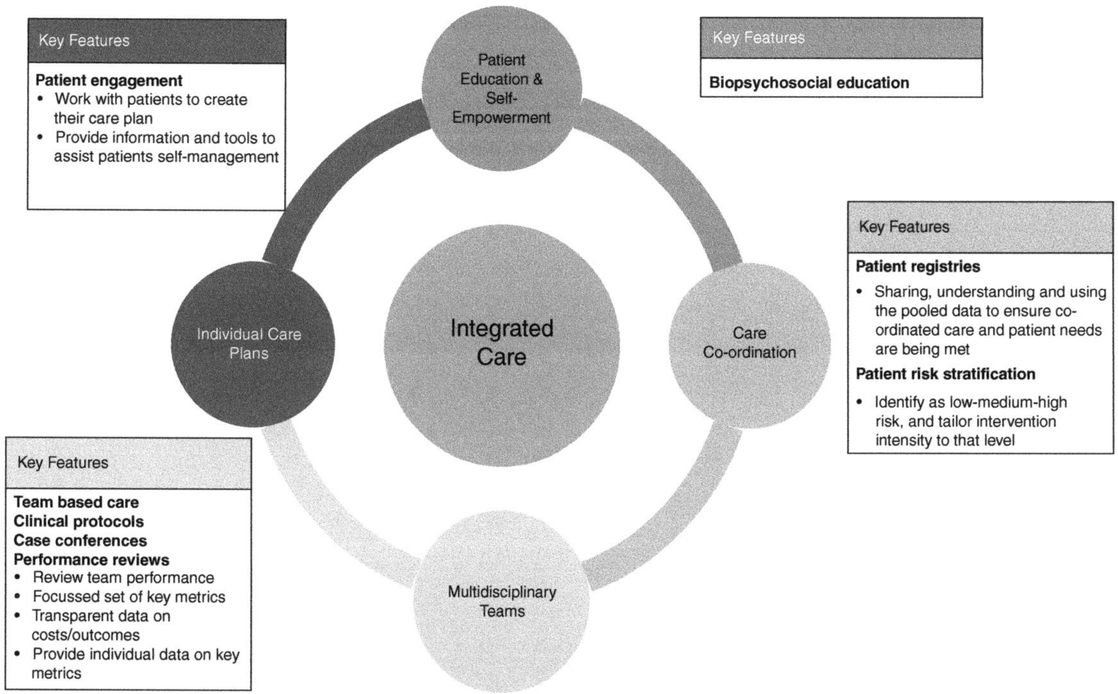

Figure 30.2 Key components of successful integrated care systems.

[14]. An integrated approach to the diagnosis and management of FGIDs, beginning at the first point of medical contact, could greatly improve patient outcomes and reduce costs.

McKinsey research has identified four elements which are critical to successful integrated care: patient education and empowerment, care coordination, multidisciplinary teams and individual care plans (Figure 30.2) [7].

Current recommendations for integrated care

Although most clinical guidelines highlight the biopsychosocial approach to the management of FGIDs, which may involve the primary health-care provider (PHCP), gastroenterologists, dieticians and/or psychologists, little direction is given on the manner in which this should occur [15–18]. The recently published Rome IV criteria recommend a tiered approach to the management of FGIDs, according to symptom severity (Figure 30.3) [17]. In the UK, NICE guidelines recommend that patients with FGID be diagnosed and managed within the primary care setting, and that psychologists, dieticians or gastroenterologists be consulted when symptoms do not improve after one year of implementing general lifestyle changes [19]. Regardless of the restraints of a country's health system or FGID guidelines, there is current opportunity to provide better patient care by integrating and co-ordinating the biopsychosocial providers/treatments.

With the potential number of specialty practices involved, the challenge remains to ensure patient care is integrated [5]. Ultimately, primary care may be ideally placed to facilitate integration and continuity of care for patients with FGIDs in health settings where PHCPs co-ordinate secondary and tertiary care (e.g., Australia) [20]. However, there are significant barriers that need to be overcome, such as funding structures.

The evidence for models of integrated care

Despite the current recommendations for a biopsychosocial approach to the diagnosis and management of FGIDs, to date, only five published studies have evaluated an integrated model of care for FGIDs from diagnosis through to management (Table 30.1). Studies assessed models of care for functional

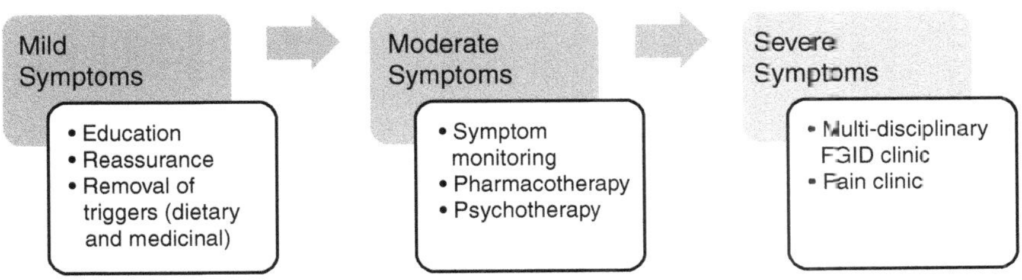

Figure 30.3 A symptom severity–based approach to FGID management.

Table 30.1 Models of care for FGID diagnosis and management.

Model/setting	*Description*	*Evidence*	*Advantages/disadvantages*
Nurse navigator (tertiary care) prior to GE consult	• Initial screening, treatment trials • Multidisciplinary group session with nurse, dietician, mental health therapist • Onward referrals for persistent symptoms	Abstracts [21, 22]	Advantages: • Cheaper for patients, enhanced patient care, experience and outcomes, and more efficient to the practice • Not reliant on GE consult, able to be implemented in primary care. Disadvantages:
Nurse navigator (tertiary care) following GE consult	• To provide ongoing holistic management –including education, counselling & referrals	Level IV [23]	Advantages: • Patient more likely to accept diagnosis and management recommendations following specialist consultation. Disadvantages: • Dependent upon specialist consultation
Private nurse clinic (secondary care) independent of GE consult	• To provide diagnosis, reassurance, education, management strategies • Including low FODMAP diet and exploration of psychosocial issues • Onward referral as needed	Level IV [24]	Advantages: • Improves patient satisfaction and QoL and reduces frequency and severity of symptoms • One-stop shop for diagnosis and management by a specialized practitioner • Could be integrated into primary or tertiary setting Disadvantages: • Requires a specialist nurse practitioner
Algorithm-based approach (primary or tertiary care) independent of GE consult	• To screen and diagnose FGID, and identify patients requiring GE review without face-to-face contact • To provide reassurance, education, management strategies, resources which can be discussed with PHCP • Including low FODMAP diet and psychological therapies	Abstract [25]	Advantages: • Reduces stress, anxiety and maladaptive cognitions and improves symptoms • Clinical pathway for use in primary or tertiary care • Can be implemented by nurse, physician or GE • Allows rapid triage and assessment in health systems with long waiting lists Disadvantages: • Patient is not assessed in person • No guarantee of patient follow-up in primary care

dyspepsia in Canada [21, 22] and the United States [23], for irritable bowel syndrome (IBS) in New Zealand [24] and FGIDs in general in Australia [25]. Four studies assessed variation of nurse-led care models [21–24], and one an algorithm-based approach to integrated care [25]. There is a lack of robust peer-reviewed data, as several of these have been published only in abstract form [21, 22, 25]. While all studies demonstrated the benefit of integrated models of care, much more high-quality research is required to evaluate the best model of care.

Nurse-navigator models

The nurse-led or nurse-navigator (NN) models differ from each other in the role assigned to the nurse and at what point in the patient journey nurse-led care was initiated (see Table 30.1 for advantages and disadvantages of each model). The first NN model of integrated care for IBS consisted of an initial consult and provisional diagnosis by a gastroenterologist and a 30-minute nurse-led educational session covering pathophysiology, review of medications ordered and discussion on lifestyle, stressors and triggers/elimination and diet, followed by 30-minute follow-up sessions (as needed) [23]. Supportive counselling surrounding stress and psychosocial issues was also provided as needed.

The second NN model (2014) used a nurse to perform active telephone triage of patients referred to the tertiary centre with gastroesophageal reflux or functional dyspepsia and involved a one-hour multidisciplinary small group session with an expert nurse, pharmacist and dietician, followed by a brief physician visit for medication/endoscopic evaluation as needed.

In another functional dyspepsia NN model, the nurse conducted initial screening (coeliac screen, urea breath test), and arranged a trial of PPI therapy prior to leading the multidisciplinary group session with a dietician and mental health therapist [21]. Patients with persisting symptoms were referred on to the specialist for upper endoscopy.

Only one small study in New Zealand trialled an integrated model of care in a secondary care setting in the form of a private nurse-led IBS clinic [24]. The care model included an initial nurse consult to collect full history, physical exam, blood and stool tests, as well as a food and symptom diary and IBS questionnaire. A follow-up nurse consult was conducted to review findings a fortnight later. Abnormal test results or physical exam findings triggered a referral back to the GP, gastroenterologist or other specialists. Normal test results were used as a basis for reassurance and education, and management strategies were tailored to the individual. Strategies offered included low FODMAP diet, referral to dietician, nurse reassurance and discussion of psychosocial issues, with referral to a psychologist where needed and accepted.

Non-specialist dependent algorithm-based model

Early results from a small Australian trial suggest the usefulness of an algorithm-based approach to the diagnosis and management of FGIDs which does not depend on specialist consultation [25] (Table 30.1). Patient referrals to a tertiary centre triaged as 'likely' FGID were screened for organic disease with a standard online questionnaire for alarms and routine panel of blood/stool tests (CBE, CRP, iron studies, TFTs, biochemistry, coeliac serology and *H. pylori* serology and/or faecal calprotectin and elastase). Where clinical alarms or abnormal tests resulted, records were reviewed by a gastroenterologist and, if appropriate, a prompt appointment was offered. Those without screening concerns were classified according to Rome III criteria, and received a letter (copied to their PHCP), explaining their FGID diagnosis and dietary/psychological management options.

Conclusions

Although there are very few studies to date, research suggests that integrated care for patients with FGID is likely to improve patient outcomes. Key features of all models include a standardized diagnostic pathway, patient education and reassurance, and resourcing the patient to self-manage his or her condition. Most models reviewed centre around an ongoing supportive relationship with a nurse who co-ordinates and reviews care. It is envisaged that integrated care approaches will also facilitate patient education, diagnostic acceptance, access to and uptake of, multidisciplinary management and improve outcomes, such as symptoms, daily functioning, health-care costs, stress, anxiety and maladaptive cognitions. Its uptake is also likely to decrease the frustration currently experienced by patients and PCHPs alike.

Practical recommendations

- Integrated, multidisciplinary care is an emerging field in the management of FGIDs.
- Integrated care should begin at diagnosis.
- An early confident diagnosis with minimal investigation and reassurance of lack of organic causes is required.
- Patient education about the chronic, recurrent nature of the disorders and effectiveness of the low FODMAP diet and psychological interventions are key tools in integrated care.
- Team-based care coordinated by a central figure is recommended as is the use of standardized clinical pathways and multidisciplinary case management reviews.

Current limitations/future considerations

- There is no published research into the long-term effectiveness of integrated models of care in FGIDs.
- Small care providers may struggle to run specialist nurse-led clinics; this limitation may be circumvented through the use of a virtual FGID network.
- Health-care systems need to review funding models to ensure financial incentives for specialist or doctor-led care do not prevent novel solutions.

Acknowledgements, competing interests and funding

Authors are the investigators of one of the studies included in this review. No other competing interests.

References

1 Alander, T., Svardsudd, K., Agreus, L.: Functional gastrointestinal disorder is associated with increased non-gastrointestinal healthcare consumption in the general population. *Int J Clin Pract* 2008, **62**(2): 234–240.
2 Brown, M., McCool, B.P.: Vertical integration: Exploration of a popular strategic concept. *Health Care Manage Rev* 1986, **11**(4): 7–19.
3 Current European concepts in the management of Helicobacter pylori infection. *Gut* 1997, **41**(1): 8–13.
4 Dorling, G., Fountaine, T., McKenna. S. (2015). The evidence for integrated care. McKinsey & Company. Washington, USA.
5 WHO: WHO global strategy on people-centred and integrated health services. *Interim Report*. In: WHO/HIS/SDS/2015, 6th edn, 2015.
6 Kodner, D.L., Spreeuwenberg, C.: Integrated care: Meaning, logic, applications, and implications – a discussion paper. *Int J Integrated Care* 2002, **2**: 1-6.
7 Carter, K., Chalouhi, E., McKenna, S., Richardson, B.: What it takes to make integrated care work. *Health Int* 2011, **11**: 48–55.
8 Halder, S.L.S., Locke, G.R., Schleck, C.D., Zinsmeister, A.R., Melton, L.J., Talley, N.J.: Natural history of functional gastrointestinal disorders: A 12-year longitudinal population-based study. *Gastroenterology* 2007, **133**(3): 799–807.e791.
9 Spiegel, B.M.R., Kanwal, F., Naliboff, B., Mayer, E.: The impact of somatization on the use of gastrointestinal health-care resources in patients with irritable bowel syndrome. *Am J Gastroenterol* 2005, **100**(10): 2262–2273.
10 Levy, R.L., Korff, M., Whitehead, W.E., Stang, P., Saunders, K., Jhingran, P., Barghout, V., Feld, A.D.: Costs of care for irritable bowel syndrome patients in a health maintenance organization. *Am J Gastroenterol* 2001, **96**(11): 3122–3129.
11 Ålander, T., Svärdsudd, K., Agréus, L.: Functional gastrointestinal disorder is associated with increased non-gastrointestinal healthcare consumption in the general population. *Int J Clin Pract* 2008, **62**(2): 234–240.
12 Longstreth, G.F., Wilson, A., Knight, K., Wong, J., Chiou, C-F, Barghout, V., Frech, F., Ofman, J.J.: Irritable bowel syndrome, health care use, and costs: A U.S. managed care perspective. *Am J Gastroenterol* 2003, **98**(3): 600–607.
13 Talley, N.J., Gabriel, S.E., Harmsen, W.S., Zinsmeister, A.R., Evans, R.W.: Medical costs in community subjects with irritable bowel syndrome. *Gastroenterology* 1995, **109**(6): 1736–1741.
14 Linedale, E.C., Chur-Hansen, A., Mikocka-Walus, A., Gibson, P.R., Andrews, J.M.: Uncertain diagnostic language affects further studies, endoscopies, and repeat consultations for patients with functional gastrointestinal disorders. *Clin Gastroenterol Hepatol* 2016, **14**(12): 1735–1741.
15 *Irritable bowel syndrome IBS*, 2nd edn. Gastroenterological Society of Australia, 2003. Digestive health Foundation: Sydney, NSW Australia.
16 Quigley, E.M.M., Fried, M., Gwee, K-A, Khalif, I., Hungin, A.P.S., Lindberg, G., Abbas, Z., Fernandez, L.B., Bhatia, S.J., Schmulson, M., *et al.*: World Gastroenterology Organisation global guidelines irritable bowel syndrome: A global perspective update September 2015. *J Clin Gastroenterol* 2016, **50**(9): 704.
17 Lacy, B.E., Mearin, F., Chang, L., Chey, W.D., Lembo, A.J., Simren, M., Spiller, R.: Bowel disorders. *Gastroenterology* 2016, **150**(6): 1393–1407.e1395.

18 *National Institute for Health and Care Excellence: Irritable bowel syndrome in adults: NICE quality standard [QS114]*. National Institute for Health and Care Excellence, 2016, London, United Kingdom.
19 Dalrymple, J., Bullock, I.: Diagnosis and management of irritable bowel syndrome in adults in primary care: Summary of NICE guidance. *BMJ* 2008, **336**(7643): 556–558.
20 McWhinney, I.: *A textbook of family medicine*. New York: Oxford University Press, 1997.
21 Buresi, M.C., Andrews, C.N., Novak, K.L., Swain, M.G., Johnston, C., Kathol, B., Heitman, S.J.: A cost-utility analysis of novel and current strategies for the management of uninvestigated dyspepsia. *Gastroenterology* 2014, **146**(5): S558–S559.
22 Novak, K.L., Kathol, B., Swain, M.G., Johnston, C., Kwan, J., Bucholtz, L., Hignell, D., Schoombee, W.S., Buresi, M.C., Andrews, C.N.: Nurse-led, interactive group sessions for dyspepsia and GERD referrals: A prospective controlled study of the "nurse navigator" clinic. *Gastroenterol* 2014, **146**: S-192–S-193.
23 Dill, B., Dill, J.E.: The RN's role in the office treatment of irritable bowel syndrome. *Gastroenterol Nurs* 1995, **18**(3): 100–103.
24 Moore, J.S., Gagan, M.J., Perry, R.E.: The benefits of a nurse-led service in the identification and management of symptoms of irritable bowel syndrome. *Gastroenterol Nurs* 2014, **37**(6): 416–423.
25 Linedale, E., Mikocka-Walus, A., Gibson, P., Andrews, J.: Performance of a novel care pathway for functional gastrointestinal disorders: A pilot study-interim results. *Clin Gastroenterol Hepatol* 2016, **14**(12): 1735–1741.

Index

Note: Page numbers in italics refer to figures or tables.

For Product Safety Concerns and Information please contact our EU
representative GPSR@taylorandfrancis.com
Taylor & Francis Verlag GmbH, Kaufingerstraße 24, 80331 München, Germany

www.ingramcontent.com/pod-product-compliance
Ingram Content Group UK Ltd.
Pitfield, Milton Keynes, MK11 3LW, UK
UKHW022011180926
475701UK00003B/303

* 9 7 8 0 3 6 7 1 9 8 7 3 2 *